FIGHTING FOR SPACE

TRAVIS LUPICK

FIGHTING

FOR

SPACE

HOW A GROUP OF DRUG USERS
TRANSFORMED ONE CITY'S
STRUGGLE WITH ADDICTION

ARSENAL
PULP PRESS
VANCOUVER

ARSENAL PULP PRESS
Suite 202 – 211 East Georgia St.
Vancouver, BC V6A 1Z6
Canada
arsenalpulp.com

The publisher gratefully acknowledges the support of the Canada Council for the Arts
and the British Columbia Arts Council for its publishing program, and the Government of
Canada, and the Government of British Columbia (through the Book Publishing Tax Credit
Program), for its publishing activities.

Chapters 31 and 33 include sections from articles by the author that were previously
published: Travis Lupick, "A Community Response: How the Worst Overdose Epidemic
in Vancouver's History Left the Downtown Eastside to Fend for Itself." *Georgia Straight*,
December 10, 2016. Travis Lupick, "Legal Heroin: As the Fentanyl Crisis Continues, One
Vancouver Doctor Moves People out of the Alleys and into a Clinic." *Georgia Straight*,
March 11, 2017.

Text design by Electra Design Group
Cover design by Oliver McPartlin, cover photo by Amanda Siebert
Edited by Susan Safyan

Printed and bound in Canada

Library and Archives Canada Cataloguing in Publication:
Lupick, Travis, 1985-, author
        Fighting for space : how a group of drug users transformed one city's
struggle with addiction / Travis Lupick.

Issued in print and electronic formats.
ISBN 978-1-55152-712-3 (softcover).—ISBN 978-1-55152-713-0 (HTML)

        1. Drug addicts—British Columbia—Vancouver—Social conditions.
2. Drug addicts—Health and hygiene—British Columbia—Vancouver.
3. Drug addicts—Civil rights—British Columbia—Vancouver. 4. Drug
addicts—Political activity—British Columbia—Vancouver. 5. Drug
addicts—Legal status, laws, etc.—British Columbia—Vancouver. 6. Drug
addiction—Treatment—British Columbia—Vancouver. 7. Drug
addiction—British Columbia—Vancouver—Prevention. 8. Opioid abuse—
British Columbia—Vancouver. 9. Drug addiction—British Columbia—
Vancouver. I. Title.

HV5840.C32V36 2017   362.29'150971133   C2017-904038-3
                                                   C2017-904039-1

Our governments and police have waged a war on people who use drugs. This book is for their victims; for those in prison, for those whom they have pushed into the shadows, and for those who are no longer with us.

Contents

Downtown Eastside
Nonprofit Organizational Chart

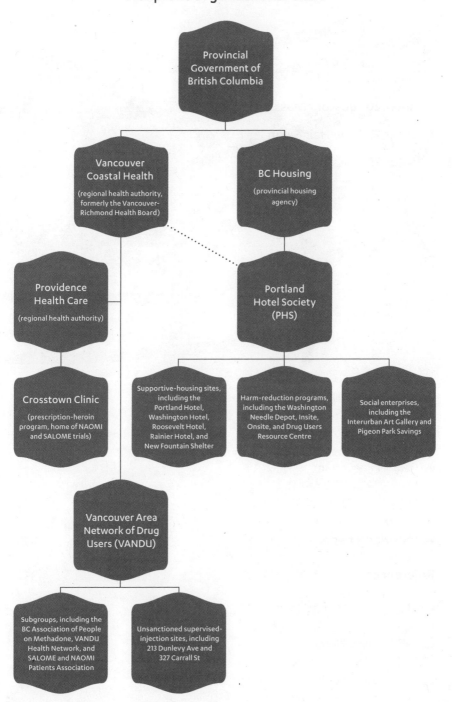

Harm reduction in Vancouver's Downtown Eastside

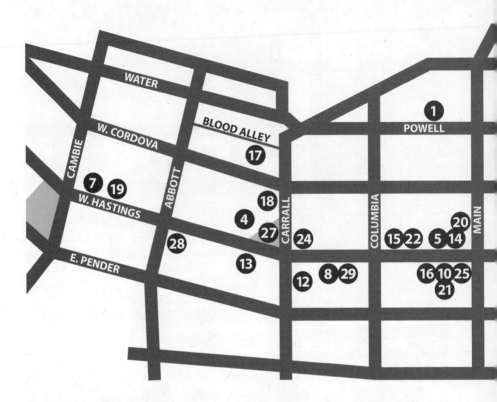

Vancouver Area Network of Drug Users (VANDU)

1 Ann Livingston home
2 Back Alley injection site
3 Dunlevy injection site
4 Carrall injection site
5 Street Church (VANDU HQ 1)
6 LivingRoom Drop-In (VANDU HQ 2)
7 VANDU HQ 3
8 VANDU HQ 4
9 VANDU HQ 5
10 Main & Hastings needle exchange

Portland Hotel Society (PHS)

11 Liz Evans & Mark Townsend home
12 Old Portland Hotel
13 New Portland Hotel
14 Washington Hotel

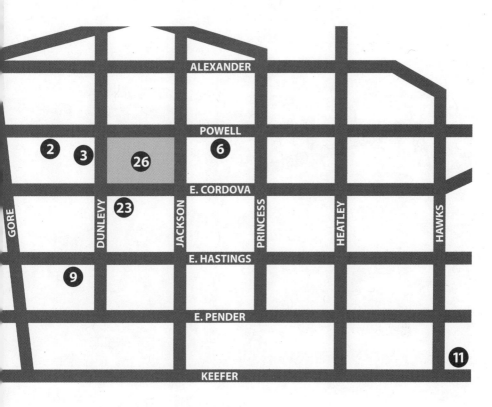

15 Sunrise Hotel (Dean Wilson home)
16 Roosevelt Hotel
17 New Fountain Shelter/Stanley Hotel
18 Rainier Hotel
19 Woodward's Community Housing
20 Washington Needle Depot
21 Thunder Box injection trailer
22 Insite/Onsite
23 Drug Users Resource Centre
24 Interurban Gallery

Other
25 Carnegie Community Centre
26 Oppenheimer Park
27 Pigeon Park
28 Crosstown Clinic
29 OPS injection tent

"There are two kinds of people in the Downtown Eastside: the ones that desperately want to leave and the ones who know they're home." —Melissa Eror

INTRODUCTION

In a beat-up old hotel, Mark Townsend watched one of his tenants, a woman named Mary Jack, crawl up the stairs, so crippled by the symptoms of withdrawal that she couldn't lift her body to walk. It was 1992, Townsend recalls, and doctors required a thorough examination and patient history before they would prescribe methadone to someone addicted to drugs.[1] Often that took several days.

"How can we make this woman's life bearable?" he remembers thinking. The rules were wrong, Townsend decided. He found a doctor who put Mary on methadone immediately. They broke the law. That still didn't solve Mary's addiction to heroin; she would struggle with that for many years. But they addressed her immediate pain and made her well enough to fight another day.

Like Townsend, activists, health-care workers, and some politicians in cities across North America are realizing that they will have to break and rewrite the rules on how society addresses addiction. The continent is in the grips of an overdose epidemic. In 2016, there were an estimated 64,000 fatal drug overdoses across the United States, up from less than 15,000 twenty years earlier.[2] Roughly seventy-five percent of 2016 deaths were attributed to heroin and similar drugs like OxyContin and fentanyl.[3] For people under the age of fifty, an overdose associated with an opioid is now the number one cause of death in the United States. Heroin has reached the middle class

---

1 Bruce Alexander, Barry Beyerstein, Teresa MacInnes, "Methadone Treatment in British Columbia: Bad Medicine?" *Canadian Medical Association Journal* 136 (1987): 25-28.
2 "Provisional Counts of Overdose Deaths, as of 8/6/2017" (Atlanta, GA: Centers for Disease Control and Prevention, 2017). https://www.cdc.gov/nchs/data/health_policy/monthly-drug-overdose-death-estimates.pdf
3 Josh Katz, "The First Count of Fentanyl Deaths in 2016: Up 540% in Three Years," *New York Times*, September 2, 2017.

and suburban America. At the same time, public opinion is turning against the "war on drugs." Many policymakers are beginning to look at addiction as a health-care issue as opposed to one for the criminal justice system.

One Canadian city has seen this sort of crisis before. In response, a grassroots group of drug addicts waged a political street fight for two decades to transform how Vancouver treats its most marginalized citizens.

Beginning in the early 1990s, activists pushed the city to adopt a "four pillars" approach to addiction. Authorities would continue with the pillars of prevention, treatment, and enforcement, but also deploy a series of complementary programs described as harm reduction. The city defined it like this: "The principles of harm reduction require that we do no harm to those suffering from substance addiction, and that we focus on the harm caused by problematic substance use, rather than substance use per se."[4]

In Vancouver, the municipal government accepted that it could not immediately help every addict stop using drugs. Therefore, for those people who had failed to get clean, or who simply were not ready for that step, it would attempt to make drug use less harmful.

Inherent in harm reduction is an understanding that it is not necessarily the drugs themselves that do the most damage to a user; the laws and systems of prohibition—which make drug procurement and possession illegal—are what hurt people the most. When a person addicted to cocaine injects with a dirty needle, it is not the cocaine that poses a risk of infectious disease but the syringe. So why not make a clean needle available? Yes, the risk of overdose remains, as does the much larger issue of the addiction itself, but the potential harm of an infectious disease is removed. When someone uses heroin in an alley, hurriedly injecting for fear of police, it is not the

---

[4] "Four Pillars Drug Strategy" (City of Vancouver, 2017). http://vancouver.ca/people-programs/four-pillars-drug-strategy.aspx

drug that causes them to rush and miscalculate their dose, possibly leading to an overdose. It is their fear of persecution. If they were offered an injection site where they could take their time and use under the observation of health-care professionals, the risks would be reduced. Again, the addiction remains. But if they overdose at an injection site and a nurse is there to monitor them, they live to make another attempt at long-term treatment.

Harm-reduction strategies are about keeping people alive and as healthy as possible until they can arrive at a place in their life where treatment or abstinence works for them.

———————

Today, there are dozens of cities across North America at the point where Vancouver was in the 1990s. Toledo, Miami, and San Francisco, for example, have sprouted activist groups that are working with health-care professionals to slowly warm public opinion to this issue.

"Ninety percent of new heroin users are white. A rising number are middle class or wealthy," a US official told *Frontline* on PBS in 2016. "It's been true throughout American history that when drugs penetrate into the middle class—the white middle class—politicians panic much more than they do when the drugs are concentrated in poor neighbourhoods. It's not fair and it's not right, but that is the kind of country that we are living in."

Jurisdictions across the United States are looking to Vancouver's example with increasing interest. One of the founders of Vancouver's harm-reduction movement, Mark Townsend, spent April 2016 in New York, helping the city expand needle-exchange programs. In October 2016, a delegation from Seattle visited North America's first supervised-injection facility, Insite, in Vancouver. In early 2017, former BC coroner and mayor Larry Campbell was in Sacramento helping lawmakers draft policies that would allow for the establishment of supervised-injection facilities in California. Interest in Vancouver's model has grown with the increasing severity of America's opioid problem.

———————

Fighting for Space is about people who slipped through the cracks. It is about those who have suffered the consequences of addiction and prohibition and who did not have family or friends to help them get back up. It is about those who, for a myriad of reasons, failed with treatment and rehabilitation. It tells their stories and explains harm reduction for communities that are struggling with overflowing jails, crimes fuelled by desperation, and people left in the streets to die.

It's also about the activist movement that fought for harm reduction in Canada, which came out of a small neighbourhood in Vancouver called the Downtown Eastside. It's only twenty square blocks and has long held notoriety as the poorest urban neighbourhood in the country. But in the 1990s, its residents banded together to demand a say in drug policy.

They called for harm-reduction services to provide the stability, space, and time that some people need to find treatment services that might help them eventually control their addiction. It's a simple yet revolutionary idea: that everybody deserves a home regardless of their drug abuse or destructive behaviour, and that an addict is a human being who should be treated with dignity.

Despite officials' reluctance, a conversation about harm reduction is being forced on North America by an unprecedented increase in opioid addiction and an almost-unfathomable spike in overdose deaths.

Chapter 1
Toledo, Ohio

Matt Bell was in a coma for five days. He woke up in a hospital in downtown Toledo, Ohio. Although disoriented, he knew where he was and that he'd overdosed to get there.

"Fuck," Bell remembers thinking as he opened his eyes. "I messed up again." It was November 2014.

After another two days at ProMedica Toledo Hospital—while his body learned how to walk again—Bell was ready go home. He grabbed the bag that the hospital had stuffed his possessions into when he arrived, and his girlfriend drove him home. As he was unpacking his things, he found a business card. "Lucas County Sheriff's Office," it read. Bell moved to throw it in the trash but then slipped it into his wallet instead.

Bell had been a freshman at the University of Toledo. He'd graduated high school with a straight-A report card and received a full scholarship for baseball. Major League teams, including the Baltimore Orioles and Toronto Blue Jays, were already scouting him. How he found himself waking up from a heroin overdose in a Toledo hospital is a story that will sound very familiar to thousands of opioid addicts across North America today.

"I hurt my shoulder," Bell begins. "They did surgery, and they gave me ninety Percocets. And that's all she wrote. I abused Percocets to an extreme," he continues. "And then somebody introduced me to Oxy[Contin] because those were stronger. And then I started doing Oxy. That became a $400-a-day habit. And then it went to heroin."

In the eight years between his first time using heroin and the five days he spent in a coma at ProMedica Toledo Hospital, Bell tried and failed at rehab twenty-eight times. He was arrested thirteen times in four different states. He previously overdosed twice. Once he found himself in a back alley, where his dealer had dragged him and left him to die. The second time was at his mother's house, where Bell woke up covered in vomit. Bell's third overdose, in November 2014, was the one that came closest to killing him.

There were 2,744 drug-overdose deaths in Ohio that year, placing it among the top five states in America for drug fatalities.[5]

Twenty-seven hundred deaths is triple the roughly 900 fatal overdoses that Ohio saw one decade earlier, in 2004. Since 2014, the number has continued to climb, to 3,310 in 2015 and then to an estimated 4,000 deaths in 2016.[6] In June 2017, NBC News reported that based on deaths during the first five months of the year, Ohio's Montgomery County coroner predicted the state will see 10,000 fatal overdoses in 2017.[7] That's more than the entire country recorded in any given year during the early-1990s.

The overdose crisis that Ohio is experiencing is part of an epidemic playing out across the United States and Canada. In the 1980s, there were less than 10,000 drug-overdose deaths in America each year. Twenty years later, in the mid-2000s, that number had grown to 30,000. In 2017, it's projected that America will see some 60,000 people die of a drug overdose, according to a comprehensive analysis by the *New York Times*.[8]

The very day that Bell checked himself out of that hospital in downtown Toledo, he was using heroin again. After another nine months on the drug, he put a gun in his mouth.

---

[5] Statistics throughout the book for drug-overdose deaths in the United States up to 2015 are sourced to the US Centers for Disease Control and Prevention. www.cdc.gov/drugoverdose/data/statedeaths.html

[6] "Ohio Had More Than 4,000 Overdose Deaths in 2016," The Associated Press, May 28, 2017.

[7] Jacob Soboroff, Mitch Koss, Aarne Heikkila, "'Mass-Casualty Event': Ohio County Now Tops U.S. in Overdose Deaths," NBC News, June 19, 2017.

[8] Josh Katz, "Drug Deaths in America Are Rising Faster Than Ever," *New York Times*, June 5, 2017.

He was tired of heroin and tired of the hustle it kept him on. Tired of waking up every morning in a panic over where the next fix was coming from, scheming every day for enough money to keep withdrawal at bay. He was tired of being an addict.

Then, with the gun in his mouth, he remembered the card in his wallet.

"I wasn't even supposed to be around a gun," Bell remembers thinking. "I had two active felony warrants in two different states. I had drugs and I had paraphernalia. But I called [the sheriff's office], and they came there and they took me to treatment instead of to jail."

Bell ended up at Zepf Recovery House, where he spent the next ten days going through detox and then beginning down the road to long-term recovery. At Zepf, he got to know a few guys who were in there for using the same drug, and they grew close. Before each group-therapy session, Bell and these four other men would form a circle, put their hands in the centre, count to three, and then break, raising their hands in the air like a baseball team does before taking the field. "One, two, three—Recovery!" they'd shout. Then they'd get on with their group-therapy session.

"It was a joke," Bell says. "We were feeling like shit and we were just trying to do anything to make each other feel better." But the nickname "Team Recovery" stuck.

Society doesn't make life easy for people coming out of recovery for a drug addiction. Most job applications have a box you have to tick if you've ever been convicted of a felony, and a lot of former drug users have. They tick that box and then seldom receive a call back. Meanwhile, a lot of an addict's friends are often still on drugs, which makes reconnecting with them a bad idea for anybody who's trying to stay sober. It all makes for a lot of free time. "When we got out, we were bored," Bell recounts.

"Let's go down and hold signs on Cherry and Summit," one of the guys suggested. Cherry and Summit is a busy intersection in Toledo where panhandlers sometimes congregate. The idea was to break the stereotype of a heroin addict as an unwashed homeless person standing on the side of the road asking drivers for drug money. Toledo is part of America's Rust Belt. The region was devastated by North

America's loss of factory jobs. Then, in the early 2000s, prescription opioids swept into town. Heroin followed shortly after. In Toledo—and right across North America—addiction was a disease affecting families. Team Recovery wanted families to be able to talk about it. Just like the homeless addict people imagine when they think of heroin, Bell and the guys decided they would go down to the intersection of Cherry and Summit and hold cardboard signs. But instead of asking for money, they would give it away.

"Honk if you hate heroin," one of their signs read. "Heroin's killing our town," read another. And a third, "We used to take, now we give."

Into the hand of each driver who stopped to chat for a second, they placed a one-dollar bill. "Completely flipping the stereotype," Bell explains.

People loved it.

Just about everyone who drove by Team Recovery that day knew someone who was struggling with an addiction. Many had already lost someone. Stigma prevented them from talking about it, Bell remembers thinking, but everyone knew what was going on.

The guys had created a Team Recovery Facebook page a few days earlier. It only had twelve followers, but nobody cared. It was just an inside joke and an easy way for the guys to stay in touch. If it spread a little awareness about addiction and recovery, that was a bonus. The evening after they'd taken signs down to Cherry and Summit, Bell uploaded a few photos to the Facebook page. The next morning, when he woke up and logged online, the pictures of the guys and their "Honk if you hate heroin" signs had more than 200,000 likes. In February 2016, Team Recovery decided it wanted to organize something bigger.

After they put the word out on social media, more than a thousand people gathered in the parking lot outside Zepf Recovery House one chilly afternoon. There was free food, coffee, and hot chocolate for kids. It was a family event. They had a bouncy castle and face-painting stations. On a small stage, politicians, police officers, and recovering addicts spoke about a need to break the stigma around drug use in Toledo.

A journalist with a local newspaper reported that the head of the

Toledo Police Department was there that afternoon and stood on the stage to say that it was time Ohio take a new approach to addiction. "Chief Kral called the heroin addiction a 'public health crisis' and said, although it might seem counter-intuitive to some, the police department is 'moving away from putting everyone in jail to putting the right people in jail,'" the article reads.[9]

From Zepf Recovery House, the crowd marched down Collingwood Boulevard, making a public call for government action on Ohio's overdose epidemic.

The city had never seen anything like it, Bell remembers. Toledo is a conservative town, and people seldom spoke publically about a friend or family member's drug problem. If somebody died of an overdose, that was never mentioned in the obituary. The February 2016 rally began to change that.

Team Recovery grew from there. They established a twenty-four-hour hotline for help accessing treatment services as well as for people who called just to talk. They launched an education and prevention campaign, visiting more than fifty high schools and speaking with more than 27,000 students in the first year. Team Recovery now holds twice-weekly support groups for the families and friends of people who are struggling with an addiction or who have lost someone to drugs.

In mid-2016, Team Recovery partnered with Ohio Mental Health and Addiction Services to teach overdose response. Its family-support groups usually meet at a church, and at the end of those meetings, attendees can stick around to learn how to use naloxone (the generic name for Narcan), a prescription drug that reverses the effects of an opioid overdose.

"In Lucas County, we've put out more Narcan than the health department, all pharmacies, and every other facility combined," Bell says. "And it's confirmed that some of these kits have saved lives."

Bell won't call it harm reduction. He emphasizes that Team Recovery focuses on abstinence-based treatment. They don't even encourage widely accepted opioid-substitution therapies such as methadone.

---

[9] Taylor Dungjen, "Ohioans Rally against Heroin Abuse," *The Blade*, February 26, 2016.

"We realize that everybody has their own path, but the way that we got clean and sober was through twelve steps," he says. "Harm reduction is not our purpose. Yes, it will stop the spread of disease and it will stop people from sharing syringes and all that stuff, but we think that getting somebody clean and sober will stop those things too. I can't actually support any kind of needle exchange," Bell continues. "I just can't wrap my head around it. I get that it works in other places and I know the data behind it ... but that's just not in our mission. In Ohio, it would never happen."

Few people involved in that February 2016 march down Collingwood Boulevard had ever heard the name Bud Osborn. Bell concedes that he never had. Osborn grew up in Toledo. Many years later, in Vancouver, Canada, Osborn was a key figure in a grassroots movement of drug users who transformed how Canada responds to addiction. He helped pioneer North America's first harm-reduction programs, expanding needle exchange and eventually establishing the continent's first supervised-injection site.

Some thirty years before Team Recovery existed, Osborn arrived in Vancouver, in a rundown part of the city called the Downtown Eastside.

Chapter 2

Hundred Block Rock

Walton Homer Osborn Junior was born on August 4, 1947 in Battle Creek, Michigan. But he discarded the name at a very young age.

"I was terrified of that name," Osborn recalled. "I had been told—and this really screwed me up, this was, I think, the worst thing you could do to a child—I was told that I never knew my father, that he died in the war. The thing is, because I had memories—actually memories of him, yet I was told I never knew him—I thought there was something wrong with me. Something really wrong with me, mentally, and my perception of reality."

When Osborn was still just a little boy, his family moved to a rough part of Toledo, Ohio. "A white trash neighbourhood," as he described it. "These little kids in the alley asked, 'What's your name?' And I said, 'Robert,' or something. And one little kid said, 'No it's not. It's Bud.' And so I insisted, from then on, on being called Bud."

Bud Osborn passed away on May 6, 2014, at the age of sixty-six. Just before he died, he was hospitalized for pneumonia and a heart condition. But the larger cause of his death was simply living a very hard life.

The last lengthy interview that Osborn gave was in September 2012, to a British journalist named Johann Hari. Hari wrote a book about the war on drugs called *Chasing the Scream* and, in researching that book, spent hours with Osborn at his home in the Downtown Eastside. Hari shared the tapes of those conversations.

Osborn's father, Walton, fought in World War II, flying a fighter plane for the United States Air Force. He was shot down over Austria, captured by the Nazis, and spent the rest of the war in a POW camp. Walton's legs were badly injured in the crash and while he never spoke of the experience to Osborn, there's little doubt that his imprisonment was a traumatic ordeal from which he never recovered.

"When I was three, my father hanged himself in jail," Osborn said. One night, while on a bender, Walton had tried to throw himself out of a window. Police showed up and took him to the Toledo jail to sleep it off. "He was taken there for safe-keeping, ironically," Osborn said. "While he was there, he tore his coat into strips, tied it to the grating, and hanged himself."

Later that week, the newspaper where Osborn's father once worked published a lengthy and bizarre account of events leading up to the suicide. Osborn's mother, Patricia, had been having an affair, and the newspaper shared private parts of her life in detail and explicitly blamed her for Walton's death. "These are the consequences of violating the morals of the community," the article reads, alongside a large photograph of Osborn's mother.

"After that, she began running," Osborn said. Patricia fled Toledo and the gossip and accusations that tormented her there. "She ran mainly to bars. She was either working in bars or hung out in them. So bars felt more like home to me than anywhere I'd ever lived."

As a child, Osborn regarded one person as a refuge: his grandmother. She was shot and killed by his aunt, who then turned the gun on herself.

Osborn recalled that his mother regularly brought men home to whatever trailer or small room they were renting at the time. "Really brutal drunken people," Osborn said. She would sleep with them and some would beat her. "I saw her raped right in front of me when I was four," Osborn continued. "I ran after [the man], and he just flicked me away," Osborn said. "I mean, he was a really big guy. Certainly, to me, he was really big. And then I went after him again, and he really hit me hard. This time I hit the wall. My mother just screamed, 'Stay there! Stay there.' And it was a one-room place, so I just tried not to feel, to not be aware." Osborn described the experience as "evil stabbing me."

"I vowed I would never again be intimate with another human being," he said.

Osborn was made acutely aware of pain and death at a very young age. One year after Osborn witnessed his mother being raped, he made his first attempt to kill himself.

"We had moved to some other place, and it had a really high porch on it," Osborn began. "I just hated the life I was living, the way it was. I mean, all those men, moving all the time, all the violence, all the trouble and everything." He hurled his little body off the porch and angled himself so that his head came down first, connecting with a large rock on the ground below. Osborn managed to crack open his skull.

As he got a little older, his mother began to routinely disappear on him. "That my father left one day and never came back, and my mother was always leaving—she'd say, 'I'll be back in a couple of hours,' and wouldn't come back for a few days—I thought, 'Well, the reason these people, my parents, aren't with me is because there is something really wrong with me.'"

It was a coping mechanism. If he wasn't the cause of his parents' abandonment—if it wasn't he who had driven his father to suicide and led his mother to leave—that would mean he didn't matter at all, that he was totally worthless, as if he didn't even exist. It was better to think that, although he was only five years old, he'd done something to make them leave.

"I hated myself," he remembered.

———————

Throughout his teenage years, Osborn remained extremely depressed but was able to channel all that negative energy into an obsession with sports. He would walk to a public basketball court in Toledo and shoot hoops there by himself for hours on end, running to one end of the court and back to the other. "It was like a trance," he said. Then, in his final year of high school, Osborn discovered alcohol.

"I drank for oblivion. I knew, if I drank enough, it would just knock me out." He spent the better part of a decade that way, some years intermittently attending AA meetings but often drunk for years on end. He drifted from one town to the next, aimless and depressed. One Christmas, when he was thirty-five, Osborn was back in Toledo, staying with his sister. "I had totally bottomed out," he said.

On Christmas Day, he got drunk. "I fuelled myself on alcohol." Then he took his car out for a drive. "I didn't want anybody else to be around, I didn't want to hurt anybody." On the expressway that runs through Toledo, Osborn got his speedometer up to sixty or seventy miles an hour and then steered the vehicle straight into a concrete barrier. "The last thought I had before hitting that wall was, 'I'm dead now,'" he said.

For some people who have attempted suicide, waking up in a hospital room feels like a new life, a second chance. For others, it's the ultimate defeat and the resumption of a nightmare. When Osborn regained consciousness, there was "a surgeon picking glass out of my face. And I thought, 'Oh no.'"

After alcohol came heroin. "I felt that I didn't want to kill myself anymore," Osborn said about his first time injecting the drug. "It made me feel like I wanted to be alive, as long as I could get more heroin. And also, poetry. Poetry helped keep me alive."

Osborn had begun to read the works of Charles Baudelaire, Arthur Rimbaud, and their late-nineteenth century contemporaries. "I saw their lives were a total mess and that they used drugs and all that," he said. "But what they gave me was a reason to live another hour, another day, another week, another something. I decided that this is maybe something I could do. Because I'm so totally fucked up and they're so totally fucked up. But they were able to do something that actually gives something."

Osborn purchased used collections of these writers' poetry and cut individual lines into tiny little pieces. Then he would eat them. It was an attempt to bring the greatness and the comfort he found in those words inside himself.

"What I wanted to do was help someone in that way," Osborn said. "I mean, to really connect deeply in their pain, in their suffering, the same way these poets did with me."

The state had other plans. Osborn had been drafted to fight the war in Vietnam. "There was certainly no way I was going to go somewhere and learn how to kill people," he said. "I was just adamantly opposed to it." He drove to the nearest draft office, proceeded to the first clerk he saw, and told her: "I don't accept your authority over me."

For years, the military's draft cards continued to find him, somehow arriving in the mail wherever Osborn laid his head. Eventually, Osborn was indicted by a federal grand jury and fled to Canada. After a few years in Toronto, he ended up in Vancouver, in the Downtown Eastside. It was 1986, and the neighbourhood was flush with potent China white heroin.

"[A]fter the board of directors meeting at the carnegie community centre I walk outside the theatre where the meeting was held to the balcony overlooking an alley to smoke a cigarette," Osborn wrote of one early memory from Vancouver.

> in the alley I see a man methodically going through the trash in an overflowing dumpster and it reminds me of men I've seen panning for gold in rock creek
>
> I see empty syringe packages floating or sunken in dark and dirty pools of water and I see a pink blouse in a heap and drug addicts scurrying to fix and I hear shouts and screams and curses and sirens blaring
>
> and I see a woman wearing a sleeveless white blouse with large purple polka dots and a short white skirt with blue stripes
>
> she's barefoot and has a multitude of bruises up and down her legs and black needle marks on the backs of her knees like a swarm of ants feasting on something sweet
>
> and there are needle tracks on her arms and on her jugular vein and she has open cuts and scratches and a white gauze bandage around one wrist the bandaging of a kind I've known to cover stitched and slashed wrists. for even china white can't quiet the flashbacks united from a childhood of rape and beatings and abandonment so common down here.[10]

---

[10] Bud Osborn, "the passion of the downtown eastside," *Hundred Block Rock* (Vancouver, BC: Arsenal Pulp Press, 1999), p. 79.

East Hastings Street running through Vancouver's Downtown Eastside.
Photo: Amanda Siebert

Osborn felt at home like he never had before. He was still chronically depressed, self-destructive, and now wired for a heroin addiction. But he was home.

To an outsider, the Downtown Eastside can be a difficult place to describe. It's not scary, if you know it, but it can look scary if you don't.

It's crowded and noisy. Through the Downtown Eastside runs East Hastings Street, Vancouver's skid row. Sidewalks on either side of Hastings are wide but still congested until late at night. Street vendors lean against buildings with blankets set out before them and used goods displayed for sale. People injecting drugs or smoking crack don't hide it here. Dealers similarly operate in the open. The neighbourhood hosts a large homeless population, many of whom struggle with a mental illness. Vancouver is one of the only major cities in Canada that seldom receives snow in the winter, and so a disproportionate number of the country's down-and-out end up here, in decrepit hotels, hectic shelters, or on the street. There's the occasional person wandering in nothing but a hospital gown, and young men wearing the gray sweats and white sneakers that the prison system gives inmates upon release. The alleys buzz with just as much activity, but with a gritty subculture to them. It's chaotic, but embedded in the commotion is a strong community. There is crime and bad things happen here. But if a woman is alone and crying on the street, another woman doesn't have to know her before she'll offer a hug. People look out for each other. The bodegas give short lines of credit to those who can be trusted with it. Most people don't have much, but they share what they can. It feels like everyone knows everyone. The Downtown Eastside is a place where you can't walk far before bumping into a friend with whom you'll stop to chat.

Osborn was thirty-nine years old when he moved into the neighbourhood. He was dramatically good looking but worn from a hard life and the last decade spent using drugs in New York City and Toronto. He had brown hair cut just above his shoulders that he wore unkempt, letting it flow in the wind, and usually dressed in faded blue jeans and a loose button-up shirt.

"For the first several years here, I was one of the drug addicts on the 100 block of Hastings and on the corner in front of Carnegie Centre," he says in a 1997 documentary called *Down Here*. "I had no life, I had no hope, I had nothing. I had done everything I could to end my life and destroy it. And yet here I am, much more alive than I ever thought I would be."

The Carnegie Community Centre is the heart of the Downtown Eastside and the 100 block is its soul. The grand old building at the corner of Main Street and East Hastings is built of Vancouver Island sandstone with imposing four-storey pillars on either side of its entrance. Those doors open onto the corner, and inside is a large lobby with an adjacent winding staircase. Stained-glass windows give it the feel of a church.

Originally built as Vancouver's main library, the Carnegie building was constructed between 1901 and 1903. When the city moved its books elsewhere in 1957, Carnegie was mostly left empty and fell into disrepair. Through the 1950s and '60s, the commercial centre of the city moved southwest, contributing to a long decline of the

Downtown Eastside. A 1965 report describes what the area that was once Vancouver's centre had become: "Many people live here because they have little choice. Some are physically disabled and live solely on welfare assistance; some are pensioners eking out their allowances in the cheapest accommodation they can find. Some, by lack of skills, are virtually unemployable, and some live here simply because they enjoy the constant activity of the area. Compared to the rest of the city, few people here have any family ties. Many have acute personal problems—almost all are poor."[11]

Carnegie eventually reopened as a community centre in 1980. It was viewed as a major victory for the Downtown Eastside but didn't slow the neighbourhood's descent into poverty. By the time Osborn arrived in 1986, dealers had owned the corner of Main and Hastings for many years. An open-air drug market attracted a constant flow of seedy foot traffic.

From that corner, the 100 block runs west. It's a crowded strip of destitution, home to a number of single-room occupancy hotels, or SROs. The Downtown Eastside was and still is largely a collection of SROs, though that has begun to change with the arrival of gentrification in recent years. An SRO is a building characterized by small rooms, usually less than 250 square feet (twenty-two square metres), with shared bathrooms on each floor. In the early years of the twentieth century, this layout was fine for the lumberjacks for whom these hotels were built. The men stayed a few days, enjoyed city life, and then returned to British Columbia's forests, where the booming logging industry was then in full swing. By the 1980s, however, most logging jobs were gone and the Downtown Eastside's SROs were filled with the region's mentally ill, physically disabled, drug users, and poor.

In the neighbouring city of Coquitlam stands Riverview, a massive complex of buildings that opened in 1913 as the Hospital for the Mind. In the 1950s, it was home to a peak patient population of 5,500 people who struggled with a range of severe mental illnesses.[12] In the decades

---

[11] *Downtown East Side* (Vancouver, BC: The City of Vancouver, 1965).

[12] John Higenbottam, *Into the Future: The Coquitlam Health Campus: A Vision for the Riverview Lands* (Coquitlam, BC: City of Coquitlam, 2014).

that followed, the institutionalization of the mentally ill became increasingly unpopular in North America, and Riverview stopped taking new patients. Many argue that was for the best. Riverview was the sort of stereotypical institution that treated people poorly and led to a backlash against the entire concept of forced care. But as Riverview stopped taking new patients and was slowly decommissioned, the provincial government failed to build a new system of care for the mentally ill to take its place. The thousands of people who struggled with a mental illness and lacked family support ended up in the only place where they could afford housing or, failing that, where they were accepted on the streets and in the alleys: the Downtown Eastside.

The neighbourhood's downhill slide continued until 1993, when the Woodward's department store closed its doors. This event is widely remembered as the Downtown Eastside's arrival at rock bottom. The once middle-class shopping complex occupied an entire square block. When it went out of business, the majority of shops that lined Hastings Street closed shortly after, their windows boarded up. Some properties were left vacant, though dozens of pawn shops and beer parlours opened. The Downtown Eastside no longer had anything to offer the middle class.

In 1999 a journalist with the *New York Times* visited and described it this way: "The area of no more than a dozen square blocks, with roughly 16,000 residents packed into various shelters, single-room-occupancy hotels and apartments, is the site of eighty percent of Greater Vancouver's drug-related arrests, though it represents only three percent of the region's population. Of the 16,000, about 6,000 are addicted to intravenous drug use. And with those numbers comes a darker statistic as well: with an HIV infection rate as high as fifty percent among the area's intravenous drug users, according to the police, the Downtown Eastside had the highest rate in the developed world." [13]

Osborn took comfort in the rawness of the neighbourhood, in what he called its "soundtrack," the sirens of police cars and ambulances, the shaky clacking of shopping carts pushed along the sidewalk, and

---

[13] Murray Whyte, "Fighting Addiction by Documenting Its Wretchedness," *New York Times*, November 7, 1999.

the soft calls of drug dealers selling crack, cocaine, methamphetamine, and heroin.

"Rock? Powder? Jib? Down?" they asked passersby. The same poem, over and over, all day and all night.

The early 1990s were hard years for addicts in the Downtown Eastside. There wasn't a single clinic in the neighbourhood and access to clean needles was severely restricted. Osborn recalled one weekend he spent in a flophouse injecting heroin with a group of gay sex-trade workers that he'd met on the street. "There would be, like, six of us lined up on this one raggedy needle," he said. "How I dodged HIV, I have no idea."

Osborn's opinion of heroin was never totally negative. Even in the years before he died, after he was clean for some time, he spoke fondly of the drug, arguing that for him, it had its uses. Heroin ended his frequent nightmares, let him sleep, and curbed suicidal thoughts that had followed him since he was just a little boy. "I felt good, I didn't hate myself," he said. "I felt this warmth in the pit of my gut, which had always been really cold."

Osborn maintained that it wasn't the drug that does the most damage, but rather its criminalization. "Prohibition has made a nightmare of my life," he said. "I was so screwed up. If I could have had heroin through those times, through those years, until I stabilized in some kind of way ... my life would have been very different." He did, however, dislike how the drug affected his ambition and, by extension, his poetry.

"I was running back and forth on drugs and alcohol—on anything—and I just felt a complete failure with poetry," Osborn said. "I wasn't accomplishing what I had intended, which was to write a poem that could speak to another human being, as all those poets I read initially had spoken to me, had helped me to live, to go on."

By the mid-1990s, Osborn was doing better for himself than he acknowledged. In 1995, a book of his poetry called *Lonesome Monsters* was published to critical acclaim. It was followed by others that achieved similar success. He was also keeping a busy schedule of readings and playing in two bands that did well on a local level. His writing was gritty and deeply rooted in the neighbourhood in which he lived.

"The one credo I have is just to write the truth," he said. "What I see. And if someone says something, exactly what they say. That's the one thing I figured I could do. I may not be the most gifted poet or anything like that, but at least I can tell the truth about what I see and what I hear. I made that an absolute vow."

Eventually, Osborn did achieve the one measure of success he sought more than any other.

"I went on this reading tour around BC with some other poets," he began. "We were way up north at Smithers, and there was a high school there. I'd written a poem called 'When I was Fifteen,' and it was about when I was fifteen years old and took more than 200 aspirin, trying to kill myself." It wasn't the typical sort of poem most people would pick for a reading at a high school, but Osborn explained it was a selection that was honest. After the reading, a young girl rushed up to him, "just glowing, actually," he continued. "And she said that she had, earlier that week, taken a great many aspirin trying to kill herself, and had just come back to school that day."

A teacher unlocked a door to a classroom where there was a photocopier so that Osborn could leave the girl with a copy of the poem he had read. "She told me about herself at some length," he said. The girl explained that she felt alone and alienated. "My parents tell me I can't be depressed because they give me everything," she said.

"When she was leaving, she was clutching the poem and was just radiant," Osborn said. "And thinking about living, not about dying. I thought, 'Finally, a poem has accomplished what I had attempted all those years before.'"

Chapter 3

A Chance Encounter

In 1986, Mark Townsend was a bit of a punk. His hair was tied in scraggly dreadlocks, bleached, and then dyed pink and blue. He was tall, thin, and always wore skinny black jeans paired with a leather jacket. In June of that year, he was on his way back to London after several months travelling in Northern Ireland. On a warm spring day in a quiet country town called Frinton on Sea, he and his friend Steve were walking to the post office along Connaught Avenue when they bumped into a young woman from Canada who recognized Steve as an old friend from childhood.

"She was called Liz," Townsend says with affection. "She was looking for a place to stay in London. So I said, 'Why don't you come with us?' And she did, the very next morning."

Liz Evans was a twenty-year-old nursing student at the University of Ottawa. She had long, dark hair and seldom wore jewellery or much makeup, if any. She was a bit of a tomboy, with a look and demeanor that was gentle while strong. On vacation in Frinton to visit her mother, Evans had plans to live in London for the summer, working with a Christian mission serving meals to the poor.

"I was having a crisis of faith," Evans remembers. "I came up against the hard, cold reality that Christianity was incapable of meeting people where they were at. It really upset me. I didn't like the church anymore, so I couldn't go and do this thing that I had committed to. I arrived in my mom's hometown and I didn't even know if I believed in God anymore."

There on Connaught Avenue in idyllic Frinton on Sea, Evans poured her heart out. "I just started ranting about how I didn't know what I was doing and I didn't have a job in London and I was having this faith crisis and I didn't know who God was anymore and I didn't know what the meaning of life was anymore and I was just so angry."

Liz Evans in 1992, roughly a year after she started at the Portland Hotel.
Photo: Steve Bosch / Vancouver Sun

Townsend thought it was all a bit funny, but the two hit it off.

"I went back to Steve's house," Evans continues, "and we stayed up and talked for hours about politics and God and religion, and listened to tapes." The next morning, Townsend and Steve were waiting outside her mother's house.

"I got in a car and drove with them to London and ended up living with them in their flat," Evans says. "They had a big house and tons of roommates. We all lived in East London for the summer, and I fell totally in love with Mark."

Townsend, however, was dating a girl named Mary. It was quite a while before he shared Evans's feelings, but the two immediately became best friends. "I would sneak up into his loft each night and we would just spend the whole night talking. We were really good friends for a long time."

The house was a tall and narrow brick structure in an area of London called New Cross. "Mark had a lot of friends and kind of a crazy community of people who came by the house all the time," Evans remembers. "They were all interesting characters ... It was great. We did a lot of weird things."

Townsend was employed at The Old Vic Theatre, working in the stage-lighting department on a production of Bernard Shaw's "Widower's House." He found the work exciting but, like Evans, he sought something with a larger purpose. "It was a very meaningful play," Townsend says. "But I thought, 'Can this really change things? Can it make things a little better for people? No.' And it was in that moment that I thought, 'I don't know if I want to do this.'"

Money was short that summer. Evans worked in a cafeteria at the Greenwich Maritime Museum "for about a minute" before she decided she couldn't bear it. They survived on tea and toast but were never bored. Semi-famous stars of the London underground occasionally dropped by the house. They travelled to Bristol, hitchhiked all the way to the south of France, and spent a weekend camping in an old tent on the outskirts of Cornwall. The summer flew by.

Mark Townsend in 1991, shortly after he moved from the UK to Vancouver. *Photo: Mark Townsend*

"It was the '80s in London with goths and parties in church basements and weird movie projections everywhere," Evans remembers. "It all seemed so exciting to me, coming from nursing school in Ottawa."

Then Evans returned to Canada for the next semester at school, "very depressed." She spent the next two years completing her nursing degree and working part-time at two women's shelters in Ottawa's Sandy Hill neighbourhood. She contemplated further education in psychiatry but found she didn't like the mental-health professions, or at least not the way they were practiced at the time. "I found it depressing and dehumanizing," she says.

Without strong ties to Ottawa, Evans and her roommate decided to move west, to Vancouver. Meanwhile, Townsend was trying to convince her to move to London (despite his relationship with Mary). But Evans had just spent four years working to obtain a degree in nursing, and it would go to waste if she moved to the United Kingdom, where it wasn't recognized.

Common sense won out. She moved to Vancouver and took a job in the emergency department at Vancouver General Hospital. That was the summer of 1989. Townsend would follow her there a couple of years later. Back in London, he had developed an activist streak.

Townsend's family comes from an area of Bristol called St. Paul's.

It's a poor working-class, multi-ethnic inner-city suburb that takes pride in itself. It's St. Paul's to which Townsend gives credit for his inclination to rebel. In the spring of 1980, he recalls, a force of more than 100 police officers was sent into the neighbourhood to raid the Black and White Café, a notorious drug den run by immigrants from Jamaica. Police trucks blocked each end of the street and officers poured forth. More than a thousand St. Paul's youths engaged in a violent standoff with police.

"The community defended the café against the police, and the police were actually chased out," Townsend says. He wasn't at the Black and White Café that day, but he recalls hearing about the riot and feeling that the protesters' victory over the police emboldened him to challenge authority.

The same year, Townsend's younger brother, Glen, entered his freshman year at Aberystwyth University. The semester had just begun when he suffered some sort of a mental breakdown. Townsend was only twenty-two at the time and away at the University of London, but his mother called him and asked for his help. Glen had been transported back to Bristol and admitted to Barrow Gurney Hospital, an old-fashioned psychiatric institution that had fallen into disrepair some two decades earlier. It was an isolated place in the forest. "The doctors are there, and they're all very nice at the beginning," he says. "Then they tell me about the treatment, which is going to be electro-convulsive therapy."

Showing a will, persistence, and bit of a temper that would terrorize political opponents many years later, Townsend spent the next twenty minutes locked in an argument with the psychiatrist overseeing his brother's treatment. "I kick up such a fuss," he says. By the time Townsend was finished, not only was his brother no longer going to receive electro-convulsive therapy, but he was no longer going to remain at Barrow Gurney Hospital at all.

His brother, who had locked himself in a bathroom and remained uncommunicative throughout the ordeal, was transferred to another, more modern facility where he received therapy and fully recuperated. But Townsend never forgot the situation in which he found Glen at Barrow Gurney. "I saw what a pile of shit the system was, a system that thinks it knows what it's doing but doesn't."

Ten years later, on March 31, 1990, thousands of Britons across the country took to the streets in what became known as the Poll Tax Riots. The Conservative government of Margaret Thatcher was about to implement a major set of tax reforms that many criticized as saving money for the rich while increasing the burden placed on the lower classes.

Townsend remembers the day as if he was at the front of a crowd of 20,000, marching up Langham Place in Central London to the doors of the all-mighty British Broadcasting Corporation. "We felt like we were leading the crowd," he says, chuckling. "So we decided, let's go to the BBC and broadcast that we had taken over the country. We ran up the steps and tussled with the security guards. We looked behind us, and this mob just stood at the bottom of the stairs at Langham Place. It was just me and my friend inside with all the security. So we turned and ran away."

Townsend recalls the day as a learning experience. "I thought, 'Well, that sums up how it all works. Change is a tough thing to get.'"

Meanwhile, in Vancouver, Evans quickly grew disillusioned with the job she had only just started. At the city's largest hospital, she worked in the emergency psychiatry and assessment unit, seeing patients who were brought there in the depths of their mental-health crises. She hated how the system categorized and broke people down to nothing more than symptoms and solutions. "People were reduced to labels and to a disease model, and so the problems that you were able to address were not really the whole person's problems; they were a tiny fraction of an issue," Evans says. Worse, she noticed that when the hospital could not address a person's mental-health issues, that patient was simply ejected from the system. "They would literally give up on people, and that was their MO. 'I can't do anything with this person. There is no outcome that is worth my time. So I can write them out of my caseload.'"

Evans wondered how anyone could ever really get better when health-care professionals never even attempted to look beyond the symptoms a patient displayed to what was truly bothering them below the surface. She wanted to look at each patient as a whole and begin to address what had caused them to experience a crisis. "I was only seeing them in the emergency department," Evans says. "So there was this giant disconnect between what mattered to people in their day-to-day lives and these brief episodes of emergency."

Her superiors noticed her restlessness and reluctance to embrace the norms of psychiatric care. "In one of my evaluations there, I was told that I rebelled against seeing people as sick," she says. "I found that years later in a review from a head nurse."

Evans had grown up around mental illness. Her childhood was happy but confusing for her. She was born in New York City where her father, Emyr Wyn Evans, worked as a pathologist. When Liz was three, the family moved to Newmarket, Ontario, where Wyn (he used his middle name) settled permanently. Her mother, Jane, left a few years later, when Evans was six. In the years that followed, Jane came and went, occasionally taking Evans for short periods to wherever she was living. One year it was London, another it was Colchester, the next it was Frinton on Sea.

"I was pretty much raised by my dad," Evans says. "My mum really didn't ever feel competent to be a mother. So when I was born, she took one look at me and decided I didn't need her, because she was not really fit. And so even though she was around, on and off, she never really was very present."

Evans recalls one weekend when she was eight years old, her parents sent her on a Girl Guides trip to a lake in Ontario. "I didn't know any of the other girls there and I really hated it," Evans recalls. When the weekend was finally over, her mother and father picked her up for what she thought would be the drive home to Newmarket.

"My mum was wearing a black fake-fur coat," Evans remembers. "I was sitting in the back seat of the car, and she said, 'Oh, Lizzy, we're driving to the airport.' I said, 'Really, why?' And she said, 'Oh, because I'm going back to England.'"

Evans buried her head in her mother's big fur coat and sobbed the rest of the way to the airport. "So it's just me and dad again," she remembers her little eight-year-old mind thinking. "It happened many, many times. There was no warning ever." Evans never blamed her mother. "To me, she was my mum, and I just loved her," she explains. "I didn't think she was sick or mentally ill. I just thought she wasn't very happy."

———————

It wasn't long before Evans quit her job at Vancouver General Hospital.

"I would come home [from work] and cry all the time, I hated it so much," she says. "I just wasn't particularly drawn to looking at people as sick. I didn't find it a helpful mechanism for helping people. So I left."

It was the spring of 1991, and Evans had just moved from Vancouver's West End to the edge of the Downtown Eastside. Shortly after, a friend of hers employed as a social worker told Evans about a community group called the Downtown Eastside Residents Association, or DERA.

Formed in 1973 as a nonprofit organization that focused on affordable housing, in the decades that followed, DERA became a political force in Vancouver and successfully lobbied the government to support several large housing projects in the Downtown Eastside. Just before Evans moved into the neighbourhood, DERA was awarded a contract to run a mental-health program in a few rooms of a rundown old hotel called the Rainbow.

"I didn't know anything about the Downtown Eastside at that time," Evans says. "But I just showed up and went in and started talking to Jim Green."

Green was DERA's larger-than-life leader. An old-school organizer like you might find on the front lines of a rowdy union picket line, he was an effective champion of affordable housing for the working class, but he didn't know a lot about about mental health. And the Rainbow Hotel was a dilapidated building filled with problem tenants who had been kicked out of just about everywhere else. Nobody in DERA was sure what to do with it. Green renamed it the Portland Hotel after the city in Oregon had implemented a series of progressive social-housing policies.

"Really, that was as far as Jim got in his thinking about what to do with the actual building," Evans recalls. She didn't know what she would do with the hotel either, but Green just about hired her on the spot. "I walked in the door of my house after the interview and the phone rang and they asked if I could start right away."

Chapter 4

Hotel of Last Resort

The Portland Hotel is located on the southeast corner of Carrall and East Hastings streets. The hotel shares the intersection with Pigeon Park, a small collection of benches screwed into a concrete space with a couple trees hanging over them. An open-air drug market operates there, and the benches make it a popular spot for the neighbourhood's homeless people and alcoholics.

The hotel itself was built in 1908, and when Evans took the keys in March 1991, that was apparently the last time anyone had bothered to give it so much as a fresh coat of paint. Vancouver's old cable-car line once ran down East Hastings, making the hotel a prime location in the early twentieth century. But those days had come and gone. The Portland was now a slum; paint peeled off the walls, the pipes leaked, the floor was filthy, and the lighting was dim. The Portland's tenants were only there because it was one step better than living on the streets.

"We ended up being known as the 'hotel of last resort,'" Evans remembers.

On paper, Evans's job was to support ten of those tenants who were diagnosed with severe mental-health issues. In fact, the entire hotel was hers to run as she saw fit. "To start, I focused a lot on practical things: vacuuming and cleaning, changing door locks, and trying to figure out how to paint a room and hang curtains," she recalls. "I did everything from cleaning to personal care to helping people with their welfare workers or whatever issues people had. It was absolutely, completely overwhelming."

There were a lot of empty rooms in the hotel, so Evans also began to fill them up, taking people in off the street who were blacklisted from everywhere else. After just a few weeks, Evans was responsible for sixty or seventy people. "People who came with mental-health issues, HIV, criminal histories, and drug use," she says. "That is who needed the support."

Outside of the hotel, the Downtown Eastside was just as beat-up as the building Evans was given.

In British Columbia, welfare cheques are issued on the last Wednesday of every month, so once every four weeks, the Downtown Eastside is flooded with cash. Drug dealers circle the banks like sharks, looking for anybody with an outstanding IOU and potential customers who can rack up new debts. Government officials call it "Welfare Wednesday." Residents of the Downtown Eastside call it "Wely" or "Mardi Gras."

Liz Evans remembers her first Welfare Wednesday working at the Portland.

On the ground floor of the hotel, just around the corner from her office, there was a rough bar called the Rainbow. "The bartender was a big guy who kept a baseball bat behind the counter," Evans says. "On my first welfare day, he smashed some guy's head open with that bat. Someone came screaming into the hotel to get me. I went running out—I remember, I was wearing the most inappropriate clothing, a cotton skirt and my hair in pigtails."

The man lay on the sidewalk with his skull broken open. "I'm holding this guy's brain in, and there's blood everywhere, all over my skirt. I remember waiting for the ambulance to show up, wondering if he was going to live or die," Evans recalls. "It was just one of those moments," she adds. "What the fuck am I doing in the middle of all of this? Holy shit." It was May 1991, and Evans was twenty-five years old.

"He was a Hispanic drug dealer, was what I was told," Evans continues. "But as far as I was concerned, he was another drug user. That's one of so many stories that illustrates the hatred of people who used drugs in the community, not just by the outside world, but by people in the community too. Drug users were seen as scum."

In the early 1990s, the Downtown Eastside's drug scene was blowing up. The city had begun a slow but sustained effort to thin out a concentration of bars in the Downtown Eastside that had come to give it a rough edge. But closing the bars had the unintended consequence of pushing some people into drugs and creating room for that market to grow. Around the same time, injection cocaine arrived on the scene.

Everyone who lived at the Portland was severely addicted to drugs or alcohol. Evans estimates that ninety-five percent were injection users. "They were treating themselves badly and treating each other badly because they didn't feel like their lives were worth much," she says. "I was getting to know people and listening to their stories. And always the common denominator was, 'My life is worth shit and I don't matter.' That was the piece that really made me think about my mum and think, 'Well, fuck, these are just people in the world who don't feel like their lives have a right to occupy space.'"

While she was never abused, Evans saw her own life in the lives of her tenants. "I had grown up with a mentally ill mother. I never had thought of her as sick; I just thought she was a really nice person who was broken and sad," she explains. "And so I just saw [the Portland tenants] as broken and sad. These people are lovely, but they don't fit. For whatever reason, there is no space for them. They don't fit anywhere in the world, and the world, to them, feels like a very unwelcoming place." Inside the Portland, she worked to create a sanctuary.

Her tenants were the hardest to house in Vancouver. A survey she conducted that year found that Portland tenants had lived, on average, eleven different places during the previous twelve months. "They literally moved every month because they were so complex to deal with," she says. At the Portland, Evans found ways for those people to keep a roof over their heads. "That meant, when people were psychotic, not forcing them into a hospital," she says. "When people were doing eccentric things, it meant not arresting them for it, and learning how to accommodate a lot of different, eccentric behaviours and characteristics." Instead of pushing people to fit into the rules of the hotel, Evans bent the Portland's policies and safeguards to fit around its tenants.

"One of the first guys we housed was a really sweet guy named Joe," Evans begins. "He had a tendency to hear voices and then smash his fist through glass windows. That was just sort of his thing. He would hear something and then he would put his fist through glass or he would throw something out his window. He was a very gentle person, actually, very charming, sweet. The staff all loved him. But he would do this thing where he would smash windows, and that made him hard to house."

Evans bolted his television set to his dresser so Joe could not throw his television out the second-storey window. To prevent him from punching through the windows, she installed large sheets of fire-grade Plexiglas that were impossible to shatter. The same measures were taken throughout the hallways on Joe's floor.

"We did lots of crazy things like that," she says. "It was about accommodating people, really understanding who people were and creatively making space work for them."

Another tenant, a chronic alcoholic named Stan, repeatedly attempted to kill himself. He "was tortured with suicidal thoughts and very, very sad," Evans says. "I'd go up and knock on his door and go and check on him, and I would find him sobbing and sobbing and sobbing." He had come into the hotel off the streets. There were other homeless people like him—First Nations guys who were barred from most other SROs in the neighbourhood, discarded as hopeless alcoholics. Evans identified a few who were Stan's friends and found room for them in the hotel. "We got some of his buddies from the street into the building and created more of a community for him," she says. Stan slowly grew a little less despondent.

There were many subcultures within the Portland Hotel: heroin addicts who flopped around the building; stimulant users who stayed up all night smoking crack cocaine; and drinkers like Stan who got blind drunk on the alcohol in mouthwash and hand sanitizer. Evans quickly found that people were happier when there was a bit of balance among the different groups and enough of these different communities for everyone to feel at home.

Other tenants just took a little getting used to. In these cases, behaviour that would have resulted in an eviction somewhere else simply became a personality quirk.

"We had this woman, Linda, who was six-foot-two and screamed at the top of her lungs all the time," Evans recalls. "The first day she moved into the building, she screamed so loud, everybody in the lobby jumped three feet off the ground. It was terrifying. It was like somebody was being murdered—a terrible gut-wrenching screaming."

The Portland's staff and tenants realized that Linda's shouting didn't actually signal that anything was wrong. It was just an involuntary outburst. "When she moved into the hotel, there was a process of getting used to her," Evans says. "But after about a week, I remember her walking through the lobby and screaming and everybody just going, 'Oh, that's just Linda.'"

Others required different creative solutions.

"One of the first people I met and who I cared for a lot was an old guy named Fred," Evans says. After forty years of chronic alcoholism, his body was giving out by the time Evans found him. That meant constant bouts of diarrhea. And because the Portland had only shared bathrooms, Fred kept a bucket in his room and used that when he needed to relieve himself. "I'd go in and change his bucket and it was really smelly. There was a strong stench in the hallway. And so, we installed an extra door in the hallway." With a second barrier in place, the smell wasn't quite so terrible.

"It was never an option to kick somebody out," Evans says. "It was like, 'Okay, what can we do to manage this situation?' Everybody was a new challenge. So what new solution did we have to create to make sure that person stayed housed?"

The primary goal was not to fix people but to give them a space to live in the greatest degree of comfort that the Portland could create. There were a lot of unhappy endings at the hotel, but endings that would have been worse had they occurred on the street.

Fred passed away in his room at the Portland two years after Evans met him. "He aspirated on his vomit," she says. "He was hanging out of his bed when I found him. That was one of the first and really incredibly depressing realities that I was confronted with. I couldn't fix things. I couldn't make Fred better. I couldn't fix forty years of chronic alcoholism. But I could bring him inside and be kind to him, and I could give him a clean bed. I could check on him every day, and he could have a home."

Evans was able to give other tenants more time. Many lived long enough to reconnect with family. One of those tenants was Tilly. "She was a sex-trade worker. Tilly was a beautiful First Nations woman, but she had had a really complicated childhood and had been severely abused," Evans begins. "When I met her, she was still working in the sex trade. One night, she came back to the hotel after she had been extremely badly beaten. She was bloodied and bruised head to toe. She'd been raped. But she didn't want me to call the police, and she didn't want me to do anything."

Evans walked her up to her room, cleaned her up best she could, and cradled her in her arms for hours that night. "I was holding her, and she was crying and sobbing. And what she kept saying to me over and over again was, 'It's my fault. I deserved it. I'm a bad person.'" It took Evans back to her childhood, when her mother's detached nature and repeated absences left Evans feeling like she had done something wrong and that she was the reason her mother abandoned her. "I thought, 'Holy fuck, there is no difference between me and Tilly, except that she had nothing and no one and no support, and I did,'" Evans says.

She worked with Tilly for years, helping her take small, incremental steps to improve her life. The victories were far from total but still real. "She was always in extremely violent, abusive relationships," Evans says. "So it was really sad. I worked with her, but I couldn't force her to charge any of the people who abused her, and I couldn't force her to leave any of the abusive relationships she was in. But I could give her a home." Tilly died of AIDS, but not until many years later.

"We were too late for her because by the time I met her, she was already HIV-positive because nobody ever gave a shit about her when she was using. [No one] gave her a clean needle," Evans says, still audibly angry. But before Tilly passed away, Evans had stabilized her heroin addiction with methadone and reconnected her with children with whom she'd previously lost touch.

At the time, the medical community would not have classified Tilly's case as one where progress was made. But she had made a lot of progress. "In so many people's minds in those days, what we did was seen as without value," Evans remembers. "Because people only respected interventions that led to recovery or to rehabilitation."

Evans was simply giving a home to people who, up until then, had been told they weren't good enough to have one. The months flew by in a blur, but this chaotic period marked the beginning of something much bigger than the Portland's tiny staff could have imagined.

"The hotel of last resort," Evans says with fondness for the term. "We accommodated people, no matter who they were."

Mark Townsend reappeared in Evans's life in the summer of 1991, just a few months after she started at the Portland. He travelled to Vancouver for what he still insists was just a vacation.

"It's very hard to get a commitment out of me," Townsend says. "I was just visiting Liz for fun." He stayed at the house Evans had just moved into and shared with a rotating cast of roommates. It straddled the eastern edge of the Downtown Eastside and the more residential neighbourhood of Strathcona. One evening, Townsend went for a walk to buy milk. That was his first visit to the Downtown Eastside. "I thought, 'Shit, what the hell is this?'" he recalls. Townsend likens it to apartheid South Africa—a situation so obviously and fundamentally wrong that there was no way one could witness it without taking further action.

A few days later, Townsend returned to the neighbourhood to visit Evans at work and take her out for a cup of tea. While he was waiting for her in the lobby of the hotel, a pipe sprung a leak, so Townsend offered a hand and patched it up. Later that month, a maintenance worker that DERA had assigned to the Portland decided that he'd had enough of the hotel's unique tenant population. His resignation was symptomatic of a growing problem between the Portland and its parent organization. But it worked out for Townsend, who became the hotel's new handyman.

In addition to maintenance, Townsend quietly began implementing programs that he hoped would alleviate what he viewed as harms inflicted on tenants by the criminalization of their drug addictions. Among the first of these was a needle-distribution program that they ran at the hotel's front desk.

In the Downtown Eastside in the early 1990s, even a used needle could go for a dollar or two. "There was a guy on the corner selling needles for five dollars," Townsend recalls. The government of the day and its nonprofit partners insisted that clean needles would be distributed only on a one-for-one exchange for used needles. That sort of policy was about to contribute to an explosion of AIDS in Vancouver. But for many years the dominant logic among health-care providers stated that uninhibited needle distribution would encourage drug use and spread disease. (One-for-one requirements still exist today across much of the United States. In some jurisdictions, needle exchange remains completely illegal.)

"I thought, what is this needle-exchange crap that we're doing?" Townsend recalls. "So immediately, we got needles in the building. But that was horrifically politically complicated, because that was seen as a bad thing that encouraged drug use."

In the late 1980s, before anyone in Vancouver had heard the term harm reduction, a recovering addict named John Turvey began walking the Downtown Eastside's back alleys, handing out packaged syringes from a backpack he carried. Soon enough, he turned those walks into a registered nonprofit that became the neighbourhood's distribution system for clean syringes. Turvey called it the Downtown Eastside Youth Activities Society, or DEYAS. Today, dozens of sites across Vancouver offer clean needles free of charge and with no exchange requirement and no questions asked. But Lou Demerais, the executive director of another nonprofit called the Vancouver Native Health Society and an old friend of Turvey's, recounts how risky the idea was back then.

"I was sitting here in my office working on some other issue and John phoned me and said, 'Guess what I've done?' And I said, 'You've what!?'" Demerais recounts. "It scared the living hell out of some of us. It was against the law. But then you started thinking, 'Well, who gives a shit about the law? The law doesn't give much of a shit about us or our folks.' So when I calmed down, I thought about it and realized, you know, that's probably what we need as much as anything else. But it had shock value."

Demerais emphasizes the impact that the arrival of injection cocaine had on the Downtown Eastside beginning in the 1980s, around the same time that he connected with Turvey. He explains that while a heroin addict can get by on three or four injections a day, a cocaine addict might require a dozen or more. That meant a lot more needles were needed, and since clean gear was so hard to come by in those days, it meant a lot more people sharing needles.

"When injectable cocaine hit the streets, the [HIV/AIDS] numbers began to spike," Demerais says. "What we found among our people down here was that it genuinely took about a year and half from the time that they knew that they were [HIV] positive until they passed away. Often it was about six months. Six months. So it was happening very fast."

When the AIDS virus hit Vancouver's injection-drug user community, it spread like wildfire. A 1996 BC government report drew specific attention to this group, noting that in 1989, forty people who identified as intravenous drug users were diagnosed with HIV in BC. Five years later, in 1994, that number was 198.

"Of the 688 people who first tested positive in 1995," the report continues, "333—about one a day—cited injection drug use among their personal risk behaviours."[14] The vast majority of IV-drug users diagnosed with HIV then were not distributed across the province but were living in one neighbourhood consisting of less than twenty square blocks.

DEYAS's pioneering work in harm reduction and specifically needle exchange is worthy of incredible praise but also fair criticism. A lack of clean supplies for intravenous drug use had brought a tide of hepatitis C to the Downtown Eastside. HIV and AIDS followed shortly after. Turvey was the first person to insist that the best way to combat the spread of those diseases in the Downtown Eastside was to make clean needles more readily available. But DEYAS kept a tight bottleneck on the supply of needles from the time it initiated its programs in 1988 right through to the early 2000s.

A DEYAS pamphlet from 1996 makes clear how difficult it was for a drug user to find a clean rig: "All trading is done on a point for point basis," it begins, "You can get no more than one needle at any time

---

14 *A Report on the Health of British Columbians: Provincial Health Officer's Annual Report 1996* (Province of British Columbia, 1997), 120, C-51.

if you don't have any to trade. We do not issue needles to non-users. Clients not registered with the Exchange will be asked to confirm IV drug use by showing tracks [track marks] to the Exchange worker, or to the STD nurse."

Dr John Blatherwick was head of the regional health authority at the time and the man who ultimately oversaw the restrictions under which DEYAS operated. He recalls that authorities had to overcome successive learning curves, first within the health-care community and then in political circles. "A small group of activists got their own needle exchange going before any funding was available—they got private funding for it. I marvelled at what they were able to do," Blatherwick says. "The activism came first, and it was John Turvey and [the activists like him] who paved the way."

Soon enough, there was an understanding among health-care workers that exchange requirements limited those programs' ability to minimize the spread of disease. But health care for drug users was a highly politicized area. "You had to sell it to the politicians," Blatherwick says. "And we sold it to the politicians on the basis of a needle exchange. In other words, if we were putting 10,000 needles into the Downtown Eastside, we were taking 10,000 needles out. If you had told them we're going to put 10,000 needles in and maybe get 2,000 out, they probably would have said, 'No, the citizens of Vancouver won't support that.'"

Townsend had other ideas. Over the course of their first year at the hotel, it became obvious to him and Evans that prohibition-style drug laws were inflicting as much pain on their tenants as the drugs themselves. The criminalization of addiction—a condition that was just beginning to be understood as a disease—was inflicting tangible harms on the Portland's tenants. They began to attempt to reduce those harms.

Townsend especially was highly critical of DEYAS's limited needle-exchange programs. At the front desk of the Portland, he began doing needle distribution. When they could get away with it, if someone at the hotel needed a clean needle to inject drugs, they were going to get one. A few years before the term began appearing at drug-policy conferences in North America, the Portland Hotel was doing harm reduction. Townsend says they simply acknowledged that their tenants were using drugs and so they tried to take away a few of the risks.

At first, even the residents didn't know how to react. "I remember the very first time someone overdosed in the building, there wasn't a sense that they could tell us," Evans recalls. "They would almost rather have died because they were so scared of being caught and getting evicted."

The biggest mistake that an intravenous drug user can make is to use alone, behind closed doors. When Evans arrived at the Portland, that was the norm. People were afraid that if anyone in any sort of position of authority saw that they were using drugs, they would be evicted, so they were injecting drugs in their rooms with the doors closed. "That reflected the level of fear and anxiety and criminalization and dehumanization that was the norm ... in the community," says Evans.

"Building trust and changing that space from a criminalized space to a human space was really complicated," she remembers. "It first meant that you had to explain to people that you weren't judging who they were in the world, that you didn't actually give a shit about their drug use, and that you just wanted to be there for them."

Slowly the Portland's tenants began to leave their doors open a crack when they injected drugs. It became a subtle signal, letting people know that there was somebody inside that room who was using heroin or cocaine and that it wouldn't be a bad idea if somebody poked their head in and checked on them every so often. "It was interesting watching how the culture inside the building shifted to one where people actually started to trust the staff and ask us to come and help them," Evans says.

Tenants began to feel comfortable shouting down to the front desk when somebody overdosed. "Then we would run up to the rooms and resuscitate people," Evans says. It happened so often that she quickly lost count of the number of lives she saved performing CPR in the Portland's tiny rooms.

The year that Evans and Townsend arrived in the Downtown Eastside, 1991, was also the start of the province's epidemic of drug-overdose deaths. In 1989, sixty-four people across the province died of an illicit-drug overdose. There were eighty deaths in 1990, 117 in 1991, 162 in 1992, and then 354 in 1993.[15] A vastly disproportionate number of them were in Vancouver, in the Downtown Eastside.

"If I walked down Hastings, it was not uncommon for me to stop and have to do CPR once or twice on my way to work," Evans recalls. "Those were the days I would be puking because I was so stressed out. I used to walk into a room [in the hotel] and literally find two people down at the same time and be running from one body to the next trying to resuscitate two people and screaming, trying to get an ambulance. It was terrible and awful and sad. And it was stressful."

But for tenants who moved into the Portland that year, it was the exact opposite.

Today Stephanie Blais lives a stable life. She has a mental-health diagnosis, but not obviously so. Her speech pattern is somewhat irregular and her body language is slightly over-animated. In 1992, however, Blais was what service providers called a "million-dollar woman." That is, she was so well-known by police and ambulance services, interacting with them so regularly and spending so much time in emergency rooms, that it was estimated she singlehandedly cost the government hundreds of thousands of dollars every year.

"My mental-health diagnosis was very disruptive," Blais says, explaining that she was diagnosed with borderline personality disorder and emotional dysregulation disorder. "For about a year, I ended up calling ambulances almost every day and going to the hospital," she explains. "I'd overdose and self-harm. Not overdose on heroin or whatever—I never got into any of the actual drugs—I'd overdose on Tylenol or on antihistamines or whatever."

Almost daily 9-1-1 calls meant there wasn't a hotel in Vancouver that let Blais keep a room for very long. "I was living in a single-room occupancy suite just up on Granville Street, near Davie," Blais says. "But my mental-health diagnosis was very disruptive. So I got kicked out of the hotel and had to go stay at Lookout's emergency shelter for a bit." Essentially living on the streets of the Downtown Eastside,

---

[15] Statistics throughout the book for drug-overdose deaths in British Columbia are sourced to the BC Coroners Service. http://www2.gov.bc.ca/assets/gov/ public-safety-and-emergency-services/death-investigation/statistical/ illicit-drug.pdf

Blais' mental-health case worker suggested she try to get a room at the Portland Hotel. A few weeks passed, but she never got around to it. Then, one sunny afternoon, she was sitting on a bench in Pigeon Park.

"People kept coming up and asking me if I wanted to buy weed. I didn't know what people meant by up or down," she says, referring to dealer slang for cocaine and heroin. "I was like, 'Oh, well, I guess it's up.'"

While sitting on that bench, Blais eventually noticed the Portland Hotel just across the street. She walked over there, found Townsend at the front desk, and asked if she could have a room.

"I moved into the Portland Hotel on Wednesday, June 17, 1992, at four o'clock in the afternoon," Blais says. "Mark had dreadlocks! And he told me I could have a cat," she continues. "I didn't have a cat. But if I wanted one, I could get one."

Blais had met Liz Evans two years earlier, when she was still working as a nurse at the emergency psychiatry and assessment unit at Vancouver General Hospital. "She got to meet me when I wasn't doing very well," Blais says. But she proudly adds that encounter means that she was one of the first people Evans met in Vancouver, even before Townsend had arrived.

Blais remembers how Evans and the Portland's small staff helped her understand herself better and the problems her behaviour created by giving her more responsibility over her own life.

"The way they helped me get out of that pattern is, if I overdosed or hurt myself, the staff wouldn't call an ambulance for me unless it was a definite emergency," she says. "So if I wanted an ambulance but I was still alive and breathing, then I could call it myself." Blais explains how this made her feel a new sense of personal responsibility. At the same time, she realized that she no longer had to live in constant fear of a potential eviction notice. An enormous source of relentless stress was removed from her life.

"It was them just letting me do what I needed to do," she says. "I started wanting to do well again, to open doors again."

———————

While Evans and Townsend struggled through their first year at the Portland, Kerstin Stuerzbecher, a young nurse, was employed at a Vancouver group home for troubled teenagers. It was difficult work. The kids were there because they had been abused by their parents or forced from their family's home by other difficult circumstances. They were angry, some had serious mental-health issues, and many were violent. During an average day at work, Stuerzbecher would be cursed at, spat on, and punched or kicked by the young people for whom she was trying to provide care.

Stuerzbecher was born in Canada but spent her formative years in Hamburg, Germany, where her parents are from. After she completed high school there, she returned to Canada on her own and settled in Vancouver.

In December 1991, Stuerzbecher and her boyfriend, Kevin Grand, accompanied another couple who lived in their building to a Christmas party. It was the first of what turned into an annual gathering that Evans and Townsend hosted for the next twenty years.

Evans laughs when she remembers meeting Stuerzbecher. "She was very severe-looking, very German, with short hair, wearing a leather jacket and looking very alternative, punky, and scary," Evans says. "I was terrified of her. And Mark, of course, right away, was like, 'You should work with us!'"

There were about twenty people at the party that night, but Evans, Townsend, Stuerzbecher, and Grand spent most of the evening with each other at the kitchen table talking about social justice and their shared distaste for the cold nature of clinical health care. It took Stuerzbecher several months to decide to quit her job and take the position that Townsend had offered her at the Portland, but it was immediately clear that they all had a lot in common.

"Working in that home for teenagers and working more in an institutional-type setting just was not my cup of tea," Stuerzbecher says. "Some of the aggression and violence that we were experiencing was as a result of the restrictions that we put on people's lives, and fundamentally I did not agree with that. That evening, Mark and Liz had already convinced me that, politically and in our hearts, we believed the same things."

Stuerzbecher also had some experience with the sort of overdose crisis that was then just beginning in Vancouver. "In the '70s, heroin hit Germany quite bad, and a lot of kids died," she says. "At the main train station in West Berlin all these street kids congregated and were shooting up and dying. So people in Germany, people I knew, died."

In 1981, the German filmmaker Uli Edel made a gritty picture about the city's heroin scene that gained cult status, due in part to a supporting role played by David Bowie. In *Christiane F. – Wir Kinder vom Bahnhof Zoo* (*Christiane F. – We Children from Bahnhof Zoo*), a thirteen-year-old girl is drawn into an underground drug culture that revolves around a subway station. Townsend had seen the film and taken an interest in German cinema. He and Stuerzbecher bonded over conversations about their shared interest in such films and their growing disdain for accepted norms in mental-health care of the time.

In the decades before Evans, Townsend, and Stuerzbecher moved to Vancouver, jurisdictions across North America drastically cut services for the mentally ill. That left police and prisons as the first points of interaction many vulnerable people had with the state. Researchers at the University of Chicago compared America's prison population to that of mental hospitals. They found that since the 1970s, the rate of the former has quadrupled while the rate of the latter has fallen three-fold, to close to zero.[16] A graph tracking the sizes of the two groups over seventy years consists of squiggly lines that form an X. It suggests that the US literally transferred the people who it once housed in hospitals and health-care facilities into correctional institutions. Left to pick up the pieces of BC's mental-health-care system were nonprofit organizations and people like Evans and the team she was putting together in the Downtown Eastside.

Stuerzbecher's first day at the Portland was a case of trial by fire. Evans and Townsend had left town for the weekend and so Stuerz-

---

[16] Bernard Harcourt, "Reducing Mass Incarceration: Lessons from the Deinstitutionalization of Mental Hospitals in the 1960s," *University of Chicago Public Law Working Paper* 335 (January 26, 2011). http://dx.doi.org/10.2139/ssrn.1748796

becher was greeted at the hotel by a man named Raul wearing a white lab coat. "He said hello to me, handed me a set of keys, showed me where the mop bucket was, and said, 'Okay, here you go,'" Stuerzbecher recounts. Raul left for the night, and the hotel was hers. "I was the only staff there for seventy residents. I had never set foot in the building before, and Mark and Liz were on a ferry to Victoria. And then Raul left. So I thought, 'Okay.'" Stuerzbecher spent the next few hours exploring the hotel and attempting to introduce herself to its tenants. "I got sworn at a bit," she says. But most people just said, 'Hello, and nice to meet you.'"

Stuerzbecher was given the regular night shift at the Portland Hotel. "There was a group of people who were always up," she says. "You had people running around the building." There were safety concerns for a woman working the night shift alone at a time before cell phones were common. Stuerzbecher found the best way to address any potential risk of violence was to build relationships. She found at least one tenant on every floor who wouldn't be too startled should she have to burst into their room in the middle of the night and take shelter there.

"Once I had this teenager who was flying on something," she recalls. "God knows what. And he was chasing me down the hall with a skateboard trying to kick my head in. I had to be aware of my space and where I could go if something went sideways. Another time I was chased down the hallway by a guy who was a torture survivor from South America. He was high on coke. He'd ripped a sink off the wall and grabbed a machete and chased me down the hall. I was chased down the hall a fair amount by people with various instruments. So you wanted to make sure that you could be okay somewhere."

In addition to drug abuse, many early tenants shared a history of violence that was almost always related to a mental-health issue and for which they had been judged not criminally responsible. These people came from the Forensic Psychiatric Institute (later renamed Forensic Psychiatric Hospital and commonly referred to as Colony Farm), located in Vancouver's neighbouring city of Coquitlam. "We took loads of their people because nobody else did," Evans says. "I think they only had about forty people on their caseload, and we had ten of them living in our building."

Back then, the Portland was the only housing agency in Western Canada that was willing to offer these people a room. "We were housing all of these people that the system itself couldn't deal with, and we had one staff member on at night with seventy people in the building," Evans says. "It was insane." It wasn't until six years later, in 1997, that they were finally able to secure enough funding to keep a minimum of two staff members on at all times. "We had so many people with mental-health issues that were attached to the forensic system that eventually [the Forensic Psychiatric Institute] gave us some money," Evans says. "They considered it a safety issue."

The first year at the Portland was a learning experience for every-one. No one on staff was ever hurt, but Evans has stories similar to Stuerzbecher's. "There was a woman screaming at somebody in the hallway," Evans begins. "I had to ask her to leave. And she reacted to that badly and came after me, chasing me all through the building." Evans raced down the stairs to her office on the ground floor with the woman running after her. "I tried to shut the door behind me but she shoved her foot in the door and grabbed my necklace. She started twisting it with her finger around her giant hand until I was choking. And I thought, 'Oh, she's going to kill me. This is actually a way I could die.' It had never occurred to me before that a necklace could be used that way." Evans laughs as she continues telling the story. "It was scary, but I did get the necklace off before she actually killed me. She was very psychotic, but she was actually a lovely woman and, of course, she came back to the hotel and it was all fine."

Incidents involving a direct threat to staff were a relatively rare occurrence, and in the majority of cases, Evans, Stuerzbecher, and Townsend found they could rely on the relationships they'd established to return a disturbed tenant to a state in which they could walk them back from the edge. Evans recalls one such episode with a woman she was close to named Angela.

"One time, Angela pulled a knife on me," Evans says. "I just grabbed the knife out of her hand and was like, 'Angela, don't be an idiot. It's me. Don't pull a knife on me.' And she said, 'Oh. Oh yeah.' So rela-tionships can go a really long way."

To that end, Evans had the brave idea to take Portland residents on an annual camping trip. Stuerzbecher recalls the weekend from 1992. "The first year that we went, it was literally into the wilderness," she says.

Bright and early one summer morning, Evans pulled up outside the Portland Hotel in a big minivan. Stuerzbecher and a couple other staffers similarly arrived with their cars, and everybody piled in for a drive more than 125 miles (200 kilometers) east, away from Vancouver and into the forest. Evans and Stuerzbecher only had two or three other staff members with them on that trip.

"You were taking fifty residents who are using various substances and who may or may not be on meds to stabilize their mental health into the middle of nowhere," Stuerzbecher says. "So a few things happened that were somewhat distressing. But we dealt with them and they were always managed."

Evans bought meals from McDonalds for everybody on the bus ride up, she remembers. And then the whole weekend was filled with activities that would normally be completely out of reach for anyone living on social assistance, addicted to drugs, or struggling with a mental illness in the Downtown Eastside.

Stephanie Blais remembers these camping trips as the highlight of each year. "We'd go go-kart racing, and horseback riding," Blais says. "We'd go down to the lake and go inner-tubing, pulled behind a speedboat! It was a blast."

There was one incident where the police did have to be called. A tenant with a history of violence had come along and, on the second night, had fallen into a psychotic episode. "He's manic, he's in the woods, he has a knife, and he's saying he's going to kill people," Stuerzbecher recalls.

There were fifty other Portland campers there, plus another 200 members of the general public who were also sleeping in the park that night. So Evans took a van they had rented for the trip up to the gate of the park, where there was a payphone, while Stuerzbecher remained with the Portland campers. "This was pre-cell phones," Stuerzbecher notes. "It took the police three hours to get there."

The psychotic individual with the knife was found and taken into police custody without too much trouble, but his trip was over. By that point, it was approaching four in the morning, just about time for Evans and Stuerzbecher to wake up—had they slept—and begin making breakfast for everyone.

For just about everybody on those camping trips, however, the camaraderie Evans aimed to build at the hotel worked wonders. "I remember brushing Andrea's hair one time, just sitting by the lake," Evans says. "She was a woman who worked as a sex-trade worker, used drugs a lot, and was very, very uncommunicative when she was running around doing her stuff all day, often getting into fights with people. And there we were, sitting by the lake. She had gone into the water and I remember brushing her hair and having a really wonderful conversation. The fact that she let me brush her hair felt very intimate."

Staff at the Portland sought to build relationships with every one of their tenants. But Stuerzbecher recalls one man she had trouble with named Max. "He was a heavy drinker, and he would come in every single evening blasted out of his mind," she begins. "Then he would stand in the entryway of the building and try to tear off his shirt and swear up a storm and be extremely nasty to me." Every single evening, she emphasizes.

"And he came on a camping trip. I was thinking, 'Oh, God, of all the people, really, did you have to come too?' But then I thought, 'What am I doing here? Why am I actually here at the Portland?'"

That year, the group was camping at Manning Park, which sits on the edge of a picturesque lake surrounded by forested mountains. Stuerzbecher decided she would ask Max if he would accompany her on a canoe trip, and he agreed. They set off, but once they were up an arm of the lake, away from camp, it started to rain. "Pouring, heavy rain," Stuerzbecher remembers. "Of course."

An hour into the trip but still without having said a word to each other, Max and Stuerzbecher paddle under a bridge to wait out the storm. "We're in the canoe, sitting under this bloody bridge," Stuerzbecher says. "So we started talking. He told me about his life. We sat there and chatted for two hours, starting with his life story and then just chatting about the world."

Two nights later, Stuerzbecher was back at the front desk of the

Portland and Max was out somewhere drinking. When he returned to the hotel in the early hours of the morning, he resumed his usual routine.

"I'm on the night shift, he comes in, and again he's drunk," Stuerzbecher says. "He started to swear, he started to tear off his shirt, and then he looks at me." Max froze, caught Stuerzbecher's eyes with his, held them for a second, and a calm fell over him. He walked up the stairs to his room and never resumed his nightly lobby outbursts again.

———————

The Portland Hotel became something of an oasis. The building itself was falling apart, but it was safer than the streets. The tenants whom Evans brought to live there no longer feared being robbed while they slept in a stairwell or harassed by police for using drugs in an alley. At the Portland, they had a room where they could be themselves, however difficult a person that might be.

Chapter 5

Rat Park

In 1970, Bruce Alexander was a rookie professor of psychology at Simon Fraser University (SFU), located on a small mountain that overlooks Vancouver from the neighbouring city of Burnaby.

"Because I was new, I had to teach whatever they told me to teach—what nobody else wanted to teach," he recalls. "So I had to teach a course called social issues, which, in those days, meant heroin addiction."

It was a topic Alexander knew nothing about. So he paid a visit to the Narcotic Addiction Foundation of BC, a quasi-government institution that primarily existed to distribute methadone (before the task was passed on to pharmacies). He was put to work as a counsellor, seeing heroin addicts who were mostly from the Downtown Eastside.

"They would say, 'I dropped out in grade nine and really, I'm not very good at school or anything like that, but this is a place where I belong,'" Alexander says. "I would go back up [to SFU] and tell those stories to my class." For many students, that message resonated and sparked new ideas. Perhaps feelings of social isolation had something to do with drug abuse, some of the students hypothesized. Were these people using drugs because they were unhappy? If that was the case, there could be implications for treatment.

Other students dismissed the question outright, insisting they already had the answer. "Don't you know about the rats?" they said.

A Skinner box is an uncomfortable place for an animal to live. It is small, keeps whatever is inside of it in total isolation, and can be equipped to deliver different forms of rewards and punishments. Subjects can be given a treat when they exhibit one kind of behaviour and an electrical shock when they perform another. A Skinner box (also known as an operant conditioning chamber) can also give the animal inside a small amount of control over intakes such as food and water with a button or lever that, when activated, will release, for example, a food pellet.

In the early 1960s, experimental psychologists at the University of Michigan developed a new application for the Skinner box. In addition to food and water, they added a device that allowed the rats inside to produce another kind of substance: narcotics. In this sort of Skinner box, there is a lever on a wall of the cage and when a rat pushes down on it, a simple machine releases a set amount of morphine, amphetamine, cocaine, or heroin, depending on the experiment. From a tube that enters the cage, the narcotic flows down to where it is taped to the rat. The drug then rushes through a catheter inserted straight into the animal's jugular vein. The animal presses on a lever, and nearly instantly, it receives a flood of powerful and mind-altering drugs. It's a cause and effect that even a rat figures out very quickly.

"The rats would just press and press and press," Alexander says. "Sometimes they would starve to death while they were pressing the lever for dope. So they were very dramatic results."

A few years later, similar results were observed in experiments with monkeys that were strapped into restraining chairs and given the ability to inject themselves with morphine. The rats and then the monkeys were obviously addicted. But why? For quite some time, nobody bothered to ask. The assumption was that the rats were addicted because they were doing drugs.

This was the pharmaceutical theory of addiction, or what Alexander calls the "demon drug" view. Experiments that appeared to support this analysis were repeated and, over the course of two decades, the theory gained widespread and firm acceptance among academics and then politicians across North America.

In a typical example of the thinking of the day, a 1979 paper by Avram Goldstein, a highly distinguished addictions expert and the founder of Stanford University's pharmacology department, describes the power of narcotics observed in such experiments as irresistible.

"If a monkey is provided with a lever, which he can press to self-inject heroin, he establishes a regular pattern of heroin use—a true addiction—that takes priority over the normal activities of his life," it reads. "Since this behaviour is seen in several other animal species (primarily rats), I have to infer that if heroin were easily available to everyone, and if there were no social pressures of any kind to discourage heroin use, a very large number of people would become heroin addicts."[17]

Substances so powerful could not be allowed to freely circulate within a productive society. Earlier the same decade, on June 17, 1971, US President Richard Nixon declared that illicit substances like cocaine and heroin would be considered "public enemy number one." The war on drugs was underway.

But Alexander's conversations with addicts from the Downtown Eastside made him and a growing number of his students wonder if the drug itself was really where the story of an individual's addiction began. "I was, at that time, not at all a rebel against the accepted theory," Alexander says. "I thought it was probably true ... But I thought of myself as a scientist, so why not test it?"

Alexander and his team got to work. They focused on the rats' environment, the Skinner box, and strategized how to test whether or not different living conditions would affect an animal's decision to press the button that injected them with drugs. At Simon Fraser University, the researchers constructed what they envisioned as the opposite of a Skinner box: a paradise for rats, or Rat Park.

Instead of a Skinner box's steel floor equipped to deliver electric shocks, the animals at Rat Park enjoyed a thick layer of wood chips. They were given all the food and water they wanted as well as free access to rats of the opposite sex. There were little boxes the rodents could sleep in and running wheels they could use for exercise. One of Alexander's students even painted a forest-themed mural that wrapped around the park's entire perimeter.

Rat Park also included water tanks that were filled with liquid morphine. (The freedom of movement the animals enjoyed at Rat Park meant they could not be implanted with catheters.) If the drug, an opiate that comprises the key ingredient in heroin, was the ultimate

---

[17] Avram Goldstein, "Heroin Maintenance: A Medical View. A Conversation between a Physician and a Politician," *Journal of Drug Issues* 9 (1979): 341-347.

cause of addiction that previous researchers were sure it was, the animals at Rat Park would consume it with the same hopeless abandon they exhibited in the Skinner box experiments. Paradise would be overrun with desperate rat dope fiends. But it was not.

In 1978, Alexander and colleagues Robert Coambs and Patricia Hadaway co-authored the first paper based on his team's experiments at Rat Park. It describes how a control group of rats kept in isolation in Skinner boxes was given the same level of access to morphine as the animals living together in Rat Park. To the researchers' surprise, there were clearly observable differences in the two groups' behaviours. "Isolated rats drank significantly more morphine solution than the social rats," the paper states.[18] "Housing conditions appear to play an important role in determining morphine self-administration," it continues. "A possible explanation for the environmental effect is that for isolated rats, the reinforcement values of morphine ingestion was enhanced by relief of the discomfort [caused by] spatial confinement, social isolation, and stimulus deprivation."

The paper was not greeted warmly, Alexander recalls. A few local reporters took notice, among them a young scientist and broadcaster named David Suzuki. "But in the larger academic world, it sank like a stone," Alexander says. "No one wanted to hear it."

However, the group felt it was on to something. They poked at the experiment from different angles. Sometimes the animals would enter Rat Park already addicted to morphine, sometimes the researchers would start the control group free of drugs. "It didn't matter if they were tasting it for the first time or going through withdrawal symptoms," Alexander says. "The more time you have in Rat Park, the less you like to drink morphine."

But still the research failed to gain widespread attention. Worse, when it was paid notice, it was usually in the form of open hostility. Narcotics as an irresistible plague on society remained the dominant narrative.

In 1984, an inspector paid a visit to Rat Park. He decided the facility

---

[18] Bruce Alexander, Robert Coambs, Patricia Hadaway, "The Effect of Housing and Gender on Morphine Self-Administration in Rats," *Psychopharmacology* 58 (1978): 175-179.

did not have sufficient ventilation to provide for the rats on which Alexander was experimenting. "Rat Park was closed down," Alexander laments. The room was reconfigured and shortly after opened as a counselling centre for students. "With the same ventilation system," Alexander notes.

The natural next step was to conduct a similar experiment with humans and attempt to test whether the environment theory of addiction held in the more complex minds and bodies of *homo sapiens*. Of course, recreating the sort of conditions for people that the rats had endured wasn't possible. The researchers could not confine humans in a monitored paradise where they had access to all the opiates they could ever desire. And they certainly could not sequester other humans in solitary confinement with a powerful drug as their only way to make the experience less torturous.

"We tried a number of cheesy experiments in which we tried to set up role-playing situations. And then we would ask people, 'Do you feel like taking drugs now?'" Alexander recalls. "They didn't go anywhere."

Next, Alexander went looking for real-world examples. "Natural experiments had already occurred with people," he recalls discovering. "We didn't need to set up experiments. What we needed to do was read history in a very, very careful way. And the primary history that I read and that, for a while, I was totally immersed in, was a history of Native people in British Columbia."

More than 10,000 years ago, Indigenous people populated what today we call British Columbia. They lived there in prosperity until the 1800s, when British traders began to arrive in substantial numbers. For the next 150 years, the Indigenous populations of BC were oppressed by settler-colonial violence. They were confined to small reserves, and their children were taken from them and forced to attend residential schools that forbade them to speak their languages and practice their customs.

Throughout the 1980s, Alexander travelled to many reserves and interviewed the First Nations people who lived there. "We went around questioning elders and looking at the historical records of the old anthropologists in British Columbia and the missionaries and so forth," he says. "What we found is that there is very little indication there was anything like addiction prior to the cultures being destroyed and people being forced onto reserves." After colonization, addictions, primarily to alcohol but also to other drugs, spread on reserves with the ferocity of smallpox outbreaks.

"Their culture had been completely broken down," Alexander says. "Their traditional ties to the land and the sea and nature and everything else had been destroyed, and they had been put into these little reserves. They weren't in solitary confinement or cages, but they were so far from a natural situation for those people that it seems it was close enough. And when you do that experiment, which has been done all over the world, not as an experiment but as colonization, then you find that the results are consistent."

He recalls a visit he made to Fort Ware, a remote First Nations community in northern British Columbia. Before colonial settlers dammed the Peace River, creating Bennett Lake, the people of Fort Ware lived in a river valley there.

"They lived by hunting moose," Alexander says. "All of their tribal territory and all of their history is under water now. They were devastated. And now it is one of these places where you can say there is 100-percent alcoholism. That is one of the places where I asked, 'Tell me about addiction before you guys were colonized.'" No answer ever came. "That natural experiment is as good an experiment as any you could ever design," Alexander says.

He found a second example in another population as different from the Indigenous people of BC as one could imagine.

In June 1971, US President Richard Nixon's drug czar, Dr Jerome Jaffe, travelled to Vietnam to assess concerns about heroin becoming a problem among young American soldiers who were fighting there. The doctor established a urine-screening program and then returned with his data to the US, where he enlisted the help of Lee Robins, a professor of psychiatry at the Washington University School of Medicine.

The men analyzed the data, and the results were terrifying. Nearly forty percent of all American serviceman stationed in Vietnam for whom they had obtained urine samples tested positive for opium.[19]

---

[19] Robins, Lee, "Vietnam Veterans' Rapid Recovery from Heroin Addiction: A Fluke or Normal Expectation?" *Addiction* 88 (1993): 1,041-1,054.

In follow-up interviews, Jaffe and Robins found twenty percent of soldiers reported physical withdrawal symptoms associated with opiates. Eleven percent of the soldiers tested positive for opium or heroin in a urine test administered upon their departure from Vietnam. Because the soldiers knew about the test before taking it, Robins later wrote, it stood to reason that eleven percent was addicted to an extent that they could not stop consuming the drug. Using the eleven-percent figure to calculate the scale of the problem that was being transported back to the United States, Jaffe and Robins warned the White House that there were 1,400 men with full-blown heroin addictions flying from Vietnam to their homes across America each month.

"President Richard Nixon himself announced that the country was in for an incredible disaster because these hordes of addicts were about to return to the United States," Alexander remembers. "This was going to be an overwhelming wave of addiction. But it never happened."

Jaffe and Robins conducted follow-up visits with the veterans who returned addicted, expecting the worst. But what they found was that of those soldiers who returned to America addicted to heroin—some 16,800 men each year as the war began to wind down—only five percent were still using heroin one year after they had left Vietnam. Continuing to follow a sample of the men, they next learned that just two percent entered treatment for an addiction and only about a third even attended a short detox program. Fifty percent of this group did use drugs again. The veterans had access to hard drugs and lacked treatment options, yet only a tiny minority remained addicted.

"This surprising rate of recovery, even when re-exposed to narcotic drugs, ran counter to the conventional wisdom that heroin is a drug which causes addicts to suffer intolerable craving that rapidly leads to re-addiction if re-exposed to the drug," the paper concludes.

The reaction to Jaffe and Robins's study of the Vietnam veterans—like the response to Alexander's Rat Park study—was one of borderline hostility. "The press and the research community were ... skeptical," Robins wrote.[20] "They resisted giving up the belief that heroin was a uniquely dangerous drug, to which a user became addicted very

---

[20] Robins, "Vietnam Veterans' ..."

quickly, and addiction to which was virtually incurable."

Bruce Alexander's reaction was the opposite. He was fascinated and found that the results of the Vietnam studies strongly reinforced those of his own experiments with narcotics.

"Their addiction was very much environmentally determined," Alexander says today. The men—barely more than boys, in most cases—were taken from their families and dropped into the jungles of Vietnam. They lived in terrible conditions, sleeping in rain that could last for weeks on end, in constant fear of attack and death. They experienced violence and watched their friends die in gruesome ways. They were on the wrong side of history, aware that their cause was one that many of their peers did not believe in. "So the addiction rate went way up," Alexander says. "But it didn't remain up when they got back to the relative comfort of being state-side." The term that Alexander eventually applied to this phenomenon is "dislocation."

"People need to have a place in their community, in their family, in their world, and in their supernatural world," he says. "They have to feel connected on all these levels. And when they are not, they have to find something which connects them, something which engages them. And it turns out that drug addiction is a wonderfully engaging thing."

How this problem manifests itself in great numbers of human lives was best explained to Alexander by an elder Indigenous woman—a grandmother, he recalls—whom he met on one of his trips to BC's remote communities in the 1980s.

She described herself as sitting on the bank of a raging river that cuts through the mountains. "We see a head out there, bobbing up and down," the woman told him. "We know somebody is drowning. So we swim out. And we know how to swim out there because the elders have told us where the rocks are. We go around the rocks. We don't crash on the rocks. And we get the person. We grab them by the scruff of the neck, we drag them back through the water and, with the last of our energy, we throw them up on the bank.

"Sometimes they get up, and they walk back onto the land and all is well. They return to the people. And sometimes they stand up on the slippery bank and they slip right back in. They go back in the water and over the falls, and they are gone.

"When we do that, when we drag someone back, even if they don't make it up the bank and back to the land, we feel like we are warriors. We feel like we are powerful and strong. Until we realize that some son of a bitch upstream is throwing more and more people into the river every year."

The old woman never named the force that was throwing her people into the river. But to Alexander, it was obvious. "It's a hostile society," he says. "A society which is hostile to community and hostile to human well-being, in the broader sense ... It doesn't make homes for people."

Over time, Alexander developed theories that applied what he learned at Rat Park to a variety of societal conditions, perhaps none starker than those of the war on drugs itself.

"The ultimate effect of prohibition is to put people in cages," he says. "To marginalize people and say, 'You're not like the rest of us; you are possessed by this drug, and you are out of control.' Well, immediately, you've made that person less than a human being. That is another way of putting them in a cage. The difference between people and rats is, with rats, you can see the cage, and with people, you can't always see the cage. You have to look for them carefully, and that's what I've been doing for a few decades."

Eventually, the original set of experiments at Rat Park did attract considerable attention from researchers working on drug issues and addiction, though to this day, not all of it is positive. What Alexander calls the "demon drug theory" remains deeply entrenched in mainstream North American society. But Alexander's ideas about the impacts that environment and social conditions can have on an individual's propensity to addiction have gained a degree of acceptance.

For Mark Townsend, who discovered Alexander's work shortly after he arrived in Vancouver, it had the force of a bolt of lightning.

"Rat Park was a very big deal for us," he says.

Chapter 6
Growing Up Radical

When Ann Livingston arrived in Vancouver in the early 1990s, she was thirty-nine years old but looked a decade younger. She usually wore a beautiful light summer dress paired with trademark combat boots. Her long hair, parted in the middle, and kind eyes behind wise-owl glasses evoked a contemporary portrait of a 1960s flower child. Livingston was a single mother with three boys. David was twelve, John was six, and Angus was four.

It was June 1993, and the month before, she'd left her partner in a hurried move from Victoria, looking for a fresh start.

She had lived in Vancouver for several years in the 1970s and had happy memories of the Downtown Eastside. Back then, East Hastings Street was a long row of middle-class shops anchored by Woodward's Department Store. But in the two decades that followed, most of those businesses had closed and were mostly replaced by pawnshops and cheap beer parlours. Still, Livingston retained a fondness for the area, and in 1993 settled in the Four Sister's Co-op, a family-friendly housing complex that the Portland Hotel's parent organization, DERA, had brought to the neighbourhood. Comprised of three buildings positioned around a central courtyard, it was a fine place to raise her boys.

One hot afternoon toward the end of August of their first year in Vancouver, David, John, and Angus were outside playing with other children in the co-op's grassy courtyard. Livingston was in the kitchen of their second-floor apartment when she heard a woman call for help from outside on the street.

"She's passed out! Call 9-1-1," the woman cried. Livingston did and then rushed outside to find her boys and more than a dozen other children peering through the fence that separated their complex from the alley it bordered. A young Indigenous woman had overdosed and another was working to resuscitate her.

"She lay in the alley, legs folded underneath her, arms straight out to her sides," reads a journal entry Livingston wrote about the experience. "Her midriff showed, and I saw it heave and fall rhythmically as she sluggishly seizured."

There was no sign of the ambulance that Livingston had called, so, thinking it would be faster, she proceeded on foot to the closest fire hall, which was located just around the corner from the Four Sister's Co-op. There, Livingston found a group of firefighters smoking cigarettes and watching dancers come and go from the No. 5 Orange, a strip club directly across the street.

"We've got someone down over here," Livingston told them. The guys didn't respond with any urgency but followed her back to the woman in the alley, where they took over. While the firefighters fixed an oxygen mask on her, the children watched from the other side of the fence. One of them spotted a man they had seen with the woman before she overdosed. "That's the man who put the needle in her arm," Livingston recalls the kids shouting. "A lynch mob of innocent children," she jokes.

The firefighters grew annoyed with the crowd and asked Livingston to leave. But she stood her ground, unable to pull herself away. A second later, the woman's chest heaved as life returned to her and she gasped for a large breath. "It was an intimate moment," Livingston says. "How the air just gets electric. The children really noticed it."

Livingston recalls that when she was growing up, there were three lessons that her mother and father reiterated over and over again. The first, from her mother, was to be a good neighbour. The second, from her father, was that she should understand her surroundings, her environment, and her place within it. And the third, from both of them: "Don't believe everything you're told at school," Livingston says. "Really question things."

"We were always trained to be these troublemakers," she continues. "So following all that, I start making calls: 'What are all these overdoses about?'"

Ann Livingston at a demonstration for drug-users' rights in the spring of 1997.
Photo: Duncan Murdoch

Ann Livingston was born in Nelson, BC, on November 30, 1954. Her family lived in the nearby mining town of Salmo, where her father, Ed, worked as a geological engineer. He moved the family to the larger interior town of Kamloops when Livingston was two years old and settled the family there for the next five years. Livingston's mother, Dorothy, had a degree in social work and had previously worked in New York City with recovering heroin addicts and, before that, disadvantaged children in Harlem. It's that tendency of her mother's to care for others that characterizes Livingston's earliest memories.

"We were always going to Indian reserves," she says. "There must have been a dirt road running through the reserve near Kamloops because I can remember this haywire dirt road that we used to drive up with piles of kids' clothes."

In the 1950s, most Indigenous communities in Canada existed in varying states of poverty and disrepair. They were neglected by the government, held few opportunities for meaningful employment, and were prone to social problems largely related to alcohol abuse and addiction. Livingston remembers that her mother was shocked by the underdeveloped conditions in which the government allowed the Indigenous reserves to remain. Livingston was the middle child of five and aged five or six by this time, just old enough to assist her mother with chores and not yet old enough to seek independence from her parents. "I was kind of like my mom's little helper," Livingston says of that time.

"I remember one day this young woman came to our house, and I thought she was ill or something," she recalls. "My mother took her upstairs and put her in her bed, and we were all shushed because she was taking a nap and sleeping."

The woman wasn't sick, Livingston realized years later. She was drunk. A resident of the nearby reserve, the woman had run into some sort of trouble with police. When the officers threatened to take her to jail, she had given them Livingston's mother's name, betting correctly that with an association to a white family, the police would treat her with enough respect to refrain from throwing her in a cell.

"My mother didn't put her on the porch in case she vomited or something," Livingston says. "She got my parents' bed. And only anyone who was a special guest to our house got put in my parents' bed, because it was the only part of the house where you wouldn't be harassed by these five children."

Livingston took the lesson to heart. An entire lifetime later, at her apartment at the Four Sister's Co-op, neighbours repeatedly reprimanded her for bringing homeless people in off the street and allowing them to crash on her couch for a night or two, or sometimes for much longer. "It's just being neighbourly, really," Livingston says.

She laughingly recounts how her youngest son would get annoyed with her for the habit. "He used to freak out at me because sometimes people smelled bad," she says. "He could get really militant."

Livingston's mother, Dorothy, played a significant role in shaping her daughter's activism. Today, Livingston acknowledges that influence but remains amused by its unlikeliness. "My mother was so straight," she says. "I'd never even heard her swear."

Among the lessons Dorothy instilled in Livingston when she was still just a child was a reminder that people can break the rules and should do so when a rule is unjust. In 1967, when Livingston was thirteen years old, she first understood the extent to which her mother was willing to ignore or challenge authority in instances when she believed it was wrong.

In the 1960s, abortion was still illegal in Canada and the United States. A Canadian coroner's report from those years notes that did not mean that abortions weren't happening; it meant that the law made it impossible for women to receive an abortion legally—and often safely. The daughters of wealthy families paid professional physicians to perform the procedure. But women of lesser means were generally forced to deal with the situation themselves or, if they could afford it, to pay for a "nurse" to help them. A "nurse" meant a woman who was usually not an actual trained nurse, but someone who knew how to perform an abortion outside the medical system with as little risk to the mother as possible. The coroner's report states that the procedure often involved pumping Lysol into a woman's womb. The mortality rate is described as "high," the risk of infection greater than fifty percent.[21]

This was one of the situations for which Dorothy felt breaking the rules was required. She was working as a psychiatric social worker for a regional care provider on Vancouver Island called Saanich Mental Health. She crossed paths with young women who were struggling with unwanted pregnancies, and the meetings she attended placed her in a position to help them. She began "counselling" them, which meant connecting them with safer means of receiving an abortion, helping them obtain birth control, and assisting in other ways related to women's health.

Livingston was barely a teenager at the time but vividly remembers answering the phone calls of young women asking for help from her mother. "She knew that women were doing illegal abortions, getting infections, and dying," Livingston says. "So she had given out her home number so people would call our home and say, 'I'm pregnant.

---

[21] *Report of the Royal Commission to Investigate Allegations Relating to Coroners' Inquests* (Government of Ontario, 1968).

Can you help me?' They would call, and then my mother would meet them somewhere."

This led the Victoria police to tap their phone, Livingston swears, recalling a clicking noise she heard a few seconds into every call. "When they used to bug your phone, you could hear noise on the line," she explains.

Livingston knew that her mother was not a criminal by any moral definition of the word. "She was a professional with a degree who was mild-mannered, a lay chaplain in the Unitarian church, and respected in the neighbourhood," Livingston explains. "That she would be defying the law to the extent that the police were tapping our telephone, that was really startling."

It prompted the entire family, including thirteen-year-old Livingston, to grow acutely aware of state power and understand that not every exercise of authority is an application of justice.

"My mother's approach was, 'If there is a problem, let's solve the problem. And if the law is in the way, we'll deal with that,'" Livingston says. "If the law is in the way, you can ignore the law and do what needs to be done."

Chapter 7

Back Alley

In 1994, Melissa Eror lived in what she describes as "the suburbs." In fact, it was barely a stone's throw from Vancouver's downtown core—a nice neighbourhood consisting of family homes with a good school nearby, but it wasn't the suburbs. Her idyllic description might have something to do with where she came from. In 1994, Eror was a wife and mother who spent much of her free time volunteering at her daughter's elementary school. Yet she still considered herself a member of the Downtown Eastside's down-and-out.

"I was a typical child of the hippie years," she says today with the comforting voice of a grandmother. "I certainly enjoyed my time with different hallucinogens and pot and that kind of thing. At the time, we started hearing about things like opium and heroin. And I tried it. And, jeez, I liked it."

That was the early 1970s. Eror was a teenager, and one thing led to another. Before long, she was addicted to heroin and doing what she had to do to support her habit. She recalls spending more than a decade that way, becoming a well-known resident of what was then called the Hastings Strip.

When she had her first child, a baby girl, in 1981, it was time for that chapter of her life to end. "I realized that wasn't going to work," Eror says. Beating the odds on which so many fail, she successfully transitioned from heroin to methadone, married the father of her child, and escaped the pitfalls of the Downtown Eastside.

But she kept in touch with friends there and maintained ties to the community. When more and more people began to die of overdoses in the early 1990s and the AIDS epidemic grew worse, she felt called back. In June of 1994, she attended a meeting at the Carnegie Community Centre.

Community meetings about the growing number of drug-overdose deaths were happening more frequently. This one featured the province's chief coroner of the day, Vince Cain, who was there to hear from drug addicts for a major report he was researching about addiction in BC. The man who would soon succeed Cain, Larry Campbell, was also in attendance. He had taken a keen interest in the area's drug problem. And so on a hot summer day, the Carnegie Community Centre was packed with drug users—people who normally were not even allowed to set foot in the building.

Campbell, today a senator who splits his time between Vancouver and Ottawa, recalls the energy in the room. "It was pretty sombre," he begins. "It brought people back to their worst fears and to memories of people who had died. And they all knew people who had died. So it got pretty raw."

Eror had heard the name Ann Livingston before, but the two women had never met. She spotted Livingston across the room at Carnegie with her two youngest boys, noticeable because they were the only children in the room. Livingston had them in a wagon that she wheeled back and forth during the entire meeting in an effort to keep them asleep or at least quiet while the sizable group of drug users took turns sharing stories of abuse and memories of friends they'd lost.

"I had been talking at the meeting, and she had been talking at the meeting," Eror recounts. "The ones who had been talking sense—we all kind of noticed each other. It was all about the overdose deaths. And, finally, there was something that we could hang the issue on: human rights for drug addicts."

The idea was revolutionary at the time, at least in North America. Eror remembers how it excited her. She gave Livingston her number with the feeling that something big was about to begin. "She said, 'We ought to get together.' And I said, 'Yeah, that would be really interesting.' But I didn't hear from her for about a year."

In 1994, Livingston was living on welfare and her eldest boy had just been diagnosed with cerebral palsy. Her economic condition led her to monthly meetings with a group called the Innovative Empowerment Society at a café called La Quena on Commercial Drive. Loosely led by a thirty-four-year-old man named William Kay, the group mostly talked about how to fight for better conditions for the unemployed and

In 1994, Ann Livingston (front row, far right) and Bud Osborn (sitting behind her) attended a meeting at the Carnegie Community Centre where drug users pleaded for government attention to overdose deaths. *Photo: Duncan Murdoch*

held workshops on how to navigate different government bureaucracies in which the poor so often find themselves lost. The meetings at La Quena were not about drugs, with the exception of a little beer and pot that sometimes accompanied Friday-night sessions.

In a past life, Kay had practiced as a lawyer but was disbarred in 1989. (He shrugs off questions about those years. Livingston recalls rumours that it had something to do with a bank robbery.) His intellect was sharp, and he maintained an inexhaustible work ethic that proved a significant benefit wherever his attention turned.

"I was a revolutionary communist," he says today from his home in Edmonton, Alberta. "Someone with a lot of anarchist sympathies. And the strategy that I was operating on was that you don't just preach revolutionary politics to the oppressed. You've got to get involved in their actual day-to-day struggles."

Kay was an agitator with several projects on the go. Addiction was not one of them, he recalls. "I was never someone who was, initially, passionately moved by the harm-reduction cause."

But drugs and the overdose epidemic were primary interests of Livingston's, and Livingston fast became a primary interest of Kay's. He and Livingston met at those meetings on Commercial Drive and soon the Innovative Empowerment Society was headed in a new direction.

The same year, Livingston met Liz Evans. Livingston needed somewhere to store a shovel and other tools she was using in a somewhat futile effort to tidy up East Hastings Street. Livingston walked into the Portland Hotel one day to ask if they would mind if she stored the tools there. Whoever was behind the front desk that day said that would be fine, and so Livingston began to come and go from the Portland and soon enough bumped into Evans.

"Of course, the tools were stolen right away," Livingston says. "I went back once and they were there, and then I went back a second time and nobody could find them."

One night a few months after that meeting at Carnegie, Livingston and Evans were out together handing out clean needles. Their route along East Hastings Street took them into a few of the neighbourhood's very worst hotels. "These were abandoned buildings that sat there for I don't know how long," Livingston recounts. "Your classic shooting galleries. There was actual shit and then humans and then garbage and people dragging mattresses through that and then sleeping on these mattresses. And at that point, they couldn't get needles, either. You could just *feel* the HIV spreading. It clawed at your heart."

The two women never became best friends. Evans found Livingston difficult to work with—an opinion shared by many—and Livingston never particularly liked Mark Townsend. But both Livingston and Evans recall an immediate sense of mutual respect and admiration for one another. They quickly found they could work together on a shared cause.

"She was very saint-like in those days," Livingston says. "She had this hotel that was really, really difficult to manage and just falling down. It had an area with a TV where people would be laying on the couch in various states of disrepair. [Townsend and Evans] were really considered ground-breaking simply because they were nice to people."

The desperation of the scene she found with Evans that night sent

Livingston into action. In the weeks following, she spent hours every day writing letters, begging for funding for programs that might help drug users. Not by coincidence, Kay's meetings at La Quena became less about rights for the poor and more about the Downtown Eastside's drug problem. Before too long, a subgroup had formed within the Empowerment Society that followed its members' interests from Commercial Drive to the Downtown Eastside.

Vancouver Native Health Society had a building on the 400 block of East Hastings Street that was left unused each evening. The group's executive director allowed Livingston, Kay, and whoever else showed up to use a room on the building's second floor. Their meetings were initially irregular, and they operated on a budget of just $100 a month, but a new group had taken shape. They called it IV Feed.

Around this time, Livingston got back in touch with Eror. "I had given her my phone number at that meeting, and now she was ready to do something," Eror recalls. "She said, 'You want to come together and talk and see if we can put together some plans?' I said, 'Yeah, sure.' She got the meeting together, and I invited people from the street that I knew might want to attend. And some of them did."

It was April 19, 1995. "The first meeting we ever held was on the day of the Oklahoma City bombing," Livingston recalls. "Weirdest fucking thing." Kay recalls that their objective was still vague. "Our goal was to get involved with local people's issues, listen to what their issues were, and then help them fight for their issues. So we started organizing bi-monthly meetings of addicts themselves. We always tried, as much as possible, to let the addicts run it themselves. But it was like letting the mental patients run the asylum."

Livingston similarly recalls how those first meetings were challenging. "We were completely overwhelmed with the people who came," she says. But they stuck with the plan for self-empowerment. "We followed exactly the way you are supposed to do grassroots activism," Livingston says. "You have your education thing, there is a discussion, decisions are made, decisions are recorded, and then word goes out that that's what we're doing this week. And then you go on to the next thing."

Vancouver Native Health Society had been an early advocate for needle exchange. But its executive director, Lou Demerais, didn't like the direction that Livingston and Kay were heading with the group to which he had given the keys to his second-floor boardroom. "If they were just using the space on a pretext and were going to start to allow people to shoot up and so on, that's not why we [Native Health] were here," he says. "They got that message and moved on."

Even before IV Feed was off the ground, it was earning detractors. "There were a lot of people connected with different agencies that didn't like [Ann Livingston], because she was very blunt and had a way about her," Demerais says. "Maybe she interpreted that as, 'Well, if nobody's going to do it, then I'll do it.' And then off she went."

Livingston describes the next step they took with IV Feed as almost inevitable. "There was a real sense that we were in the right," she says. "You can't be around that much death and think it's okay to let it go on."

At the time, John Turvey's nonprofit, the Downtown Eastside Youth Activities Society (DEYAS), was distributing money to smaller groups focused on health initiatives. Livingston convinced him to share some grant money it had received from two more mainstream charitable organizations, Central City Foundation and the Vancouver Foundation.

IV Feed—or IV League, as in ivy league, as some drug users playfully called it—could now afford to move out of the Native Health Society's boardroom, where they were no longer welcome anyway. Kay found them a storefront on Powell Street, near Oppenheimer Park in the Downtown Eastside. Livingston paid the first month's rent of $650. And on November 15, 1995, IV Feed officially held its first meeting there. With a touch of black humour, they dubbed the place "Back Alley."

At 356 Powell Street—their own space, a first for drug users, certainly in Vancouver and likely in North America—people could just hang out. Livingston called it a "clubhouse." Nothing more.

Eror—who takes credit for the name IV Feed but notes she's not positive it was she who came up with it—agrees that a supervised-injection facility was not the reason the group formed, nor was it why they moved into the space on Powell. "It started out as a basic, 'What should we be doing?' kind of thing," she says. "And then that evolved, eventually, into Back Alley."

They were activists, and activists paying rent. So IV Feed began to look for a more specific purpose. Why did they exist? It was a question that Livingston and Kay very consciously avoided answering themselves.

In those early days, there were two issues that drug users raised at every IV Feed meeting at Back Alley: police harassment and overdose deaths. A front-page story that ran in the *Globe and Mail* on May 4, 1996, describes how dire the situation had become. It notes that during the first four months of that year, sixty-four Vancouver residents had already died of illicit drug abuse. "That's one death every two days," the article reads, "and the city coroner thinks that there could be a record number of bodies by the end of 1996." That prediction was correct. There were 151 overdose deaths in Vancouver that year, up from 116 in 1995. They accounted for a little more than half the number of fatal overdoses recorded across the entire province. The same article states that one in fourteen Downtown Eastside addicts was HIV positive, describing the neighbourhood as "an incubator for AIDS."[22]

While it might have been news to the *Globe and Mail*'s national readers, the drug users who gathered at Back Alley already knew all of that, Livingston says. She recounts how their concerns turned to action.

"When you do this process, you say, 'What are the issues? Why do we have those issues? And what are we going to do about it?' We went through it step-by-step. They said that the main problem we have is that we need a place to inject drugs that's safe. Why don't we just do it here?"

Livingston recalls users who came to 356 Powell with injuries they'd incurred not from drug use but from police. People who had been caught in the act of injecting drugs were sprayed with mace. One user had the end of a needle break off inside their arm during a particularly rough encounter with a pair of officers. "We were trying

---

[22] Miro Cernetig, "Death Likes Canada's Overdose Capital," *Globe and Mail*, May 4, 1996.

to figure out how to deal with mace burns in ear holes," Livingston says with exasperation. "So, yes, it was conscious, and, yes, we knew we were taking a big step. Now the place was an injection site."

She gives a lot of credit to Kay as the individual who made Back Alley's move. "William said the most important thing to do is that we should just rent a place," she explains. "I would have gone slower. I wouldn't have done that."

A manifesto of sorts written by Kay announced the news to the community: "IV FEED no longer holds its meetings at the Native Health Clinic," it begins.

> We recognized the need for a full time meeting space so—Yes, we're back in the alley—in name only, thank goodness. One of the main reasons for having rented a space was to ensure that there would be at least one spot on this earth where we would be welcome, other than the streets and back alleys of the downtown eastside and as you know we are not exactly accepted in the alleys and streets, only tolerated. We've had our ups and downs and will probably experience more but as these sorts of things go we've been quite lucky. If you haven't been to a meeting, they are still held every Tuesday at 6 pm, with a light supper following. We're at 356 E. Powell St.

Word went out that cocaine and heroin users could inject drugs there without having to fear they would die of an overdose alone on the street.

Back Alley was a big step up from a literal back alley but it still wasn't much to look at.

"A bunch of fucking anarchists had been in there before," Livingston says. "The place was just a pile of rubble. People would come in later and say it was really squalid. And I'd think, 'Wow, we should have taken some before pictures.'"

It was a fairly large space. At the front, near windows looking out onto the street, there was a desk and a table people could sit around. A bit further back, there were two rows of couches that faced one another. The very back of the storefront had been sectioned off by a previous tenant and divided into a series of dark rooms for photographic development. Before long, IV Feed members covered the walls with murals, poetry, and whatever else came to mind.

Twice a week, Livingston led evening meetings there. Always wearing one of her trademark flower dresses paired with combat boots, she stood at the front of the group and scrambled to write on big sheets of paper as much as she could of what was said. It was semi-official, with Livingston keeping regular meeting minutes. There was free coffee, powdered creamer, and a pouch of tobacco, all purchased at the corner store next door in a bid Livingston made to keep the neighbours happy.

Aside from Livingston, Kay, and Eror (sometimes clean but often not), the group's membership was entirely drug users. It wasn't long before casual use at Back Alley became the site's primary function.

The police were aware of that transition almost as soon as it happened, Kay recounts. "A month or so into it, a police officer in a starched white shirt comes in with two supporting escort officers. And he wants to talk to William." One of them told Kay, "We're not condoning what you're doing. But as long as there is no trafficking going on in here, and as long as we're not getting called here a lot, we're not going to do anything about it."

As the conversation continued, one of Back Alley's regulars wandered over from one of the couches near the back and took an interest in Kay's conversation with the police officer. The man leaned into them and casually put a butane flame to a crack pipe with a sizable rock stuffed in its end. He was quickly arrested.

"You said we could do this in here!" the man yelled at Kay, who replied, "Well, don't do it right in front of them!"

Ground rules were established. No dealing and keep the worst of it out of the cops' sight. "Basically, that was the attitude of the police," Kay says. "They were going to tolerate it."

Members of the Vancouver Police Department weren't the only

people in positions of power who took note of IV Feed and Back Alley. In an effort to keep the organization political, Livingston invited members of the local and provincial governments to speak at 356 Powell. One of her first guests was Larry Campbell, the coroner whom Livingston and Eror noticed at that meeting at the Carnegie Centre where they had all met one year earlier.

"It was scary," Campbell recalls. "One night, I went down and the place was packed. People were shooting up. I think the thing that stuck for me was, if somebody overdosed, they would call [an ambulance], but put them in the alley because they were afraid of the police. It was a real moment of change for me. I realized the really dire straits that drug users were in."

Campbell gave a bit of a speech that evening, mostly made up on the spot. "You've got to do something," he told them. "You've got to be heard. You've got to raise a little hell."

Larry Campbell was ahead of most members of the establishment when it came to views on harm reduction. It wasn't that he was especially enlightened or even very liberal. He had travelled a long road to get there.

In 1973, Campbell was a young officer with the Royal Canadian Mounted Police (RCMP), assigned to a drug squad called the "Street Crew" that patrolled the Downtown Eastside. In *A Thousand Dreams*, a book about the Downtown Eastside that Campbell co-authored in 2009, he describes the neighbourhood as a place less dangerous than it later became.

Campbell remembers "crawling onto ceiling tiles to spy into the washrooms in the rundown Brandiz Hotel, because it was still a challenge then to catch someone using drugs," he wrote with the help of journalist Lori Culbert. "Police targeted users and dealers by setting up sting operations in other notorious hotels like the Sunrise, which was located at the centre of the action: the corner of Columbia and Hastings. Officers knew who the dealers were, but they were hard to arrest ... The street crew members, who worked in plainclothes without protective equipment, would follow tips about the locations of dealers, busting down doors in sleazy hotel rooms to catch them with a stash."

In 1981, Campbell left the police force to work as a coroner. He credits those complementary experiences with shaping his views on addiction and harm reduction. "Leaving the police and then becoming a coroner and moving from enforcement to just trying to keep people alive, that was when the light went on," Campbell says. "Realizing that many of the people who are involved in drugs are, basically, self-medicating," he continues. "Coming to the realization, perhaps belatedly, on my part, that this was a medical problem that we were dealing with as if it was a criminal problem."

In the early 1990s, Campbell's desk at the Vancouver coroner's office began to grow crowded with files on people who had overdosed on heroin. He recalls how through the mid-1980s, there was seldom more than a handful of such cases across the province each year. Then, by 1993, there were 354. "We didn't know what it was until we started analyzing the samples we were able to get," he says. "That led to the conclusion that there was a glut of pure heroin out there—that it was coming in pure, and they were putting it right onto the street."

That data supported anecdotal reports he received from the streets. "There was a sense of panic in the community, in the Downtown Eastside as a whole," Campbell says, "that something was happening here. It was very palpable."

A sad reality of the Portland Hotel was that a lot of its tenants died. They were people who were sick with AIDS, using intravenous drugs, and facing marginalization so extreme that even the health-care system avoided dealing with them whenever possible. Campbell sadly notes that this often meant their first encounter with the government was when he paid a visit to collect their bodies.

Around the same time, Campbell met Liz Evans and then Bud Osborn. It was only very shortly after Evans's takeover of the Portland Hotel that Campbell got to know her fairly well. He recalls the evening they first met. "It was Halloween night," Campbell begins. "I had a new coroner with me and we went in, and you couldn't really tell who was dressed for Halloween and who wasn't. And in the midst of this was this young woman, above the fray, boiling hot dogs on a big gas stove." Evans offered Campbell and his partner each a hotdog and then calmly took them upstairs to the room where one of her tenants lay deceased.

"There was such a whirlwind of activity inside that hotel," Campbell says. "She was a sense of calm in the middle of what appeared to be disorder, but she actually had a good handle on it."

Campbell similarly recounts one afternoon he was walking along East Hastings when he bumped into Bud Osborn on the corner of Columbia Street, just outside the Sunrise Hotel. "He was talking about supervised-injection sites, and I said, 'Bud, I just can't go there. I don't think I can go there,'" Campbell recalled. "But he started explaining to me that this was not some weird, out-there idea. That this was, in fact, health care. And that I had to remember that addictions are a health problem." The seed was planted.

"Bud Osborn had a huge, huge influence on me," Campbell says. "I can't think of anything that was more important to me than what he told me that day."

———————

Everyone at Back Alley was acutely aware of what the city's coroner had finally noticed: addicts were dying like never before. By this time, an eclectic cast of characters had collected there and entered the very early stages of forming a movement. Livingston and Kay were still playing lead roles as organizers, but other people spent more time there than they did.

Ron Hudlin, better known by his street name Spanky, practically lived at Back Alley for much of the time it was open, literally for at least a few months. "I was a Downtown Eastside dope fiend," he says now with a laugh. "I'm not normally a person who goes in for places like that. But I knew Livingston, so I showed up and hung around there sometimes." (A vast understatement, according to everybody who remembers him from those years.)

Hudlin explains that the appeal of Back Alley for users was straightforward. Along with overdose deaths and the spread of HIV and other diseases, homelessness in Vancouver was also on the rise. "So it was a place to hang out," he says. The added security was sort of a bonus,

Hudlin continues. The separate darkrooms installed by Back Alley's previous tenant made perfect booths for injecting drugs.

"There was one room there and another room there and you go in, and you get high. If you don't come out in time, somebody comes to see if you're okay. It was a fairly peaceful place," Hudlin continues. "That was probably some of its allure. You knew if you got in there, there probably wasn't going to be violence, and if violence started, there probably was going to be enough people to stop the violence."

On the management side of things, Eror was often at Back Alley as a volunteer manning the front desk. Talking about her role in IV Feed, she's extremely modest and reluctant to agree that Back Alley, as a supervised-injection site, actually was "supervised." But there's no doubt that Eror's work saved at least a few people's lives.

"If there was an overdose or problems, I dealt with it," she says matter-of-factly. "Call the cops or throw someone out the door or whatever. That was what I did. And it got pretty wild sometimes. One night a guy died," Eror says. "That was not nice. His heart just went. And people threatened me, for sure, on a number of occasions," she continues. "But you gotta stand your ground. People threaten you outside, too. So it was safer there because if I had a problem, at least there was going to be someone to jump in from the back. There was a very informal thing where people were helping each other."

Eror recounts two women getting into a fight inside the building and having to throw them both out. One of them walked away, but the other crashed down onto her knees on the pavement outside and began banging her head into the ground. "I said, 'Not here. Take it down the block. At the fixing site, we don't need the advertising,'" Eror recounts. "And she was really choked at me."

But incidents of real violence were rare. An eventful night was more likely to consist of Eror calling 9-1-1 after someone had overdosed and performing mouth-to-mouth and chest compressions until an ambulance arrived. "Maybe it happened once a week," she says. "That's just what you do. That's what you do on the street too."

There were many other more mundane challenges that Livingston and Kay learned come with running an unsanctioned headquarters for drug users. "All kinds of problems," Kay says. "They kept destroying the plumbing. They generated so much garbage, it defied the laws of physics. I'd have a friend of mine come with a pickup truck, and there were just bags and bags and bags of garbage. Those were things that we didn't really anticipate. The bathroom was constantly in shambles," he continues. "They would break the toilet off the wall. I don't know why they had a thing about doing that. That was one of the major problems we had there."

Toward the end, a bigger issue was the dealers and then full-on gangs who came to infiltrate the place despite efforts to keep them away.

"Here's a war story," Kay begins. "I actually ball-batted a guy in that facility in this high-noon sort of way." One man started to deal drugs inside Back Alley—not seriously dealing, but selling to support his own habit. He was constantly ripping off other low-level drug dealers from around the Downtown Eastside, and that eventually angered gang members who were higher up the chain. And because the guy was spending so much time at Back Alley, that attracted blowback on Kay, who by now was known fairly widely as the site's manager.

Kay was at Livingston's apartment one afternoon, which was just a couple of blocks from Back Alley, and Eror came over to complain about the dealer. "In the interim, I'd purchased an aluminum baseball bat from Canadian Tire," Kay recounts. "And when I heard that he was back, I put the bat in my baggy sweatpants, walked all the way down there, and just laid a beating on him."

"No head shots," he adds. "I didn't want to have a dead body to deal with. But that was the only language these people understood ... So I laid a hammering on him. And it worked. He never came back."

Back Alley was open from ten in the morning to two in the morning and, at its peak, saw between 150 and 250 people use injection drugs there every day. Not all of them were long-time addicts.

Several former Back Alley volunteers politely refused to say anything about the place when approached for this book. That could have something to do with stories about activists who started work at 356 Powell with no interest in hard drugs and who left addicted to heroin. Kay confirms it. "A few people of the core group that were running it were not injection-drug users when we started that facility, but became injection-drug users," he says.

There were also challenges keeping the facility supplied with enough clean needles to ensure everybody who was using there was doing so safely. The Downtown Eastside Youth Activities Society was supporting IV Feed and Back Alley with a monthly allowance of about $2,000. But its executive director, John Turvey, did not approve of Back Alley and would not allow his organization's needle-exchange program to supply 356 Powell with syringes.

IV Feed's former landlord, Lou Demerais, had his needle-exchange program running out of the Native Health Society, but he felt the same way. Demerais says he thought it was dangerous to go ahead with supervised-injection without the involvement of health-care professionals.

"I didn't like the idea because it was totally unsupervised," he explains. "People did go there who were not [HIV] positive and became positive there and subsequently died a very short time later."

Livingston concedes that maintaining a sufficient supply of clean needles was a challenge. "It was so bad that you could sell dirty needles," she says. "That's how scarce needles were. And that's how much fucking dope there was. Until the Centre for Disease Control nurses saved us."

The Street Nurses Program was a project the BC Centre for Disease Control launched in 1988. Pairs of health-care workers patrolled alleys in the Downtown Eastside and other poor areas of the city, handing out harm-reduction supplies such as condoms, sharing information on where people could get tested for HIV, and conducting basic checkups on people's health.

In 1995, Liz James, Fiona Gold, and a half-dozen other young nurses were employed by that program to run a small clinic on Main Street just around the corner from East Hastings, on the second floor above a needle-exchange program. Gold remembers being young, intimidated, and unable to remain on the sidelines.

"Oh my god, people are dying," she remembers thinking. "I went back and contacted the coroner's office and asked, 'What are the stats on overdoses?' So they faxed me the stat sheets, and I was horrified. It was just nuts. So we had to do something. But what were we going to do?"

The Street Nurses began going to Back Alley with clean needles. Gold describes the BC Centre for Disease Control as a reluctant supplier. "They were not convinced about an injection site at all," she says, "however, they were allowing us to do needle exchange. There was an exchange requirement, one for one, but as nurses, we were pretty liberal. You knew that if you didn't get a clean one out there, somebody was using a dirty one."

———————

That was the most support Back Alley ever received from the medical establishment. By the fall of 1996, things were coming apart.

During the summer, Eror was diagnosed with breast cancer. Her work at Back Alley ended when she began chemotherapy. Other key volunteers were spending more time in the building's back rooms shooting heroin than they were manning the front desk or helping maintain what little order existed there. Meanwhile, dealers had moved in, the cops were circling, and Kay was simply fed up with the whole ordeal.

"My main problem was, I could not keep drug traffickers out of the facility," he says. "I was ending up in outright physical and violent confrontations with these people. And it was stressing me out. You'd get rid of one and another one would pop up," he continues. "It was to the point where I was at risk of being stabbed every time I walked in there."

A newspaper article mentions one sizable drug bust occurring at Back Alley shortly before it was forced to close its doors.[23] "Vancouver police media liaison officer Constable Anne Drennan said the centre was raided last week and a forty-year-old man was arrested with eighty doses of heroin," it reads. "At the time of the raid, Drennan said, there were 100 people on the premises, including juveniles and drug dealers."

———————

[23] Frances Bula, "Addicts' Centre Shut in Furore over Funds," *Vancouver Sun*, October 18, 1996.

DEYAS withdrew its funding for the project. Meanwhile, Back Alley's landlord, a legitimate businessman, had been watching the site gather more attention and, spotting an opportunity, had steadily raised their rent as the whole thing became more controversial. IV Feed was out of cash. There were also growing accusations of financial mismanagement and outright theft aimed at Kay. While it's possible that happened, it's unlikely, given how little money Back Alley had to begin with. To this day, Kay vehemently denies taking a penny. Regardless, IV Feed had lost what little community support it had. "They took my criminal record, printed copies of it, and distributed thousands of copies around the neighbourhood," Kay says. "I couldn't have been more of a pariah."

Eror attributes more significance to health concerns. One day, John Turvey brought her evidence of a case of AIDS traced directly to Back Alley. "I knew that was the end," she says. "After that, there was no way they were getting grants."

Kay describes Back Alley's demise as the walls simply closing in. "We were shut down because the police had had enough of the facility, the ambulance people were coming there every other day, and I was at a point where I didn't even want to go in there without body armor on," Kay says. "It was getting really intense with the traffickers."

Although he had grown bitter, Kay fondly recalls the opportunities he had to get to know the addicts who found a safe space there. "I would try to get their biographies, quick, from every addict I met," he says. "I would ask what their class background was and what kind of families they had come from, how old they were and what the circumstances were surrounding the first time they put a needle in their arm. They were always working-class, lower-working-class people, with a few exceptions. And eighty percent of them had become injection drug addicts while they were still teenagers. There was some significant adult in their life—a sister's boyfriend or somebody—who got them going. And that was it. Their entire lives. From the first poking of that needle in their arm. Boom. Destiny. They turned a corner and that was the end of them."

Livingston remembers Back Alley with a smile on her face. She recounts her two youngest boys, both under the age of ten at the time, hanging out there with her when it was her turn to take a shift on the front desk. The space was large enough for them to ride their bicycles inside, and they would keep themselves entertained for hours that way. "It never felt the least bit dangerous," Livingston insists. "We really did have a team," she says. "At least we had each other. This bizarre marginalized shit-show that we were involved in."

Kay similarly speaks warmly of IV Feed today. "It was a sloppy affair, but that it happened at all is interesting," he says. But in the days and months immediately following the facility's closure, Kay recalls being very unsure of what they had done. "When Armageddon came down, one of the officials from the downtown agencies confronted me and said, 'You have set back harm reduction in this city ten years.' There certainly were people who felt I had damaged the cause."

Eror remembers the day Back Alley closed, on October 15, 1996. "It was a really good place, but there were a lot of flaws," she says. "And we learned a lot. It's too bad those lessons often didn't end up going into effect."

Asked how users took the blow, Hudlin shrugs. "They went back to wherever they were before," he says. "People hanging out in alleys. It was the same as before."

An essay published in April 1996 in the *Carnegie Newsletter*, a monthly publication named after the building where Livingston and Eror met, best summarizes the lasting impact of 356 Powell: "The idea that users can organize themselves is starting to grow, and even if IV Feed and the Back Alley were to shut down tomorrow, the idea that we must take control of our own lives, and that we have the numbers and the knowledge to do so, is here to stay."

Chapter 8
Miami, Florida

In 2009, Dr Hansel Tookes decided he was going to establish a needle exchange in Florida. At the time, he wasn't a doctor or even a medical student. He was studying public health at the University of Miami. America's annual National Harm Reduction Conference was in Miami that year. Tookes attended and was impressed by a presentation made by a group of researchers from California.

"They had walked the streets of San Francisco, quantifying the number of syringes on the street," he recalls. "And then they had interviewed a bunch of people who inject about their syringe-disposal patterns." The San Francisco team used that research to make a very compelling case for the city to open a place where intravenous drug users could go to obtain clean needles and dispose of dirty ones. Tookes thought he could do the same in Florida.

Needles were cheap and available. They were mass-produced for pennies and sold without a prescription at pharmacies everywhere, even in small rural towns. Needle-exchange centres had operated in Europe and Canada for decades. More recently, many states across the US established similar programs, albeit often with restrictions. So why not in Florida?

Tookes spent the next seven years working toward his goal before Miami finally opened the state's first needle exchange, in December 2016. "It was a journey," Tookes says. One, he emphasizes, that continues today.

Beginning in 2010, Tookes and his UM classmates conducted hundreds of interviews with street-entrenched drug users concentrated in Miami's Overtown neighbourhood. Recording data based on those conversations, they found that ninety-five percent of intravenous drug users admitted to discarding used needles on the street. After San Francisco opened its needle exchange, the California researchers found that that number was reduced to just thirteen percent. Tookes had identified a problem and an opportunity to fix it.

The team also knew that the issue was bigger than street cleanliness and that it affected people who had nothing to do with drugs. For a peer-reviewed paper that Tookes co-authored years later, he calculated that drug use-related infections cost Jackson Memorial Hospital in Miami more than $11 million (USD) every year.

Exactly what Tookes had to do was clear to him: give people clean needles. But there was a barrier. "Chapter 893 of the Florida Statutes made it illegal for anyone—a pharmacist, a doctor, a person on the street—to give a syringe to somebody if they knew that they were going to use it to inject drugs," he explains.

In Florida, a pharmacist can sell a syringe if they are told that a diabetic will use the needle for an insulin injection. But if a person with a substance-use disorder lets a pharmacist know they will use a needle to inject drugs, the transaction becomes a third-degree felony, or first degree if the purchaser is a minor. "Which is absurd, from a doctor's perspective," Tookes says. "So we had to change state law to amend Chapter 893 to allow us to have syringe access here in Miami."

By this time, Tookes was enrolled in medical school. A small group of his fellow students had taken a similar interest in the issue and together they came up with a plan. "A bunch of med students came to me and said, 'We should use the Florida Medical Association resolution-writing process ... to get legislation sponsored to authorize syringe exchange in Florida,'" he recounts. "We got together, wrote a resolution, passed a resolution, got a bill, and after four years, got a law."

Almost. After four years of the idea slowly winding its way through the state's glacial legislative process, an eleventh-hour amendment severely limited the scope of everything Tookes wanted to do.

The law was changed to allow Tookes to open his needle exchange, but only his, and only for a trial period of five years. Miami Dade received legislative permission to distribute syringes for the use of intravenous drugs, but needle exchange remained illegal everywhere else in Florida. The legislation also said that not a penny of taxpayers' money could go to clean needles for drug users, so Tookes had to raise funds privately. He took what he could get and forged ahead.

There was new urgency. By this time, it was 2015 and an HIV epidemic was exploding across the state and especially in Miami. According to the US Center for Disease Control and Prevention, there were 2,332 new cases of HIV diagnosed in the Miami–Fort Lauderdale–West Palm Beach region in 2015, or a rate of 38.8 new cases per 100,000 people. It ranked Miami number one for new HIV infections among metropolitan areas in the United States. (For all of Florida, the rate was twenty-four new infections per 100,000 people in 2015, placing the state third, after the District of Columbia and Louisiana.)

The nation's opioid crisis struck at the same time. In 2013, there were 2,474 drug-overdose deaths in Florida. The next year, there were 2,634, then 3,228, and then an estimated 4,000 in 2016.[24] On May 3, 2017, Governor Rick Scott declared the opioid epidemic a public-health emergency. "The individuals struggling with drug use are sons, daughters, mothers, fathers, sisters, brothers, and friends, and each tragic case leaves loved ones searching for answers and praying for help," he said.

Tookes knew he couldn't open anything like a supervised-injection facility in Florida. But he envisioned his needle-exchange program as a centre for every sort of harm-reduction supply he could offer within the limits of Florida state law. "We didn't have to go through the steps that everyone else had to when this was implemented across the world twenty years ago," Tookes says. "We could go straight into best practices, so we were able to start a pretty robust program right from the beginning."

On World AIDS Day of 2016, December 1, the IDEA Exchange opened at 1636 Northwest 7th Avenue in Overtown, Miami. They named it after the bill that allows it to exist: the Infectious Disease Elimination Act. It's nothing flashy, just two beige storage containers like the kind one sees moving around the country via train. They were outfitted with air conditioning units, then set down in a parking lot and positioned adjacent to one another in the shape of an L. At the container closest to the street, drug users can bring used needles and trade them for clean, packaged ones. A one-for-one exchange is a strict requirement,

---

[24] Haden, Peter. "The Number of Daily Opioid Overdoses in South Florida Is Overwhelming Police," PRI Public Radio International, April 20, 2017.

Tookes notes. He says he wanted a distribution model with no exchange requirement, but the law says one-for-one. The IDEA Exchange actually collects more needles than it gives out, he adds.

There are other harm-reduction supplies available at container one: condoms, for example, and everything one needs alongside a clean needle to inject drugs, including cookers, cotton balls, tourniquets, and sterile water.

Next door, at container two, there's a small clinic. Drug users or anyone who walks by can receive help connecting with a substance-use counsellor or a detox or treatment program, if they're ready for that. They can also do a free test for HIV, hepatitis C, and other infectious diseases, and get the results there, on-site. As of April 2017, IDEA Exchange also distributes naloxone (sold under the brand name Narcan), the so-called overdose antidote that's used to reverse the effects of opioids.

The day the IDEA Exchange opened, there was a line of drug users down the sidewalk, Tookes recalls. The four-year battle in the Florida legislature that was waged to make the needle exchange happen had generated a lot of media coverage, and many drug users in Miami read every article.

But the program remained controversial in Florida and even in relatively liberal Miami. Other people were less enthusiastic. "The police did not receive the program well," Tookes says. "They arrested everybody. It was bad. It was very bad."

Anticipating some confusion to linger around the change in drug laws, the IDEA Exchange distributed needles with a card that explained the program. On one side was an IDEA Exchange member's name and on the other side was an explanation of how the exchange operates legally. The actual statute is there, plus a statement saying that whoever is in possession of the card is not breaking the law by carrying a needle, even if an officer finds evidence that they plan to use it to inject drugs. But some officers did not respond well to drug users claiming they knew the law better than police.

"The cops would pull the syringes off people and say, 'This card doesn't mean shit,' and they would throw it in the gutter," Tookes says. "We lost a lot of people coming into our program at first because of that."

And so the IDEA Exchange launched an education and outreach program, not for drug users or the general public, but for police. Tookes says that, to their credit, most of them came around quickly. He says it was narcotics officers who did the most to facilitate the shift in attitudes. After spending years around drug users, narcotics officers understood addiction and the benefits of harm-reduction programs like needle exchange, Tookes explains. They helped educate their colleagues on the force.

"The cops have ended up being a huge ally," Tookes says. "It just took them a while."

Chapter 9

The Killing Fields

A nn Livingston and Bud Osborn's paths crossed several times before the two of them actually met. In photographs taken at the 1994 meeting at the Carnegie Community Centre, where Livingston connected with Melissa Eror, Osborn is sitting directly behind Livingston, just two rows back.

Then, just before Back Alley inevitably closed its doors, William Kay invited Osborn down to check the place out. The users there had covered the walls in poetry and graffiti, and Kay thought Osborn might be able to make something out of it.

"The felt pens kept disappearing," Livingston remembers. "I have to have white paper and I have to have felt pens because I am a freak about how I do organizing. But the felt pens kept disappearing. Meanwhile, this poetry is all over the walls because everybody is writing all over them. Later, I thought, 'That's where all the felt pens went.'"

Livingston was at home with her boys the day Osborn took Kay up on his invitation. But she remembers the result of that visit. Osborn copied down everything that was written on the walls at Back Alley and put it into a book.

Livingston knew the name Bud Osborn from years earlier. She had come across another one of his books of poetry when she was still living in Victoria, but somehow it was not until 1996 that the two finally got to know one another.

The moment when Osborn first noticed Livingston was not one of her better days. For several years, Livingston had held a seat on the board of the Downtown Eastside Residents Association. On this day, she was losing that position. Made to stand at the front of a room of some 400 people, she held her tongue while fellow DERA members levelled every sort of accusation at her—charges that had to do with the illegal injection site Livingston had brought to the community and not a lot else beyond that. Livingston's fellow DERA board members didn't approve of her new interest in drug addicts.

Osborn recounted the spectacle in a 2002 interview with Nettie Wild, a filmmaker who later produced a documentary about drug users in the Downtown Eastside called *Fix: The Story of an Addicted City*. (Osborn was ultimately cut from the film. Wild shared the transcripts of their interviews for inclusion in this book.)

Osborn noticed Livingston at the DERA meeting because, while an entire room attacked her, she didn't attack back. "I remember she said, 'I hope whatever comes out of this will strengthen the community and be for the benefit of the community,'" Osborn told Wild. "She was the only one that had the community in her mind ... I was very impressed that she did. And so, that was the first time that I really, really saw Ann."

In 1996, the two bumped into each other at the Carnegie Community Centre and finally actually said hello. "I remember he was checking me out," Livingston recalls.

By this time her relationship with Kay had fallen apart. "At one point, I said, 'So, William, you're going to keep coming over to my house?'" Livingston says. "'We're not moving forward with our relationship, so what is this? Like, squatters' rights?'"

That was the end of it. Then, a few months later, Livingston noticed Osborn at a meeting of the Vancouver-Richmond Health Board, a regional arm of the provincial government whose jurisdiction included the Downtown Eastside.

John Turvey had pulled strings and gotten Osborn a seat on the board. Livingston recalls that she liked his poetry but that wasn't what really impressed her about him—it was that he had a say in public policy. "He gets appointed to the health board, and I'm like, he might as well have had a fucking Ferrari."

The two began spending more time together and one thing led to another. Livingston would often hold small community meetings at her apartment that would end late. One evening, Osborn spent the night.

Osborn had also gotten to know Liz Evans and Mark Townsend, which made him an important intersection between the Portland's world and Livingston's.

Evans reached out to Osborn and asked if he would come to the hotel to hold a series of writing workshops for her residents. He loved the idea and quickly agreed. The only problem was that they didn't have a space to hold these meetings, so the group that came to gather once a month with Osborn settled in a stairwell of the old building's emergency fire escape. Residents shared their stories with him, mostly of hardship, and Osborn helped them commit those stories to paper. "He did that for years," Evans recalls fondly.

Osborn remembered the Downtown Eastside in the mid-1990s as a neighbourhood on edge. "There was nothing but sirens, sirens, sirens, all the time. I mean, people were dying," he told journalist Johann Hari. "And every time there would be a siren, I would wonder, 'Do I know this person?'"

One morning in July 1997, Osborn was walking down East Hastings Street and bumped into an Indigenous woman named Margaret Prevost. She was in a wheelchair and so Osborn leaned in slightly to say hello. She told him that her cousin had overdosed and that when her husband had found the body, he had hung himself there in the same room. Their young boy was left without a home, Prevost continued, and so the extended family was meeting that afternoon to decide where he would go.

"By then I had learned it was preventable, it was unnecessary," Osborn told Nettie Wild. "I had learned about harm reduction, I had learned about the reduction of overdose deaths in Europe and elsewhere. Something—it was physical—rose through my nervous system like a charge of some kind and just went right up into my brain and exploded," he continued. "That's enough, that's it—that is just too much of death." Osborn was totally overwhelmed, not with grief but with anger.

At that moment, Evans was sitting in her office on the ground floor of the Portland, chatting with Townsend and Kerstin Stuerzbecher. "Bud came in and was fuming," Evans recounts. "He was like, 'I'm just done. I'm done. This is too much. We've got to do something and I don't know what, but we have to do *something*.'"

He wasn't the only one feeling that way. Stuerzbecher, who by now was considered a co-founder of the Portland alongside Evans and Townsend, recalls how bad things had gotten. "I was reviving people two or three times a day," she says. "We needed to symbolize that, somehow."

Evans remembers that in those years, the vibe of the Downtown Eastside could get so intense that some mornings she would vomit on her walks to work. "I used to get incredibly stressed," she says. "I was really anxious about what I was going to come across each day. There were funerals every day for people dying in the neighbourhood. I was literally walking to work passing blue bodies in the stairwell every day."

On top of it all, they felt alone, as if nobody outside the Downtown Eastside was even aware of how many people were dying. "There was a general, wide-spread abandonment of thousands of people, and nobody gave a fuck and everybody turned a blind eye," Evans says. "We were sitting there in the middle of it, thinking, 'What the fuck is going on? Why doesn't anybody care? Why isn't anyone talking about it? Why isn't there a giant public outcry?'"

In Evans's tiny office, the four of them got to work brainstorming. "That's when we decided to create this giant banner in red and stretch it across the intersection of Main and Hastings and call the neighbourhood the 'Killing Fields,'" Evans says. "And then we thought we'd get a thousand crosses and build one for each person who had died in the last five years from drugs."

Townsend recalls that they planned the protest to be a deliberate attempt to grab the specific attention of the city's journalists. "So many people were dying, but the media hadn't taken it up," he says. "We needed visuals." How would the crosses look on camera? Was there a vantage point from which a news crew could capture the entire scene? Who would speak at the protest? What could they say that could serve as a succinct and punchy soundbite? All of these questions were given careful consideration.

The year before, the federal government had published a report on HIV/AIDS in Canada, and Townsend had gone crazy for it. But nobody else had paid the document any attention. He made a phone call to Ottawa and ordered 500 copies of the report. They would shut down the intersection of Main and East Hastings and there set them all on fire. "We wanted to block the traffic and burn these reports to say, 'There are all these reports that gather dust on government shelves while nothing happens,'" Townsend explains.

Next they needed quotes for print media. Townsend placed a call to Dr Steffanie Strathdee, then a young researcher with the University of British Columbia. He asked her how they could describe the extent of the HIV/AIDS crisis in the Downtown Eastside. Everyone knew it was bad, but how could they describe it in a way that would grab headlines? "Was the Downtown Eastside's rate of infection the highest in the world?" Townsend asked Strathdee. No, it wasn't, she informed him. "Could we say that the rate of HIV/AIDS infections in the Downtown Eastside was the highest in the Western World?" Strathdee checked and confirmed that was accurate.

Evans, Townsend, and Stuerzbecher continued to spitball ideas. Meanwhile, Osborn went to find volunteers willing to assemble 1,000 crosses. He found them in the Political Response Group, a loose organization of Christians he was close with who lived in a row of colourfully painted houses located on Jackson Street, on the eastern edge of the Downtown Eastside.

"There was a gang of us," recalls Dave Diewert, a close friend of Osborn's. The two of them went to another friend who owned a carpentry shop and asked if they could borrow the back room for an evening or two. "We nailed the crosses at the wood shop through the night leading up to it," Diewert says. "And then, early in the morning, we had a bunch of people ready for the march."

At the Four Sister's Co-op, Livingston had also gone most of the night without sleep. She woke up hours before dawn to make sandwiches for the dozens of drug users that she and Osborn had organized to take part in the demonstration. "I did all the fucking work, but Bud got all the credit," Livingston says with a laugh. "That was the usual relationship that we had."

She describes him as the ideas man. Osborn seldom put in the hours and days and weeks of leg work that it takes to bring a protest together, but he often would serve as the spark that got everybody moving. Nobody interviewed today is sure who came up with the plan to plant crosses to symbolize the dead, but everyone agrees it sounds like a Bud Osborn idea.

On July 15, 1997, about 200 people gathered in the middle of the intersection of Main and East Hastings Street. A fire burned in a barrel in which Townsend threw the government reports he had ordered from Ottawa. Drug users dragged a chain across the street and fastened it to poles on either side to block all six lanes of traffic. From the chain they hung a banner. "The Killing Fields," it read. "Federal action now."

This was Liz Evans's first time participating in a public demonstration. She recalls actually feeling guilty about it. "All these cars were stopped, and I just kept feeling sorry for them all not being able to get to work," she says. "They would roll down their windows, and I would shove pamphlets into their car, saying, 'I'm so sorry to bother you, but did you know people are dying?'"

From Main and Hastings, the demonstration marched three blocks east to Oppenheimer Park, where Diewert and his friends with the Political Response Group had worked since before sunrise, banging their 1,000 crosses into the ground.

Oppenheimer Park is a square block of green space in the Downtown Eastside that for decades has served as a living room for people who don't have a home. There's a baseball diamond at one end and, in 1997, a shuffle board and area for chess at the other. It's a cherished community space shared by children and adults.

With 1,000 crosses spaced evenly to cover the entire block, Townsend recounts how the crowd thinned and fanned out as it moved into the park. "People started to write names on the crosses, which is something we hadn't really thought of," he says. "It was emotional and very upsetting."

As the crosses were assigned names of the dead, Osborn recited a poem he had written for that day. It reads in part:

These thousand crosses silently announce a social curse
On the lives of the poorest of the poor in the Downtown Eastside

They announce an assault on the community
These thousand crosses announce a deprivation of possibility
For those of us who mourn here
The mothers and fathers and sisters and brothers
The uncles, aunts, grandmothers and grandfathers
The sons and daughters the friends and acquaintances
Of those members of our community
Of a thousand dreams of a thousand hopes
Of a thousand yearnings for real community
Lost to us but memorialized today
Brought finally into a unity here in this community park
This park which is the geographical heart of the Downtown
Eastside
These thousand crosses are a protest
Against the abandonment of powerless and voiceless human
beings
These thousand crosses speak to us resoundingly
Collectively to warn us that to abandon the wretched
The miserable the scorned the scapegoated
Makes a legitimate place for abandonment in our society
And this abandonment will go right up the social ladder
But to truly care for lives at the bottom
Will make a place for care
And this caring will ensure that no one be abandoned
These thousand crosses represent the overdose deaths of drug
addicts
Who are not the only drug addicts in our society
But only the most visible the most naked because the poorest
But these thousand crosses reveal a culture
Pretending to be about life and health and hope
But permeated with death and disease and despair
These thousand crosses bear witness not to a culture of care and
freedom
But of carelessness and addiction.[25]

---

[25] Bud Osborn, "a thousand crosses in oppenheimer park," *Raise Shit: Social Action Saving Lives* (Vancouver, BC: Fernwood Publishing, 2009), p. 20.

In July 1997, Downtown Eastside poet and activist Bud Osborn helped organize the city's first major protest calling for action on overdose deaths. *Photo: Duncan Murdoch*

They were all on the news that night and in the papers the following morning. "It was a day of tears and sombre symbols in a Vancouver neighbourhood," narrated an anchor over a CTV News broadcast. "All orchestrated to bring attention to the growing number of people in the area who are dying from heroin and AIDs. The city's east end has gained international notoriety for the deadly resurgence of drugs, and residents say it's time something is done."

A number of Vancouver papers quoted a report that BC's chief coroner of the day, Vince Cain, had published in 1995. "Governments were made well aware of the crisis more than two years ago," reads one of those articles. "And what has happened on this front since Mr Cain issued his report at the beginning of 1995? Virtually nothing."

"Testimony of the Crosses," read a headline above a story about the demonstration in the *Montreal Gazette*, all the way on the other side of the country.

Reflecting on that day more than a decade later, Evans described it in a letter to friends as a "turning point, a point when people began to ask questions about what was going on … and a turning point at which people began to see that those images of people with needles in their arms were people who were suffering, alongside families who were suffering, alongside an entire community that was suffering."

––––––––––––––

With the Killing Fields protest, as the day became known, Osborn and Livingston and the Portland's management team finally grabbed the public's attention. Among those who took note was Libby Davies. Just one month earlier, she'd been elected to her first term as a member of parliament.

Davies knew the Downtown Eastside well. More than twenty years earlier, in 1973, she was out for a beer with her boyfriend, Bruce Eriksen, at an East Hastings bar called the Patricia Hotel, which is still there today. Davies was a twenty-year-old student at the University of British Columbia at the time and Eriksen, twenty-five years her senior, was an artist and activist. When the waitress at the Patricia came to take the couple's drink order, she asked for Davies' ID, and the three of them began to chat. The waitress introduced herself as Jean Swanson. Eriksen, a recovering alcoholic, responded by admonishing her for the Patricia's reputation for over-serving customers. Swanson liked them both right away and asked Eriksen what she could do to get involved in the sort of activism he was then already well-known for.

Within a year, the three of them had transformed a small nonprofit group Eriksen was working for, called the People's Aid Project, into a political force in the neighbourhood. That was the beginning of the Downtown Eastside Resident's Association, or DERA, the housing nonprofit that in 1991 had given Liz Evans the keys to the Portland Hotel. (Forty-three years later, in 2016, Jean Swanson received the Order of Canada—a civilian honour comparable to the United States' Presidential Medal of Freedom—for the work on housing and homelessness that she began with Eriksen and Davies at that chance encounter at the Patricia Hotel.)

Cancer took Eriksen's life in March 1997, four months before the Killing Fields protest. He and Davies were never married but were common-law partners until the day he passed away. She recalls being utterly devastated by the loss but marching ahead as best she could. On July 15, Davies met protestors at the intersection of Main Street and East Hastings, hoping to learn more about the rising number of overdose deaths that were occurring in the constituency she was recently elected to represent in the nation's capital.

"I remember walking into Oppenheimer Park and the emotional impact of seeing 1,000 crosses neatly lined up in rows," she recounts. "The park was empty because everybody was behind us in the march. And the visual impact was something I will never, ever forget. It was moving and it was also very empowering, in a strange way. This sense of the community being together ... There was a silence, a deep sense of grieving, but also togetherness. People were united for a common purpose."

Davies and Osborn had been friends for years and had grown very close throughout 1996. Eriksen was mostly bedridden that year, and Osborn visited often. The two of them talked for hours, Davies says, with Osborn asking questions about Eriksen's work as an activist.

"He was so eager to learn what organizing was about and how it happened," she remembers. "Then when I ran [for office] in '97, Bud came canvassing with me. He just laughed his socks off. He had never done anything like that in his life, and he didn't like politicians. But we actually went door to door ... him with his little clipboard, putting marks for supporters and people who were undecided. He just thought it was hilarious that he was out doing political canvassing."

At Oppenheimer Park, Davies looked across the field of crosses to where Osborn was reciting the poem he had written for that day. "It propelled me to Ottawa," she says. "I knew what I had to do. I didn't have a clue how I was going to do it. I didn't know how Ottawa worked. I just knew I had to make this a critical issue. My constituents were dying, and these were preventable deaths."

She took Osborn's words to the House of Commons. The first statement she made there was from the poem he had recited in Oppenheimer Park:

> These thousand crosses of the contemporary martyrs—
> Bear witness not only to their drug overdose deaths
> But to the uncounted deaths in the Downtown Eastside
> Deaths of drug addicts from suicide and AIDS
> And so we are all abandoned if one is abandoned
> So we are all uncared-for if one is not cared for.[26]

The seat that John Turvey had secured for Osborn on the health board was an accomplishment that might sound minor but was, in fact, unprecedented. "We used to meet in this greasy spoon," Osborn said. "And there he asked me if I wanted a seat on the health board, the Vancouver-Richmond Health Board. I didn't even know what a health board was. I said, 'Is that a good thing?' And he said, 'Yeah.'"

For the first time, the seat gave someone who was open about an addiction to drugs a say in how a government spent its money on addiction services. But Osborn didn't know how to use the position to turn the needs of the Downtown Eastside into policies that would address them. Davies continued the lessons in activism that her partner had started with Osborn the year before he passed away.

"When he was on the board, it just about drove him mad," she remembers. "It was a new environment for him, and he was pulled here and there within the bureaucracy. And so I began to give him a lot of advice." Throughout 1997, Davies met with Osborn on just about every trip she made from Ottawa back to Vancouver. Together they strategized on how to use Osborn's seat to bring action to the Downtown Eastside. "My job with him was to give him patience," Davies continues. "How to work it on the inside, how to figure out who your allies are, how to figure out who your obstacles are, and how to work the system. He was very frustrated, so my job was to help him keep the faith."

---

[26] Bud Osborn, "a thousand crosses in oppenheimer park."

At one meeting, Osborn read a preamble to a motion he brought forward by describing his words as "a composite cry of anguish expressed to me by both service providers and drug users in the Downtown Eastside, the people I represent on this board." He called what was happening a "genocide" and one for which he blamed the very people to whom he was speaking.

"To ascribe the eruption of this tragic phenomena to the behaviour of addicts, to injection drug users crowding into the Downtown Eastside in unsanitary conditions and injecting cocaine in large numbers is a subtle form of blaming the victim for their conditions, when the production of this epidemic can be found in the near criminal neglect and abandonment of our poorest and most afflicted citizens by all three levels of government," Osborn said. The crowd he faced was often skeptical of Osborn's arguments, to put it mildly.

Livingston, who attended many of those health board meetings as a citizen, recalls how they could end with Osborn standing up, sometimes knocking over his chair in the process, and literally screaming at the other board members. Other times, he would completely lose his temper and storm out. She recounts a particularly memorable one of those incidents.

"Bud was in a board meeting and somebody was looking at the graphs of AIDS deaths," she begins.

For years, HIV/AIDS raged through the Downtown Eastside unchecked. In 1989, there were eighty-six deaths attributed to HIV/AIDS in the City of Vancouver. By 1994, that number had jumped to 203. By 1996, HIV/AIDs deaths were on the decline, but the disease still claimed 146 of the city's citizens that year. [27]

What's more, authorities were now closely tracking the rate of infection in Vancouver and knew more deaths were coming. "Vancouver has the highest reported HIV incidence rate amongst injection drug users in North America," reads a 1997 government report.[28] The majority of

[27] Statistics throughout the book for HIV/AIDS deaths in British Columbia are sourced to the BC Vital Statistics Agency. http://www2.gov.bc.ca/gov/content/ lifeevents/ statistics-reports/annual-reports

[28] Parry, Penny. *Something to Eat, a Place to Sleep and Someone Who Gives a Damn: HIV/AIDS and Injection Drug Use in the DTES* (Victoria, BC: Ministry of Health and Ministry Responsible for Seniors, 1997).

those people were Osborn's neighbours in the Downtown Eastside.

Livingston recounts that one member of the board looked at the statistics charted on the wall, turned to the rest of the group, and said, "If we don't do anything, they are going to come down, because we'll hit a saturation point." The suggestion was that eventually, so many drug users would die that there simply wouldn't be enough left to keep the statistics as high as they were at the time.

"Bud lost his shit," Livingston says. "He jumps up, the fucking chair falls over, and he starts screaming. 'Are you fucking serious?!'"

Interviewed twenty years later, Dr John Blatherwick, who held the position of board chair during that meeting, acknowledges that the deaths hitting a saturation point is very likely what occurred. "There wasn't something that we did that helped," he says. "It was simply a numbers game. When so many people got infected, there were fewer people left to get infected. And so the number of cases went up and up and up, and then dropped fairly precipitously. I'd love to say that things like the needle-exchange program changed the course, or that the Street Nurses changed the course. But, in fact, the epidemic burned itself out. It's very sad."

In 1997, Osborn saw this explosion of HIV/AIDS in his community as an emergency. He couldn't understand why others didn't feel the same, and so he went to the public library to look up the definition of the word. What was happening in the Downtown Eastside was definitely an emergency, Osborn confirmed.

On Davies' next visit to Vancouver, Osborn met her at a diner, presented her with the definition of the word "emergency" he had copied down, and asked for her advice on a next move. They decided he should propose a motion at the health board that would give the HIV/AIDS outbreak in the Downtown Eastside official status as a public-health emergency. "He didn't know how a motion was formulated," Davies says. "So I helped him craft the right sort of language."

At the health board meeting on September 25, 1997, Osborn arrived with his motion, ready to present it and call for a vote. But one of his colleagues had another idea. "I got to the meeting and was greeted by one of the executives of the health board who had an alternative motion for me that they wanted me to introduce instead of the public-health emergency," Osborn said. "I refused."

That exchange left Osborn discouraged, but he followed through as planned and tabled his motion. And it passed. It was a great victory but also a point of unbearable frustration.

"Declaring a public-health emergency really rang an alarm, and it caught a lot of media," Osborn said. "And I felt that the health board would have to then explain to people what a public-health emergency is or define it. Well, that isn't what they did at all ... They didn't do anything."

Davies recalls Osborn's intense anger at the situation. "He expected everything to change with this emergency resolution, and, of course, it didn't," she says. "Getting it through was one thing; giving it meaning and having action taken is a totally different thing."

Eventually, after another year of people dying, the declaration did begin to bring tangible results. Slowly, more funding for health-care programs found its way to the Downtown Eastside. In addition, Osborn and Evans and Townsend and everyone fighting for the Downtown Eastside in those years were able to hold the declaration up and say to government, "A public emergency has been declared. We need you to respond." Davies describes it as "pivotal."

"It was a tipping point in how the public-health system responded," she says. "And it would never have happened if it hadn't been Bud on that board, presenting it, arguing for it, lobbying for it, and getting it through."

Chapter 10

A Drug-Users Union

In the summer of 1997, Livingston remembers feeling a strange disconnect between the beautiful weather and the tension and fear that had emerged in response to so many deaths in their small Downtown Eastside community.

"It was just fucking ghastly," she recalls. "If you added up the suicides and alcohol poisonings, it was huge. We were losing over a hundred people a year to alcohol poisoning in this neighbourhood. And then about 200 to overdoses. It was just fucking horrible. But I remember how sunny it was that summer. Every day, Bud and I would wake up, and it was just glorious weather. And I would think, 'How can the weather be this good when all these terrible things are happening?'"

On one of those sunny afternoons in September of that year, Livingston decided it was time to take another stab at organizing drug users. She drafted a simple flier and went around the Downtown Eastside fixing it to telephone poles. "Meeting in the park," it read. "Discussion items: police conduct, violence and safety, 'Is this your home?,' washroom facilities, neighbourhood relations ... Let's talk about a community approach."

Through Livingston's work at Back Alley two years prior, she was well-known among the neighbourhood's community of drug users. A lot of them had felt empowered by participating in the meetings she had led there. Osborn enjoyed a modicum of fame in Vancouver for his poetry and anti-gentrification activism. And so on September 9, 1997, several dozen people were there to meet the pair of them at the east end of Oppenheimer Park.

A few years earlier, Osborn had made a serious attempt to get clean, spending more than a month at one and then two treatment centres for drug addiction. "I needed to get away," he recalled. "I was just wretched. And I had started getting arrested for shoplifting and stuff like that. And I thought, 'I gotta do something.'" Osborn didn't kick all of his bad habits, but he did gain enough clarity to find a new meaning in life. "When I came back from those treatment places, I decided, 'Okay, what am I going to do now?'" Osborn said.

"I want to keep writing poetry," he thought. "I'll always do that. But I also want to give as much of myself as I can to help the Downtown Eastside. Because it had become, really, the only home that I had ever known."

Osborn gave part of the credit for this transformation to a counsellor he met at Kinghaven Treatment Centre, a rehab facility that still operates today in the rural Vancouver suburb of Abbotsford. "I ran down the same weary story that I'd been running down all my life," Osborn recounted. "My father hanged himself, my mother was mentally ill, there were all these beatings.

"I thought what [the counsellor] would say is what others had always said: 'Oh, you poor guy, no wonder you use drugs. That's terrible.' But he didn't. He leaned back in his seat and looked out the window, and then he looked at me and said, 'It's your lightning.' Which completely stunned me, so much that I didn't even ask him what he meant. And from then on, I began to puzzle over what that meant. I even looked it up: 'What is lightning?' It's the most powerful physical force on Earth, really. A natural force."

A good friend of Osborn's in those days was Donald MacPherson, who held a manager's position at the Carnegie Community Centre. He recalls how seriously Osborn took his position on the health board, assigning himself the role of a liaison for the Downtown Eastside. The flip side of that work on the health board would be the meetings he and Livingston held in Oppenheimer Park. "They were an attempt to do something like a needs assessment," MacPherson says.

Livingston brought all her felt pens and the big chart paper on which she had recorded meeting minutes at Back Alley. While Osborn led the group, calling on drug users for their input, she scribbled frantically to record everything they said. "We would compile the [notes], and I would take them to all the [health] board members, so they could actually see what a real junkie says," Osborn explained.

Two large pages of Livingston's notes from their very first meeting in the park survived to today. A note added to the top describes the scene: "A community meeting was held to get input from people who use and care about the park," it begins. "The meeting held at six p.m. outside on the checker board was attended by about sixty people. The weather was warm and although there was some heated debate the tone was positive. Agency people, seniors, neighbourhood activists, drug users, and people who sleep at the park participated and shared food."

Thirty-three bullet points are recorded below. There are complaints about used needles and trash left around the neighbourhood and concerns about violence in the community. Abuses perpetrated by police are mentioned a couple of times. But the one concern raised more than any other was that drug users simply had nowhere to call their own. "When the Back Alley Drop-In was open, we had our own place to go," one point reads. "You shut it down."

In response to some attendees' complaints about discarded needles that made the park unsafe for children, drug users argued that a designated site like Back Alley might address that problem. "If we provide users with a place to go shoot up, it will improve things in the park for all of us—users and non-users."

Livingston recalls the meeting as bare bones but powerful. "It was just me and Bud, and we had a big piece of paper and I made notes," she says. "It wasn't that it was massively well-attended. But I wrote down everything people said, and they could see me writing down what they were saying." That alone had a huge impact, Livingston recalls. Drug users were speaking and somebody was listening.

At the end of her record, another note is appended. "After the meeting, people visited with one another and the atmosphere was friendly. Many people are looking forward to some kind of regular get-together at the park to discuss serious community issues and to get to know each other."

Livingston drafted a second poster and put it up around town, this time with a message that was more focused. "Where can users go?" it read. "How do users feel about having no place to go, nowhere to wash, inadequate detox, constant police harassment and no one who cares?"

Meanwhile, Osborn found them a place where there would be a roof over their heads. He was heavy into a religious "twelve-steps" approach at the time, and had come to know the pastor of the Four-square Church, also known as the Street Church. It was a congregation of low-income people who met each Sunday on the second floor of a building on the 100 block of East Hastings Street, across the street from the Carnegie Community Centre. The church's pastor, Randy Barnetson, in 2017 still holds twice-weekly meetings there. Today, he's usually found minding a stove with a large pot of hot dogs boiling, just as he was in the mid-1990s. Back then, a twelve-pack cost a dollar. Today the price is more than double that, but Barnetson still serves them for free. It's from this routine that the building gets its better-known nickname, the "Hot Dog Church."

Barnetson recalls the day Osborn approached him to ask if they could use the space for a weekly meeting of drug addicts. "We got to talking about harm reduction," Barnetson says. "I was saying, 'Well, in our own way, by giving free food out to addicts, we were doing harm reduction.' But Bud had a different attitude toward people who just give out food. He said, 'We don't need a sandwich, we need justice!'"

Barnetson says he never thought the idea of hosting a regular meeting of drug users was anything to balk at. The destitute were the church's regular patrons anyway. "That's what the Street Church is," he adds. "We're a church for the people on the block."

In November, Osborn's group of drug addicts convened there for their second meeting together. Livingston had stayed up late the night before, preparing sandwiches for everybody (an effective incentive for attendance, she had learned). Upon arrival, people signed in, took a seat on the floor, and then introduced themselves. Again, Osborn led the meeting while Livingston furiously recorded every attendee's contributions to the discussion.

"Bud would say, 'Many people are dying. I'm an addict like you guys. I'm straight now, but blah blah blah,'" Livingston recounts. "So he says all this inspiring shit, and people are like, 'Oh shit, I want to be on this guy's fucking team.' He was very charismatic. People wanted to be part of what he was doing."

Livingston's notes from that first gathering at the Foursquare Street

Church reflected addicts' wishes for a place where they could feel comfortable without fear of harassment by police. "It is important to have these meetings to hear from drug users," one note reads. "Drug users aren't illiterate. They need a voice in the matters affecting their lives."

On January 10, 1998, the group's tenth consecutive meeting, they invited a guest: the rookie MP who was so affected by the Killing Fields protest the year before: Libby Davies.

"The room was so jam-packed I could barely get in there," Davies recounts. "Ann had all her flipchart paper all the way around the walls, like she always did, just scribbling everything that people said. She really understood that giving witness to what people were saying was very important."

No federal politician had ever spoken to a group like this one, and Davies recalls the room was highly skeptical and more than a little suspicious of what she was doing there.

"Ann introduced me, and I was literally stepping over people to get to the front of the room," Davies continues. She told them she was in Ottawa working for them, and that one day, they would create a safe space for injection-drug users, an idea that was just beginning to attract more discussion among residents of the Downtown Eastside.

"I remember a couple of them said, 'It's never going to happen, Libby. We'll never get a safe-injection site,'" Davies says. "I said, 'It's going to happen. It will happen, I promise you. We are going to fight for this.'"

She attended a couple of subsequent meetings and likens the experience to an education on the issues facing street addicts. "I realized that one of the issues was that nobody listened to them," Davies says. "That once you were labelled a drug addict or a criminal, nobody ever again saw you as an individual. You were part of this stereotype, a screwed-up criminal. And so just listening to people and knowing people as individuals was really important."

With the church as a space they could call a home, Livingston recalls that things began to move more quickly. "I kept saying that we needed to organize and then we would get somewhere," she recalls. "And it was true. Within I don't know how many meetings, we had fifty people."

Around this time, a young couple by the names of Kenn Quayle and Brian Mackenzie took notice of the collection of people Livingston and Osborn brought together each week. Quayle and Mackenzie were not living the street life on the Downtown Eastside, but they did use drugs.

"They were more rave guys," Livingston recalls. "They contacted me and said, 'We know you did this thing at the Back Alley.'" They suggested that Livingston's group would have a greater influence if it expanded to include the more recreational sort of drug users that they hung with, which at the time were mostly interested in MDMA (then called ecstasy or "e" and today called molly), methamphetamine, and hallucinogens like acid, as well as Vancouver's marijuana community. Livingston and Osborn thought that made sense.

"We were doing harm-reduction outreach in the rave scene," Mackenzie says. Quayle was also involved in the city's medicinal-marijuana movement. "And because we were all affected by the same anti-drug prohibition laws, we thought that it made sense for us to all pool our resources and our energy."

Livingston started having Quayle and Mackenzie over to her apartment more frequently (Quayle fondly recalls that the children were a constant interruption), and they began to strategize their next move. Following the example of a group in Australia, the Australian Injecting and Illicit Drug Users League, they decided they would make a play for government funding.

Well past midnight of the day their grant application was due, Quayle and Mackenzie were still up hastily trying to complete the paperwork when one question stumped them. What was their organization called? "I was working on the floor of our apartment on Commercial Drive in the middle of the night, putting together this funding proposal," Quayle says, "and it needed to have a name."

Mackenzie recalls that Quayle began playing around with the components they wanted to incorporate and what letters worked well as an acronym. Neither Livingston nor Osborn were there that night, but when Quayle was finished completing the grant application, the weekly meeting of users at the Street Church had a name: the Vancouver Area Network of Drug Users, or VANDU for short.

They did not get the grant. "The first proposal we wrote was for an outrageous amount," Quayle says. Mackenzie remembers that it asked for half a million dollars. Quayle says it was for an even million. Either way, "The bigwigs there snorted and laughed us out of the room," Quayle says.

Toward the end of January, Osborn was able to use his seat on the health board to secure a small line of funding for the group. It wasn't much, a couple hundred dollars for each meeting that went to sandwiches plus an honorarium for attendees equal to bus fare. But it marked a significant milestone: a group of drug addicts was receiving financial support from the government. "Not much at all," Osborn noted. "Money to get it started, to rent the place and to give some money for a bit of tobacco and bus fare and stuff like that." But, he added, he considered those small sums one of his life's greatest accomplishments.

Unfortunately, it wasn't long before the group was back out on the street, no longer welcome at the Street Church.

"Some asshole got into their office and started making 1-900 calls to a sex line," Livingston explains. "That's when they kicked us out. One day, we went there with our key to get in and the lock had been changed. I think it was the guys doing those 1-900 sex calls. The church didn't like that."

Barnetson laughs when he's reminded of that incident. "The phone company was ... nice enough to cancel the bill for us," he says.

When that door closed, another opened when Livingston spotted an opportunity to secure real funding. A grant of $50,000 was available for a group that said it could prevent hospitalizations of marginalized people. No one was going to give $50,000 to a group of drug users, Livingston realized, and so she applied for the money through a Downtown Eastside nonprofit organization called Lookout, which at the time ran a shelter and drop-in centre for people with mental-health challenges. Against all expectations, Livingston's application was approved. Then, later the same year, that grant was topped up with an additional $47,000. Now VANDU had real funding, which it used to rent a room at Lookout's drop-in, called the LivingRoom.

At one of VANDU's first meetings, in late 1997, attendees made a list of names of friends and family they had lost and attached it to the wall behind them. *Photo: Duncan Murdoch*

"We had an office with a broken computer, a phone, and a leaky roof," Livingston says. "And Lookout could not grasp what we were doing. Not a clue."

Just as VANDU was gaining an air of legitimacy, Mackenzie and Quayle were offered another opportunity. The drug-user group in Australia that they had essentially copied to help found VANDU wanted them to relocate to Sydney. The offer was too good to pass up, and they took the job. Had they not, VANDU might have turned out very differently, perhaps with a far wider membership than the group of mostly injection-drug addicts that it's composed of today.

Quayle and Mackenzie left but their name stayed. On August 15, 1998, the group debated—endlessly, Livingston recalls—the drafting of a constitution. At the end of it, a new nonprofit was formed. "The name of the society is: Vancouver Area Network of Drug Users," the constitution reads. That document consists of just one page and outlines a simple mandate to "improve the quality of life for people who use illicit drugs." Those objectives would be achieved through organizing, educating the public, and by developing "local networks and coalitions of informed and empowered people who will work to ensure public policies and practices are favourable to people who use illicit drugs."

The next step was to elect a leader. Livingston and Osborn kept their names out of the race, instead encouraging the group to vote in an active drug user. Another raucous debate ensued. At the end of it, Melissa Eror, the unsung hero who had kept Back Alley together, was elected the first president of VANDU.

She recalls that the experience was not a positive one. "I got really frustrated quite quickly with the whole thing," Eror says. She enjoyed the hands-on work she had done keeping Back Alley open as long as she had. In contrast, VANDU's less tangible activism left Eror feeling disenchanted. She worried their efforts would never get them anywhere. "I didn't think there was a future in it," Eror explains. "Those things don't really impress me. They get your name in the paper and everybody gets to beat their breast but that's about as far as it goes."

Eror was also trying to keep herself clean for the sake of her two daughters. Hanging out with a group for which a membership requirement was active or recent drug use didn't help her do that.

"The more things got bad with the group, the more drugs I started to use," Eror says. "And at the end of it, it just wasn't a good thing."

———

She did stick around long enough to make one notable contribution. There's a document dated September 1998 that was drafted for the Vancouver-Richmond Health Board that bears Eror's name at the top of its list of authors. The title of the report is "Proposal for the Development of a Pilot Project to Implement and Evaluate the Use of Safe (Injection) Sites: a Strategy for Reducing Drug Overdoses in the Downtown Eastside."

The previous January, Osborn had pushed the health board to

adopt a motion in support of harm reduction. It's quite possibly the first time that a government body had ever incorporated those words into a policy document anywhere in North America.

"The first priority of harm reduction is to decrease the negative consequences of drug use for the individual," the motion reads. "As a strategy, harm reduction establishes a hierarchy of goals that ranges from reducing the immediate harm associated with use or consumption to abstinence." In accordance, the board established a committee to "explore the possibility of establishing safe-injection sites within the Downtown Eastside."

Osborn had ensured that a number of VANDU members were appointed to the group. His name was included as were Eror's and Livingston's.

The board was represented by Heather Hay, who at the time was responsible for community health services in a large area of Vancouver that included the Downtown Eastside. She had gotten to know Osborn and, through him, Livingston, in an effort get a better grip on the needs of the community.

In the late 1990s, those needs were dire. "There was an epidemic of HIV and AIDS, there was an outbreak of syphilis—we hadn't had transferable syphilis in North America in thirty years, and all of a sudden it broke out there—we had an outbreak of hepatitis C, which we couldn't get under control, and transferable TB. So there was a huge need. What we called a public-health emergency."

On top of all that, the number of illicit-drug overdose deaths in BC—which at this time were mostly occurring in the Downtown Eastside—had continued to climb. There were 217 in 1995, 301 in 1996, 300 in 1997, and then 400 in 1998.

So twice a week for a period of several months, Hay met Osborn at the Ovaltine Café, an old-fashioned diner near the corner of Main and East Hastings that's still there today. "He would educate me," Hay says. "And then I met Ann through VANDU. We used to rely on her to organize the IV-drug users. And they soon became the eyes and ears and support for us to get the work done."

By September 1998, the working group had its draft report ready, a plan to bring four sanctioned injection sites to the Downtown

Eastside. Their idea was to create a space for IV-drug users that was a combination of a more casual, "coffee shop" sort of atmosphere, but also fairly medical in nature, with separated cubicles for injecting drugs and professional health-care staff on-site, including counsellors. Equipment for injecting drugs—clean syringes, for example—should be supplied, the report said. It also recommended that these supervised-injection sites be staffed by "peers," the government's term for past and present drug users. "It is proposed that IVDUs [intravenous drug users] take on responsibility for reception, security, cleaning, and counselling; creating job opportunities for those within the user community," the document reads.

For those positions that could not be filled by peers, "It is considered critical the professional staff is trusted by the users," it adds in bolded text.

A short article published in the *Vancouver Sun* includes a description of the facility that was imagined by the report: "The proposal describes a uniquely West Coast amalgam of half coffee bar, half social service outlet," it reads. "While the front coffee shop would offer coffee and snacks at a nominal price, a space behind the coffee shop would provide private cubicles equipped with apparatus for injecting, mirrors, lockers for clients' belongings, and washrooms with sinks."[29]

In 1998, however, this first official plan for a supervised-injection facility in Vancouver went nowhere. The same newspaper article recounts how the draft report got to the health board for a discussion but never made it to a vote.

Hay blames politicians in Ottawa. "The feds caught wind of this early on, and the whole thing went sideways," she says. The federal health ministry had assigned a woman named Simin Tabrizi to the committee. She was fired for the report the group had put together. "It totally died, and I think it was pressure from the feds to make it die," Hay says.

Tabrizi had put a considerable amount of time and effort into the project. She even travelled to Switzerland, Germany, the Netherlands, and Sweden, visiting supervised-injection sites in those countries to

---

[29] Cori Howard, "Safe Site for Addicts 'Saved Lives,'" *Vancouver Sun*, September 25, 1998.

inform their proposal for Vancouver. Tabrizi took her dismissal in stride, acknowledging the controversial nature of their work, but still feels it was a missed opportunity. "Nobody wanted to touch this," she says. "And I thought that was irresponsible. The model had proven to be effective. And it was not a huge departure from what we were already doing in terms of needle exchange. It was a natural extension, in my opinion ... But they vetoed the idea."

Eror took the entire experience especially hard. A few months later, in early 1999, she resigned from her position as VANDU's first president and left activism for good. Eror took an entry-level job with the Portland Hotel Society, helping with HIV/AIDS outreach. She found she preferred hands-on work and settled in there.

"The Portland was a zoo," Eror says with a laugh. "But it is what it is, and they managed to keep a lid on everything. I might have a lot of criticisms for Mark Townsend, but at this point, I'm going to give him nothing but praise for what he did. They were effective."

––––––––––––

Eror's successor was Bryan Alleyne. He came from Nova Scotia where, in the early 1990s, he worked in a home for schizophrenics, watching himself go insane. Alleyne spent half of every shift down in the basement of the building, locked in a bathroom, smoking crack. Paranoia could set in, and he would get stuck in there for hours. It was time for a change.

"A buddy of mine just happened to call me from Vancouver," Alleyne begins in his booming, raspy voice. "He said, 'Do you want to come out here?' I said, 'Do they got any work out there?' He said they got lots of work. I said, 'They got any cocaine?' He said, 'Oh, man, you wanna come out here.' And I came out, and that's what I came looking for."

For a while, Alleyne had a job removing asbestos. But the cocaine in Vancouver was great those years, and an addiction to the drug was soon a lot more powerful than his ability to maintain steady work. "Things started to get hard, and then someone told me, 'Go down around Hastings and you'll get a sandwich and a little help and stuff,'" Alleyne says. "Everything I wanted was right there. Or everything I thought I wanted."

He settled into a life on the streets. On the edge of the Downtown Eastside, Alleyne found a store called the Chemistry Shop, where he could buy crack pipes in bulk for two dollars each. He would take them back to East Hastings or Oppenheimer Park and sell the pipes there for three dollars apiece. Alleyne stayed up for seventy-two hours at a time that way, fuelled on crack cocaine for days before an inevitable crash.

"I became a fucking burnout drug addict, there is no doubt," he recalls. "A full-blown junkie. It was a tough time. I was standing out on the street selling pipes, waiting in the food lineups, fucking sleeping in alleys sitting up, not sleeping all night long. It was a hard time."

One day in early 1998, Alleyne was feeling especially burned out. "I was really, really hungry," he says. "I asked this girl if she wanted to buy a pipe. And she says, 'If you're hungry and want something to eat, go upstairs. This lady's having a meeting. And after the meeting, you get three dollars and a hamburger.' Boom. I heard that and I went upstairs."

There were fifteen or twenty people inside the Street Church that day, Alleyne recalls. "This woman is standing up at the front of the room, and everybody else in the room is either a crackhead or a pin cushion or whatever," he says. "We were all drug addicts. And she was trying to tell us, if we listen to her and if we followed her and if we lined up, that the government was going to listen to our voices.

"I went, 'No, that's bullshit. Government ain't ever going to listen to us,'" Alleyne continues. "She said, 'I'll tell you what, if you join this here group, I'll prove to you that the government will listen.' I had to take her up on that challenge. A year later, I was the president."

Alleyne was Livingston's right-hand man in those days. "VANDU gave me purpose," he says. "I loved the fucking power. It gave me something. I wasn't just a junkie on the street. I was a junkie who was doing something, making noise, and being heard."

Livingston was still dating Osborn, but he had somewhat lost interest in VANDU. "Bud was a recluse at this point," she says. "He stopped coming to the Saturday meetings. I guess he was home shooting dope. I don't know. He pulled away."

Livingston recalls how Alleyne, heavily using cocaine and heroin, was still able to pour his energy into VANDU with the single-minded focus that she's noticed is a common trait among functional addicts. "He would show up at my house every morning at 8:30 a.m.," Livingston says. "I would be trying to get dressed and then we would talk about what we were going to do that day."

VANDU only had access to the rooms they were offered at Street Church and then LivingRoom for a couple of hours each Saturday. And so, as the group grew more active, Livingston's apartment became its de facto headquarters.

"We were always making sandwiches at my house and then sticking a hundred of these sandwiches in a Safeway cart and pushing them up the street to a meeting," she says. "So the people in my co-op were freaking out because these drug people were coming to the door who were just bent out of shape and super marginalized. But we had nowhere else to make the sandwiches."

Livingston describes those sandwich assembly lines that formed in her kitchen as a crucial component of the strategy for empowerment that she deployed within VANDU. Long-time addicts were marginalized to such extremes that years had passed since anyone had trusted them with any sort of responsibility, she explains. On the sandwich assembly lines, they were charged with seeing that someone else was fed that day. They also received a very small stipend for it, usually equal to bus fare. Alleyne notes that even back then, a couple bucks wasn't much money to someone with a fifty-dollar-a-day heroin habit. It was the sense of belonging that gave the stipend its real value.

Alleyne likens hanging out with Livingston to a master class in activism. "Like a little dog, I'd go everywhere Ann went," he says. "Just to see what was going on. I'd go to the health board meetings and Bud would be standing there and cursing and getting his point across doing whatever he had to do. And I just loved it. I thought, 'I'm going to do this now.' So when I went up to city hall, I talked how I wanted to talk, not how they wanted me to talk. And they listened. It was amazing how it came together. It was fucking amazing. They actually listened to us."

Ann Livingston and Bud Osborn began dating in 1996. *Photo: Ann Livingston*

Alleyne expresses puzzled bemusement with how little Livingston knew about him before she gave him her total trust. He was still homeless then, and she would let him sleep on her couch whenever he'd had a particularly rough couple of nights outside. Soon enough, Livingston's children were calling him Uncle. The affectionate nickname could turn heads in public, he says, laughing. The boys were skinny white kids, and Alleyne was big and black.

"I used to babysit her kids," Alleyne recounts. "And one day I'm walking down Hastings over by Powell Street and I'm pushing baby Joseph in a stroller. I was just walking there with the kid, and the police pull me over. They want to know who owns this baby and what I'm doing with it."

"None of your fucking business," Alleyne replied to the cop. "Are you just bothering me because I'm a black guy with a white baby?"

That didn't end the altercation, so Alleyne got Livingston on the phone, and he recalls how she unleashed a string of expletives on the officer.

"Why wouldn't I have cussed him out?" Livingston says now with a mix of amusement and outrage. "Why would a black guy go down the street with a white kid in a stroller? What did he think—he was selling him or something?"

Alleyne and baby Joseph were told they could continue on their way.

"She put so much trust in people," Alleyne says.

———————

About a year before Osborn passed away, Johann Hari asked him if, after nearly three decades of activism, he could name a high point.

"The highest moment was the organization of VANDU," Osborn replied after a moment's hesitation. "I would never in my life, as a lone junkie on the street, have ever believed in a million years that a whole bunch of low-bottom drug addicts from the worst places could come together as an organization and accomplish something."

Chapter 11

Out of Harm's Way

The Portland Hotel Society was founded in March 1991 under the umbrella of the Downtown Eastside Residents Association (DERA). Its leader, Jim Green, was supportive of everything the Portland was doing, primarily by taking a hands-off approach that left Liz Evans and her team to act on their own.

Green passed away in 2012. In Vancouver today, he deservingly holds the status of a hero of the Downtown Eastside. But in regards to the Portland, in the early 1990s, he didn't understand what was going on at the hotel and didn't much care to. Back then, his mission was to provide affordable housing for the working class. Evans and her hotel of drug-addicted lunatics—in the eyes of so many blue-collar workers—were viewed as dragging DERA through the mud.

At the same time, Evans and Townsend weren't advertising their work. "There was a very deliberate decision on our part, that we made in the early '90s, when we started, that we would not talk out loud about what we were doing, because we worried it would jeopardize our ability to house people," Evans recalls. "Jim was great. But when the Portland started and we had all these active drug users, he really did not have any kind of clue what the fuck we were doing."

The result was a bit of a disconnect between the Portland and its parent organization. Tensions slowly built over the years and as the Portland became more involved in activism.

One evening, the rift spilled into the streets, literally. "A DERA staff member was drinking in the bar on the ground floor [of the Portland Hotel] and came out drunk at eleven at night," Evans recounts. "And they bumped into one of our residents and beat them up right outside the hotel. A staff member! There was just this sort of hatred of the people that lived at the Portland. They were viewed as the people that needed to be extricated from the community."

It was time for Evans and the Portland Hotel to go off on their own. She approached Green and explained the situation from their perspective.

"This is about protecting a more radical space that doesn't really exist anywhere else," she explained. "In order to make sure that we don't water down what this is, we feel that we need to have a society created to protect what the Portland is doing." Green gave them his blessing.

"There was enough internal frustration and anger and hatred, frankly, of what we were doing, for DERA to happily let us go and be our own entity," Evans says.

Late one night in August 1993, Evans, Stuerzbecher, and Townsend stayed up late around the same kitchen table where they had met. They drafted a constitution for what would soon be a registered nonprofit organization called the Portland Hotel Society, or PHS. Summarized, the organization's stated purpose would be to provide housing and support for the people that no one else would house. "To promote, develop, and maintain supportive affordable housing for adult individuals who are poorly served elsewhere in the community due to their physical health, mental health, behaviour, substance dependencies, forensic history or for those who are homeless," it begins.

It's explicitly stated in this document that PHS would not push people into treatment or rehabilitation for any of those challenges. Among key principles described there is self-determination, defined as "Allowing each person to determine for themselves the time, place, course, and method of therapeutic treatment chosen if any."

The constitution concludes with an eviction clause: "The Portland Hotel Society endeavours to find an alternative to eviction in each and every situation," it reads. "This clause is unalterable."

On its own, the Portland Hotel Society began to expand. The Portland Hotel was falling apart long before it was given to Evans to manage. And so she had been looking for a suitable building nearby to which they could move its tenants. Townsend, never in his life accused of lacking ambition, decided they would try for a brand-new building, designed specifically for PHS from the ground up. And who did he want for the job?

"Who is considered the best architect in Canada?" Townsend recalls asking himself. The answer was Arthur Erickson.

Erickson, who passed away in 2009, was in his mid-seventies at the time and had enjoyed an illustrious career that made him wealthy. His work includes many buildings famous for their designs that drew inspiration from Canada's First Nations people, including the University of British Columbia's Museum of Anthropology, Simon Fraser University's Academic Quadrangle, and the King's Landing building in Toronto, among others.

"Instead of treating these people like Bedlam [psychiatric hospital] patients in the old days in England, instead of keeping them in deplorable conditions, we'll have Arthur design the building. As a political statement," Townsend explains. "Arthur was a way of saying, 'These people deserve space.'"

It was easier said than done. "We had so little money," Townsend continues. "The budget was, like, $12 million, and we only managed to cobble together $6.5 million. And we were going to design a building for fire starters and very difficult people."

Townsend approached Erickson with a challenge: Could he design a social-housing complex specially fitted to accommodate the Portland's unique tenants on a budget that was barely a fraction of what such a project would normally cost? Erickson quickly accepted.

"He was really sweet and really generous and really kind, as was the rest of his team," Townsend says.

It was nearly a decade before funding was secured, plans were drafted, permits were acquired, and the building was constructed and ready for tenants. In the meantime, PHS seized on an opportunity that arose when BC's provincial government took a new interest in low-income housing.

In 1998, the province purchased a number of old SRO hotels in the Downtown Eastside that were similar to the Portland Hotel. They were run-down buildings that had once housed transient labourers but long ago had fallen into total disrepair. The government issued a request for proposals from nonprofits interested in managing them. PHS applied and, to everyone's surprise, was awarded contracts for two—the worst two. "The hotels were crap," Townsend says. "It wasn't going to be great housing, but they were better than nothing."

In addition to the Portland Hotel, PHS now ran the Sunrise Hotel (today called the Irving) and the Washington Hotel (today the Maple), both located one block east of the Portland Hotel, on the opposite side of the street.

Evans remembers the expansion as exciting and obviously a victory, but also as uncomfortable. Almost overnight, her role had shifted from that of a nurse caring for tenants in one hotel to that of a manager responsible for staff working at three hotels. "I remember being very nervous and anxious, like a scared mother," she says.

What had been one tight-knit group had to grow into a much larger team, and so 1998 serves as the beginning of a second iteration of the Portland. Many new hires joined around this time, an unusual number of whom came from Vancouver's indie music scene, giving rise to a longstanding joke about PHS as an employment program for out-of-work musicians. Among them was Darwin Fisher.

He hates to admit it, but Fisher is devastatingly good-looking. He has a slim build, thick wavy-brown hair, and a youthful demeanour. In the late 1990s, he was living in Vancouver, but where he first connected with the Portland was in Europe, at a café in Amsterdam.

"Stop me if you've heard this one before, but prior to the Portland, I was playing some music," Fisher says with a laugh. "I was with some musicians, and I knew Kerstin [Stuerzbecher] and her husband Kevin Grant from the local music scene. I'd see them at the Railway Club. I was in a band called the Ronnie Hayward Trio. We were touring some festivals in Europe at the same time Kevin and Kerstin were on holidays there."

The three of them got together for breakfast and, instead of bonding over their shared love of music, fell into a deep conversation about harm reduction and social-justice issues. At one point, Fisher made a joke about how work at the Portland didn't sound very different from the life of an eccentric band on the road. Stuerzbecher laughed and extended a casual invitation for Fisher to stop by the hotel after his tour wrapped up.

A month or so later, he got in touch and they met at the Portland Hotel. "Then Liz burst into the room, and she was pissed," Fisher recounts. "My first impression of Liz was as somebody who is acutely pissed off about something ... and being very sharp-tongued about that. And so that put me back a little bit. But long story short: it was a good, full conversation. Not a stereotypical job interview. The idea was, 'Why don't you come down here and try it out?'"

The day the Portland Hotel Society officially took over the Washington Hotel, Fisher was given the night shift there and was working the front desk.

"First night on the job, the first night that we're open, it's getting close to nine p.m., so I've got to make sure the place is safe for folks coming in and introduce myself to everybody," he recounts.

One of the Washington's new tenants was a sex worker, Fisher continues. She was bringing a client back to her place, and her place was now at the Washington.

"She came by with one of her gents, and I had to tell her, 'It's a bit late for guests right now,'" Fisher continues. "I'm saying that through the glass door there. And she kind of smiles, red dress on and the classic red spiked heels. She backs up and does a high kick and kicks that locked door right open." The Plexiglas stood up to the kick but the door did not, almost breaking from its hinges.

"They walk in right past me," Fisher says. "Like, whelp, that happened. So we're going to show a little bit of that flexibility for which we're famous. And I think I'll make sure the place is safe for the night just the same."

In recent years, a social policy that's gained attention from governments across North America is called "housing first." It posits that by giving people a roof over their head, you begin to stabilize a person's life to a point where they can then work on their addiction issues, mental-health problems, prospects for employment, and relations with family and friends. If you first give a person a home and ensure that they can stay there, research shows that this degree of stability will give them the space and the time that they require to figure out the rest.[30]

More than a decade before anybody called it housing first, in three beat-up hotels on two blocks of East Hastings Street, people with complex combinations of mental-health and substance-abuse problems received rooms from which they would not be evicted.

———————

There was still a lot of confusion among Vancouver nonprofit service providers about what the Portland was doing. Drugs were not allowed anywhere else in the neighbourhood—in homeless shelters, for example. Evans recalls meeting with managers running those facilities and attempting to get them to stop evicting addicts for fixing in the middle of the night. Needle exchange was still only happening under strict limitations. And more radical harm-reduction policies, such as a supervised-injection facility, were barely even topics of discussion.

Townsend increasingly focused on the question of how to begin getting people to talk about the ideas that he was already sure had to be deployed in order to bring the neighbourhood's HIV and overdose problems back under control. "We became obsessed with providing education and information," he says. "People aren't unkind and people aren't stupid. So we thought they just needed the information."

The Portland had to watch where it stepped. As a registered nonprofit with charity status, there were legal limits on the extent to which it could engage in activism.

Tom Laviolette is considered another founding executive member of the Portland Hotel Society, but he wasn't employed full time by PHS until 2003. Why he gets credit for being there alongside Evans, Townsend, and Stuerzbecher since the beginning reveals the secret weapon that the Portland developed to push radical harm-reduction policies as far as it did.

[30] Lauren B. Currie, Akm Moniruzzaman, Michelle L. Patterson, and Julian M. Somers, *At Home/Chez Soi Project: Vancouver Site Final Report* (Calgary, AB: Mental Health Commission of Canada, 2014).

In 1996, Laviolette took a job with the Carnegie Community Action Project (CCAP), a group of political activists based out of the Carnegie Community Centre, which is just two blocks east of the Portland Hotel. From his office there, Laviolette worked closely with Townsend and PHS, serving as the public face of what was really a PHS-driven campaign.

"The Portland needed an avenue to give a source to its direct action," Laviolette explains. "It needed a proxy." That was him and CCAP. As PHS increasingly engaged in activism, it used this strategy—deploying a front organization that was largely under PHS control—to hold protests against the government that were otherwise too risky to conduct under the Portland name.

In early November 1998, pamphlets appeared on Vancouver telephone poles advertising a conference called "Out of Harm's Way" that was planned for later that month. "Carnegie Community Association presents an international symposium on solutions to drugs, crime and addiction in the inner city," they read.

Curiously, however, the task of organizing the conference went to Tanya Fader, a mental-health worked on the payroll of the Portland Hotel Society. Fader had joined PHS just a few months earlier. A close friend of hers had died of a drug overdose when they were in grade eight, and she'd helped another childhood friend battle a heroin addiction.

"I went to hell and back with her so many times," Fader says. She remembers being aware of the good families that those friends came from and the strong support networks that didn't save them from addiction. And then there was the Downtown Eastside, where so many people didn't have families and lacked support of any kind. "That was a big motivation for working down here," she says.

Fader recalls how Townsend vetted her. When she arrived at the Portland Hotel at the time they had agreed upon, she was buzzed into the building and proceeded up to the second floor, where there was a small common area. Townsend was nowhere to be found. But there were a number of the building's higher-needs tenants to keep Fader company. She was left there not knowing what to do for twenty minutes. Finally, Townsend showed up and invited her into an adjoining office where Evans and Stuerzbecher had been waiting all along.

"I had never done that type of work before, and so I made a promise to myself that if I didn't feel totally comfortable with it from the get-go, that it wouldn't be fair to the people I would be serving," Fader recalls. "And then I loved it, right away."

Fader spent her first couple months at the front desk of the Portland Hotel, which is more work than it might sound. "It was action all the time, nonstop," she says. "People needing their meds, people needing medical attention, people just wanting to talk, people losing their minds, people fighting, people getting drunk on rice wine and becoming completely unmanageable. Then Liz said to me one day, 'We have this money to organize an international conference. Can you do it for us?' And I was, like, 'Sure, okay.'"

The idea was to host the sort of conference that one might find in a ballroom at a Hilton Hotel. They would invite experts from various fields related to drug policy and health care from cities around the world where harm-reduction programs were already implemented. But instead of hosting the event in a fancy hotel, this conference would take place in Oppenheimer Park, where the Killing Fields protest had culminated in July of the previous year.

"The speakers weren't told," Townsend says with a chuckle. "They were just invited there to give their normal talk." That might not have mattered had the event occurred in the summer.

"Unfortunately, this was in November and it was pouring rain," Townsend adds. "If the conference had gone on one more hour, the tent would have collapsed under the weight of the water."

Fader recalls it all coming together as a mad scramble. "I had to get permits and organize all the international speakers' travel and timing, and then figure out the actual timing of the conference and try to get the word out about it." All tasks she had never dealt with before. "I had to do a lot of stuff where I was just flying by the seat of my pants," she says.

The speakers list was impressive. Werner Schneider was the name around which there was the most excitement. He held the position of drug-policy coordinator for the city of Frankfurt, Germany, and had spent the previous decade integrating harm-reduction programs into the city's response to illicit drugs. Schneider had overseen the establishment of supervised-injection rooms that by this time had operated successfully for years. Representing a modern European metropolis, the hope was that Schneider would take the stink of activism off what in Vancouver was still a very radical idea, present the concept of a supervised-injection site from the perspective of the establishment, and therefore normalize it in the minds of Canadian authority figures.

There was also Steffen Lux, chief of the Frankfurt police department's drug squad, who Townsend thought could catch people's attention as a progressive voice from the realm of law enforcement. Hannes Herrmann came from Switzerland, where he had implemented a "four pillars" response to illicit drugs consisting of enforcement, prevention, treatment, and—notably—harm reduction. Herrmann had also established a program called "heroin maintenance," where long-time addicts were administered the drug in controlled doses supplied by the health-care system. That novel concept had caught Townsend's attention especially. It was something nobody in Canada had ever heard of before. Vancouver's own Bruce Alexander was also there to share the results of his Rat Park experiments and findings on how environment can affect drug use.

Stuerzbecher remembers that a conscious decision was made to keep VANDU members and Portland staff off the speakers list. "We knew that in order to save people's lives, we needed to bring some of these experts in so that people who had the ability to make decisions would listen," she says. "Because they were not going to listen only to activists. If that is the only voice you have, you are not going to be able to convince bureaucrats."

The idea was to show Vancouver that so-called serious people—a judge, a police officer, doctors, and lawyers—were talking about harm reduction. And to attract the attention of politicians and policy makers in Vancouver while also making the event accessible to those affected most acutely by drug policies: the residents of the Downtown Eastside.

"We were talking about things like prescription heroin and supervised injection, and there was very little support for these ideas,"

Evans says. "But we were, like, 'Fuck it. Nobody is going to listen to us. We're just a bunch of crazy people running a hotel. So let's get some of these experts from other places to come.'"

They planned for 200 or maybe 300 people to attend. Close to 800 people showed up. The tent was packed all day long. "When we opened the tent in the morning, there was a lineup all around the park," Evans says. "Drug users, nurses, social workers, community workers from Carnegie, cops—anybody and everybody, really.

"People sat and listened all day," she continues. "There were literally rows of people at the front the whole day taking notes. Seriously, note-taking. And by the end of the next day, people in the community were saying, 'Hey, have you heard about this thing called a supervised-injection site?' All of the sudden, these totally radical and crazy ideas were no longer crazy or radical; they were things that other people had done."

An article published in the *Vancouver Sun* ran under the headline "Tent Revival Message" and began, "An extraordinary event occurred in Vancouver's Downtown Eastside ... It brought together disparate and often antagonistic groups: residents, business people, city bureaucrats, provincial cabinet ministers, federal health officials ... Coroner Larry Campbell and the drug squad sat along one row, a group of junkies and young adults with day-glo hair sat nearby. It was a remarkable scene full of mutual respect."

As the Killing Fields protest the year before had jolted Libby Davies, the "Out of Harm's Way" conference caught the attention of one politician in particular, Philip Owen, the city's right-of-centre mayor. "It had a big impact on me," Owen says. The Frankfurt story especially struck him as one from which he thought Vancouver had a lot to learn. In the years that followed, officials from Germany stopped by city hall whenever they were in Vancouver and met with Owen. "I learned a lot," he recalls.

The day was a brilliant success, with one postscript.

In 1998, Angela Jardine was twenty-eight years old and living at the Portland Hotel. She had short brown hair and looked barely older than a teenager. The perception that she was younger than her age was helped by a mental disability that stalled her intellectual development at the level of a child's.

"She was a little girl trapped in a woman's body," her mother, Deborah, told a newspaper. "Her dream was to someday be married to her Prince Charming, have her own family and live happily ever after." Stuerzbecher recalls Jardine as a great help at the conference that day. "She wore a pink satin dress," Stuerzbecher recalls. "She was hosting and helping people. She was so lovely and so proud. And that was the last day she was seen."

That evening, Jardine never returned to the hotel, which was not unusual, Stuerzbecher continues. She was a sex worker and sometimes would spend the night with a john or at a friend's place. But she would always call.

"We were her home," Stuerzbecher says. "We were mum and dad. When she wasn't going to come home at night, she would call ... The day after the conference, she didn't call. We knew right away."

Years later, Jardine's DNA was found on a farm in Vancouver's neighbouring city of Port Coquitlam. The property's owner, Robert Pickton, confessed to murdering forty-nine women there, the vast majority of whom were taken from the Downtown Eastside during the 1980s and '90s.

Stuerzbecher is absolutely adamant that she and Evans called the police and reported Jardine missing the very next day, on November 11, 1998. According to the Canadian Press, police didn't open a file on her disappearance until December 6.

The CP article includes a description of Jardine's room at the Portland Hotel. "Posters of kittens and unicorns were tacked to the walls, a jumble of pictures, World Wrestling Entertainment paraphernalia and colouring books," it reads. "Go-go boots to wear during the day, teddy bears for whispering secrets to in bed at night."

Evans is quoted in that article. "She certainly had an incredible imagination," she said. "She had a way of drawing you into her imagination, into the world she was living in, which wasn't always the world everyone else lived in."

Shortly after the Out of Harm's Way conference, the Portland picked up its fifth and final founding member: Dan Small.

Small didn't join PHS full time until 1998, but his history with the organization began in 1992. That year, Small was employed at the Forensic Psychiatric Institute as a recreational therapist. His patients were extremely marginalized—people who had committed violent crimes but, due to a severe mental illness, were deemed not criminally responsible for their actions. There wasn't a housing agency in Canada willing to give these people a home.

"Nobody would take my patients from Colony Farm," Small says, using the institute's nickname (it's on Colony Farm Road). "Not even mental-health centres. So I organized this thing called a 'coping fair,' and that is when I first met Liz and Kerstin, at forensic."

PHS became the one organization that did take forensic patients, creating a relationship between Small and the Portland's management team. "There's something special about these people, I thought, even though I didn't know anything about them," Small says. "So I made a little footnote in my mind that I would one day visit them."

Evans recalls walking away from that meeting thinking the same thing. "He just understood what we were doing," she says. "One thing we all had in common from the very beginning, very strongly, was an anti-psychiatry kind of bent."

Small already had an interesting background related to drugs, addiction, and psychiatric care. His mother has a mental illness and his father was an RCMP officer who worked on the drug squad in the conservative Canadian province of Alberta. "Which isn't to read into any kind of deep, psychological, Freudian analysis of things," Small says. "But it did give me a point of view about drugs and the war on drugs."

As an undergraduate student at Simon Fraser University in the 1980s, he grew very close to one of his professors, Bruce Alexander. "I thought he was crazy," Small says. "The fundamental idea that he had at that time was that drugs were not inherently addictive and that you had to look at other issues in terms of people's suffering to understand the nature of addiction. But I believed that drugs were inherently addictive."

Small made clear that he intended to disprove Alexander's work on addiction, to which the professor replied: "Why don't you become my honours student?"

"I spent every ounce of my being as a young undergraduate writing an honours thesis to prove his theory wrong, to prove that drugs were inherently addictive and that the war on drugs was a legitimate response to these issues," Small says. "I attacked his theory quite relentlessly. I made a poignant, hard-working effort. But I didn't succeed ... At the end of that honours thesis, I started to have questions," he continues. "And then I realized that Bruce was right, but actually hadn't gone far enough."

Then Small went to work for Colony Farm. There, he made himself a student of the problems that lay below his patients' mental-health issues. "When I went to forensic, the first thing I did was read every single file," he says. "I saw every person's story. And then I started seeing what a soul-destroying place it was. It was meant to care for people, but it was very abusive."

In 1996, he left forensic and took a part-time job at the old Portland Hotel. "I had worked with people who were even more challenging than the Portland residents, so I was no stranger to this," he says. "What was unusual to me is that I could see they had a paradigm at work here, one that was completely antithetical to any paradigm that I had ever seen before. It was intuitively congruent with mine."

He was a perfect fit, but in 1996, felt he wasn't done with his education. Despite having already obtained a master's of philosophy from the University of Cambridge, Small left the Portland to pursue a PhD in cancer genetics at the University of British Columbia.

The following year, he accepted a job at another Vancouver nonprofit, Coast Mental Health. When Evans and Townsend heard he had taken that position and was now based at an office just outside the Downtown Eastside, they decided to get back in touch and pay him a visit. Townsend sat on the corner of Small's desk and said, "The mental health field doesn't need you. Come work for us."

Small thought about it for a few days, but they all knew right away that he was going to accept the offer. When he did, the three of them sat down for a brainstorming session about what it was exactly that Small would do for PHS. One idea that Townsend had was for Small to work with what they described as a "drug-user union."

"Yeah, that sounds interesting," Small remembers saying.

Chapter 12

From Housing to Harm Reduction

Before November 1998, the Portland Hotel Society was essentially a housing agency. After the Out of Harm's Way conference in Oppenheimer Park, it became Vancouver's foremost advocate for harm reduction, albeit with the Carnegie Community Action Project or VANDU usually taking the credit (and the blame). In the months and years that followed, PHS pioneered harm-reduction programs that nobody had tried before anywhere in North America.

Townsend had broken the rules on needle exchange for years, essentially having staff run distribution centres from the front desks of the three Portland hotels. Tanya Fader recalls that this was no simple task.

"We had to account for every needle. But of course we had people who said, 'I need more than one needle.' And if you didn't give it to them, you knew they were going to reuse the same needle, which is not good."

PHS was getting its needles from the Downtown Eastside Youth Activities Society, which was still enforcing a one-for-one exchange requirement. DEYAS wasn't forcing nonprofit staff to count dirty syringes by hand. It provided yellow plastic bins for the safe disposal of needles, and they held a volume of needles equal to the number distributed. That left room to game the system, to which Stuerzbecher devoted significant time.

"Kerstin spent hours measuring and counting needles in those disposal bins with markings on the side, so we knew what our return amounts needed to look like," Evans says. They found creative ways to ensure the boxes always appeared full. Stuerzbecher recalls the situation as almost comical. "When funders came to tour the building, we were hiding needles in the bloody desk, for crying out loud," she says.

In a partnership with VANDU, PHS began to push the limits on needle exchange in an effort to break the rules outright. Ed McCurdy was the man Townsend assigned to liaise with the drug-user group. The arrangement was similar to Fader organizing the Out of Harm's Way conference and then putting the Carnegie Community Action Project's name on it. Except VANDU wasn't quite the team player that CCAP was.

"I met with Mark Townsend and Dan Small and they said, 'Here's the thing,'" McCurdy recounts. "They [VANDU] have this volunteer coordinator position but they only want a drug user to do it, and they certainly don't want anyone affiliated with the Portland doing it. So you cannot ever let on that you work for us."

McCurdy said he'd give it a try. But the Downtown Eastside is a small place with a tight community that loves to gossip. He was immediately outed as the spy that he was. "My fucking god they hated me," McCurdy remembers. But somehow he convinced the VANDU board to give him a chance. They agreed—with one catch. "Someone got me a rock and a crack pipe, and I smoked it in front of them. Then I was hired," he says. "That's how I started my job at VANDU."

The first project that McCurdy led through this partnership between PHS and VANDU was not a glamourous one. "One of the many things VANDU was working on at the time was public washrooms," McCurdy begins. "There was a problem of feces in the neighbourhood, so we had this ongoing crusade to get more bathrooms in the Downtown Eastside."

The city's homeless population was growing rapidly. Many of them used intravenous drugs, and if you looked like an addict, no private business would let you use their washroom. McCurdy acknowledges that it sounds like a mundane issue, but just finding a toilet became a major struggle. Finally, VANDU convinced the city that something had to be done. But action still wasn't taken until after the usual bureaucratic hoops were jumped through.

"The city sent us an engineer to basically be guided through the alleys with a map to mark an X wherever we'd find a poop," McCurdy says. "We had a poop map to prove to the city that people were in fact shitting in the alleys. "

Finally, city hall supplied a pair of portable toilets. But it insisted they be deployed with a security guard—god forbid that drug users be trusted with their own toilet. Around this time, Ann Livingston was mostly home with her two young boys. But she always remained in the background of events at VANDU, and when the city said it would deploy security guards, she got involved.

"I said, 'If you put security guards on those toilets, the people who are shitting in the alleys will keep shitting in the alleys because they'll think they can't use those toilets,'" Livingston says. "So VANDU would guard the toilets. That was the beginning of that project."

The location selected for the toilets was a small alcove adjacent to the Carnegie Community Centre, just around the corner from the intersection of Main and East Hastings. That crossroads is a beehive of activity. Its epicentre is the southwest corner, outside the entrance to Carnegie. There, an open-air drug market operates twenty-four hours a day, 365 days a year. The cast of characters that occupies this intersection of mental illness and drug addiction is an eclectic one. Dealers from Central America controlled most of the cocaine and heroin trade at the time. A lower caste of addicts sold just about everything else, mostly single prescription pills and the occasional psychedelic (never that popular among the Downtown Eastside's entrenched user population). Young Indigenous men peddled cigarettes and dishevelled customers of all these substances came and went in constant flows from every direction.

Now there was a pair of porta-potties there and a VANDU member stationed to keep them safe and clean. From that vantage point, the need for a needle exchange was so obvious and so dire that Livingston just went ahead and set one up.

"You called them poison parties," she recalls. "You would see someone handing a needle they had just used to someone else to use it. So I thought we had to have [clean] needles. If you're going to see that much public drug use and you're going to see someone hand someone else a needle, you can intervene and say, 'We have some needles here.'"

So on the corner of Main and Hastings, right outside the Carnegie Community Centre's front door, out in the open and obvious for everybody to see, VANDU and PHS set up a table, pitched a small tent over it, and opened a needle exchange.

"The VPD came and smashed the table and broke up the tent," says Townsend.

A game of cat and mouse ensued. The needle exchange was busiest at night, and so each evening, around ten, Vancouver police officers parked a pair of squad cars on the corner outside Carnegie and left them there for a few hours. With police vehicles stationed directly beside the VANDU table, drug users refused to stop there for clean needles.

Townsend watched this from the Washington Hotel, directly across the street from Carnegie. Each evening, he created a distraction, the cops left, and then, from the Washington, a team grabbed the table, tent, and a large bag of clean needles, and rushed across the street to set it all up.

"We'd call the police and tell them that people were unbolting the mufflers of all their cars that were parked outside the Carnegie," Townsend recounts. "So they would run back and move them. And then, when they moved them, we put the tent up."

The cops wouldn't bother with this hassle every night, so once the table was up, they often left it alone. The trick was to take the corner. "It was a weird battle for space," Townsend says. "This police sergeant said he was going to break the table over his knee if it was put up again. So late at night, in the evening, there was a mini battle between us and this sergeant over who was in control of the area." The war of attrition eventually wore the police force down. "We just kept on putting [the table] there," Townsend says.

While Townsend waged his guerilla war, Dan Small fought on a bureaucratic flank. He and the rest of the Portland's management team had built alliances with prominent health researchers working in HIV/AIDS and related fields. When the VPD took VANDU's needle-exchange table, Small reached out to a doctor at the BC Centre for Excellence in HIV/AIDS named Martin Schechter and asked if he would put the prestigious organization's name on a letter to the police department. Schechter agreed.

It read, "Every night this needle exchange is gone, there is one more HIV infection. You are killing people." The letter was received by the police department on July 16, 2002. Two days later, VANDU, with significant but silent support from PHS, took to the streets.

"I said, 'Let's make a 100-foot-long needle,'" Small recalls.

Enter the Portland's notorious maintenance team, which consisted of a scrappy Vietnamese guy named Phong Lam, a thick-accented German named Christoph Runne, and an older remnant of the hippie era named Patrick O'Rourke. This trio, sometimes a team of four when joined by O'Rourke's son Allen, played a quiet but crucial role in just about every protest, memorial, and black-ops mission that the Portland Hotel Society has ever held. They also kept the hotels together, in a very literal sense.

"The maintenance crew are heroes," Evans says. "They worked incredibly long hours doing repairs, helping with de-hoarding rooms, preparing for pest control, moving people in and out, managing every aspect of maintenance in very old buildings housing very complex people." Day or night, Lam was almost always the first person on the scene of a fire or a flood, "Of which there were many," Evans adds.

The team's official job description included plumbing and carpentry. "My job, basically, was fixing doors," Runne says with a laugh. "Because doors were constantly being kicked in. So I would start on the top floor, work from the top down, and then by the time I made it down to the bottom floor, I could basically start again from the top down, constantly fixing doors."

But the official job description only accounted for half of the team's work for the Portland. "They were our ops crew," Evans says. "They showed up at everything. They were always everywhere."

She remembers how, while she was taking care of the Portland's paperwork, Townsend would scheme with this crew and come up with ridiculous plans, some of which were never carried out but many more of which were. "Sometimes they didn't tell me what they were doing because they didn't want me to know," Evans says. "Mark and them had all the fun."

There were some interesting projects—building fifty black coffins, for example, or finding a way into a hotel where the health minister was speaking. In July of 2002, Small asked the maintenance team if it would build him a 100-foot-long needle.

"That was one of the stranger projects," Runne says. Using a large cardboard tube that had previously encased a concrete pillar, the maintenance team gave Small and Townsend the 100-foot needle they wanted. Then, on July 18, more than 100 VANDU members met at Main and Hastings to carry it through the streets.

"Drug addicts and advocates brandishing a giant ... hypodermic needle rallied yesterday to protest against the recent closing of a controversial needle-exchange program," reads one newspaper's report about the day. "City police moved in to close down the program last month, alleging that VANDU volunteers who were staffing the tables were both using drugs and trafficking in them. Since then, both sides have engaged in a war of words that spilled onto the streets with yesterday's demonstration."[31]

VANDU's participation in the protest was largely organized by Thia Walter, a prominent activist during those years who passed away in February 2012. Quoted in that report, she alluded to rising tensions among different arms of the government. While the health-care system was slowly acknowledging the benefits of harm reduction, law-enforcement agencies were not yet ready to do the same. "There appears to be a war between the health board and the police, and unfortunately the users are in the line of fire," Walter told the paper. "Police tactics toward addicts have become extremely brutal," she said. "They pepper-sprayed two dozen of them the other day because they didn't move out of an alley quick enough."

Small explains how several moving pieces would come together to create an action like one as large as the needle protest. "When I would have an idea like that, Mark would build the infrastructure in the background with Phong and the maintenance team," he says. "And then VANDU would be there ... with picket signs and would populate the event."

It wasn't just cooperation between two organizations with shared goals but a conscious strategy. "We made a decision at that time to create some avatars," Small explains. "So we decided to explicitly put VANDU forward—we never discussed it with VANDU, but Mark and I discussed it. We put VANDU forward as the symbolic front of this movement. In part, it was done to protect the residents of the

---

[31] Adrienne Tanner, "Needle-exchange Fight Hits Streets," *Globe and Mail*, July 18, 2002.

Portland from having services cut, in part to help build up the social capital of the drug-user movement, to validate their personhood. It was a strategic move. So they were shielding us," Small continues. "That was the other piece of it. Absolutely, they were. This was a strategic move."

Meanwhile, Townsend's game of cat and mouse continued to create a nuisance for whatever poor beat cops were assigned to the corner of Main and Hastings on any given night. Then came the letter from the BC Centre for Excellence in HIV/AIDs that practically accused the police department of murder. And then VANDU went marching with a hypodermic needle so large it shut down six lanes of traffic.

"In the end, the police agreed to support a fixed site for needle exchange," Townsend says. "There was a peace settlement."

The police would not allow VANDU's table to return to the corner outside the Carnegie Community Centre—that was a little too public for the establishment's liking. Instead, PHS would finally break DEYAS's monopoly on needle exchange and operate a public distribution point of its own. At the Washington Hotel, just across East Hastings from where VANDU had pitched its table, tucked in an alley about fifty feet (eighteen metres) back from the main street, PHS installed a little sliding window.

The health authority said it would deploy a nurse there who would sit at a desk in an office facing into the alley. Drug users could knock on the window and receive clean needles. It was a huge victory, but Small kept pushing for more. He wanted VANDU members—drug users, that is—employed at the window, effectively working as low-level health-care workers.

"I ended up negotiating with the health board, with a contract, that VANDU workers would be paid wages," Small says. "They were stipends but they looked like wages. Which was huge. It symbolically validated the fact that people with addictions and their experience could be used by the clinical system officially."

The government's initial answer was a firm no. "I had been told, 'Dan, there is no way that this health board is ever going to pay drug users to do clinical services. It's not happening,'" Small continues.

"So when that did happen, it was a key moment in the evolution of the health board and people with addictions."

Today the Washington Needle Depot is believed to distribute more syringes than any other harm-reduction program in North America.

––––––––––––

What began as a fight for public toilets had morphed into a needle exchange. Progress emboldens, and PHS kept going.

"Through the course of time and through peers, it was identified that there was a real need for injection materials at these supervised bathrooms," McCurdy says. "And then people started injecting in the bathrooms. So we decided, 'It's fine. We'll let people inject in the bathrooms.'"

But portable toilets are unpleasant, and for intravenous drug users they can also be dangerous. On several occasions, someone went into one of the porta-potties, closed and locked the door behind them, and overdosed, only to be found just in time. So, after a few weeks, McCurdy and his new VANDU friends began to brainstorm how they could make things a little more comfortable for everyone.

"I said we could rent one of those half-moon trailers [used by the film industry], park it somewhere, and use that as our bathroom," he says. They got an old trailer, the kind one finds on movie sets (low-budget movies, in this instance). Inside were two toilets in separate compartments with doors that conveniently did not go all the way to the ground, so PHS staff could see if someone happened to overdose while they were in there.

VANDU and PHS agreed it would be entirely counter-productive to hire a security guard. But they had invested some money into it, and so PHS needed to find someone who was willing to hang out on the sketchy corner of Main and Hastings all night and keep an eye on everything.

Enter Coco Culbertson, another musician the Portland had recently brought on staff during its expansion into additional hotels. Culbertson had enjoyed a fair amount of success in music, even making it onto late-night shows with David Letterman and Jay Leno.

Liz Evans (centre) and Mark Townsend (far left) had their first child, Kes, in March 2000. The community loved him, Evans remembers. *Photo: Mark van Manen* / Vancouver Sun

But by 2001, she had a young son who was tired of being dragged around on tours, and so she was looking for something else. A friend introduced her to Liz Evans, who arranged another unconventional job interview.

Evans and Townsend had just had a child of their own around this time. Baby Kes was born on March 23, 2000. The pair had been living together since Townsend had first arrived to Vancouver in the summer of 1991. Beyond that, it's impossible to get a date from either of them for when the relationship turned romantic. "I liked him very much right away," Evans says. "But then it took quite a few years, to be honest. I mean, *properly* romantic?" She laughs. "I don't know. It's embarrassing." Culbertson met with Evans while baby Kes played on the floor between them. "We met and talked and hit it off right away," Culbertson says.

Continuing what by this point was a well-established pattern for Portland hires, Culbertson had had an unconventional childhood that she now found she could put to work for her. Her first shift was at the Washington Hotel, and there was a mattress fire to deal with.

"One of the arsonists we housed had set his room on fire," she recalls. Darwin Fisher was also working at the Washington that night and he rushed upstairs with another staffer to take a look. They doused the flames with a fire extinguisher and before too much longer, everything was back to normal.

The police were called as a matter of standard procedure. ("We're mavericks but we're not outlaws," Culbertson explains. "Most of the time.") But the tenant was not evicted. The mattress he'd set on fire was thrown out and he was found another room. "We do call the police because that's their job," she says. "But our job is to keep the door open for them [tenants] when that process is completed.

"They handled it with such decorum and without any level of panic," Culbertson remembers. "They even had a sense of humour about it, not in a light way, but in a way where everyone else was made to feel safe and cared for ... They dealt with it so beautifully, it completely blew my mind," Culbertson says. "I just thought, 'Fuck, I want to be able to do that.' I immediately wanted in."

Like Tanya Fader—and just about everyone else Evans had hired thus far—Culbertson says she felt comfortable in the organization's chaos. "All of the weird things I'd picked up through my dysfunctional upbringing completely applied to this unique scenario," Culbertson says. "I realized I had the skills to be in this really chaotic, fucked-up workplace. It was like magic for me."

When Townsend came looking for volunteers to take the night shift at the bathrooms, Culbertson raised her hand.

"That was my first management project, because nobody else wanted it," she says, laughing. "Funnily enough, none of the other PHS employees wanted to be outside of Main and Hastings overnight, running a toilet and a needle exchange with only people high as fuck working with you.

"PHS was gently managing VANDU, which was really complicated," Culbertson continues. "We'd have volunteers come onto their shift, go to the needle table, grab a couple of rigs, go into the bathroom, and smash a speedball." (A speedball is a mixture of cocaine, an upper with intense effects that don't last long, and heroin, from which a mellow high can last a while.) The trick for Culbertson was to channel that energy.

"One individual, who still works with us, loved to do up and down," Culbertson continues, using a another slang term that describes a mix of cocaine and heroin. "And he would come out of the bathroom ready to go but just completely fucked out of his head. He would be mopping out in the alleyway ... running around maniacally and then, like seven or eight minutes later, he'd be sleeping. And for the rest of the night, he'd just be nodding out." She laughs. "I got three minutes of completely unproductive hyperactivity."

Somehow it all made sense. There was a drug market in the middle of which VANDU had dropped a pair of portable toilets. Then, in response to open drug use there, the toilets became a distribution point for clean syringes. A trailer was better than porta-potties, so that was a logical improvement. Now there was a supervised-injection site.

"Folks would get rigs from the table and check in with VANDU and then go to the bathrooms right next door, inject, and then leave," Culbertson says. "And if there was an overdose, we were there and we did respond."

There hadn't been a plan to open a supervised-injection site, but that's what PHS had done.

The Thunder Box, as Portland staff came to affectionately call it, never attracted media attention during the few months it ran, and since then, it has all but been forgotten. But McCurdy recalls it as crucial to the evolution of PHS and harm-reduction in Vancouver. "The bathrooms became one of the prototypes for what a safe-injection site would be," he says. "We learned a lot there"

Today, Townsend says he considers the Thunder Box a major step toward the founding of Insite, North America's first sanctioned supervised-injection facility, which PHS would establish a few years later, in 2003. "You'd have clean rigs, and if something went wrong, we'd actually save your life and you wouldn't have to die."

There were hiccups. People selling drugs would occasionally try to set up shop inside the trailer, especially when it was raining. Culbertson recounts having to literally drag "the odd dealer" out by their ear. And some VANDU members resented having to operate the needle exchange under the umbrella of PHS. That meant there were often disputes between the two organizations about how exactly everything should run. But overall, everyone got along.

"VANDU was a great partner to have because they would never take shit from anyone," Culbertson says. "But we were always on the sharp end of that stick."

She describes the relationship as mutually beneficial. VANDU got the Portland's managerial resources, bureaucratic know-how, and, crucially, banking infrastructure that their larger initiatives required. And PHS got to put VANDU's name on more radical programs—for example, a toilet that was really functioning as an unsanctioned supervised-injection site—and pretend everything PHS was doing was above board.

"It was very symbiotic," Culbertson reflects. "And at the end of the day, we were all rolling in the same direction and kicking against all the same pricks. So that unified us, regardless of our differences."

Chapter 13

Childhood Trauma and the Science of Addiction

D r Gabor Maté did a poor job of following the rules. He wasn't a troublemaker. He didn't break the law or intentionally go out of his way to disobey professional guidelines. It's more accurate to say that rule-breaking came to him naturally.

"The thing about me and medicine was, I was always uninterested in rules," he explains. "I didn't regard them as the ultimate guides to anything."

This was not a quality that his employer found beneficial. Vancouver General Hospital removed Maté from his position as its medical coordinator for palliative care. "Part of the issue was, I just did things the way I thought they should be done," Maté says, two decades later. "I would do things quickly and rather spontaneously, with good effect. I didn't have any negative outcomes. But I didn't necessarily do things by the rules ... or explain things very clearly. I didn't document stuff. I just had no patience for that kind of thing. So friction arose," he adds. "I engineered my own firing. Not deliberately, but I did."

A few weeks later, as fate would have it, Maté received a call from Liz Evans. "I don't think she knew very much about me," Maté says. "And then I was hired. Not that I think there were too many others breaking down the door."

Evans recalls she actually did know quite a bit about Maté. "It wasn't random," she says. "We head-hunted him. I knew that he would be somebody who would be willing to go out on a limb."

Evans did not know that Maté had just been fired but now says she doubts that would have swayed her from bringing him on board. "We had phoned a bunch of doctors and asked if they knew Gabor Maté," she says. And what were his reviews?

"He was difficult to work with, opinionated, headstrong, arrogant, thought highly of himself, and didn't listen to advice," Evans recounts.

"He got lots of negatives. But I knew that the negatives meant that he would fight the system."

Maté became the latest member of Evans's team of medical-establishment misfits. Evans had left her previous job at Vancouver General Hospital's emergency psychiatry and assessment unit because she had trouble seeing her patients as sick. Mark Townsend carried with him the memory of his brother locked in a bathroom at Barrow Gurney Mental Hospital, facing a sentence of electro-convulsive therapy. Kerstin Stuerzbecher resigned from the home where she took care of troubled teens after she came to believe that the restrictions that she and her colleagues placed on youths could often do more harm than good. Dan Small obsessively read his forensic patients' life histories at Colony Farm and concluded that the system he was working within was unlikely to bear positive outcomes for them.

Evans describes bringing this sort of like-minded group together as something that occurred naturally. "I think, on reflection, I never really felt like a misfit," she says. "But I clearly was one. I identified very strongly with other people who didn't fit in." This became the Portland's unique advantage.

"For me and Mark and Kerstin, a lot of the other things that we'd done in psychiatry had felt off-base—overly controlling or coercive, robbing people of their individual rights and freedoms," Evans continues. "What the Portland represented for all of us, in the beginning, was an opportunity to not be controlling, not be coercive, and to leave people to be human beings first."

Now Maté joined them.

"I walk into this grungy hotel that had fallen upon hard times at some point—faded elegance," he recalls. "There are all these people and a hubbub, people scrambling around. I felt right at home."

He was given a small office on the second floor and the freedom to treat patients as he saw fit. From there, a new care model for addiction began to take shape and, eventually, a new understanding of addiction itself. "We saw the addiction not as characterizing the person, but as a coping mechanism," Maté says. "And underneath, there was a very sensitive or creative, interesting human being, who had just suffered so much that the addiction became their way of coping."

Expanding on the definition of an addiction beyond biological terms, Maté says he began to see it as a "normal response to an abnormal situation," as a coping mechanism for trauma, and for the life-time effects of childhood trauma.

Gabor Maté was born to Jewish parents in Budapest, Hungary, on January 6, 1944. Two months and one week later, Adolf Hitler ordered Operation Margarethe and the Nazis invaded the city.

Maté recounts what happened next in a section of his first book, *Scattered Minds: A New Look at the Origins and Healing of Attention Deficit Disorder.* Two days into the Nazi occupation, his mother, Judith Lovi, was compelled to call the doctor.

"Would you come to see Gabi," she requested. "He has been crying almost without stop since yesterday morning."

"I'll come, of course," the doctor replied, "but I should tell you: all my Jewish babies are crying."

Seventy-three years later, at his home in Vancouver, Maté wonders aloud about the effect the Nazi threat had on him as an infant. He notes there is nothing that such a young child could have known about the war, the violence, or the dangers his parents felt around them in every direction.

"My first year of life was under Nazi occupation," Maté says. "With the threat of deportation and death hanging over my mother. Terror and fear." The Hungarian Army had taken his father, Andor, for forced labour. Judith, just twenty-four years old, didn't know if her husband was alive or dead. Shortly after, her parents were taken to the gas chambers of Auschwitz. Before Germany surrendered in May 1945, some half a million Hungarian Jews were sent to the Nazi death camps, ninety percent of them murdered upon their arrival.

Maté breaks from the story to quote from a book by Hameed Ali, a Kuwaiti-born spiritual teacher and author who writes under the pen name A.H. Almaas. "The child is very open and can feel the pain and suffering going on in its immediate environment," he reads. "The child is aware of its own body and can also feel the tension, rigidity, and pain in the body of the mother or of anyone else he is with. If the mother is suffering, the baby suffers too. The pain never gets discharged."

Maté explains how that sort of childhood trauma physically alters the brain. "My mother could barely ensure my survival," he says. "She could not give me the joyful, playful parenting that might help the brain develop. Then, when I'm a year old, I'm handed over to a stranger in the street, which was my mother's attempt to save my life," he continues. Maté's mother left him with a Gentile woman who took him to live with relatives in an attempt to save his life. It was a logical choice, but it left him feeling abandoned and unwanted. "Under such circumstances, how does a child deal with that much stress?" Maté asks. "You disassociate, which then gets programmed into your brain, because that is when your brain is developing."

Maté never became addicted to drugs. Of course, not everyone who has a hard childhood does. But he's spotted other unhealthy tendencies in himself that he explains as coping mechanisms left over from Nazi-occupied Budapest. In his adult life, Maté became a workaholic; that is, he became addicted to work. "If you are a workaholic doctor, you are wanted all the time," he says. "Your beeper is going off, and so you must be important." He developed a compulsive shopping habit for classical music, spending thousands of dollars on CDs, many of which he never listened to. Then, in his fifties, he was diagnosed with attention deficit hyperactivity disorder, or ADHD.

"I started looking at personality development and brain development in a scientific way," Maté says. "That's when I first found out about how the brain is actually shaped by the environment."

At the Portland Hotel, Maté was tasked with keeping as healthy as possible a population in which many were literally dying. A majority were diagnosed as multiple-disorder patients. They had an entrenched addiction to drugs (almost all of them using intravenously), a severe mental-health issue, and were living with HIV or AIDS. He also made regular rounds to three other hotels the Portland was running by the time he was hired.

He looked after tenants' basic medical needs, treating them for symptoms associated with hepatitis, HIV, and frequent infections. Maté also wrote a lot of prescriptions for methadone. But, breaking from the dominant logic of the medical community, he did not see his job as curing an addiction or fixing a mental illness, per se. Instead, his job was to meet his patients where they were at, and then to help them there.

"We had no intention of controlling anybody," Maté explains. "We had no visions of getting people off their addictions. We would want to help people do that, but we did not have an agenda for them to do that. There was no coercion in any way. If you were going to be an addict, if that is where you are at in life right now, the question was, how can we support you? How can we get you as healthy as possible? How can we, potentially, make other choices available to you?"

He concedes that many people will struggle to understand harm reduction as treatment, and responds with a comparison.

"If somebody has diabetes and their pancreas is not functioning—it doesn't produce insulin or enough insulin—you balance their sugars as best you can, you provide them with the right dietary advice, and you give them whatever medication they need. You don't say to them, 'Don't be a diabetic.' You say, 'You're a diabetic and here's what we can do for you.'

"Harm reduction does not rule out the possibility of abstinence, but it does not demand it," he adds. "It just says, 'Right now, this is where you're at, so how can we work with you to make your life better?'"

The nature of the doctor-patient relationship and the psychological trauma that so many of the Portland's tenants had experienced inevitably meant that Maté also served as a counsellor. Before too long, he began to draw connections between what he'd learned about the brain while researching his own neural development and the stories of childhood trauma that his patients recounted to him in their rooms at the Portland Hotel.

"All of these people were traumatized as children," Maté says. "In the Downtown Eastside, not a single patient of mine had *not* been abused as a child. Nobody, not in twelve years."

He is emphatic. "Every single one of them, horribly neglected and abused—sexually, physically, emotionally."

In his second-floor office at the Portland Hotel, Maté came to understand that in seeking destructive drugs like cocaine and heroin, his patients' brains were not functioning abnormally; rather, they were "responding in a very normal way to abnormal circumstances."

Those abnormal circumstances usually began many years ago, he learned, when the Portland's tenants were still just children, or even earlier. There might have been a boy who watched his father beat his mother or a girl who was raped by an uncle. Or an infant who, like Maté, was separated from their mother in circumstances beyond anyone's control. The effect of such adverse experiences is that the child's brain was altered.

Later, in researching his seminal book on the subject, *In the Realm of Hungry Ghosts: Close Encounters with Addiction* (2009), Maté combined the observations he made working at the Portland Hotel with exhaustive research on the subject. People addicted to drugs were not criminals, he concluded. They were victims.

"I didn't study the individual brain chemistry of any of my patients, but looking at the scientific literature, it was clear to me what happened," Maté says.

There is no one area of the human brain responsible for addictive tendencies. An addiction primarily plays out in four brain systems, each one of which is vital in shaping human behaviour. This is why an addiction is such a difficult problem to solve. If, in an attempt to address an addiction, we could flip a switch that eliminates any of these networks, doing so would simultaneously terminate a system required for human survival.

Maté lists them off: the dopamine incentive-motivation apparatus, the opioid pain-relief and pleasure-reward apparatus, the impulse-regulation apparatus, and the stress-regulation apparatus.

Each one responds to the external stimuli of childhood abuse and neglect, he continues. These changes can have positive effects in the short term. For example, in situations of abuse or neglect, the brain adjusts to help a child tune out reality and soften the emotional blows of those experiences. But in the long term, the outcome of those adjustments is a development of the brain that makes it significantly more susceptible to addiction.

The dopamine incentive-motivation apparatus

When a child is abused, its brain develops with fewer dopamine receptors. In the long-term, what happens is a person develops a need for an external supply of dopamine; cocaine, for example.

A vicious cycle begins. An addict snorts a line of coke and their brain is flooded with dopamine. Seeking to restore balance, the brain reduces the number of receptors this artificial and unusually plentiful source of dopamine has to latch onto. The addict's sense of pleasure subsides, leaving them with a greater desire for more cocaine.

Dopamine is also crucial to the brain's processing of incentives and motivation. This is part of the reason why an individual addicted to cocaine will prioritize drug abuse over relationships with friends and family. More generally, when the brain lacks dopamine, it feels less motivated to do anything.

The opioid pain-relief and pleasure-reward apparatus

The human brain's natural opioid system also plays a crucial role in addiction. It has three functions vital to human survival: it regulates feelings of pain, both physical and emotional; it allows us to experience pleasure and related feelings of reward; and it is largely with the opioid system that we feel attachments to other humans.

For example, without an opioid system, a mother would feel less of a bond to her infant. Caring for a newborn baby is one of the most demanding tasks there is. Without the opioid system creating feelings of love and ultimate responsibility for a young child, the task could be abandoned and the infant would die. That is, when we talk about heroin's effect on the brain, we are discussing a fundamental system crucial to survival—both for the individual and for the human species—and of the chemicals responsible for the very strongest of human emotions: love.

Ask a heroin addict what if feels like to inject the drug. "It's like a warm hug," will be among the most common responses one hears.

The relevant chemicals in these processes are called endorphins, a direct contraction of the words "endo," meaning "within," and "rphine," from "morphine." They are part of the body's natural pain-management system, attaching to opioid receptors in order to blunt feelings of physical and emotional discomfort.

If, as a child, an individual is abused, or even if they don't receive adequate attention, their brain's endorphin activity will decline. Over a sustained period of abuse or neglect, a reduction in supply can become the norm. The individual is therefore more vulnerable to feelings of pain. In such cases, the person becomes more likely to seek external sources of opioids—an organic one like the opium poppy, which we process into heroin, or a chemical one like Purdue Pharma's popular painkiller, OxyContin.

The impulse-regulation apparatus

The effects that narcotics have on the dopamine and opioid systems have profound consequences for impulse control.

One section of the brain where receptors for those chemicals are concentrated is the orbitofrontal cortex, which is located just behind our eye sockets. It is the orbitofrontal cortex where we rapidly process potential decision outcomes on the basis of short and long-term results; that is, whether or not we should act on an impulse and what consequences any action might bring. The orbitofrontal cortex is also strongly connected to the brain's limbic centres, the primary home of emotions, which makes it susceptible to responding inappropriately because of past traumatic experiences. The area of the brain that influences decisions about the potential pros and cons of a considered action can be impaired by early childhood adversity in ways that make us more susceptible to addiction.

Take the example of a woman who sells her body for money. The idea was once likely unconscionable, given the high emotional cost versus the relatively low material gain. But trauma and addiction can change the outcome of that equation. In the woman's limbic system, she feels emotional pain related to childhood memories of sexual abuse. In the orbitofrontal cortex, she subconsciously recalls the power of heroin to dull those feelings. The impulse to acquire the drug becomes difficult to control—almost impossible, for many addicts. The woman finds she can tolerate the shame and disgust that many people associate with sex work in exchange for a few hours numbed on heroin.

The stress-regulation apparatus

Finally, childhood trauma will affect how a brain feels and responds to stress.

In manageable doses, stress is good. It helps us complete work assignments on time and study for tests in university. But prolonged periods of elevated stress can adversely affect our health.

Humans address feelings of emotional discomfort caused by stress with different methods. Often, these are external. A warm bath works for some people but not everyone. What does relieve stress for just about all humans are narcotics like cocaine and heroin, at least in the short term. The extent to which an individual seeks external comforts is affected by how well internal stress regulators are functioning.

If a girl or boy is raped as a child, they will be overwhelmed by stress. At chronically elevated levels, their biological systems for the natural regulation of stress hormones will develop improperly.

At birth, humans are completely helpless to regulate stress. A newborn baby can scream for hours in response to even the most minor of discomforts. They depend entirely on their parents to respond and help manage their emotions. The stress-regulation system remains in its early stage of development for some time. If a toddler experiences prolonged periods when stress-hormone levels are elevated, the development of their regulation apparatus will suffer. They will experience difficulty regulating impulse-responses; for example, perhaps they feel anxiety concerning who receives the first piece of a cake, and in response they physically attack another child. Years later, teenagers will shout at their parents and stomp their feet when they feel anxious about a social gathering they are forbidden from attending. It takes humans a very long time to develop appropriate responses to stress.

Faced with stressful circumstances later in life, someone who suffered abuse as a child will have grown more likely to seek external sources of comfort.

"People who use opiates, very often they are medicating post-traumatic stress disorder," Maté says. "It is a way of reducing the symptoms temporarily."

There is data supporting Maté's emphasis on childhood trauma as a determinant of one's likelihood of developing an addiction to drugs. The landmark Adverse Childhood Experiences Study found that a person who underwent four or more traumatic events as a child was 7.4 times more likely to develop a problem with alcohol compared to someone who experienced no significant trauma as a child. The same group was 10.3 times more likely to use injection drugs.[32] A related study found that a child even just witnessing traumatic events (spousal abuse, for example) resulted in a positive-graded risk (the more events, the greater the likelihood) for later developing problems with alcohol and illicit drugs.[33]

In the under-developed brain of an adult, stress becomes significantly more likely to perpetuate an addiction or prompt an individual to relapse and return to an abusive habit that was previously under control.

Maté recalls that this effect was everywhere he looked during his time as a physician in the Downtown Eastside. The primary source of stress was the prohibition of drugs. "If you had to design a system to stress people, you would design the current legal system," he argues.

---

[32] Vincent Felitti, Robert Anda, Dale Nordenberg, David Williamson, Alison Spitz, Valerie Edwards, Mary Koss, James Marks, "Relationship of Childhood Abuse and Household Dysfunction to Many of the Leading Causes of Death in Adults," *American Journal of Preventive Medicine* 14 (4) (1998): 245-258.

[33] Shanta Dube, Robert Anda, Vincent Felitti, Valerie Edwards, David Williamson, "Exposure to Abuse, Neglect, and Household Dysfunction Among Adults Who Witnessed Intimate Partner Violence as Children: Implications for Integrated Health and Social Services," *Violence and Victims* 17 (1) (February 2002): 3-17.

Most people addicted to drugs are engaging in one form or another of self-medication, says Maté. They are attempting to suppress memories of childhood trauma or sooth feelings of lifelong abandonment. But the substances that many of these people chose to use as medication have been made illegal—arbitrarily, Maté insists. And since they are addicted, forced to seek these substances out several times a day, their life becomes one that is as stressful as anyone could imagine. "If they are caught with it, they are jailed," he says. "If they deal it a little bit to support their habit (which most of them do), they are jailed for longer."

The first thing prohibition does is create a feeling of anxiety for supply. Where will the next hit come from? When the consequence of failing to obtain the drug is as severe as heroin withdrawal, the associated stress is extreme. Next, like a squirrel in a park, a drug addict is forced to remain vigilant at all times, constantly on the lookout for threats posed by police. Will their dealer cheat them? Forced to buy drugs in an alley, there's a risk they will be robbed. What would a friend or family member think of what they are doing? It all creates stress, which builds a desire for more of the drug that can relieve them of those feelings.

"You make them afraid, you make them live outside the law, you ostracize them, and you demean them," Maté says. "That is a great way to create stress in people. It is a great way to keep them mired in addiction.

"I saw it every day," he continues. "Their very lives were a reflection of the effects of prohibition. Having to spend all their energy looking for the drugs, having to scrounge around for the next hit, having to shoplift, getting arrested all the time, moving through the revolving door in and out of jail, the experiences they had in jail, their furtiveness, their fear. Everything. Everything I saw in them was a reflection of prohibition."

In the Portland Hotel, Maté, Evans, and Townsend acknowledged that the majority of their tenants were victims and would be treated as such. They began breaking the rules to free tenants who were addicted to drugs from those stresses caused by prohibition.

Maté would, for example, perform an act he says he never would have imagined engaging in: in a dingy hotel room, he helped an addicted man find a vein in his arm to inject some illegal concoction. "If I hadn't done so, he was going to inject in his neck, risking a brain abscess," Maté explains.

"Liz and Mark are the same way," he says. "It's not even that they are rule breakers. They created new rules. They saw a necessity and they fashioned what they would do around that necessity.

"Most institutions try and fit the clients and everything into a set of top-down priorities," Maté continues, "whereas Liz began with a simple question: What do these people need? What's actually required?"

Chapter 14
Raleigh, North Carolina

The first time Minister Michelle Mathis saw Robert Childs was in 2012, in a parking lot outside the Cooperative Christian Ministry in Hickory, North Carolina.

"There was a guy, this scruffy, bearded little fellow with a weird accent, who was handing out packets of stuff from the back of his car," Mathis recounts in a southern accent of her own. "I didn't know who he was, but I knew he wasn't from around here."

Mathis was right about Childs. He's a bit of a nomad. Originally from the United Kingdom, he immigrated to Chicago and then lived in Portland, New Hampshire, and New York. Since 2009, he's lived in Chapel Hill, a town of about 57,000 people just west of Raleigh. While not from North Carolina, Childs knows the place well. For years, he operated as a one-man needle-exchange program, roaming the state with a backpack full of clean syringes.

Each morning, Childs filled a backpack with packaged needles and naloxone, called for his dog, and set off in his little Honda Fit.

In 2012, distributing needles was illegal in North Carolina. But, of course, there were still intravenous drug users. And so an underground network developed. "We started going to methadone and buprenorphine clinics all over the state, distributing naloxone, doing know-your-rights training and harm-reduction training," Childs says. "Something else we used to do to engage people is have barbeques in people's yards. And in North Carolina, people can't say no to barbeque."

In Fayetteville, Childs connected with a pastor named James Sizemore who was running an illegal needle-exchange program out of the basement of his church.

In High Point, he found Steve Daniels, central North Carolina's so-called "godfather of needle exchange." Daniels was an older man whose body was weathered by decades of drug addiction, HIV, and hepatitis C, but he was always on call. Twenty-four hours a day, drug users knew they could call Daniels and soon enough he'd pull up with a supply of clean needles and alcohol swabs. He saved countless lives from HIV before the disease took his life in January 2017.

In Hickory, Childs met Michelle Mathis and Karen Lowe. The couple run their own congregation, called the Olive Branch Ministry, which does homeless outreach and advocacy work for the LGBTQ community. They were distributing naloxone in the area around Hickory and hanging out in parking lots outside methadone clinics, offering people free tests for HIV and hepatitis C.

"We began to get requests for clean rigs," Mathis recalls. "We didn't have any. But Robert had explained to us that while there were no protections, if we decided to do underground syringe exchange on our own—if we were willing to take the risk—that he could get us rigs. We said, 'Absolutely, we're in.'"

Just a few weeks before that meeting, a pastor in Charlotte, NC, was arrested for running a needle exchange out of his church. There were real risks involved. But there was also a real need. By the time Mathis met Childs in 2012, the prevalence of HIV in North Carolina had risen steadily for more than a decade. There were 127 infections per 100,000 people in 2000; in 2012, that number was 280.[34]

"So we began to kind of covertly get the word out," Mathis says. "Hey, if you know anybody who needs a clean rig, you can put them in touch with us."

To keep their exchange program off authorities' radar, Mathis and Lowe asked people to donate an item not usually associated with harm-reduction programs: they asked for boxes of corn chips.

Using the syringes that Childs provided in bulk, the couple prepared little Ziploc bags of harm-reduction supplies. Then, in each bag of donated corn chips, Mathis and Lowe cut a small hole near the bottom at the back and stuffed one of the Ziploc harm-reduction kits inside, hiding them among the corn chips. Then they used a clear piece of tape to reseal each bag to make it look like it had just come off a store shelf.

---

[34] *2013 North Carolina HIV/STD Epidemiologic Profile* (Raleigh, NC: North Carolina Department of Health and Human Services, 2015).

"And then we would deliver chips to people," Mathis says. "We would meet people in a fried chicken restaurant or in the parking lot of a big box store or, as people became more comfortable with us, we'd actually go to their house."

It's a travel-intensive business to offer needle exchange in a mostly rural area like central North Carolina. "Ninety percent of what we do is mobile," Mathis says. "We put five-to-six hundred miles a week on our personal vehicles just making syringe drops in the evenings ... There are some people who we deliver to who don't even have running water or electricity."

While Childs was working with Mathis and Lowe's Olive Branch Ministry and similar groups spread out across the state, a larger nonprofit he'd joined called the North Carolina Harm Reduction Coalition was advocating for policy reform in the capital, Raleigh. In 2010, Childs hired a young woman named Tessie Castillo and she quickly proved herself adept with the legislative process.

The underground exchanges were doing a lot, not only without the government's support but with authorities actively working against them. But there was only so much of the state that a few church groups could cover.

"The situation before there was needle exchange was really dire," Castillo recalls. "I would talk to users who had found needles by scrounging through trash cans for them, picking up used needles off the ground. We knew about diabetics who were selling their used needles ... People would use the same needle fifty times before it would finally break and they would have to try to figure out a way to get another one."

In the spring of 2011, Castillo found a state legislator willing to introduce a bill that would decriminalize syringe distribution. That was the beginning of a long and complicated process.

Along the way, they picked up a number of unexpected allies. Castillo says that perhaps the most influential in convincing politicians was law enforcement.

Before too long (but only as a result of an education and advocacy campaign that she and Childs led for the North Carolina Harm Reduction Coalition), police departments that had previously spoken out against needle exchange were quoted by North Carolina media as in favour of harm reduction. "I support syringe-exchange programs, a common sense tactic to address the issue of drug use in our communities," Fayetteville police chief Harold Medlock said. "It's clear to me that these programs do not encourage drug use and that they can work in conjunction with the continuing enforcement of drug laws."[35]

On July 11, 2016, five years after Castillo found her first sympathetic legislator, an amendment attached to a bill about police body cameras made it legal to distribute clean needles in North Carolina.

Childs says that by 2016, North Carolina's underground-exchange networks were pretty well established. So when the law changed, it didn't bring on a massive expansion of services. Rather, it brought above-ground the exchange programs that were already running.

"We had gotten to know a lot of people. We've set up syringe exchanges at methadone and buprenorphine clinics," Childs says. These distribution points are usually as simple as a table and a couple of chairs set up in a clinic parking lot. "If people are coming to dose [methadone], they can also get supplies for their mates or bring their mates with them who can then get supplies from us," Childs says. "When we talk to them, we talk about risk reduction. And then if they are ready to go on methadone or buprenorphine, we say, 'Great, go across the parking lot.'"

Mathis says that even though needle exchange has been legal in North Carolina for more than a year now, a lot of drug users remain cautiously suspicious. "We still have people who don't trust the system," she says. "Even though what we are doing is legal, there is a stigma attached to it."

But Mathis adds that attitudes are changing. "Thank God we don't have to deliver in corn-chip bags anymore," she says.

---

[35] *North Carolina Law Enforcement and Syringe Exchange Programs* (North Carolina Harm Reduction Coalition, 2016).

Chapter 15

A Drug Dealer Finds Activism

Dean Wilson is one of those people who has lived a lot of lives. He was a delinquent teenager and did time in prison. Later, he grew into a family man and, for many years, he was a highly successful computer salesman for IBM. He was also a single father. Later still, he was a drug dealer, and then an activist and something of a movie star. Finally, he became "Canada's most famous junkie."[36]

Wilson was born in Winnipeg, Manitoba, in 1956. His family moved to Chicago and then settled in Toronto when he was still just a baby. As a teenager with middle-class parents, Wilson was a handful. He got into drugs early and they often got him into trouble. The first of a number of times he was arrested was in 1972, when he was just sixteen years old. Wilson was picked up for marijuana possession and got away with a warning. When the same thing happened a few months later, a judge threw the book at him, and he was sentenced to six years in prison. Interviewed forty-five years later, Wilson grows visibly angry when asked about those years.

"That judge looked at me and said, 'Fuck you,'" he says. "Ruined my fucking life."

Wilson declines to talk about the time he spent in prison. But a passage in Dr Gabor Maté's 2009 book, *In the Realm of Hungry Ghosts*, offers clues to what happened inside. "What's the worst thing you've ever done?" Maté recounts asking him. "Dean winces as he tells me about an incident in jail that still revolts him for its cruelty and physical sordidness—nothing would be served by repeating it here."

In other interviews over the years, Wilson has mostly dodged requests for details and responded with vague statements about doing

---

[36] Mike Howell, "Downtown Eastside: Canada's 'Most Famous Junkie' Comes Clean," *Vancouver Courier*, February 27, 2014.

what he needed to survive. He gave a little more in a 2002 interview with the documentary filmmaker Nettie Wild. Wilson described the prison they sent him to as a "hate factory."

"I wasn't racist before that, but you have to be racist in there, otherwise you die," he explained.

"First thing, I walk up to one of the biggest white men I've ever seen in my life, just built unreal, just covered in swastikas. He said, 'You're in the Aryan Nation.'"

"You're bloody right I am," Wilson replied to him.

"There were only eighty white guys in that facility that had almost 5,000 people," Wilson told Wild. "But we ruled the joint. So you had to do what you had to do, 'cause if you go it alone, you would have died."

Today Wilson describes his youth warmly. "I had a wonderful upbringing," he says. But he later reveals he was affected by his parents' divorce. "When my parents split up, my mom had to go to work. And I was ten. My dad left on my tenth birthday; he handed me the chess set that I wanted, and said, 'I'm gone.' And it just blew my fucking mind. I didn't talk about that for years."

Wilson first injected heroin at the age of twelve. He's insistently vague when asked about the experience. It was at his family's home in Toronto and Wilson and his older brother, Bobby, had been left the place to themselves for the weekend. The only other detail Wilson mentions is the feeling the drug gave him.

"Bobby was there, and I turned to him and said, 'I feel normal for the first time,'" Wilson recounts. "I thought that was kind of an odd thing for a twelve-year-old to say."

Drugs were the priority for the next few years, and then Wilson met that judge who sent him to prison when he was just sixteen. After he was released, Wilson followed his estranged father west, to Vancouver.

In 1983, his own first child was born and then, in 1984, his second. Wilson settled down for a while. Things didn't work out with their mother, so he found himself living in South Vancouver as a single father. A good one, it turned out.

"I sold computers. I wore a suit and tie and fucking everything like that," Wilson says. He never went completely straight. While Wilson proved an expert at selling computers, he was also very good at trafficking large amounts of marijuana.

"I would [make] $100 on every pound and sell a thousand pounds a month."

That paid for the house in South Vancouver. "Then my kids grew up," Wilson continues. "They didn't need the twenty-one meals a week anymore. They didn't rely on me as much. And I found I began migrating back into the drugs again that I had put away when the kids were born."

Wilson gives a slightly different account of his on-again-off-again relationship with drugs in the interview with Wild.

"During those years, it was more of a managed drug thing," he told her. "I'd use my shot in the morning so I wasn't sick and then I'd have one shot at night and that was it. There was never any really getting high. It was just a management thing, because you had to keep the monkey off your back.

"And occasionally, if the [kids] went over to their mom's on the weekend or were away or something, I would take that weekend to shut the blinds, shut the door, and let's rock," he continues. "But, no, they were definitely the apple of my eye and there was no bullshit with them."

The drug scene in South Vancouver was somewhere between boring and nonexistent, and before too long, Wilson had blown through the small fortune he'd made selling computers and marijuana and could no longer afford to live in the suburbs.

"People go where the dope is, and the dope was down here," Wilson says about the Downtown Eastside, where he still lives today. "And then I got to shooting cocaine, and that was the real beginning of ten years of hell. I sold a lot and I did a lot."

In 1996, Wilson moved from the four-bedroom house where he'd raised his children to the Ivanhoe, a seedy hotel located above an even seedier bar next to Vancouver's main bus station. He was kicked out a few months later and ended up in a similar place just down the street, called the Pacific Hotel. His small room was a convenient three blocks from the open-air drug market at Main Street and East Hastings.

A hardcore addict in rough shape by this point, Dan Small found

Wilson and moved him over to Portland's Sunrise Hotel. In his room on the second floor there, Wilson became a constant headache for the PHS staff and especially for Small.

"Dan used to call me in about my drug dealing," Wilson explains. "He called it my 'entrepreneurial adventure.'"

Small managed him as best he could. "Look, man, you went up and down the stairs eighty-nine times last night!" Wilson remembers Small telling him one morning. "Dan goes, 'You can't be going in and out and having people up to your room.' I said, 'I never have people up to my room. That's why I'm going up and down the stairs.' He says, 'Well, we can't protect you much longer.'"

This being the Portland, Wilson wasn't evicted. He and Small actually became great friends. And while they didn't like it, PHS staff did protect Wilson for a while longer.

"I had the best fucking security in the world," Wilson says with a laugh. "To get to me you had to get by the Portland staff first."

Every night at seven, Wilson left his second-floor room at the Sunrise to pick up two ounces of cocaine and a quarter-ounce of heroin. "The number that everybody phoned was then forwarded to my phone for the next twelve hours," he recounts. "I would answer the phone, I would sell all that, and it typically came to $5,000 or $6,000. It was funny how it worked out. Every single night, $5,000 or $6,000.

"Except on Wely," he adds, using a slang term for the last Wednesday of each month—Welfare Wednesday—when government money pours into the Downtown Eastside. "On Wely I would do up to $20,000. In a night." (That's about $27,000 CDN in 2017 dollars or $21,600 US). "And I worked every night."

Those dozens of trips down and up the stairs of the Sunrise each night equated to a lot of cocaine and heroin. "I did well over a million dollars in twelve months," he says. "For three years, I went out every night and never missed a shift. Three years solid."

It was a remarkable work ethic, made more impressive by the fact that Wilson was injecting cocaine every day through all of that. "I remember one November when I only slept three nights," he says. "The whole month, three nights ... But I was really fucked up. That's when you have involuntary movement in your body and shit like that."

Andy Bond, a frontline Portland staffer who joined the organization the same year that Wilson moved into the Sunrise (and another musician of some success), recalls the headaches Wilson's drug dealing caused him.

"I was working at the front desk of the building and there were a lot of people coming by asking for him. 'Is he here? Is he here?'" Bond says. "There would be twenty people coming by, going in and out. It was obvious what was going on. So then there would be a power struggle.

"Your whole shift would become focused around Dean's guests, people trying to sneak in, or someone wanting to collect or assault him, or whatever it was," he continues. "I remember one time getting really frustrated and calling Mark or Liz." An hour or so later, Bond received a call back from Dan Small.

"Look, you're losing the plot a bit," Small told him.

"I thought, 'How am I losing the plot?'" Bond says.

"He's driving the other residents crazy. Why do we keep him?" he asked Small.

"Well, there's nowhere else for him to go," Small replied. "It's bigger and more complicated than that. He's not doing well. And if we don't support him, no one else will."

Bond says that made sense to him. "He couldn't find another place. Back then, we were the last stop. Otherwise, he would have been homeless."

Small remembers that this sort of dust-up with Wilson happened somewhat regularly. "Someone would tell me, 'Dean is drawing a line that is unreasonable, that pushes the flexibility of even the Portland beyond what it can possibly sustain,'" he says. "Then I would meet with Dean and we would have coffee, and I would say, 'Hey, you're getting a lot of exercise on the stairs, huh?' We would have a discussion and at the end of the day, he would know what I was saying, and that he would need to pull his horns in a little bit. And he would do that."

To this day, Wilson refuses to even give a hint about who he was dealing for. "You're never going to nail that down," he says. "Just people. People who ran the Downtown Eastside at the time. They had six or seven hotels. And I just did their bidding at the Sunrise."

Wilson was making a lot of money, but there's no such thing as a street addict with a healthy bank account. One afternoon in January 2000, he was out with a friend named Sammy and they were three dollars short of the ten dollars they needed for a hit.

They were at the intersection of East Cordova and Gore Avenue, where they found a long line of people leading down into the basement of the St. James Anglican Church. It was the annual general meeting of the Vancouver Area Network of Drug Users. Wilson was told that if he made it through the meeting, he'd get three dollars.

"People started talking about supervised-injection sites and heroin maintenance and all that," Wilson says. "But to tell you honestly, I thought, 'Yeah, that will fucking happen when pigs fly. Big fucking deal.' I sold a lot of dope, and I wasn't big on this harm-reduction shit. It just didn't matter to me. I'd survived, I had money, so fuck off."

But if he and Sammy both made it through the VANDU meeting, they'd get six dollars between them. So into the church they went.

A VANDU AGM is a special event to witness. There are elections for board positions that can involve a little money so everybody is competing for them hard. And because drug use is a VANDU requirement for membership, a lot of the people there are high.

"We walked into this room and there are 200 fucking junkies just going wild," Wilson recalls. He and Sammy took a seat at the back and waited for the whole thing to be over. Then Wilson spotted Ann Livingston across the room.

Dean Wilson (left) met Bud Osborn at a Vancouver Area Network of Drug Users meeting in January 2000. *Photo: Ann Livingston*

"I leaned over to Sammy and I said, 'I'm going to get that girl!'" Wilson says, laughing.

Sitting directly behind them was Bud Osborn, Livingston's steady boyfriend of several years.

Osborn leaned forward, stretching his neck in between Wilson and Sammy, and flashed a big grin. "That's alright, but that's my girl, man," Wilson recalls Osborn telling him.

"I didn't know who Bud was and I didn't know who Ann was," Wilson says in his defence.

"That was a Saturday afternoon," he continues. "I walked into the office on Monday, and within four months, I was president of VANDU. I took over and I ran with it. It was exactly what I wanted. I wanted to have a voice," Wilson explains. "Because I was sick and tired of shit. I had been doing drugs for so long, I had spent time in jail and all this shit because of drugs." He pauses a moment, and then adds, "And I thought Ann was pretty good looking."

A few weeks after the AGM, Wilson was working at VANDU's new office at West Hastings and Cambie Street, getting ready to close the doors and lock the place up for the weekend. A young Indigenous girl—no older than sixteen, Wilson remembers—wandered in off the street and over to the desk where he was sitting.

She was pretty, Wilson remembers, petite, with straight brown hair, wearing jeans and a zip-up hoodie over a T-shirt. A subtle baby bump revealed her to be pregnant. "But a normal fucking kid," Wilson says.

"Oh, it's my birthday," the girl said to him.

Wilson cheerfully replied, "Oh yeah? Happy birthday."

"I really don't like birthdays very much," the girl said. "It's the day my dad passed me around to all my uncles. I just wish they hadn't done it on my birthday."

Wilson remembers how flat and devoid of emotion her voice was. He looked her in the eyes and said the only thing he could think of. "It should have never happened, dear," Wilson told her. "That stuff shouldn't happen."

He grows furious recounting this memory today. "She was pregnant, she was HIV positive, she was sixteen, and she was living on the street. And I thought, 'This is bullshit.'"

Wilson was still an addict and a heavy one at that point, injecting cocaine forty or fifty times a day. He needed to support his habit, and for him dealing was the easiest way to do that. So for quite a few years he continued to sell enough to at least pay for drugs. But more often, he took a step back and instead of dealing himself, made a living cutting cocaine and heroin for other dealers. Wilson's involvement in the drug trade finally ended for good in 2008, when police executed a large bust against the crew that was supplying him. "I was happy to get out of it by then anyway," he says.

Even if he didn't transform into a model citizen overnight, Wilson credits that girl who he met on her birthday as the beginning of the end of his days as a drug dealer.

"That was the moment I really said, 'This has got to change,'" he says.

"People in my position don't realize how lucky we are, in many cases. I was articulate, I was educated, I was white. All these things come into play. Then you come down here and you really start to get to know some people down here and you go, 'How the fuck did they survive? How could it happen? How could they have even gotten this far?' I started thinking, 'Somebody has got to fight on behalf of these people.' Because, you know, I find it easy to be a lion. And I looked around, and I thought, 'I could prey on these people and I could sell them dope or whatever, or I could protect them.'"

Wilson's energy could appear to be without limits. In the early 2000s, that was partly thanks to cocaine. But he still possessed a natural stamina that let him maintain that addiction while remaining remarkably functional. Now he turned that strength to activism.

Livingston remembers that she spotted that energy right away but wasn't sure if it would save Wilson or kill him. "If you have a weak constitution, you toy with drugs and pretty soon you face the fact that you are either going to die or you are going to have to stop," she explains. "But if you have really good stamina, you can just stagger on for a decade or two, and then you might have to face it. Or not."

Wilson recalls how Livingston began to school him.

"I started reading everything. I'd read an entire report, not just the executive summary or whatever," he says. "So we knew how many people were dying and what they were dying of. We started to see the actual numbers; it was an appalling situation for everybody. Something had to change.

"Ann turned us all into a bunch of epidemiologists," he says. "That's one of the things that Ann did that was really important."

Chapter 16

Taking the Fight to City Hall

Milestones are often counted in years. But by 2000, residents of the Downtown Eastside were measuring the overdose epidemic in bodies. Thousands of bodies.

In 1997, Osborn and the Portland Hotel Society had hammered 1,000 crosses into the grass of Oppenheimer Park to symbolize that that many people in BC had died of an illicit-drug overdose during the preceding five years. (The actual number of people to die from 1992 to 1996 was 1,342, but it appears that in 1997, the activists believed the number was closer to 1,000.)

In the three years that had passed since the Killing Fields, as the day became known, roughly another 1,000 people had died after taking drugs. (From 1997 to 1999, the exact number of fatal overdoses across the province was 972.)

With the 1997 demonstration, activists had caught the media's attention. Politicians were talking about drugs. A public-health emergency was declared. But it felt like a concrete response had never come.

The garage at Liz Evans's house had a thousand crosses stacked in a corner. Someone noticed them there and suggested they do the whole thing again to mark the passing of another 1,000 lives lost. Mark Townsend and a few Portland staffers dug the crosses out of storage and got to work building another thousand of them. "Nothing had happened," he explains. "So let's build a few more and slam them in the park."

The night before the demonstration, the Portland's maintenance team—Phong Lam, Chris Runne, and Patrick O'Rourke—met Townsend at the house he shared with Evans. Many of the crosses from the 1997 demonstration were broken or had gone missing. Runne estimates they started with about 500 when they began working toward their goal of 2,000, and the protest was scheduled to begin in barely more than twelve hours.

"We bought cheap wood and just kept going at it and called it another thousand at some point," he says with a laugh. "We bought a nail gun. One of us was cutting the crosses, and the other one was shooting them together all through the night."

Shortly after sunrise on July 11, 2000, Tom Laviolette pulled up in a jeep. The maintenance team piled in, along with 2,000 crosses, "give or take," and made the short drive to Oppenheimer Park. Now came the task of hammering them into the grass.

"Police actually showed up pretty quick," Runne says. "They told us not to do that. And we basically told them why we were doing it and ignored them ... They didn't know what to think about it. But they didn't arrest us."

Bryan Alleyne was the president of VANDU at this time. In the days leading up to the demonstration, he and Livingston made posters and attached them to telephone poles around the Downtown Eastside. "'Has anyone you loved died?"some read. For just about everybody who lived in the Downtown Eastside, the answer was yes.

Early in the afternoon of July 11, they met at the intersection of Main and East Hastings to make the short walk to Oppenheimer Park together. By the time they got there, the maintenance team had transformed it into a cemetery.

A newspaper report from that day quotes Osborn, speaking to the crowd: "We need a largely expanded methadone program, safe injection sites, heroin maintenance, and a variety of treatment models. We're not talking about wild, experimental stuff here. We're talking about practical solutions that have worked in Switzerland and Germany and other places in Europe."[37]

At Oppenheimer, a set of speakers played Bob Marley's "Redemption Song" on repeat. Meanwhile, Alleyne handed out small pieces of paper on which he had written many names of the dead. "I had to always go to the coroner and find out who died and what information they could give us," he explains. "So then we had names and we put them on the crosses.

---

[37] Hubert Beyer, "Canada's Killing Fields," [Prince Rupert] *Daily News*, July 21, 2000.

"It looked like Arlington Cemetery in the States," Alleyne continues. "There were thousands of crosses. And anyone who knew somebody who had died came and put a cross up and put their name on the crosses. It was a sad day."

Tanya Fader had worked closely with VANDU since starting with PHS two years earlier, taking a lead role in how the two organizations often worked together. "By that point, unfortunately, I'd known quite a few members who had died," she says. "We obviously had a huge heroin overdose problem, but it was also combined with AIDS. People were dropping. It was hard to imagine."

She remembers how heavy it felt, hammering crosses into the ground. "We were on a different plane for a while that day," she says. "I was writing someone's name on a cross and then I looked out and saw all these people crouched over, writing other names. It made it real. It was really intense."

Among the people Fader saw crouching among the crosses was VANDU's vocal rising star, Dean Wilson.

"It was very solemn," he says. "It was just people wandering through those crosses. And people were taking ownership of a cross. It really became a shrine ... Everyone was reflecting on their lives, that they were alive, and that many of us weren't."

Wilson walked with them, lost in his own world of grief.

A friend of Livingston's named Elaine Brière was at the park, taking photographs for VANDU. She walked among the rows of crosses for hours and eventually came across Wilson, who was sitting on the grass with his knees up, his arms folded across them, and his head buried low.

"I usually don't take a lot of photographs if somebody is in an emotional state like that, grieving," Brière says. "They feel you. Even if they don't see you, they can kind of sense you taking this picture."

She snapped two quick shots of Wilson and then continued walking. "It was very moving," Brière says.

———

A photograph of Dean Wilson taken in Oppenheimer Park on July 11, 2000, became an iconic image of Vancouver's struggle with addiction. *Photo: Elaine Brière*

VANDU was still seeing its funding funnelled through the Portland Hotel Society but had grown into a political force of its own. Its office was up on the third floor of a building located at the intersection of West Hastings and Cambie streets, perhaps a bit too far west for some people's liking. Livingston recalls how they were held responsible for any damage to the floor's shared bathroom or graffiti out on the street anywhere within a block of the place. "They wanted to blame us for everything," she says.

Which is not to say that VANDU was totally innocent. The weekly meetings that began in Oppenheimer Park had since moved from the Street Church to the Lookout building, and the group had essentially been evicted from both locations. Now they were bigger than ever and still growing.

"We had twenty-five-member boards, and for the first year or two, ten of them would show up," Livingston says. "Which is fine. You can deal with that. But by the second and third year of VANDU, twenty-five board members were showing up at every fucking board meeting."

The weekly gathering usually numbered more than forty people by the time everyone was crowded around the long boardroom-style table they had there, and everybody had their own priorities and grievances.

"All the crack cocaine people are saying, 'If I have to listen to one more story about fucking methadone,'" Livingston says. "What a shit show."

Tanya Fader sometimes helped keep VANDU meetings moving as orderly as she could, and remembers distinct challenges. For example, a member on heroin might nod out in the middle of a debate and then, upon regaining consciousness, not realizing that the conversation had moved on, continue with their argument. "I remember having to actually get people to not fist fight around the table. That happened more than once for sure."

Amidst all of that, Dean Wilson was putting himself through school. "For the first little while that I was at VANDU, I didn't do anything but listen and watch," he says. "I'd sorta migrate to the people who were in charge. I started learning things and watching Ann facilitate. And then I realized that I could do this." The first project over which Wilson really took ownership was a VANDU subgroup that focused on methadone. The rules in BC around methadone prescriptions and distribution were archaic and undignified. The opioid substitute was only available at select locations, and many of the pharmacists treated their patients like criminals. There were also rules around how an individual could obtain the drug that simply made no sense. For example, one's urine had to test positive for opiates before a doctor was allowed to write that person a prescription for methadone.

"I can't tell you the number of times I paid someone to go score some fucking drugs to get enough in their pee to get on methadone," Livingston says. "You had to do a two-week wait and you had to test positive for opiates. People were starting to go into withdrawal and they wanted to get on methadone, but then they didn't have enough opiates in their piss."

Wilson formed a subgroup called the BC Association of People on Methadone and began to lobby authorities on these issues. He was quickly finding his footing as an activist. "Then that ninety-day moratorium hit," he says.

Since the Killing Fields protest of 1997, a lot of the city's attention had turned to the Downtown Eastside, and money had begun to follow. A lot of people didn't like that. "Fed-up Merchants Tell City to

Arrest Junkies," reads the headline of an August 2000 article in the *Province*.

A small business owner named Grant Longhurst is quoted there: "It's time to say this doesn't work," he told the newspaper. "The public needs to know that not everyone in the downtown neighbourhoods is advocating on behalf of drug users."[38]

Longhurst was a spokesperson of the Community Alliance, an umbrella organization of twelve neighbourhood groups that can loosely be described as business-friendly and anti-drug user. In another article published the same day, he spoke on behalf of the communities that surrounded the Downtown Eastside—Gastown, Chinatown, and Strathcona—to argue for an end to harm reduction.

"We are asking that all three levels of government cease to support or fund resources for anything that facilitates or maintains use and dealing of illegal drugs such as needle exchange, resource centres, safe-fixing sites and quality of life counselling," Longhurst said. "These approaches are futile. It says we are giving up—that there's no hope."[39]

While VANDU and the Portland were organizing, so were their opponents.

Vancouver's mayor of the day, Philip Owen, led a right-of-centre political party called the Non-Partisan Association (NPA). The plight of the Downtown Eastside and especially its drug users had caught his attention. But his constituency was on the west side of town among the upper-class, conservative voters who preferred the drug problem stay out of sight and out of mind.

On August 10, 2000, Owen gave in to the pressure of downtown business owners and enacted a ninety-day moratorium on further spending and new services for drug users in the Downtown Eastside.

VANDU's Bryan Alleyne did the math on how many addicts Owen's spending ban would kill. "In the Downtown Eastside, a three-month moratorium on harm reduction measures is equal to ninety drug overdose deaths," Alleyne said. He and Wilson interpreted the

---

[38] Shane McCune, "Fed-up Merchants Tell City to Arrest Junkies," *Province*, August 10, 2000.

[39] Shelley Solmes, "City Calls Moratorium on Facilities for Drug Users," *Vancouver Sun*, August 10, 2000.

mayor's order as a literal death sentence for dozens of VANDU members and—as they were both injection-cocaine users during this time—quite possibly for themselves. They were angry.

"We said fuck that," Alleyne recalls. "We went up to city hall and we took over. That's how we got our voices heard. And we did get our voices heard."

One month into the moratorium, Wilson had an idea. He asked Dan Small if VANDU could borrow a few of the Portland's 2,000 crosses. If city hall was going to kill ninety drug users, VANDU was going to make sure that the politicians and the people working there knew it.

On September 12, 2000, Livingston rented a big white van and Wilson and a few other VANDU members piled in. On the way to city hall, Livingston discussed strategy.

"Go easy on the mayor," she said to Wilson. "He's in a tough place, but he is an ally. Don't yell, don't do anything that could be attributed as violent," Livingston continued. "Because you are an organization of drug users and drug users are written off all the time as being unreasonable. And so you're going to go in as a voice of reason and compassion. And protect the mayor. Listen to the mayor. Understand that he may not be saying anything that you want him to say today, but that he is an ally who is in a really difficult position."

Meanwhile, Bryan Alleyne was on a bus with another fifty drug users. They joined up outside city hall just before two p.m. On the grass that surrounds Vancouver's city hall, they hammered ninety crosses into the ground. At the same time, a larger group marched straight up to the building's wide front doors. It was a siege, but one Wilson led with strategy and tact.

"I walked up to the cops and I said, 'Look, this is what we're going to do,'" he recounts. "I gave them my card—I had a VANDU card—and I said, 'If there's a problem, phone me, and I'll deal with it. We're here to state our case and that's all there is to it.'"

As Wilson spoke with two police officers, about forty people stood behind him, arm-in-arm. If the cops had flat-out refused to let them enter the building, things could have quickly turned ugly. They did make a half-hearted attempt, but pragmatism prevailed. The police allowed Wilson to lead his parade of drug addicts past them and into city hall.

That was the cue for a third group of VANDU members to spring into action. A friend of Livingston's named Robert Cort had built a black coffin. A final group of six people had hidden around the corner with it and now, with Wilson's parade keeping the doors open, they joined the end of the line. The crowd proceeded noisily up the stairs to council chambers, which they knew was in session, with the mayor present. A second pair of police officers was there waiting for them, but there wasn't much they could do to slow the group's momentum. VANDU entered the council meeting and the room went quiet.

The group with the coffin on their shoulders made its way to the front and set the black box down directly in front of Mayor Philip Owen and the councillors who were sitting in an elevated ring around him. The message was clear: people were dying, and if politicians weren't acting to stop it, they might as well be filling the graves themselves. Reflecting on that day for a documentary that was released a year later, Owen recounts the pressure he felt. "They were all looking to me," he said. "I'm chairing the meeting, sitting in the mayor's chair. And it was all eyes on Phillip Owen. What's he going to do?" The mayor decided he was going to let Wilson speak.

"They were yelling and screaming and up on the balcony dropping banners over. I asked for silence for a minute," Owen recounts today. "I said, 'Dean, we're going to take a five-minute silence period here and all of council is going to listen to you. I'm going to give you that microphone for five minutes. And after five minutes, I'd like you to just quietly leave.'"

The mayor's colleagues with the Non-Partisan Association did not support Owen's attempt at pragmatism. "Council objected," Owen remembers. "They wanted to call in the police. But I said, 'I'm chair of the meeting, I'm the mayor, and I control this agenda. And I'm telling you, council, that we're all going to sit quietly.'"

Wilson took his five minutes.

"It's time for action," he began. "You've got to do something … If you have ninety days of inaction, it almost seems like you're sentencing us to death, because every day somebody is dying. I think it is incumbent on you, as representatives of our city—you know, we did vote you in—that you have to come down to our neck of the woods and give us a solution. One a day is dying. And if one of you were dying every day—every morning, you woke up and there was one less person working at city hall—I'll tell you, that problem would be solved in two minutes. End the moratorium is all we ask." The room erupted in loud applause.

"And then do something!" Wilson shouted.

After he finished speaking, VANDU left. "I told everybody, 'Let's go, we've done it,'" Wilson says. "And the mayor was impressed by that. He said, 'I can work with that guy.'"

Livingston says this was the day she saw that the mayor was really coming around on the drug issue. "If you watched closely, you could see that Philip Owen was on our side," she explains. "He could have just said, 'Get the fuck out of here.' But because he was chair and he recognized us, we could speak.'"

One week later, council lifted its moratorium on new services for drug users, just five weeks into the ninety days for which it was originally issued.

"VANDU was a bunch of street-entrenched addicts rounded up by this naïve, young, socialist-type woman who thought something could be done with them," Wilson says. "She amalgamated them into this little force."

A bit of a problem had slowly developed at VANDU headquarters at Hastings and Cambie.

Dean Wilson was spending a lot of time at the office there, which Ann Livingston welcomed. Before the Downtown Eastside, Wilson had spent years in the corporate world and so he knew what he was doing in that environment. His potential was somewhat diminished by his considerable coke habit, but Livingston says he still quickly proved himself a huge asset to VANDU. It was around the same time that Wilson began working around the clock at the office, however, that it became known as a place to hang out in the evenings.

"They weren't parties," Wilson says. "It was just a place where people could go shoot dope and not have to worry about dying in an alley. That's essentially what our whole thing was about. Just a place for people to go."

Livingston wasn't thrilled about it. She worried about what would happen if somebody overdosed. The VANDU office was on the building's third floor. The door on the ground floor was locked each evening at five, and there wasn't even a buzzer for people to signal when they were outside.

"Even if you called 9-1-1, how did you even let them in the fucking building?" Livingston asks. "I could see the headline: 'Ann Livingston Lets People Die in Her Office.'"

The social scene that developed at the VANDU office became more of a problem when a young academic named Gordon Roe received a grant to explore "the questions of whether an IDU [intravenous drug user] group could develop and implement effective, peer to peer services, and whether the group could sustain these services after the research was concluded."

Roe's project brought a small influx of cash to the organization, which was used to create the VANDU Health Network (VHN). The health network operated as an outreach program and low-barrier service provider. Led by Roe but with significant input from VANDU members, it established alley-patrol teams that walked the streets of the Downtown Eastside, checking on drug users and offering clean needles. It also opened an emergency shelter, launched a program that saw VANDU members pay regular visits to drug users who were stuck in hospital, and created teams inside the Downtown Eastside's private hotels that could respond to an overdose and other emergencies. A paper Roe later published on the project describes how its development was shaped by drug users.

> At the beginning, the boundaries of what that project would
> do were kept deliberately loose—so loose that one of the
> ideas under discussion was a member-based safe-injection
> site, and another was a heroin-buying co-op as a means to

reduce deaths from 'bunk,' or bad dope. There was some interesting discussion about how these could work, but they were ultimately rejected as impractical.

Projects such as a heroin-buying co-op or safe-injection site were things that certainly would have met the needs, and contributed to the health and safety, of users in the area, but they would not have met the goal of producing something that would work in the long term, because they were political actions that would likely have been shut down by the police. The final goal was for an outreach program of some kind that would promote harm reduction.

With VANDU operating as a service provider, the office at Hastings and Cambie was increasingly crowded with business late into the evenings. That slowly gave rise to tensions between the members who were working in the evenings and those who were using the space as a clubhouse. "It was a place where an awful lot of people were hanging out," Roe says. "There were some drug issues late at night. That was partially the influence of—I've got to say—Dean. Dean was kind of a wild card."

It became too much activity for one location.

"Once we started doing outreach out of Cambie and Hastings, things started getting really tense in the office," Roe says. "Supplies were going missing. Boxes of syringes were disappearing and things like that. We were in and out at all hours, there were accusations of favoritism—it was just getting disruptive."

In addition, Roe and Livingston had a clash of ideologies. Livingston had founded VANDU as a grassroots group of activists. She worried that by morphing into a service provider, VANDU risked losing the radical voice that was just starting to hold power in Vancouver. "I thought that this [needle distribution] was an avenue to independence for VANDU," Roe says. "If through these programs they could prove that drug users were reliable stewards of money and could reliably deliver services, that would be a good thing for them. But Ann was very upset that an activist organization was falling into the service-provision trap."

The growing divide threatened to break VANDU in two. "Then it happened that I had rented this other little storefront, just using my own money, on Dunlevy," Livingston recalls. Earlier in the year, she had applied for a small portion of federal money that was promised for health-care programs in the Downtown Eastside. When VANDU missed out on that round of funding, Livingston lost her temper and impulsively paid the first and last month's rent on a storefront she intended to open as another supervised-injection site. "The money never arrived, and that's when I started taking the fucking gloves off," she says.

Then, when Roe and his VANDU faction of peer-service providers grew to the point where they needed a space of their own, Livingston offered them the storefront she was renting in order to give everybody a little more elbow room.

Livingston and Wilson remained on the third floor of the building at Hastings and Cambie, and Roe and his crew moved into the new space at 213 Dunlevy. "That solved a lot of problems between us [the health network] and VANDU," he says.

Located across the street from Oppenheimer Park, 213 Dunlevy is described in Roe's research paper as a haven in a very rough part of town. "The home and heart of the project," it reads. "It was ideal— close to the action, with big front windows."

The drug users who hung out in Oppenheimer took notice, as did the sex workers who at the time congregated nearby along Cordova Street—the "Low Track," it was called then. "The office volunteers were visible to people on the street, and they would knock on the door to ask what was going on," reads Roe's report. "When they heard it was VANDU and that they were operating a needle exchange, they wanted to exchange the needles they had. The office volunteers had the supplies and nothing much else to do, so they started keeping the door open to exchange needles across the desk while they were waiting for the patrols. As the number of patrols increased, so did the time the office was open for needle exchange, and soon the volunteers were letting people hang out there as a drop-in."

Today Roe remembers it with little romance. "It smelled like un-washed bodies and recycled tobacco," he says.

There was one table at the front and off to the side where volunteers took shifts with a clipboard, checking people in and out. A second, larger table used for meetings was farther toward the back. And at the very back was a cubicle washroom, where people injected drugs.

"As soon as that started happening, Ann wanted to declare it an injection site, but it wasn't much of one," Roe says. "We were using it as a base to run street patrols out of. That's where we could safely keep syringes and all that kind of stuff."

Among those VANDU members who migrated six blocks east with Roe was Earl Crowe, VANDU's vice-president at the time.

Crowe is a tall Indigenous man with dark-brown hair that falls just past his shoulders. He's intense and at first can come off as unfriendly, but he has a big heart. Crowe was born in the US. "I'm a visitor here," he says, but other than that will share little about his past. Asked how he got to the Downtown Eastside, he replies: "She kicked me out."

Crowe maintains that 213 Dunlevy was entirely a community effort and that he was never the head of operations there. But everybody else says that he was. "Sometimes I'd stay three days there, just to make sure everything was okay," he admits.

In establishing the health network across the street from Oppenheimer Park, Crowe says the first thing that VANDU needed to do was make peace with the locals. "At the time, Oppenheimer Park was one of the most dangerous parks in Canada," he explains. "A lot of fights, a lot of stabbings, a lot of gun shots happened in the park during that time. And so we had to be careful that it didn't go from the park into our building."

Hoping to prevent the sort of dealers' takeover that sank Back Alley, Crowe served as a liaison between 213 Dunlevy and the hustlers that operated in and around Oppenheimer. "There was a communication," he says. "It wasn't like, 'Get the fuck out.' It was like, 'Let's talk. This is what this space is about. We need you to respect it. We respect what you're doing out there. Respect what goes on in here.' And you know what happened? They made sure that other people did respect that."

"There was no drug dealing in there," Crowe continues. "People would bring their drugs in, but it never happened inside. That was the one thing that we really made sure of. Because that was the one thing that would have got us closed down."

Crowe also earned the Dunlevy injection site a lot of support from the community when he began letting many of the area's sex workers spend the night there. "They were homeless and using drugs and they were working the street," he says. "So they just needed a safe place for a couple of hours to get some sleep before they went back out there. They slept on the floor. They slept where they could—on my desk, under my desk, in the restroom."

A doctor who was volunteering with VANDU at this time, Alana Hirsh, says that for many people, 213 Dunlevy was more of a safe space for female sex workers than it was an injection site. "There was a really good relationship between the women and 213 Dunlevy. It had a really wonderful feel."

Hirsh was just twenty-four years old at the time and VANDU members fondly took to calling her "Dr Love," for reasons no one can explain today. She recalls the day she informed her boss at St. Paul's Hospital that she intended to volunteer her time with a group of intravenous drug users. "I'm going to be involved in something that is not legal yet, but I really believe that it is in their best health interests and that it is the right thing to do," Hirsh told her boss. "And I wanted to let you know, if I get arrested, I will not associate myself with the St. Paul's family medicine program."

In an example of how attitudes toward harm reduction in Vancouver were changing, her supervisors supported her. She became VANDU's doctor for a time. "I have memories of going in there and it was just a big haze of smoke and it was like, 'Dr Love is here!'" she recalls, laughing. "I knew I was amidst a bunch of really amazing people who were doing some amazing pro-active things. And I felt like I could play a small role." Hirsh says it wasn't always clear what that role was, or how much trouble she might get in for taking it on. She was asked to supervise the back of the store and respond if anyone needed help with best-practices for injection drug use—something she did. She was also asked to borrow basic supplies such as latex gloves from the hospital where she worked—something she declines to comment on.

"They always appreciated my questions, welcomed them, and would follow up with stuff. If I said, 'Are you sure that this is safe and the right thing?' They would get back to me the next week with a big print-out of a study from Frankfurt that answered my question."

Nearly a decade into an overdose epidemic, many Downtown Eastside drug users had essentially trained themselves as emergency responders. While Hirsh says that she never actually responded to an overdose at the Dunlevy site, Crowe remembers that he did, often.

"Mouth to mouth," he says. "That was before we even had masks to put over our mouths. But you had to keep them alive. We would make sure that we kept them breathing until the paramedics got there."

It wasn't a glamorous space for using drugs. Crowe remembers more than once having to go into the bathroom with a bottle of bleach to clean blood off of the ceiling. But it was better than the alleys and it did save lives.

"And if someone came in and wanted to detox, we were there to do that too," he adds. "It wasn't about one thing. It was about connections and many things. People came in and injected—so call it an injection site—but it was more than just that."

Crowe recounts one evening a few days before Christmas of 2000 when his brother visited from the US. The sex trade workers at Oppenheimer Park had put up a tree and hung other festive decorations at the 213 Dunlevy storefront.

"My brother is really Republican," Crowe begins. "So anti-harm reduction, it's incredible. But he comes down to see where I'm at."

That night, Crowe's brother showed up with his entire truck full of Kentucky Fried Chicken.

"Fried chicken, potato salad, mashed potatoes, and gravy," Crowe says. "The women set the table like Christmas dinner. And then everyone sat down and ate. It was really good. It showed what a community it was, how family-orientated it was. It was very powerful."

The Dunlevy site was open for less than a year. When Livingston's money for rent ran out and Roe's research project wrapped up, that was the end of it. VANDU went back to being just VANDU. But Crowe maintains that the shabby little storefront across from Oppenheimer left a big mark on people.

"I think the conclusion of Dunlevy is that it opened a vision of harm reduction to people outside of the community," he says. "We showed them what can work."

The conclusion of Roe's report focuses on the success of the VANDU Health Network as a health-care program run by active drug users.

> From a longer-term perspective, the VHN project was blazing a new trail in a new direction. After the project concluded, the trail remained, and others could travel it. We took an idea as far as we could in hope that we could persuade those organisations and policy makers to take up that idea and develop it further in their own way and for their own programs. I believe we were successful and that the idea of user-based service provision as a cost-effective auxiliary or supplement to existing services will be a feature of many new services in the DES [Downtown Eastside].
>
> The volunteers provided an excellent example of how services could cheaply and easily extend their "reach" to the "unreached" by employing drug users as active participants in the provision of service.

For the course of the Dunlevy experiment, Wilson remained at the Hastings and Cambie office, rapidly growing into one of the Downtown Eastside's most vocal political activists.

One prominent VANDU member who stopped coming around was Bud Osborn. Ironically, it was likely because he was using more than he had during the preceding few years, when he had founded VANDU.

"Bud would carefully word these things. Like, 'I'll never inject heroin again,'" Livingston says. "You didn't realize, what else he's saying is, 'And I'll do anything else except inject heroin.'"

Livingston says it still took her weeks or even months to figure out he had relapsed. "People are telling me, 'Oh, I saw Bud on the corner today,' and it's just not clueing in," Livingston says. "It's like your old man is having an affair and the whole town knows but you don't know."

Years later, with hindsight, Livingston recalls Osborn calling her around this time in fits of panic, complaining he needed money for cigarettes or who knows what. She would drop whatever she was doing and run to his place with the cash.

"One of the guys on the corner finally straightened me out," Livingston continues. "They said, 'Ann, he bought dope off me.' So I clued in why I couldn't get a phone call from him while I was working twelve-hour days."

Osborn's return to heroin during these years didn't help his relationship with Livingston, but it wasn't what ended it, either.

"I remember going there [213 Dunlevy] and Bud sitting in the car," she recalls. "It's hard to describe people like Bud. Always sick and not feeling good. And he got more and more like that."

Chapter 17

Building Allies

W e had three kids, all doing really well," Susie Ruttan begins. The Ruttans live on Vancouver's west side, in an upscale-neighbourhood called Kerrisdale. Susie is a retired teacher. Her husband, Rob, is a Crown prosecutor. In the 1990s and early 2000s, he spent a lot of his time in a courthouse near the intersection of Main and East Hastings, prosecuting addicts, the dealers who sold to them, and women who were arrested for selling their bodies in order to pay for drugs.

In 1995, their first child, Gregory (not his real name), started smoking marijuana. He was twelve or thirteen. Within the next year or so, he tried just about every other drug, and was injecting heroin in the Downtown Eastside when he was fifteen.

"It certainly opened my eyes," Rob says. "I began to realize how naïve my understanding of addiction was." He explains how, in the years that followed, definitions of right and wrong increasingly failed to have any meaning.

"We had managed to get a place [for Gregory] in a treatment program in Montreal," he begins. "We had the plane ticket. He was set to go out the next morning, and he was in the desperate throes of craving. He just couldn't face going if he didn't use one more time."

Rob recalls feeling sick as he realized his options. He could leave Gregory to sneak off in the middle of the night and hopefully return in time for his flight the following morning. Or he could help his son get the illegal drugs he was asking for, going against every impulse he had as a parent, but keeping Gregory close until his flight to Montreal.

"I finally came to the awful conclusion that if I didn't let him do this, I wouldn't get him on the plane," Rob says. "I knew that if I let him do it, I might lose him and I wouldn't get him on the plane anyway.

But also that the only chance of getting him on the plane the next day would be going with him, down to the Downtown Eastside."

Together, they drove from Kerrisdale to find a dealer around the intersection of Main and East Hastings. Gregory unbuckled his seatbelt, stepped out of the car, and disappeared around the corner down an alley. Rob sat there waiting. Minutes passed. He lost track of time as his mind raced.

"It felt like a long wait as I wondered if I would ever see my son alive again," he says.

"Is this going to be the beginning of a long relapse period, where he's disappeared?" Rob remembers thinking. "Is this going to be the time where he has an overdose in the alley and I'm not at his side? As I sat there waiting for him, all these things were going through my head. Have I just delivered him to his death?"

It felt like hours passed, but eventually Rob's passenger door opened and Gregory stepped back inside the car. "He did score heroin, he did use, but he did keep his side of the bargain," Rob says. "And we managed to get him on the plane in the morning."

That wasn't the end of Gregory's struggle with addiction. It was neither his first nor his last time entering rehab. Gregory was eventually diagnosed with an underlying bipolar disorder, which gave his family a better understanding of the causes of his addiction. The Ruttans learned that an estimated twenty percent of people with a mental illness also struggle with a concurrent substance-use disorder[40] (for schizophrenia, the odds approach fifty percent[41]). The family's battle continued for many years.

Susie remembers the moment she realized just how tricky a problem drug addiction is to solve. She was at a meeting in the basement of a church. Gregory had just entered detox for his first time. She was feeling optimistic about his future. "I can remember people sharing

---

[40] Brian Rush, Karen Urbanoski, Diego Bassani, Saulo Castel, T Cameron Wild, Carol Strike, Dennis Kimberley, Julian Sommers, "Prevalence of Co-Occurring Substance Use and Other Mental Disorders in the Canadian Population," *The Canadian Journal of Psychiatry* 12 (2008): 800-809.

[41] Peter Buckley, Brian Miller, Douglas Lehrer, David Castle, "Psychiatric Comorbidities and Schizophrenia," *Schizophrenia Bulletin* 35(2) (2009): 383-402.

[stories] as we went around the circle," Susie recounts. "My good news was I had just gotten my son into detox, thinking that everything was going to be okay. And the more seasoned members of the group were saying, 'I'm sorry to break this to you, but it's not going to be over.'"

In hindsight, Susie acknowledges that was probably obvious. But addiction was new to their family and, as parents, she and Rob badly wanted to believe that Gregory would be cured with treatment. "I didn't want to sit down with other parents or talk about it," Rob says. "At first, I was very resistant to the idea." But he and Susie did and, to their surprise, discovered that the drug problem Vancouver faced in the 1990s and early 2000s affected a lot of families that lived nowhere near the Downtown Eastside.

In 1999, Ann Livingston and Bud Osborn were looking for allies outside of their impoverished neighbourhood that nobody else seemed to care about.

"There was a group I'd heard of in Australia of parents with teenagers who were drug addicts," Osborn said. "They had become a very powerful lobbying group. And I thought, we need something like that here."

Osborn had remained in touch with Simin Tabrizi, one of the co-authors of the proposal for supervised-injection sites that the health board had shot down in 1998. He'd shared with her his idea about a group of parents. Then, as chance would have it, Tabrizi received a request from a pastor to come and speak to a similar group who attended his church on Vancouver's west side.

Tabrizi recalls that the first meeting went well enough, but she didn't think a lot of it. Then, as she was leaving, Rob Ruttan came running after her, shouting her name to get her attention just before she stepped into her car. "He told me that his son was addicted," Tabrizi says. "And that he and his wife, Susie, were at their wits end."

Osborn recalled how excited Tabrizi was at this chance encounter. "She came back to me and said, 'I think we found our group.'"

For the next six months, Osborn and Livingston drove from the Downtown Eastside to Kerrisdale every Saturday to spend the morning with Tabrizi, the Ruttans, and the group of parents that gathered with them in the basement of St. Mary's Church. "These were lawyers, administrators at the university, people with money. But they were like beaten dogs," Osborn says.

Susie jokes about how they actually called themselves the "Bud Osborn group ... He was very charismatic but in a very quiet, low-key, compelling way," she says. "He talked about his own struggles with heroin. And he talked a little bit about the Downtown Eastside."

The Downtown Eastside was a place that terrified Susie.

"When you say the Downtown Eastside, it elicits a kind of a nightmare, because that is where I would go looking for our son when he was on the street," she explains. "I would meet some amazing people down there. But it really was a scary place."

When Gregory would go missing, Susie would print small posters that included his name, a photograph, and her phone number. Then she would drive across town to the Downtown Eastside and hand them out to whoever would take one and post the rest on telephone poles throughout the neighbourhood. "Have you seen this boy?" she remembers asking strangers on the street.

"It was a needle in a haystack," Susie continues. But there was little else she could do. And sometimes she did find him, not always for the best. He would refuse to come home with her or beg for money, claiming that a dealer would hurt him if she didn't give him what he asked for.

"It is very easy for people to say, 'You've got to exercise tough love. If you're not, you're enabling,'" Rob says. "Well, there is a very fine line between enabling and doing what you can to support your child, just to keep him alive."

Tabrizi recalls how the parents got to know Osborn and became more familiar with his arguments in favour of harm-reduction services. Before long, an injection site actually became an easy sell, much to their surprise. "When parents are scared every hour of the day—scared they're going to find their kid at the morgue—they understand the idea of safe-injection rooms, where people can go and use but will be safe from overdosing," Tabrizi says. "They could see that the most immediate safety net for their children would be a safe-injection room."

By this time, the group meeting in the basement of the church had a name. They were calling themselves From Grief to Action. Nichola Hall, another of its founding members, recalls how their relationships with Osborn, Livingston, and later VANDU were consciously strategic in nature.

"Bud came to us and said, 'Something needs to be done because people are dying in the Downtown Eastside, but no one is going to listen. The public is not going to listen. But if they know that there are people like you—that it is not just the scum of the Downtown Eastside that you can brush under the carpet—if they know that it is people like you who are struggling with the same problem, then they are more likely to listen,'" Hall says. "That made sense to me."

While the Ruttans, the Halls, and other parents were meeting in Kerrisdale, staff at Vancouver's inner city hospital had grown increasingly alarmed by the outbreak of HIV/AIDS and where that crisis overlapped with the growing problem of drug-overdose deaths.

Irene Goldstone was the head of nursing at St. Paul's Hospital then. She recounts how for years, the Street Nurses who patrolled the Downtown Eastside's back alleys visited her office and described scenes of utter indignity, of people injecting with water they had collected from puddles and sharing needles despite terrible risks of infection. They were stories of desperation, Goldstone recalls. "We were really frustrated with the ministry of health and the health board, because they didn't have a strategic plan," Goldstone says. "So we formed a committee."

That was the Vancouver HIV/AIDS Care Coordinating Committee, which met once a month with the aim of sharing knowledge and experience between both government and nonprofit groups. At these meetings, it became apparent that a new population of higher-needs patients had developed in Vancouver: people with multiple diagnoses of drug addiction, HIV/AIDS, and often also mental-health issues.

In response, Goldstone organized a conference for March 2000 that she called "Keeping the Door Open: Health, Addiction and Social Justice." It opened up the work of the Vancouver HIV/AIDS Care Coordinating Committee to a wider audience, bringing together some 3,000 people who attended meetings at six locations over the course of four days.

At the very first meeting in an auditorium in the basement of St. Paul's Hospital, there were police officers, prison guards, lawyers, doctors, nurses, and every sort of health-care professional. Livingston and Dean Wilson were there with several other VANDU members. There were a lot of people who were working on the frontlines of the gay and lesbian community's response to HIV/AIDS. The Ruttans and other parents with From Grief to Action attended. Rob Ruttan delivered one of the keynote speeches on the first day. The Street Nurses were also there to deliver a presentation on how to inject drugs in as clean and safe a manner as possible. (They were cautioned to attend as individuals and not as representatives of the health-care system.)

Fiona Gold, the Street Nurse who had gotten to know Livingston during visits to Back Alley, explains the challenge that hospitals were dealing with as HIV spread from the gay community to drug users. The two groups did not get along and each one stigmatized the other. Drug users didn't want to visit a hospital's AIDS ward for fear they would be labelled homosexual, and gay men didn't want to be seen alongside drug users for fear they would be labelled junkies. "It was a difficult mix in the hospitals," Gold says. "Street-involved users can be super chaotic, and when they came in, it could be chaos in the hospital. It was difficult as nurses to manage that."

The Street Nurses had tried to bring medical care to the entrenched drug users of the Downtown Eastside, but there was institutional pushback. They had been warned that they were walking a risky line on what was legal within the health-care system of the day.

While Gold had visited Livingston's injection site on Powell Street that ran there from late 1995 to early 1996, she remembers being explicitly warned to stay away from the VANDU site on Dunlevy that was operating while the Keeping the Door Open conference was happening.

"My cell phone rang," Gold says. "It was the solicitor general's office in Ottawa. They said, 'Whatever you do, don't go and work at Dunlevy because you are going to lose your nursing licence.' They were pretty freaked out."

It was this institutional hostility toward health care for drug users that Keeping the Door Open aimed to address. "It was a really important eye-opener for important people, the people who were really running the show," Goldstone says.

Toward the end of the fourth and final day of presentations and meetings, Livingston grew frustrated. Over the course of four days during which she attended eight hours of sessions each day, she didn't hear one thing that she didn't already know. As Goldstone spoke at the front of a packed auditorium in the basement of St. Paul's Hospital, Livingston lost her temper. She stood up, raised a clipboard she held above her head, and issued a challenge for the roughly 200 people in attendance.

Wilson remembers her stealing the day. "She stood up with that clipboard in her hand," he begins, "and she says, 'I don't know about you but I'm going to open up a supervised-injection site. If anybody's into it, stay after the meeting and put your name on this sheet.'

"She said, 'Is anybody willing to actually do something?!'" Wilson continues. "That's what she said, in that way Ann does. And people thought, 'Jeez, I better get up there and sign.' She drives people to action." It was an electrifying moment. Livingston was visibly angry, and people recognized that she had a right to be.

"A bunch of people signed up," Wilson says. "A bunch of straight people signed up. That, right there, was the moment when a group of people got together for a common cause to open up a supervised-injection site," he continues. "We had the parents of young drug addicts from the rich west side, and we had all the Downtown Eastside people."

"I needed a sense of moving forward," Livingston says. "Then I passed that clipboard around and I said, 'Is anyone else sick of this? Should we just do something about it?'"

Gold took a leadership position in the group that emerged from the list of names Livingston collected with her clipboard that evening.

They called themselves the Harm Reduction Action Society, or HaRAS. There was now a group of stakeholders that reached far beyond the Downtown Eastside and that was working with the specific goal of opening a supervised-injection facility. "It was the first time that somebody had really galvanized things," Gold says about Livingston's role.

The Ruttans also added their names to Livingston's list. Rob explains how the idea of an injection site became tenable to parents. "We kept saying to ourselves, 'We hope he never uses again. But if he uses, if his addiction drives him to use, we hope that he will use in a place where there are medical personnel handy to come to his rescue if he needs it, and where there are people who can put him in touch with other medical services,'" he says. "It would also send a message to them that our society cares about [drug users]. They are still valued and respected as human beings."

After the Keeping the Door Open conference concluded, HaRAS continued to meet in the basement of St. Paul's. These meetings were co-chaired by Dean Wilson and Fiona Gold. She remembers them as unconventional; they often arrived at solutions that involved breaking the rules or even the law. But that's what was needed.

Livingston and Wilson were spending a lot of time together. In addition to the HaRAS meetings, they began travelling around North America representing VANDU at various drug-policy conferences.

"We just hit it off," Wilson says. Neither of them remembers a specific moment when they decided they were a couple. There was one night in Ottawa when Wilson showed up at her hotel-room door with a bottle of wine. A short while after that, Livingston invited him for a weekend at her mother's home on Vancouver Island, and Wilson says he thinks he impressed her by making himself useful, fixing things around the house. They were attracted to each other for the same reasons. There was mutual admiration for the other's passion and intelligence. But the relationship was doomed to fail, they both agree now.

"It was always very tumultuous," Wilson says. "I was trying to get straight and trying to have a new relationship at the same time, which is fucking impossible. As they tell you in AA, the only relationship you've got to worry about is breaking up with your heroin. So it did eventually become a terrible scene. But I still love her to death. I think she's wonderful."

––––––––––––

In June 2000, Thomas Kerr was a young researcher working for the Dr Peter Centre, a care provider for people with HIV/AIDS attached to St. Paul's Hospital on the west side of Vancouver's downtown core. He was thirty-three years old, a father to a three-year-old and a newborn, and in addition to his work at the centre, was pursuing a PhD in health psychology. Kerr was working sixty-hour weeks while still trying to devote as much time as he could to his young family. Then he received a call from his boss, Maxine Davis, who asked if he would take on a project for HaRAS.

"I've been working with this group of stakeholders, including Downtown Eastside people, toward trying to maybe set up a safe-injection site," Davis told him. "And everybody's pitched in a couple of thousand dollars, so we have a tiny pot of money."

Kerr was tasked with drafting a proposal for a government-run supervised-injection facility. Whereas the VANDU document that the health board had torpedoed two years earlier was thin, consisting of little more than ideas, the document that Kerr eventually completed was the real deal, a detailed proposal.

It begins by outlining the problems that such a facility aimed to address—primarily overdose deaths and the spread of HIV/AIDS, hepatitis C, and other communicable diseases, but also street disorder and crime. Next, it summarizes existing academic literature related to supervised-injection sites that were operating in Europe. It then details a program model for supervised injection tailored for Vancouver, right through from its establishment and an initial start-up phase to routine maintenance requirements and day-to-day operations. There are even suggested methodologies for reviews of the program.

Kerr remembers the experience as one that nearly killed him.

"One day I was ready to pack it in because I was too freaked out by Ann's anger," he says.

There are two things about Livingston that just about everyone agrees on. The first is that she gets things going. The second is that she is not an easy person to work with. At the time, one of her most important roles at VANDU was to focus Wilson's erratic energy on specific objectives. But now Wilson was often managing Livingston's increasing impatience.

"Dean came to the Dr Peter Centre and asked for me," Kerr says. "He came to my office and said, 'Look, I think you're a good guy and your heart is in the right place. We can work this out and I can manage Ann.'"

Livingston wasn't the only one who was taking out her frustration on Kerr. Even though he was on their side, Kerr was from the medical community, and Downtown Eastside activists did not trust an establishment that had never given them any reason to. Kerr remembers one HaRAS meeting convened to discuss the injection-site proposal when Bud Osborn barged in unannounced and unleashed on the group.

"Bud shows up and started yelling at us: 'You people, you're so fucking stupid!'" Kerr recounts. "I tried to speak reasonably to him, and he just screamed. I was devastated—this was Bud Osborn, an icon, a mythical figure whom I had never talked to before. But then, the next day, he called every single person [who'd been at the meeting] and apologized."

Livingston remembers the pressure that HaRAS placed on Kerr. "Thomas was treated very badly," she concedes today.

Between the Dr Peter Centre and his PhD, Kerr was working twelve-hour days before he would arrive home and have a chance to even start in on the proposal for an injection site. The entire document was written in the middle of the night, with Kerr typing away until three or four in the morning. But by November 2000, it was complete. Vancouver had a proposal for a supervised-injection site, a real one that detailed the nuts and bolts that running such a facility would require. But just as in 1998, the document went nowhere.

"We kind of hit a roadblock," Kerr says. One problem remained unresolved: everything that they proposed was still illegal under Canada's Controlled Drugs and Substance Act. "The police came out and said, 'That's a nice idea, but it's illegal, so we can't allow it,'" Kerr recounts. "And we were really screwed there. Nobody knew what to do about it."

Despite so many sleepless nights and a lack of tangible progress, Kerr maintains that the project was worth his time. It was the first time that anyone in North America had ever asked the fundamental questions about what an injection site would require to operate. He recalls how Fiona Gold sat down with him to itemize and calculate the costs of every single chair, tourniquet, and cotton swab. "Down to the last Band-Aid," he says.

While Kerr's specific proposal was not implemented, a lot of the information it included was used to inform subsequent projects, albeit without any credit. "When they opened Insite ... they used a lot of that material," Kerr says.

The document is also notable for the names it includes on a page listing its contributors. While VANDU's 1998 proposal was almost entirely credited to activists, the HaRAS proposal was backed by health-care professionals like Gold, Kerr, Kerr's boss at the Dr Peter Centre, and other prominent service providers mostly from backgrounds working in HIV/AIDS. It also had the public support of Vancouver's straight middle class via the involvement of From Grief to Action and parents like the Ruttans and the Halls.

"It massively accelerated the conversation," Kerr says. "Now we had a product. We could now talk to politicians about it. And that's what I did. I ran around with it and met with people at the city ... We flew to Ottawa and met with Health Canada to talk to them about it."

Livingston says the HaRAS proposal let them finally move beyond meetings among activists.

"At some point, you have to make the fucking blueprint," she explains. "Otherwise all you're doing is describing things. This made it concrete. This one laid it out. Here's what it's going to look like, here's the training everyone would need. Now we knew how much it was going to cost for staff, what kind of space we were going to need, and how many people per hour could come through. Now we were ready to do the RFP [request for proposals]. We were no longer kidding."

The year 2000 was a big one for PHS, too. Nearly a decade earlier, Mark Townsend had begun raising money for the new Portland Hotel, the purpose-built social-housing complex that he'd convinced the famous architect Arthur Erickson to design.

The new hotel was located just half a block from the old one, but a lot of residents were very anxious about the move. For some, the old Portland Hotel (since renamed the Pennsylvania) was the only stable housing they'd ever known. And many struggled with a mental illness that made a dramatic change difficult to handle. So PHS tried to turn the day into a celebration.

Townsend recalls that moving the entire building in a single afternoon was a logistical challenge but that they were never going to do it any other way. "If you moved your family, you would all move together," he explains. "So when we moved hotels, we did the same thing."

Liz Evans was there with baby Kes on her back that day. He was born just a few months earlier, and PHS tenants adored having a newborn around. "They loved him," Evans remembers. "One very lovely resident named Dave went dumpster diving and brought me an amazing red plastic sixteen-wheeler Tonka truck." Another man gave his penny collection to the child. Others gifted children's books they'd found rooting through the trash. Evans tidied them up and kept every one, reading them to Kes and, later, their daughter Aza.

There were only about thirty full-time staffers working for PHS in 2000, so Evans convinced them to bring their friends and families to help with the move. A parade of shopping carts filled with everyone's belongings stretched from the old hotel to the new one. "We packed up everybody's rooms and moved and had this giant celebration," Evans says. "We even had a rockabilly band in the lobby and balloons." As tenants made their way upstairs and found their new rooms, they discovered a box of chocolates and a welcome bag filled with little soaps and shampoo left on every bed.

"'Finally, I have a home where I can live for the rest of my life,'" Evans remembers one the Portland's first tenants, Stephanie Blais, telling her that day.

Blais had lived at the old hotel since 1992. She says that for everyone, without exception, the best thing about moving was the bathrooms. The old Portland Hotel only had a couple of shared toilets on each floor and the building's ancient plumbing often backed up. They were impossible to keep clean, and there was no privacy.

At the new hotel, every tenant had their own toilet and their own shower. "That first night, the Portland Hotel had the largest hot-water bill in the whole city," Blais jokes. "In the whole province! Having your own shower and your own toilet and everything—it was nice."

Evans had been stuck behind a desk for a couple of years by this point.

"It was awful," she says. "By the time I left the Portland to have Kes, I really didn't return to the frontlines again after that. Of course, I always saw people I knew in the community and still had relationships with loads of them. But my job became running this organization, which I was never prepared to do. Now I was doing scheduling and staff supervision and training and going to endless meetings and writing grants ... I hated it."

Still, Evans kept many tenants as close as family.

Mark Rossiter doesn't fit into any neat profile of the hard-to-house. He's never struggled with a drug addiction. He's different, but his mental illness is not disruptive to others. Evans simply describes him as "a very lost soul."

Rossiter recalls that his parents divorced when he was two, and he went to live with his father. After that, his mother never took much of an interest in him. "The only time I really ever saw her was at birthdays and Christmases," he says. "And then for a while there, she really just dropped out of sight."

In February 1992, Rossiter showed up at the door of the old Portland Hotel and asked if he could have a room. "I remember knocking on the door and out comes this British person with bleached blond dreadlocks," he says. Townsend showed him two rooms they had available that day. Rossiter picked one and has lived with PHS ever since.

"Not too long after that, Liz's mother was here," Rossiter continues. Jane was in Vancouver to visit Evans and had stopped by the hotel to see where she worked. She met Rossiter in the lobby and the two "just hit it off," he says.

Evans remembers introducing them. "He had always wanted a mom," she says. So Evans told Rossiter that he could share hers. "And then he saved up his welfare cheques to buy a plane ticket to England and visited my mom in Frinton on Sea."

By himself, Rossiter travelled to London, England, where Jane was there with a car to pick him up. "I scrimped and saved for one whole year," Rossiter says. Together, they drove back to her little village.

"We went to this little amusement park and we went to a cemetery where she said an actual pirate was buried," he recalls. Rossiter stayed with her there for three weeks and they grew very close.

"She is such a sweetheart," he says, "I never had a sister but now I basically classify Liz as my sister."

Today Rossiter and Jane are still in touch. They regularly mail letters and small gifts back and forth.

Evans finds the whole thing a bit amusing, given that her mother was seldom a consistent presence in her life when she was growing up. But it works for them, she adds.

Chapter 18

Rewiring the Brain for Addiction

M arc Lewis was standing on the corner of East Hastings and Carrall streets outside the old Portland Hotel. It was a sunny evening and the sidewalks were crowded around him. A dealer leaned against the wall of a nearby corner store, repeating the standard Downtown Eastside pitch.

"Rock? Powder? Down?" he called, over and over.

A man in dirty clothes was down on his knees, using his bare fingers to dig cigarette butts from cracks in the sidewalk. A woman jumped from one discarded needle to the next, quickly checking each one for anything left inside that its previous user had missed. Across the street at Pigeon Park, a couple sat together on a bench, injecting heroin in plain sight.

"I was blown away by how down and out people were," Lewis says, looking back on that day. "There were so many people who looked like they were just struggling to hang on."

How did these people get this way?

Lewis is a developmental neuroscientist at Radboud University in the Netherlands. He was visiting Vancouver to promote his book, *The Biology of Desire: Why Addiction Is Not a Disease.* PHS had invited him for a speaking engagement and now was taking him on a tour of the organization's hotels and harm-reduction projects around the Downtown Eastside.

While Bruce Alexander's work on addiction focuses on the environment, and Dr Gabor Maté's explains the significant role that childhood trauma can play in determining one's propensity to develop a drug habit, Lewis's book lays out an argument for addiction as a learned habit. It describes addiction as a normal process of brain development, albeit a destructive one. It's an explanation that can easily apply to an individual who grew up in the most privileged home: an inclination to experiment with drugs can lead to repeat use, at which point the brain will begin to change.

"The repetition of particular experiences modifies synaptic networks," Lewis writes in the book. "This creates a feedback cycle between experience and brain change, each one shaping the other. New patterns of synaptic connections perpetuate themselves like the ruts carved by rainwater in the garden. The take-home message? Brain changes naturally settle into brain habits—which lock into mental habits."

Discussing this theory, Lewis expands on his comparison to rainwater. He imagines water dripping onto a flat surface of mud. As the raindrops repeatedly land in the same place over and over again, they alter the shape of the mud so that it is no longer flat. The falling water ceases to pool evenly. Instead, it flows in the direction that previous drops carved out for it. Tracks have formed in the mud and as the water continues to fall and then find its way into those tracks, they become deeper, precipitating more water to collect there and to continue to dig deeper paths.

"When patterns start to form, they perpetuate themselves. The process is called self-organization," Lewis continues. "It's a feedback cycle. But it's a feedback cycle that takes on a history. It's a feedback cycle for a period of hours or days or weeks, but over months and years, it takes on the shape of a trajectory. A personality pattern. A growth trajectory. It becomes dug in over time so that it becomes increasingly difficult to alter."

The provocative subtitle of Lewis's book, *Why Addiction Is Not a Disease*, is meant to emphasize the extent to which the changes in the brain that occur with a drug addiction also occur as a result of healthy activities, such as exercising.

"To say that addiction changes the brain is really just saying that some powerful experience, probably occurring over and over, forges new synaptic configurations that settle into habits," the book reads. "And these new synaptic configurations arise from the pattern of cell firing on each occasion. In other words, repeated (motivating) experiences produce brain changes that start to define future experiences."

Again discussing the book, Lewis explains that the repeated ingestion of drugs rewires sections of the dopamine system, affecting how humans assess motivations and rewards to prioritize specific short-term gains over long-term outcomes. At the same time, because repeat behaviour is habitual and therefore performed with less evaluation, the prefrontal cortex—the part of the brain responsible for inhibition—is used less. Because it is used less, parts of it will essentially become weaker, an effect called synaptic pruning.

"If you continue to pursue the same attractive goals over and over again and it becomes very habitual to do so, then you're going to prune unused synapses," Lewis explains. "If you are not using that neighbourhood of cells anymore because you just do something and you do it automatically, then those synapses are going to get pruned away, with less traffic and less activation. And before long, they become less accessible."

While ruts have formed along dopamine pathways, causing the brain to prioritize short-term gains, habitual drug use has simultaneously alerted the prefrontal cortex to degrade the strength of inhibition; what makes us think twice about performing an action that's risky or that we expect to have a negative outcome.

Lewis describes the bottom line like this: "Drug use is always a choice, to begin with. An addiction is less of a choice.

"The pure disease-model advocates will say that addicts lose the capacity for choice entirely," he continues. "I don't believe that. I think the choice becomes more difficult. The choice becomes greatly modified by habit, by perspective, and by association and needs and by all kinds of other factors. It is anything but free."

Lewis struggled with addiction himself, spending years on morphine and then heroin. He remained a functional addict, and his book focuses on people like him: middle-class professionals and university students who struggled with very real addictions but who did not fall all the way into a life on the street. He admits he was shocked by what he saw in the Downtown Eastside.

He listened to support workers at Portland's Stanley Hotel relate their tenants' stories of trauma and the difficulties they face feeding drug addictions on the streets. The Stanley's tenants are generally a bit younger than those of PHS's other supportive-housing sites. Many of them struggle with a mental-health condition and are also addicted to crystal methamphetamine, staff explained.

"A lot of people think of addiction in terms of a spectrum, and there we were looking at the end five percent," he says. "I often think of addiction as a choice, to some degree. But at that level of addiction, I saw it as a blight."

Lewis emphasizes that his writing and the theories of Bruce Alexander and Dr Gabor Maté about addiction do not stand in opposition. They exist beside one another, overlapping and interacting in complex ways. "All three of us are all pretty interested in environmental precursors and experiential precursors, how the personality is shaped and moulded by experiences, and how that personality is then more or less prone to becoming addicted," Lewis says.

He acknowledges that his theory—in its simplest form, a focus on the brain's adaptation to repetition—does not directly take into account factors affecting a person's predilection to addiction.

"There are often problems in childhood that lead to depression and anxiety, and those can lead to experimentation, which can lead to this kind of self-medication," he says. "And that realization that people can make themselves feel better, that can lead to addiction."

To continue with Lewis's analogy that compares the brain to a flat surface of mud, environmental factors and experiences of childhood trauma affect the consistency of that surface, making some more susceptible to the effects of rainwater and more likely than others to develop ruts.

"Walking around the streets [of the Downtown Eastside] took me further away from the brain and more out into the social surround," Lewis says. "Unpredictability in childhood or adolescence can lead, through repetition, to a narrowing pathway that has a much more coherent, articulated shape to it, as people move into adulthood."

He acknowledges that in response to his theory of addiction, harm-reduction programs might sound illogical or counter-productive. But Lewis says that is not the case. "You're not doing someone a favour by casting them into street life instead of helping them to feel less tension, less fear, less threatened," he explains.

Lewis emphasizes that those sorts of negative emotions—triggered by a confrontational family intervention, for example, or a run-in with a police officer—do not make an addict less likely to seek drugs. On the contrary, he says, an individual experiencing heightened emotional discomfort will feel a stronger craving for the comfort they find in drugs.

"If people are going to use anyway, they are going to have that reinforcing activity, and it is probably going to be strengthened and amplified by the trials and tribulations people have to go through just to get drugs, to get what they need, and to survive," he says.

Lewis describes harm reduction like this: "It gives them time, gives them a chance, and lets them breathe."

Chapter 19

The Vancouver Agreement

By 2001, activists had the ear of Vancouver's mayor, Philip Owen. Dean Wilson in particular had managed to make an impression, establishing a friendship. For a while, he'd somehow even convinced city hall security to let him pass for pop-in visits on the mayor. "It got to the point where they actually sent a memo around city hall saying that I was not to be left alone with him," Wilson says. "Because they knew I'd get his fucking mind going."

It wasn't always that way.

Owen was a member of the Non-Partisan Association (NPA), a right-of-centre political party with a voter base consisting of Vancouver's wealthy and established. He was born and raised in Vancouver's tony Shaughnessy neighbourhood, where the city's power players have typically lived in big houses with tall hedges around them. For five years in the 1970s, his father, Walter, served as the Lieutenant Governor of BC, the direct representative of the United Kingdom's Queen Elizabeth II. They were as establishment as one family could get. They were also about law and order. Walter's father was a police officer and then the warden of BC's Oakalla Prison (which closed in 1991).

Today, Owen, eighty-four-years-old, recalls his grandfather taking him and his brother on weekend trips to a farm that was connected to the prison and where the inmates worked the land. "My brother and I would run around freely among the prisoners and the cattle and so on," he recounts. "My grandfather, he never said to us that these were bad or rotten people. He told my brother and I that these prisoners were people who had done something wrong and who had to pay a price and that is why they were in there. That made an impression on me," he continues. "These were just people who had broken the law and they had to pay a price to society. But they were all decent people."

Owen was elected mayor of Vancouver in 1993. That year, drug-overdose deaths in the city numbered 201, more than doubling the ninety-one deaths recorded the year before. "I realized that I had to find out what was going on in the Downtown Eastside," Owen says. So he started going for walks.

In the late evenings, usually around ten or eleven, Owen changed out of the slacks and shiny shoes that he wore at city hall and put on a pair of blue jeans and running shoes. Then he would make the short drive from his office to the Downtown Eastside and go for walks, striking up conversations with the people he met on East Hastings Street. It was often raining, he remembers, and so he would carry an umbrella. With his casual appearance and the umbrella over his head, nobody recognized him as the mayor.

"I would just start chatting with people and ask them about who they are and where they were from," Owen says. "One of the first people I spoke to was a girl who was missing a couple of teeth and had her arm in a sling," he remembers. "I said to her, 'Do you have a place to sleep? A place to stay? Do you have contact with your family? Where are you from? How long have you been here? What are you taking?' And you'd hear these stories ... " He trails off.

Owen invited this group of people to casual meetings he convened in different restaurants along Hastings Street. The group nicknamed them "tea parties."

"These women would have a pimp on one side of them and a drug dealer on the other—and they were being killed by those guys," Owen says. "It became apparent to me that this was painful and as the mayor of the city, I saw that we had to do something about that. It didn't take me long to come to the conclusion that the dealer was evil, and for them we had the criminal justice system. And that the user was sick, and for them we had the health-care system."

Bud Osborn's old friend, Donald MacPherson, remembers that Owen was still far from a convert to the cause of harm reduction. But he saw addiction as something that was complicated, and he saw drug use as an act that shouldn't simply be treated as a crime. MacPherson was director of the Carnegie Community Centre during this time, and he recalls that Osborn would drop by his office there and the two of them would brainstorm over how they might get the mayor's attention.

"Bud even went to his church," MacPherson says with a laugh. "Philip went to church every Sunday morning. So Bud went to his church and ended up talking to him one Sunday."

Around the same time, MacPherson resigned from his leadership role at Carnegie. After many years working on the corner of Main and Hastings, he felt burned out. The city liked MacPherson and wanted to keep him around, and so it offered him a deal.

"I said I would work for them again but only on one issue, and that was the drug issue," MacPherson says. "So my boss [at the city's social-planning department] said, 'You take your six months and then come back and we'll see what we can do.'"

In 1998, MacPherson had attended the Portland's harm-reduction conference in Oppenheimer Park. He describes the Out of Harm's Way conference as a "watershed" experience. Then, in the spring of 1999, the International Harm Reduction Conference was in Geneva, Switzerland, and "I decided I had to go," he says. "I went there and I had this epiphany."

In Europe, MacPherson met with politicians, police departments, and health-care providers. He visited harm-reduction programs including various forms of supervised-injection sites that by 1999 had operated for several years. When he returned to Vancouver, MacPherson was a convert.

The report that he produced based on that trip recounts how, a decade earlier, Geneva and Frankfurt had struggled with drug problems very similar to the challenges Vancouver was struggling with in the late 1990s. They had responded with police actions that targeted neighbourhoods where open-air drug markets were known to operate, but also with expansions of health-care services that were consciously low-barrier. Both countries reduced prescription requirements for methadone, for example. They also made significant investments in health care, implementing programs that facilitated access to treatment and other social services in areas where drug users were known to congregate.

Key to both strategies, MacPherson noted, was the establishment of supervised-injection facilities. His report explains how these sites operated, not only as places where addicts could use drugs with clean supplies and under the care of nurses, but also as service hubs that connected people with counsellors, housing, and employment assistance.

"The Swiss and German approaches to substance misuse are based on a four fold approach which includes: Prevention, Treatment, Harm Reduction and Enforcement," it reads.

"In response to increasing health risks of drug use and to public pressure to close down the open drug scene, the Swiss instituted a broad harm reduction approach that resulted in the development of a range of low threshold services or services that were easy for drug users to access. The aim of these services was to bring drug users in contact with the system of care as much as possible and to intervene earlier in their drug use."[42]

Statistics included in the report that were provided by the Frankfurt police department's drug squad show that between 1991 and 1997, when the city's harm-reduction program was implemented, auto thefts declined by thirty-six percent, apartment break-ins by thirteen percent, and assaults by nineteen percent. In addition, police recorded a thirty-nine-percent drop in police-registered first-time consumers of hard drugs.

"There was a significant decrease in the drug activity in the inner city," the report states. "As the users moved into services, primarily the safe injection rooms, shelters and drop-in centres, police were more easily able to separate the addicted dealers (dealers who sell in order by buy drugs) and the non-addicted dealers."

MacPherson was now on a mission. "I was curious and interested before that, but then I became a total crusader," he says. "So I went to the city with one goal: to find a politician who would move this issue ... But I didn't think it was going to be the mayor."

MacPherson recalls the extent to which he was pitching ideas from outside the box of accepted public policy norms of the day. Upon his return from Europe, he sat down with his immediate superior, Vancouver's general manager of community services. In a small

---

[42] Donald MacPherson, *Comprehensive Systems of Care for Drug Users in Switzerland and Frankfurt, Germany* (Vancouver, BC: The City of Vancouver, June 1999).

conference room at city hall, he took her through his report, excitedly jotting down bullet points on a whiteboard that was mounted on the wall there.

On the whiteboard, MacPherson drew a large pyramid. Copying from a policy document that was shared with him by the Swiss, he described the top of the pyramid as "high threshold services" that only reached fifteen percent of people addicted to drugs—expensive rehab facilities, for example. The middle of the pyramid consisted of "medium threshold services" such as methadone, which reached another fifty percent of users. The bottom of the pyramid is where the bulk of the Swiss government's harm-reduction programs fit—needle exchange, low-barrier drop-in centres, street outreach, and supervised-injection facilities. They were the services that connected with the remaining thirty-five percent of drug users that had previously had little or no interaction with the system.

"I was explaining the Swiss approach and drew it up on a whiteboard," MacPherson says. "And when we left the meeting, I said to my boss, 'You're going to leave that up there?' It was like it had to be kept a secret, like we couldn't even be talking about this stuff. It was really radical."

They did leave the pyramid up on the whiteboard. MacPherson's boss was sold, and agreed that his report should go straight to the mayor. "So then I gave him this report, and he loved it," MacPherson says. "Now he had an epiphany."

The next day, Owen was at a conference attended by mayors from cities across the region. In a room full of BC's most powerful politicians, he literally went down on his hands and knees, risking the fabric of an expensive suit, took a piece of large flipchart paper, and sketched out the Swiss triangle of addiction services. MacPherson recalls how the mayor's assistant could barely believe what she saw that day.

"So we had a plan," MacPherson says. "It became a tangible, concrete thing that the mayor's coalition could promote."

Philip Owen was coming around to the idea of harm reduction, but he wasn't convinced overnight. Meanwhile a pair of politicians named Jenny Kwan and Dr Hedy Fry began to cultivate the simpler idea of addiction as a health-care issue.

The three were an unusual group: at the municipal level, Owen belonged to the conservative Non-Partisan Association; representing the province, Kwan was from the left-leaning NDP and had previously been a city councillor with the even more left Coalition of Progressive Electors, the NPA's opponent; and from the federal level, there was Fry, whose Liberal Party of Canada is politically centrist but didn't have a lot in common with either of the other two parties. Three politicians from three different parties representing three levels of government; they called themselves the Vancouver Caucus.

The Downtown Eastside had gained national and then international attention as a place best known for crime and disease, and that had begun to get to Owen. He brought the Vancouver Caucus together to see what they could do about it.

Fry remembers that the first task was to just get Owen and Kwan to speak to one another. "There was no love lost there," she says. "I thought that being a physician was an apt role for me, because I had to be a marriage counsellor and get them to talk to each other."

Kwan's provincial riding included the Downtown Eastside, and she says that Bud Osborn and Liz Evans had convinced her of the merits of harm reduction in the early 1990s, long before most of Vancouver even knew what it was. Back then, Owen was still very skeptical, Kwan says.

It took more than a year of informal "caucus" meetings at city hall, but the three of them finally put something together. In March 2000, they signed the *Vancouver Agreement*. "We agreed that you had to have this comprehensive way of looking at addiction," Fry says. "We agreed that substance misuse was a public health issue and not a criminal issue. But we also felt, in order to keep law and order in the streets, that we needed to make sure that the police were still involved." The *Vancouver Agreement* made addiction a health-care issue for BC and was crucial in laying the groundwork for the city's next policy move on harm reduction.

On September 12, 2000, dozens of drug users from the Downtown Eastside forced their way into Vancouver city hall and made a case for health-care services before Mayor Philip Owen (right). *Photo: Elaine Brière*

While Kwan and Fry were meeting with the mayor, MacPherson had continued to pester him with ideas he'd picked up from Europe. Frankfurt had a drug-policy coordinator, MacPherson told Owen, an office at the municipal level that coordinated all things related to illegal narcotics. He recommended that he occupy the same position with the City of Vancouver. Owen gave it to him.

Along with his new title, MacPherson was given a task: come up with a drug strategy, an entirely new one unlike anything in North America. It was to be a master plan for how Vancouver should respond to the illicit narcotics trade and drug addiction as a health issue—no longer a problem solely left to police.

But why reinvent the wheel? "I went away for two minutes and then came back and said, 'Why don't we just take the Swiss program?'" The Swiss plan was far more progressive than anything that had been tried in North America and, in MacPherson's mind, was just about perfect. They called it *A Framework for Action: A Four-Pillar Approach to the Drug Problems in Vancouver.*

The police were still going to be very much involved—the "enforcement" pillar in MacPherson's strategy—but now they would officially be deployed alongside three other approaches to illicit drugs. Going forward, the city would give equal emphasis to prevention, treatment, and harm reduction. MacPherson defined his key pillar like this: "Harm Reduction is a pragmatic approach that focuses on decreasing the negative consequences of drug use for communities and individuals. It recognizes that abstinence-based approaches are limited in dealing with a street-entrenched open drug scene and that the protection of communities and individuals is the primary goal of programs to tackle substance misuse."

Initial feedback was overwhelmingly positive. "The city manager loved it, the mayor loved it," Macpherson recalls. "So the mayor organized a press conference. But first, he wanted to inform council about what we were doing ... I didn't even get one word out of my mouth. The councillors read it and they said, 'This can't happen.'"

When it came to enthusiasm for harm reduction, a bit of a bubble had developed around the mayor's inner circle. His colleagues on council—even those councillors belonging to his party—still had a ways to go to get onboard. "I went home that night and bought a bottle of wine" MacPherson says. "It was a total disaster."

The next day, however, Owen called MacPherson and told him to get back to work. A second draft incorporated changes suggested by the NPA councillors who had expressed concerns. The order in which the document presented sections on enforcement and harm reduction were swapped, so that enforcement received higher placement, and harm reduction only came in further down. Poems by Bud Osborn that had lined the original draft's margins were cut. Quotes from drug users that included swear words were similarly stripped out. The document was made to look a bit more official, but MacPherson got to keep the guts of it and everything he wanted on harm reduction. His Four Pillars strategy said Vancouver should finally scrap its one-for-one exchange requirements for needles, for example, and work toward establishing a supervised-injection site for intravenous drug users.

"To everyone's credit, it was a better document by the end, because it allowed more people to support it," MacPherson says. "Then Philip had his press conference and we launched it."

A six-month period of public consultation followed. Owen says he attended no less than thirty-seven meetings. MacPherson was at sixty-five, he says.

"Donald put his whole heart and soul into this thing," Owen says. Dean Wilson was often with him to represent the views of drug users directly. And together, the three made a passionate case for the document. "I realized this idea of taking a hard line on enforcement just was not the way to go," Owen says. "That's not the way my grandfather taught me."

Council formally adopted the plan on May 15, 2001. Implementation was still to come. But at least on paper, Vancouver would become the first city in North America to offer government services explicitly designed to make it safer for people to use illegal drugs.

While progress was slowly being made up at city hall, a local film-maker named Nettie Wild had been following Bud Osborn around with an idea of possibly making a film about the drug problem in the Downtown Eastside. Wild was a documentarian, but the two were exploring the idea of a dramatized script loosely based on Osborn's life and poetry. One night in March 2000, Osborn suggested that Wild attend a harm-reduction conference in the basement of St. Paul's Hospital called Keeping the Door Open. Wild didn't think that anything of real interest was going to happen there. She didn't even bother to bring along her cinematographer. But she went along with Osborn's recommendation.

"I walk in and at the front is this woman who I've never met before who was magnificent," Wild remembers. "She was funny and sexy and smart, and she was on fire, absolutely on fire. She said, 'Fuck it. We have to open this thing. No more talking. What are you going to do?'" Wild recognized that she had found something special. She thought that within four months, Ann Livingston would have North

America's first sanctioned supervised-injection site open and that she would have the whole thing on film.

"Eighteen months later, I had many hours of film and no supervised-injection site," Wild says. "But I had had the very real privilege of filming the birth of a social movement."

Fix: The Story of an Addicted City is a gritty portrayal of life in the Downtown Eastside. It's an intimate window into the lives of Ann Livingston and Dean Wilson, a complicated portrait of Mayor Philip Owen, and it powerfully captures the fight VANDU was waging for improved rights for drug users.

The film was originally going to be about Livingston and Osborn. They were still together when Wild began shadowing VANDU members. Then, when Osborn drifted away and Livingston began dating Wilson, Wild was forced to extricate Osborn from the film and refocus its story on Wilson.

"She pulled all his footage out of that film," Livingston says. "They didn't know what to do. She'd thought the film was about me and Bud. When you make a movie, you can't just put all these characters in it, or no one will be able to figure out what's going on. So Bud just fades to nothing."

Wilson wasn't the cause of their break-up, though he was there at Livingston's side as soon as she became available. And while Osborn was once again using heroin, that wasn't what did it either. In the early 2000s, he became intensely introverted and increasingly reclusive. In Livingston's life as well as in Wild's film, Osborn simply seemed to fade away.

Sarah Evans (no relation to Liz), a close friend of Osborn's during those years, agrees that around this time, he made a slow but definitive departure from public life. "His relationship with Ann was wonderful and also problematic," Sarah says. "After they broke up, I think he burned out. He started to focus more inwards. That's when he kind of dropped out of the public scene. I think it was burnout. I hope it was also healing."

Sarah remembers Osborn's focus on drug policy reform as a form of redemption, making amends for the years he had lost to his addictions. But it was also a hard fight and often discouraging. Osborn had embraced drug policy reform as an issue that gave his life meaning; now he began to back away from it as it threatened to overtake him.

"It was what he needed to do to survive," Sarah concludes.

———————

Fix was released in September 2002. Less than two months later, Livingston gave birth to Joey, her fourth child, Wilson's fourth child, and a bit of a surprise to both of them. It was a home birth, Livingston recounts, and one they had to perform in secret. She was forty-eight years old at the time, and so no midwife was willing to be involved unless Livingston agreed to check into a hospital. She refused and finally found a midwife who would remain by her side at home, as long as nobody knew what they were doing.

Wilson was there but remained in the living room playing video games. "Catch the baby!" Livingston remembers the midwife calling to Wilson in jest. "I don't think he was too happy about it," Livingston adds.

The birth went fine, and Joey was born a healthy nine pounds eight ounces.

A few months later, *Fix* was released in theatres across Canada, and Wild took it on the road. Accompanying her were Mayor Philip Owen, Dean Wilson, Ann Livingston, and Joey.

"I used to say, 'I'm on the road with the user, the Christian, the mayor, and the baby,'" Wild says with a laugh. "We would hit a town, and Ann would start organizing drug users, Philip would try to get hold of the mayor and police chief to get them to come to the show, and Dean, if he wasn't able to get a methadone-carry, would be trying to score."

The tour was intensely difficult for Wilson. He was very much addicted to heroin and cocaine and travelling to a different city every few days, often by plane, made it nearly impossible to maintain a steady supply of drugs. In those days, very few doctors were willing to write a prescription for methadone that the patient wasn't forced to ingest on the spot, and so that meant the group's first stop after the airport

Dean Wilson says he's seen a photograph of himself taken during a July 2002 march along East Hastings Street as far away as New York City. *Photo: Elaine Brière*

was a clinic or a hospital to explain Wilson's circumstances and the need for a new prescription. Or he would run around the downtown core of wherever they were until he was able to track down heroin on the street.

"It was horrible," Wilson remembers. "I was on sixty-six airplanes in a year, and I'm a fucking junkie. At one airport, I was in Ottawa, and I was just about to go through security, and this girl goes, 'Hey, there's the junkie from the film! Oh, we loved the film!' I said, 'Gee, thanks.' And then I hear, 'Sir, would you come with us?' I missed my fucking plane. That was just one of the nightmares from that year," he continues. "It was all a nightmare."

Wild recalls a surreal scene in Quebec City where Owen, the conservative mayor, was at the hospital with Wilson, literally pleading with a doctor for methadone so that they could make it to the theatre in time to present the film. Owen, dressed in a smart suit, nearly lost his temper with the doctor on call in emergency. "Listen, can you get a move on?" he snapped. "We've got a show to get on the road!"

That didn't hurry the doctor along, and Owen and Wild were forced to make their way back across town to the theatre without Wilson.

"The show is ticking along, and still there's no Dean. Then, just as we're about to walk out, Dean walks in, he's got his methadone, and he is a rock star." Wilson, who buzzes with energy even when he's sober, could become highly erratic on cocaine and extremely irritable when not on cocaine. Further complicating matters, he and Livingston bickered a lot while on the road with *Fix*, at times prompting Wild to schedule them on alternate nights on the panel for fear they would break into an argument while on stage together.

Somehow, the tour was a success. "Dean was fantastic," Wild says. "He always got to the show on time, but how he got there was sometimes hell for him. The logistics were crazy. That was an eye-opener," she says in retrospect, "about how insane this all was, to make a human being go through all that."

Along with the chaos of life on the road with an addict, Wild recalls a lot of joy and moments of tenderness, much of which came from having baby Joey along on the trip. Livingston and Wilson were both on welfare, and Wild had barely scraped together enough money to give the film its theatrical release, so they couldn't afford to leave Joey with a sitter. He attended each screening with them and was asked to remain quiet for the documentary's ninety-minute duration—not a request with which a toddler will often comply.

After one or two nights of trying to keep him on her lap, Livingston gave up and let Joey roam free. He would pop up on moviegoers' laps and crawl up and down the aisles. "It was gross—he would keep eating popcorn [off the floor], but whatever," Livingston says. "Now Joey's got a fucking immune system like you can't believe."

Wild is modest about the film's impact, but *Fix* had a profound effect on the public debate around harm reduction that was happening right across Canada. In 2004, it won the Canadian equivalent of an Oscar when it received the Genie Award for best documentary. Wilson accepted the award alongside Wild and took the microphone just before the group was ushered off stage.

"In the words of Nancy Reagan," he shouted, "just say no—to the war on drugs!"

The auditorium roared with approving applause.

Back in Vancouver, Joey was home with his grandmother that night. "That's my dad on TV!" he cried with excitement.

Chapter 20
Boston, Massachusetts

A lot of North American cities have a Downtown Eastside. Vancouver's low-income neighbourhood might be a little more concentrated than most, and perhaps a lot friendlier to drug users. But there are similar communities in cities across the continent. In Boston, Massachusetts, they call it "Methadone Mile," or, as Dr Jessie Gaeta prefers, "Recovery Road."

"It's a neighbourhood that has the city's largest safety-net hospital, called Boston Medical Center, as well as a clustering of shelters and addictions services," Gaeta explains. "There are about 1,100 shelter beds within a few block radius, two out-patient methadone programs as well as a detox program, Boston Health Care for the Homeless Program's main hub of activity, and the state's largest syringe-exchange program. All of these things are clustered in this one section of town."

There's a large population of homeless people who sleep on the streets, intravenous drug use is common, dealers work out in the open, and discarded needles are everywhere. It's not pretty, but Gaeta, chief medical officer for the Boston Health Care for the Homeless Program (BHCHP), puts a positive spin on it. She notes that so many people with addiction problems are there, roughly centered around the intersection of Albany Street and Massachusetts Avenue, because it's where there is access to social services, including detox and treatment.

About five years ago, the situation began to grow more desperate.

"In 2012, we started to see data showing us, for the first time, that drug-overdose deaths had really replaced HIV and AIDS-related deaths as the number-one cause of death in our patient population," Gaeta says. "We had been feeling this anecdotally, but it was really striking to see it so starkly in this research. It propelled us to take a critical look at our tactics."

Fentanyl had arrived in Massachusetts. According to a research paper later published by the US Department of Health and Human Services, in 2013, the proportion of opioid-related deaths involving fentanyl—a synthetic drug significantly more toxic than heroin—was thirty-two percent. By 2016, that number had increased to seventy-four percent.[43]

Fentanyl was driving an overall increase in overdose deaths right across the state. In 2012, there were 742 opioid-related drug-overdose deaths in Massachusetts, then 961 in 2013, 1,361 the following year, 1,793 the year after that, and then an estimated 2,069 in 2016.[44]

Each morning, Gaeta parks her car in a lot and then walks two blocks to her office at Boston Health Care for the Homeless Program's headquarters at 780 Albany Street. Along those two blocks of Methadone Mile, she's encountered so many overdoses that she's lost count of the number of times she's stopped to save someone's life. "I carry about six doses of Narcan in my bag to and from work because I come upon overdoses so often," she says.

At Health Care for the Homeless, staff are trained to respond to overdoses and came to do so regularly. But each one required a mad scramble that badly frayed nerves. "We just had an emergency-response team that would stop everything they were doing and respond to a code blue and resuscitate someone who had injected heroin in our bathroom and then we'd ship them off to the ER," Gaeta says. "And that was happening between two and five times a week."

There were a lot of close calls, it was extremely stressful for everyone involved and, for taxpayers, it was expensive. (An emergency room is an extremely inefficient system for dealing with an overdose.)

Gaeta realized it was no longer enough to deploy staff to respond to overdoses in the streets or wait to stumble across a body in their bathroom. They needed an entirely new approach. The problem had become so acute that she felt Boston Health Care for the Homeless had to build some form of infrastructure

---

[43] *Characteristics of Fentanyl Overdose—Massachusetts, 2014–2016* (Atlanta, GA: US Department of Health and Human Services/Centers for Disease Control and Prevention, 2017).

[44] *Data Brief: Opioid-Related Overdose Deaths among Massachusetts Residents* (Boston, MA: Massachusetts Department of Public Health, May 2017).

specifically for the purpose of overdose response.

Directly next door to Boston Health Care for the Homeless Program's head office is the Access, Harm Reduction, Overdose Prevention, and Education (AHOPE) Boston Needle Exchange. Gaeta began to wander over on her lunch breaks and ask the staff there for new ideas about how the system could respond to the growing drug problem. What they really wanted to do was open a supervised-injection site, Gaeta says. But that would have been illegal. So they got creative.

"I started to meet and brainstorm with them—the real harm-reduction specialists in our area—and we came up with this idea: We needed a drop-in centre where people could come right after they'd used," Gaeta continues. "They couldn't legally come to use, but right after they used, they could."

The first speedbump they hit was in finding a location. "We couldn't convince anybody in the neighbourhood to give us space for this," Gaeta says. "The only space we had was our conference room just inside the front door of our building, right next to our lobby." It was the organization's primary meeting space and staff would miss it. But it had everything they wanted for drug users: it was on the ground floor and easily accessible from the street, it was large enough to comfortably sit about ten people, and its proximity to the needle exchange meant the target client population was already there in the immediate vicinity.

Gaeta and her team collected the equipment they needed, which wasn't much. They gathered a series of reclining chairs, a couple of basic medical devices used to monitor vital signs, and resuscitation supplies including oxygen and naloxone. And they were ready to go. "It's pretty simple," Gaeta says. They called it SPOT: the Supportive Place for Observation and Treatment. It opened in April 2016.

Kate Orlin is a registered nurse and the program's first director. She says people arrive at SPOT in a variety of ways. Some walk in on their own accord after realizing the drugs they've taken are more potent or something different than what they're used to. Others are carried in by a friend, sometimes half-dragged. There are also out-reach workers in the area who use wheelchairs to bring people they've found on the street to SPOT.

"If somebody has used something during the day and they are looking pretty drowsy, we place them in a chair and put a vital-sign machine on them," Orlin says. "With that, we're able to monitor their blood pressure, heart rate, and oxygen, and we count their respiratory rate continually. So we watch them there and can do interventions based on what their vitals are doing. They stay as long as they need. If somebody wakes up and is ready to go, we'll let them go."

Orlin credits their success to word of mouth. Early clients vouched for SPOT, and news spread that users could trust the staff. Reluctance to visit the site faded away. "A lot of people come in, and other people in the room say, 'This is a space where you can trust [the staff], you can be honest with them. You're safe in here. These are good people.'" Those positive relationships led to a number of unintended benefits. Orlin remembers one morning in June 2017 when she showed up at work to find a woman waiting for the clinic to open.

"She sleeps outside and uses outside, and she was sexually assault-ed," Orlin begins. "And this was the first place she came to seek care." SPOT staff took the woman inside and into an adjacent room where there was privacy.

"First we listened to her story," Orlin says, "and tried to remind her that all of what has happened isn't her fault, because she had a lot of guilt and shame about what happened. And then on top of that, she was using heroin and pills and stuff to combat what she'd just gone through."

Once the woman's immediate needs were met, SPOT staff began talking about what happens next. They wanted her to go across the street to the emergency room, but the woman was reluctant. There was an outstanding warrant for her arrest and if she told doctors that she'd been assaulted, she was worried they'd call the police. So SPOT phoned ahead to the ER and ensured that the woman would receive treatment without the hospital involving law enforcement. They also gave her a backup plan: if she still felt uncomfortable when they took her over to emergency, she could leave and come right back to SPOT and they would examine and treat her there (not something the clinic is designed for but something it could do in a pinch). In the end, the woman was treated in the emergency room.

Orlin says that SPOT is "serving as a place for some of our most vulnerable patients." It's an interesting unintended benefit, but most of SPOT's successes are much simpler.

"People wake up and they don't remember how they got here. They'll say, 'Oh my god, you just let me rest in here? And now you're giving me a coffee and a sandwich? Thank you.' Or people wake up and say, 'Without you, I would be dead.'"

Chapter 21

The Hair Salon

At ten on a Saturday morning in September 2000, more than 1,500 people gathered in the parking lot of Strathcona Elementary School, two blocks south of Oppenheimer Park.

While Mark Townsend and Bud Osborn were organizing protests in the streets, business owners from the Downtown Eastside's neighbouring communities of Chinatown, Gastown, and Strathcona were doing the same.

The hundreds of people who met at the school that morning came together from those neighbourhoods—which formed a ring around the Downtown Eastside—to create an umbrella organization called the Community Alliance. The crowds that its leaders could call to the streets vastly outnumbered those that VANDU could gather, and they had the police on their side.

"Evidence of the growing chasm between Downtown Eastside residents and merchants fed up with drug-fuelled mayhem and the area's drug users and their allies came face to face in the street for the first time Saturday," reads a newspaper account of the day.[45]

"Although billed as peaceful, the march was tense from the beginning as social activists faced off against up to a dozen private security guards hired by Chinatown merchants," reads another article. "Police had no problem with the leather-gloved security workers, who could be seen frequently pushing activists and media out of the way."[46]

A third headline from two months prior sums up a sentiment that had been building in some parts of the city: "Fed-up Merchants Tell City to Arrest Junkies."[47]

---

[45] Mike Howell, "Downtown Eastside Merchants, Residents Confronted on March," *Vancouver Sun*, October 2, 2000.

[46] Clare Ogilvie, "Cops Arrest Anti-March Protesters," *Province*, October 1, 2000.

[47] Shane McCune, "Fed-up Merchants Tell City to Arrest Junkies," *Province*, August 10, 2000.

From the school, the crowd marched through the Downtown Eastside to Vancouver's old convention centre on the downtown waterfront. Their private security guards formed a line at the front.

Mark Townsend had obtained a map of the route they had planned and, with VANDU's help, set up stations along the way where volunteers explained different harm-reduction programs. "I thought what we should do is march with them for a bit and do a counter-demonstration," Townsend remembers. "So if a journalist came and asked a question, at least their report would say, 'Some people said this and some people said that.'" Portland staff and allies equipped with walkie-talkies hid in vans along the Community Alliance's protest route. As marchers drew near to each van, PHS staff jumped out to present an opposing side for the cameras. Their numbers were far fewer that day—only a few dozen compared to the 1,500 marching against them—but Townsend's strategic organizing ensured that they were at least heard.

"Eight police officers on bicycles kept the two groups separate, but tensions ran so high that within three blocks paddy wagons had to be called in and the first arrests were made for breach of the peace," another newspaper article reads. "Each arrest was met with loud cheers from the [Community Alliance] marchers. As the wagon moved away, the protesters inside could be heard chanting and banging on the doors."[48]

Bryce Rositch, an architect and the head of the Gastown arm of the Community Alliance, is quoted in media reports from that day: "We're not against any specific program or facility or anything," he said. "What we're saying is that there's been so much here now, it truly is saturated. That's what we're saying, 'no more in our neighbourhoods.'"[49]

"There is more to the community than drug dealers and others," Rositch said, quoted in another report. "We all have a responsibility to help those in need, but we also have a responsibility to make sure our communities are safe."[50]

Richard Lee was a vocal spokesperson for the Community Alliance

---

[48] Ogilvie, "Cops Arrest Anti-March Protesters"

[49] Howell, "Downtown Eastside Merchants ..."

[50] Ogilvie, "Cops Arrest Anti-March Protesters"

and the leader of its strongest contingent, the Chinatown Merchants Association. Today, he remembers the Community Alliance as the underdog.

"At the city, we had no friends, in the provincial Liberal government, we had no friends, in the federal government, we had no friends," Lee says. "All we wanted was for treatment to be the ultimate goal that we were working toward. But the other side was not prepared to yield to that. At that point, VANDU was a strong voice and they wouldn't concede that."

Lee remembers racial slurs lobbed his way at that protest and others like it. There was vandalism committed against the Chinese Merchant Association's headquarters. And Lee said people called his home late at night only to hang up when he answered the phone. But he said he holds no grudges.

"With the numbers that we had, the march could be considered a success," Lee says. "But in the end, they won the day."

———————

In May 2001, Mayor Philip Owen had successfully pushed his councillors to adopt the Four Pillars framework and its new direction for the city's response to drug addiction. Included in the plan was a pledge to establish a task force that would "consider the feasibility of a scientific medical project to develop safe-injection sites or supervised consumption facilities in Vancouver." But in 2002, there was an election and Owen didn't run for office.

He was succeeded by Larry Campbell, the coroner who had attended that meeting at the Carnegie Community Centre alongside Ann Livingston and Melissa Eror, in 1994. Campbell was onboard with harm reduction, and during his election campaign he promised to open an injection site. But drug users didn't trust him, or any politician, by this point.

On April 7, 2003, it appeared their lack of faith was justified. "Police on horseback, motorcycles and foot patrol launched an unprecedented block-by-block campaign Monday to rid this city's notorious Downtown Eastside of drug dealers," reads one newspaper's report.[51]

---

[51] Petti Fong, Frances Bula, "Crackdown Targets Drug Dealers," *Vancouver Sun*, April 8, 2003.

Campbell had increased the number of police officers assigned to the Downtown Eastside from twenty to sixty.

A few weeks earlier, Livingston and Osborn's old friend, Dave Diewert, had scraped together some money and rented another Downtown Eastside storefront for VANDU. This one was at a prime location, 327 Carrall Street, just beside Pigeon Park and across from the old Portland Hotel. Their plan was to use it to host VANDU's hepatitis C subgroup meetings, strategize actions on low-income housing and gentrification, and to host weekly get-togethers for coffee, which they called "Not Just Coffee." Methamphetamine had arrived and created a new population of drug users in the Downtown Eastside, and so another VANDU subgroup consisting of members addicted to this relatively new drug also made use of the storefront. They named the new space the Carrall Street Centre for Compassion, Solidarity, and Resistance.

The place was a dump. It didn't even have functional plumbing. Livingston remembers that the toilet in the back was elevated because it used gravity to evacuate waste. Outside, an old sign painted onto the brick is still partly visible today. "Louvre Rooms 35 cents a night," it reads.

As shoddy as it was, Livingston had a bit of a reputation by this point, and was worried that the landlord wouldn't rent it to her. "I went to Dave Diewert and said, 'Look, I've done this enough times now so I'm worried, if the lease is in my name, that there's going to be a problem,'" she says. "This was a war. We had been kicked out of the Dunlevy place because the police had gone to the landlord. So I said, 'Dave, if you put it in your name, then it won't be in mine.'"

For a while, their landlord had nothing to fear. The storefront on Carrall really was a simple meeting place. Then the new mayor sent his occupation force into the Downtown Eastside and Livingston decided she would turn 327 Carrall into a political attack.

"Adding those forty cops was the deal-breaker," she says.

Livingston was at home when she received a phone call telling her they had arrived.

"Joey was a baby, under a year old, and couldn't walk. So I threw him in the stroller, called Bryan [Alleyne] and Dean [Wilson], and said 'We've got to go do this.'"

Livingston remembers that it felt like a foreign military had descended on the neighbourhood. "There was almost no one around," she says. When someone did venture out of the hotels, they were questioned by police. It was pouring rain, and officers were forcing people to lie face-down on the wet sidewalks and remain there while they were put through body searches. "It was like an occupation."

A related police operation saw 162 arrest warrants issued, most of them for low-level dealers who were addicts themselves.[52] Drug users had been pushed to the streets and the alleys, and now the cops were taking those away from them. Diewert explains that VANDU and the entire Downtown Eastside felt betrayed. They had supported Campbell during his campaign for mayor. And while they knew the Four Pillars drug strategy was one-quarter enforcement, it was supposed to be equal parts prevention, treatment, and harm reduction. But all they'd got was more police. "It was getting unbearable," Diewert says. "He [Campbell] brought more cops into the Downtown Eastside and that was having a detrimental effect on people using. It was creating more harmful situations for them."

Since police were taking away the alleys, VANDU would give drug users a safe space indoors: 327 Carrall Street. Except they couldn't pay for it. VANDU was fully funded by the health authority at this point, and if it opened an illegal injection site, it would very likely lose that money. Another unlikely ally emerged: a backroom operator from the former mayor's conservative Non-Partisan Association, Philip Owen's son, Christian.

"In the waning days of my father's time at city hall, there was an election," Christian begins. "Larry Campbell said that he would push for the Four Pillars. Still, in many people's eyes, it was a political third rail that was rolled up in the harm-reduction issue. And so the whole initiative at 327 Carrall, as far as I was concerned, was to make him make good on his political promise to open Insite."

Christian started making twice-weekly visits to 327 Carrall to identify where he could best help out. He wasn't a nurse who could treat abscesses or an activist who had credibility on the street. "I was

---

[52] Petti Fong, "Drug Operation Results in 162 Arrest Warrants," *Vancouver Sun*, April 8, 2003.

a suit," Christian says. "I couldn't really add any value."

So he played to his strengths. "Initially, I wrote a personal cheque, just to make sure we could pay the rent and keep it alive for thirty days," Christian says. "Then my thought was, 'I've got to go out and raise money to keep the lights on and to keep this going.' We had no idea, in that moment, how long we'd be in business," he continues. "So it was done with the view that this was going to be here until we got what we wanted."

Once again, Livingston was running an illegal-injection site. "The scene was pretty squalid," she remembers. "We'd made it as nice as we could, but it was still really old and we didn't have any money."

The property was split into two large rooms. At the front, there was a big window that faced onto Carrall Street. It had a table near the door where a VANDU member checked people in and a larger table that people collected around for meetings. The back room was once a kitchen and still had a sink that produced water, sometimes. That's also where the bathroom was, in an adjacent cubby. Livingston had someone cut the bottom of the door off so they could see if anyone in there overdosed, and that became the injection room. Then, before long, the entire back half of the property was being used as a space for supervised drug use.

The Carrall Street Centre for Compassion, Solidarity, and Resistance operated as a collective where everyone who hung out there pitched in to keep the place relatively clean and orderly. A nurse named Megan Oleson put in more hours than anyone else. (She declined requests for an interview.) Coming in a close second was another young woman named Jill Chettiar.

She was working for the Portland Hotel Society at the time, helping them with administration. Chettiar says that 327 Carrall showed just how easy it could be to establish a space for injection-drug use that was much safer than the alleys. "It was just a hang-out space, and there was an injection room in the back," she explains. "It was pretty casual. There wasn't a ton of rules. We really weren't asking for the world," Chettiar continues. "This is how fucking easy it is, guys. This is just a room. We painted it, and we're keeping it clean. It's literally just this easy."

She recalls how the arrival of meth made 327 a little more chaotic a space than Livingston's previous two injection sites. "I remember so many times hanging out with Megan when we would just look at each other and shake our heads," Chettiar says, laughing. "Like, 'What's going on? What are we doing? Did we just hang out with Christian Owen? And did he just make coffee for an injection site that's open illegally?'"

In a similar vein, Livingston recalls how much the Carrall site's injection-drug users loved having baby Joey around, who she jokes was there "building up a strong immune system."

"The news guys were there one day, and they wanted it to be all dark and dreary, but then there was this baby being passed around," Livingston says. "It really fucked up the ambience thing they were going for."

Dean Wilson laughs at those memories. "CNN comes up and there's this couch there and there's fucking two-year-old Joey, playing with his blocks in the injection site," he says.

Christian Owen put up a lot of money to keep 327 Carrall open for as long as it was. Today he maintains that his motivations were mostly political, aimed at holding Larry Campbell to his promises and ensuring that his father's goal to see a legitimate injection site in Vancouver was realized. But Livingston suggests there were also more personal reasons for Christian's interest in harm reduction.

"Their family friends had a daughter," she explains, "who got addicted to heroin. She was only nineteen when she died in this neighbourhood in an SRO ... From Christian's point of view, it was the girl next door who he grew up with. That was the connection."

Christian acknowledges that story. He even brought the girl's mother, a registered nurse, onboard as a financial backer of the site. But he says it wasn't why he paid the rent at 327 Carrall.

"We just knew it was the right thing to do," Christian says.

For the next several months, police swarmed the Downtown Eastside. The Carrall Street injection site received a low degree of harassment during this period. Officers parked their squad cars directly out front as a way to dissuade drug users from hanging out there. But it nevertheless remained open as a high-profile thorn in the side of Larry Campbell's new administration at city hall.

While those battles raged in full view of the public, the Portland Hotel Society had initiated a covert operation.

By 2002, PHS was receiving millions of dollars in government funding every year. But Evans and Townsend were still running it like the small nonprofit they had formed a decade earlier. The government didn't like that and was intensifying pressure for more formal organization.

In response, Townsend recalls how he and Evans sat down with Dan Small and Kerstin Stuerzbecher to essentially fabricate official duties to list alongside everyone's name in an effort to placate their bureaucratic overlords.

"They kept telling us they wanted an org chart and so I said, 'Fuck you, we'll send you an org chart,'" Townsend says.

Small remembers the meeting the four of them held as a little more productive than that. "We broke up the organization's key roles for the directors," he says. "Everyone would have a cluster of responsibility." Evans would manage staff, essentially functioning as the Portland's human-resources department, leading training sessions, negotiating contracts, and that sort of thing. She also liaised with political partners. Much to her disappointment, it all inevitably left her with a lot less time with tenants. Stuerzbecher took the lead on program implementation and became increasingly busy with budgets and financial planning. Townsend would continue to steer the organization on political activism and also manage nuts-and-bolts operations and the maintenance team. And Small was assigned "the torture of VANDU," in Townsend's words, "attending board meetings and making sure that no one was murdered."

"Under my umbrella was all the most controversial stuff," Small says. "All the nuclear radiation: VANDU, needle exchange, and a safe-injection site."

"We decided at that meeting that we were going to do it," he continues. "That we were really going to do it."

Small and Townsend went for a long walk around the city one day, scouting an appropriate location. In the end, they settled on the exact spot where they had begun their search: the 100 block of East Hastings Street. This was the heart of Vancouver's drug scene. Bud Osborn had named an entire collection of his poetry for this strip of pavement: *Hundred Block Rock*, published by Arsenal Pulp Press in 1999.

"Hundred block rock," begins the poem from which the collection takes its name.

      shoot up shock
        police chief
          cold grief
            war on drugs
              pull the plug
                clean it up
                  nowhere to go
                    ground zero
                      overload jail
                        rock and wail
                          where a dopefiend stood
                            comin soon
                              to your neighbourhood

      blue teardrop tattoos
        what's the plan
          tear it down
            let 'em drown
              too much reality
                fixin the alley
                  blood streamin
                    naked girl tweakin
                      hundred block reelin
                        vancouver's first
                          western world's worst
                            hiv
                              public health emergency
                                fuck 'em around
                                  till their lives burst [53]

---

[53] Bud Osborn, "hundred block rock," *Hundred Block Rock* (Vancouver, BC: Arsenal Pulp Press, 1999), p. 101.

At the 100 block's east end is the Carnegie Community Centre and the open drug market of Main and East Hastings. One block in the other direction is the old Portland Hotel and Pigeon Park, another hub for dealers. On the 100 block itself is the Portland's Washington Hotel and the adjoining Washington Needle Depot, as well as two more PHS buildings: the Sunrise and the Roosevelt. There's also the Balmoral Hotel, the Regent, and Brandiz—three notorious private SROs long known as a few of the city's very worst hotels. Hundreds of intravenous drug users were concentrated on the 100 block, so it wasn't like opening an official injection site there would attract many more. They were all already there, so why not give them a place where they could use inside instead of leaving them in the alleys?

"Mark and I looked around the city for the right area where this would make sense," Small says. "Our vision was to put it in the eye of the hurricane, where the people are."

There were a few storefronts tucked in between the 100 block's rundown hotels that might have worked. But only one building was really large enough for what they had in mind. It was 139 East Hastings, a nondescript three-storey building positioned almost exactly in the centre of the block's north side. It was so ordinary looking that Townsend felt like he'd never even seen it before that day.

"I'd never even really noticed this fucking place, and it's right between the Washington and the Sunrise, which we were operating," he says. "This building was like God had just plunked it down in the middle of the block." There was a man hosing down the sidewalk. Townsend thought he was the building's janitor and started to chat with him. "Who owns this building and what's the story?" Townsend asked. "He explains that he owns the building. He's lived there for twenty years, he's brought his daughters up here, they've all gone on to UBC, and now he lives on one floor and uses the SRO rooms on the other floor for people he tries to help out." That was Kwan Lee, or "the Korean General," as Townsend later came to affectionately call him.

Technically, the building has two addresses, but they're connected on the inside. On the ground floor, Lee sold sandwiches out of one of them and at the other, pizza by the slice. He lived with his wife and two children on the second floor. The third floor was an SRO, where

Lee rented small rooms to the same sort of down-and-out tenants that occupied the rest of the block.

When Townsend and Small struck up that first conversation with Lee, they hadn't yet agreed on how they were going to convince him to offer his building to a bunch of drug addicts. At one point, they thought it might be smart to hide their intent to open an injection site and draft the lease with vague language about a health-care facility. "But we kind of wanted to have a partner on this," Townsend says.

On the street, they continued to chat with Lee. It turned out that while they had never noticed him, he had been keeping an eye on the Portland Hotel Society. "I've watched you for a long time down here, and you're the only people who do anything," Lee said.

Townsend and Small caught each other's eyes. "What are we going to do?" Townsend remembers Small's glance communicating. "Are we going to rent the store without saying what we're going to use it for, or are we going to just go for it and lay it all out on the line? And so we laid it all out on the line for the guy."

Lee didn't know what a supervised-injection site was. He was familiar with the drug issue, given where he lived. But he'd never heard of giving people addicted to drugs a safe space to inject them.

The previous year, Kerstin Stuerzbecher had travelled to Frankfurt, Germany, and Zurich, Switzerland, and Small had visited Sydney, Australia, to see the injection sites already operating in those cities. He shared photographs with Lee, explained how the facilities worked, and described how those health-care programs operated in contrast to the scenes of squalor and misery that Lee witnessed outside his storefront every day.

"We went into his office and looked at all that," Small says. "We had a glass of orange juice together—he made homemade orange juice—and we talked about this."

At this stage, the Portland's injection site was not going to be the Portland's. PHS was responsible for housing hundreds of people, the vast majority of whom struggled with a mental illness, a serious addiction issue, or both. If PHS opened an illegal injection site and the government came down hard on them for it, all of that would be at risk. By 2002, it looked like all three levels of government were just about ready to see someone open a sanctioned injection site. But that was far from certain. At the same time, Evans, Townsend, Stuerzbecher, and Small had agreed they were done waiting. This injection site was going to open even if government support never actually materialized. And so to protect PHS and its tenants, Small established a separate nonprofit organization called Health Quest.

"It was another avatar or firewall to protect the Portland," Small explains. "Because we didn't know what was going to happen."

Health Quest didn't have any money or support from government—no one at city hall even knew it existed. That made it a risky partner for Kwan Lee.

"If the shit hits the fan, I will decloak, and I give you my word, I will take responsibility," Small reassured him. "It will be me in the press, not you."

Over the course of a week or so, they met repeatedly over orange juice.

"I believe that we will get this done," Small told Lee. "I believe it will be legal eventually. We may have to set it up illegally, temporarily. It's my view that we will get the grant for it, eventually, to pay for a lease. But if we don't, I need your word that you will rip the lease up."

If the whole venture collapsed, Lee would have moved his family and shut down his pizza and sandwich businesses for nothing. Or worse, he would be sent to jail. The risk for Lee and his family was considerable, but today he remains exceedingly modest about the whole thing.

"I'd been there a long time, long enough to know the neighbourhood," he says. "And they were nice people, working hard ... Bottom line is, I leased them the space, just as I would have leased it to anybody."

They signed the deal in his office on the second floor of the building where Insite still stands today.

"Kwan took a leap of faith that this was the right thing," Small says.

———————

"Now, obviously, you were not just allowed to build a supervised-injection site," Townsend begins. You are allowed to build a hair salon.

In February 2003, Liz Evans, former Vancouver Area Network of Drug Users president Bryan Alleyne (centre), and Don Baker posed for a news photographer inside the "Hair Salon," the Portland Hotel Society's unsanctioned supervised-injection site.
Photo: Peter Battistoni / Vancouver Sun

So that's what they called it: the Hair Salon, operated by Health Quest. Townsend called in the maintenance team.

Christoph Runne recalls the task as absolutely daunting. "For some reason, we only had ten days to turn it into a safe-injection site," he says, "or a hair salon, I mean ... So we were working through the night."

The project's tight schedule is similarly the first thing Phong Lam remembers about it. That, and then its secrecy. "We worked day and night," Lam says. "Quietly, we worked inside the building, day and night. If you were tired, you went home, got some rest, and came back and continued working on it."

Small notes that they actually only renovated half the ground floor during this initial phase of construction. The sandwich shop remained as Lee had left it when he'd closed the place up a few weeks earlier. The Hair Salon was built where the pizza place had stood. They ripped out the oven and sneaked debris out at night, through the exit to the back alley. Out on the 100 block of East Hastings, there wasn't a hint of anything going on.

"Loose lips sink ships," Small says with a smirk. "The inner circle of people at the Portland didn't tell anyone. There was zero leakage."

Lam remembers it was as if an injection site appeared out of nowhere. "Nobody knew about it," he says. "Then Mark and everyone got together at four or five a.m. He got a disposal truck to come and take down the awning and wrap up. And then we were done. Like a surprise."

Small remembers the Hair Salon really as not that different from how Insite looks today. There was a lobby at the front, larger than one might expect in an effort to dissuade crowds from forming outside on the street. Then, past the lobby, was the injection room. On the left side was a space for staff, and against the wall on the right was a row of sectioned booths. Each one had a mirror, a small sink, steel table, and a chair underneath. For a demonstration that PHS organized, each booth also had a bouquet of pink tulips.

"It was exactly like Insite is today except cheap and cheerful," Small says.

Today, Lam reflects back on the crosses he nailed together and then helped plant in Oppenheimer Park, the coffins they built for a march on city hall, the hypodermic needle they assembled that was so long it could block six lanes of traffic, and a dozen other crazy tasks that Townsend and Small had assigned to the maintenance team over the years. The Hair Salon—building an injection site from start to finish in ten days—was by far the most challenging, he says.

"That is the best memory I have," Lam adds. "Making it happen."

Nobody ever used drugs at the Hair Salon. A few weeks later, everything they'd constructed as the Health Quest injection site was ripped out and destroyed.

Chapter 22

Establishing Insite

During his 2002 campaign for mayor, Larry Campbell had pledged to open a supervised-injection site by January 1, 2003.

Chris Buchner, the health authority employee on whose desk that promise landed, remembers exactly where he was when he heard Campbell say that for the first time. He was in his office at the authority's headquarters, just a twenty-minute walk south of the Downtown Eastside. Buchner stood up from his desk and walked over to the office of his boss, Heather Hay. "Well," Buchner said, "it's going to be him sitting with some rigs and spoons in a chair down on the corner, because nobody else is going to be able to be there with him by January 1."

Little did they know, the Hair Salon was ready to go.

The night that Campbell was elected mayor, his victory party was held at the Vancouver Public Library. The event was open to the public, and Dan Small dropped by to offer him congratulations. "I walked up to Larry, and I whispered in his ear, 'We already have the safe-injection site,'" Small says.

Campbell didn't respond. His eyes just grew a little wider.

"It already exists," Small told him, "and I've got the keys for it in my pocket. If you want to see it, come and see it."

"He just looked at me kind of aghast," Small remembers. He handed Campbell his business card and walked away. (Today, Campbell maintains that he wasn't totally surprised. He claims that while he didn't know exactly what the Portland was up to, he knew they were working on an injection site somewhere.)

A week or so later, news that the Portland had built an injection site finally leaked out. In 2017, Mark Townsend was still mystified as to how. The maintenance team did not talk. News about Portland black ops had never leaked before.

It turns out that shortly after the Hair Salon renovation, an acquaintance of Dean Wilson's had broken into the place. He had noticed that Kwan Lee and his family had moved out and, late one night, jimmied open the back door, hoping to scavenge anything they had left behind. But instead of the remnants of a pizza shop, he found a brand-new—he didn't know what he had found. But when he described it to Wilson the following day, Wilson recognized what it was. He told Ann Livingston, and the Downtown Eastside rumour mill spread the news from there.

"I told Ann, and then the world knew," Wilson says with a laugh.

VANDU's guerrilla injection sites were one thing. They were really nothing more than storefronts, and police knew to look the other way. But if PHS—a government partner receiving millions of dollars of taxpayers' money every year—opened an illegal, purpose-built injection site, that would be a scandal. "This was like having a time bomb," Townsend says. "It was a functional, actual site. It existed and we had a lease for it. So it was dangerous."

As they inched closer to opening, Small remembers that the pressures building against them grew more intense. "Things start to heat up," he says. "For example, I was invited to the US Consulate. They knew what was going on and that this was about to happen."

Like children called to the principal's office, Small and Evans complied with the invitation. There to meet them was David Murray, US President George W. Bush's deputy director of the White House Office of National Drug Control Policy. "He said—twenty times—'Don't get me wrong, sovereignty is important. But if you think, for one moment, that we're going to allow this, you've got another thing coming.'"

Evans remembers the experience like something out of a movie. "It was like, 'What the hell? He's threatening sovereignty! How is that even possible?'" Evans says. "We had to sit there and listen to the guy lecture us for an hour and a half and threaten us. And then we left and were like, 'What the fuck was that?' And then we started to laugh and ignored it."

Small similarly remembers they laughed about the US Consulate's warnings, but adds that they did so somewhat nervously. "There were real risks," he explains. "I had to tell my family, 'I don't know what's going to happen.' And I wasn't being melodramatic. I didn't know if I was going to be put in jail."

Evans notes that the meeting at the US Consulate did remind them of the extent to which their plans to open an injection site challenged what was a core component of US law-enforcement's very identity. "It was directly opposed to the philosophical and political positions that the United States had adopted, which was to fight against drugs. Drugs were the problem," she says. "Anything that would be seen as condoning the use of drugs—harm reduction and Insite—was diametrically opposed to their philosophical beliefs."

Would the authorities actually let them succeed with such a challenge?

Despite intense uncertainty, there were reasons for optimism. The Vancouver mayor had won an election promising an injection site, the province had come onboard shortly after, and now the regional health authority—the actual partner and financial backer that an injection site would require to operate—was finally taking a tangible interest, albeit hesitantly.

By this time in 2003, the Vancouver-Richmond Health Board had become Vancouver Coastal Health (VCH). Dr Patricia Daly, then its medical-health officer and director of communicable diseases, remembers the authority's involvement as reluctant. "In the establishment of Insite, I would not say that Vancouver Coastal Health was the one that said, 'We're going to do this. We're going to take the lead,'" she says, somewhat diplomatically. "If you look at our leadership, they were always a little bit nervous about it."

Daly was an early supporter of Insite but explains that, for her bosses at VCH, a supervised drug-injection facility was just one small piece of a very big puzzle for which they were responsible. VCH had a staff of more than 10,000 people as well as 2,000 physicians, operated thirteen hospitals, and was providing care to nearly fifty percent of BC's population of more than four million. The Downtown Eastside was always on the front page of the newspapers, but never the only file on a VCH executive's desk. "I don't recall anyone saying that we don't want to do it," Daly says. "But I think the higher-up leadership were a little anxious about [Insite] ... It was a little out of their comfort zone."

VCH did eventually pay for Insite and staff nurses there, but Daly emphasizes that PHS and the community made the injection site happen. She sums up the health authority's role like this: "They kind of went along for the ride."

Chris Buchner says the Hair Salon was the catalyst for Insite. "That was really what triggered us moving forward with the application," he says. The day they first heard it existed, he and Heather Hay jumped in a car and drove to the 100 block to take a look. Townsend was there with Evans that afternoon, and together the four of them took a walk through the maintenance team's renovation.

"It was clear it was just a demonstration site," Buchner remembers. "It was all built with IKEA. But, lo and behold, they had built an injection site," he continues. "That said, we had to rip it out and start from scratch. But it made the point that we were going to do this. It really removed any question—and removed the health authority from getting caught up in some of the things that would be more difficult for a health authority to do, like find a suitable location, like negotiate this with a landlord, and like getting building permits."

To redo all the work that the maintenance team had just finished, the health authority tapped a local architect named Sean McEwan, a good friend of Townsend's who had volunteered his time and helped PHS with a number of projects before. "I was hired by the health authority, and they put together a project schedule to make Larry Campbell's promise coincide with how they wanted to address the drug crisis in the Downtown Eastside," McEwan says. "So we had to get this site open by September. And I started work in March."

That deadline was luxurious compared to the ten days that the maintenance team had had to throw together the Hair Salon. But this time, they would be building an injection site within the bureaucratic and legal frameworks of three levels of government—something that had never been done before anywhere in North America, and for which the procedures had never been written.

"We didn't even know if we could get a development permit for this," McEwan recalls. "I said to the health authority folks, 'Well, this might work. We might be able to build this thing in four months if we hire a construction manager right now and get the right guy. But what we don't have any time for is drawings, for example.' And they said, 'Oh, well, just do what you can do.'"

Here McEwan gives credit to Mayor Larry Campbell. "He phoned down to the director of planning and said, 'I want this development permit, dammit,'" McEwan recounts. "So everything was to the letter of the city regulations but in the shortest time possible. We had a development permit and a building permit issued on the same day within four weeks of getting the process started."

Campbell remembers that he made it crystal clear with every department at city hall that nothing was to get in the injection site's way. But today he's also quick to give credit to his predecessor, Philip Owen. "It would never have happened without Philip," Campbell emphasizes. "He really laid the groundwork. People might think I'm just saying that, but it would never have opened without Philip Owen. Period."

Back in the Downtown Eastside, McEwan worked with Townsend and Small on the design and got moving on construction. Meanwhile, Buchner and Hay still had to figure out how the whole thing would come together and open without anyone breaking any laws.

How do you allow people carrying drugs to congregate inside a government-funded facility without compelling police to enforce laws prohibiting the possession of narcotics? What if a staff member at the injection site touched a client's drugs? Could they then be charged with possession? What if a staff member touched someone's drugs and then handed them to the client they belonged to? Would that qualify as a trafficking offence? What sort of registered nurse would take a job at a facility where they could face time in prison for accidentally picking up a flap of heroin off the floor?

The answers to those questions were in Ottawa, where Canada's drug laws are written.

Bud Osborn and then Dean Wilson had worked on the drug issue at the federal level for years and then, with the release of the documentary *Fix*, Philip Owen and Larry Campbell became more involved. Meanwhile, Libby Davies, the MP representing the Downtown Eastside in

Ottawa, had been laying the groundwork for this effort with Osborn since the late 1990s.

"I took Bud to Ottawa and he met Alan Rock, the health minister," Davies says. She maintains that it was Osborn's intensity and charisma that brought the capital's conservative politicians around. "A whole room full of people would go silent when he spoke, not only with his poetry, but just in conversation," Davies says. "Listening to Bud, it was like people were in prayer. You could feel him reaching people. A silence in the room would fall, and he would be inside them."

Osborn used his gift for storytelling to make the health minister understand what was happening in the Downtown Eastside. "He pressed him on the issue [of supervised injection] and the whole crisis and communicated a sense of emergency, that people were literally dying and that he couldn't wait on it," Davies says.

As Wilson became more involved in VANDU and then was made president, he similarly went to work as a lobbyist for drug users. On December 5, 2001, Wilson was scheduled to speak before a parliamentary committee, to stand in the federal legislature and share the experiences of addicts in the Downtown Eastside directly with the politicians who ran the country. Wilson obsessed over his speech. Then, that morning, his computer crashed. He lost the document.

"I've been an addict since I was twelve years old," Wilson began, speaking only from memory.

> I live at ground zero of Canada's drug problem. The Downtown Eastside of Vancouver has been demonized as a neighbourhood filled with corruption and hopelessness, when in fact it is a community of caring and concerned people. We must be allowed to respond to the crisis in a way that will fit with our neighbourhood and not with the moral and ethical rhetoric I've heard some of you speak.
>
> I honour Ms Libby Davies, for I know her tears of pain have washed the sidewalks of the Downtown Eastside. She has spoken out many times for the need for heroin maintenance, safe-injection sites, and low-threshold methadone. It is time for you to listen. She cannot do it alone.

HIV/AIDS and hepatitis are two diseases that are part of a declared public health emergency that has been called in the Downtown Eastside, yet you have failed to act and, in doing so, have literally sentenced me and my brothers and sisters to death. HIV/AIDS prevalence rates rival those of sub-Saharan Africa, and we're 100-percent saturated with hepatitis C—I repeat, 100 percent. There's nobody down there who doesn't have it. These diseases and others such as tuberculosis will eventually cost the health-care system untold millions of dollars ...

It's unacceptable. If you were to lose three friends a week, I think that you would be upset and alarmed and that you would start doing something about it. These are Canadian citizens. We may have the common thread of being very poor, but the fact is that we do not cause the social ills in the Downtown Eastside; we use drugs as a coping mechanism for those social ills.

It's time to act. It is no longer time to hide behind reports and more research. We've lost 3,000 people since 1993. That also means 3,000 mothers and fathers and probably untold thousands of brothers and sisters who probably still look at a picture every goddamn morning.

I'm going to end my speech because I'm swelling up with the rage of the Downtown Eastside right now. But it is time to act with safe-injection sites, heroin maintenance, and low-threshold methadone. These have worked.

Wilson concluded with a call for parliamentarians to follow Davies' leadership on harm reduction.

"Libby Davies is a hero in our neighbourhood," he said. "You'll be known as heroes if you act. Follow the mayor's framework for action, and you'll all be known as heroes."[54]

---

[54] Wilson, Dean. In Canada. Parliament, Senate Special Committee on Non-Medical Use of Drugs. 37th Parliament, 1st Session. (January 29, 2001–September 16, 2002). Statement made on December 5, 2001. http://www.ourcommons.ca/Document Viewer/en/37-1/SNUD/meeting-17/evidence.

What the Portland Hotel Society really needed from Ottawa to operate an injection site was a get-out-of-jail-free card. It turns out one actually existed, at least for drugs.

In 1998, Heather Hay had worked with Ann Livingston, Bud Osborn, and a few other VANDU members to draft the very first proposal for a supervised-injection site. It never went anywhere, but in that document, there's a very brief section on how the entire idea could be made legal in Canada. In preparing that report, the health board enlisted the help of a lawyer named Linda Parsons to give a legal opinion on the proposal. Whether or not she knew it at the time, Parsons discovered the key that later became crucial to the establishment of Insite.

"The Federal Health Minister has the authority to exempt any person or class of persons or any controlled substances (such as heroin) from the application of all or any of the provisions of the federal Controlled Drugs and Substance Act and the Act's Narcotic Control Regulations," this section reads, "if, in the opinion of the Minister, the exemption is necessary for a medical or scientific purpose, or is otherwise in the public interest."[55]

Buchner had gone to work with Ottawa on the idea, and eventually received back an "interim guidance document" with a mouthful of a title: "Application for an Exemption Under Section 56 of the Controlled Drugs and Substances Act for a Scientific Purpose for a Pilot Supervised Injection Site Research Project." The seventeen-page document outlines the requirements a health-care facility must meet for the health minister to grant it an exemption from Canada's drug laws. They had figured it out. In Canada, an injection site can exist without breaking the law by receiving an exemption for a specific location that said federal drug laws do not apply there.

"Section 56," Hay emphasizes. "It was the key." But it wasn't the only trick they used to get Insite off the ground.

---

[55] Melissa Eror, Alan Favell, Heather Hay, Jim Leyden, Ann Livingston, Bert Massiah, Jazmin Miranda, Bud Osborn, Sharon Ritmiller, Simin Tabrizi, "Proposal for the Development of a Pilot Project to Implement and Evaluate the Use of Safe (Injection) Sites" (Vancouver, BC: Vancouver-Richmond Health Board, 1998).

The document that the federal health ministry had sent to Buchner also stated that the Portland's exemption for an injection site would be provided "for a scientific purpose." Technically, PHS was not going to be given permission to establish a health-care program. It would be allowed to conduct an experiment on a trial basis.

Shortly after Thomas Kerr had completed his proposal for an injection site for HaRAS, another young researcher appeared on his radar who had similar interests in harm reduction and connections to the Downtown Eastside. In 2002, Evan Wood was a Master's student working at the BC Centre for Excellence in HIV/AIDS, stationed at St. Paul's Hospital just a couple of floors above where Kerr was working for the Dr Peter Centre.

"He approached me and said, 'Hey, I'm doing this sort of stuff too,'" Wood remembers. "We chatted and decided to look at this as an opportunity for collaboration."

Over the next fifteen years, the names Kerr and Wood appeared on more than 100 scientific papers that describe Vancouver's needle-exchange programs, supervised-injection sites, and other harm-reduction initiatives. These articles have appeared in prestigious publications including the *Lancet* and the *New England Journal of Medicine*, for example, creating a reputation for Vancouver as being at the forefront of harm reduction in North America. Their very first paper about a supervised-injection facility was published in the *Canadian Medical Association Journal* on August 21, 2001, two years before Insite's founding. Its title: "Unsafe Injection Practices in a Cohort of Injection Drug Users in Vancouver: Could Safer Injecting Rooms Help?"

Insite needed a scientific evaluator. Kerr, Wood, and the BC Centre for Excellence in HIV/AIDS were the natural picks. But Mark Townsend remembers being worried that if anything was going to keep people away, it would be the research component. Originally, it was proposed that researchers would work right inside the facility, conducting lengthy interviews with each client before they were allowed to proceed into the injection room. "It would be like running to have sex but then first having to fill out a twenty-page form for Dr Evan Wood," Townsend explains. "We would have died on the vine immediately in the first twenty-four hours. All we needed to know is your name—whatever you want to be called—and what you are using. The rest could come later, once we had built a relationship."

Wood and Kerr found a way to make that work for them. "When people came into Insite on a random basis, they would be offered a referral to a research study," Wood explains. If they were selected, they were offered twenty dollars, which they would receive after they completed a survey that BC Centre for Excellence researchers conducted down the street from the injection facility, on East Hastings just west of Pigeon Park. "Ten bucks to do the survey, ten bucks for a blood sample," Wood says. Nine out of ten users took them up on it.

Inside 139 East Hastings, Sean McEwan was struggling to build the facility to the specifications of three different levels of government that weren't always on the same page with one another and that were essentially making things up as they went along.

Generally, an injection site isn't that complicated. Usually, it's a room with a ring of booths around the outside where clients sit at a counter with a small amount of privacy and inject drugs. But when you get into the specifics of it, things get more complicated. For example, Vancouver police and other reluctant supporters were concerned that drug dealing would happen there. So they lobbied for measures to address that concern, such as a requirement that each booth be wide enough to prevent one user from passing anything to another. "We had a lot of decisions like that to make," McEwan says.

There were major differences in opinion over what sort of vibe the place should have. Evans and Townsend wanted it to feel welcoming. One of the injection sites that Stuerzbecher had visited in Europe almost felt like a coffee shop, like the sort of marijuana cafés they have in Amsterdam. But the health authority envisioned something that was clinical, with bright lights and steel tables. In the end, the Portland team was convinced that it was safer to go with what the health authority wanted. "When you build something that looks clinical or modern and slick, people are like, 'Oh, this is supervised injection? It's not a den of snakes?'" Stuerzbecher says.

Still, the degree to which the facility would feel medicalized remained a major point of contention throughout its construction. McEwan recounts how this fight continued even after he thought the renovation was complete. "Mark and Liz had told me they really wanted this place to feel welcoming, so finishes were to be as warm as possible and not too much like a hospital," he says. "Then the health folks had their walk-through and they went berserk and said it was too nice."

The building's layout was designed to facilitate flow-through traffic. One enters, proceeds up a short ramp to a front desk (wheelchair accessible), and then continues straight through a second door into the injection room. It has a semi-circle of booths on the far wall and to the right of the door that connects to the lobby. On the left side is a slightly elevated observation desk where a nurse stands, supervising everything and distributing the supplies people require to inject drugs. Also on the left side of the injection room is the door to the "chill room." In the chill room, there are a couple of tables with chairs around them and, on the left wall, a counter where a nonmedical staffer is stationed to offer any sort of assistance a client might need, serve coffee and juice, and keep an eye on everything. From the chill room, one exits out onto the street, so traffic moves through the building in a u-shape.

Regarding details, there were major arguments over the floor, lighting, and a coffee machine. Today Hay concedes it was all about optics. "The night before we were going to open up the supervised-injection site, I got a call at two in the morning," she says. "Our head of communications had gone to take a look at it, and she had a mini freak-out. She thought it looked too good."

In the middle of the night, Hay got out of bed and drove down to the 100 block of East Hastings. McEwan had selected a style of laminate for the floors that was made to look like hardwood. "They thought that was just out of control," he says. At four in the morning, the Vancouver Coastal Health's media relations team was demanding they cover it with garbage bags taped to the floor.

McEwan put his foot down and told them that the floor, which had come in under budget, was going to stay the way it was. It did. The coffee machine, however, was a bridge too far. "It was deemed to be part of some luxury service for heroin addicts," McEwan says. "The coffee machine got chucked. That would have been coddling the addicts.

"And then I got enormous shit for the light fixtures that I'd chosen," he continues. Again, the lights had come in under budget. "But they were too nice." In the end, the fixtures that McEwan had selected stayed, but he was made to pay for them out of his own pocket.

While McEwan was wrapping up construction details, Buchner was trying to figure out how to stock an injection site with supplies. Today, Insite provides each client who enters the injection room with a tiny metal dish that's an inch or so across, called a cooker. But those didn't exist in 2003, so Buchner ordered a massive number of cheap metal spoons. The BC Centre for Disease Control supplied syringes as well as rubber tourniquets that intravenous drug users tie around the upper arm to increase the size of their veins, thus making each one easier to find with a needle.

Construction of the supervised-injection facility was complete. Its shelves were stocked with clean needles. Now it needed a name.

One afternoon, a graphic designer, Murray Bush, who had done quite a bit of work for the Portland over the years, was out walking his dog when he bumped into Townsend, who was also walking his dog. "We need a name for this place," Townsend said to him. "It's going to be an injection site."

Bush simply shortened the two words and crunched them together. Insite.

By August 2003, it looked like everything was just about in place. Townsend and Small had found the building. McEwan, Buchner, and Vancouver Coastal Health had completed their renovation and had the place ready to go. The name "Insite" was stenciled in white on the door. And then a new, totally unexpected opponent emerged: the Vancouver Area Network of Drug Users.

"We get to opening day, and there are no peers who are going to work anywhere in the whole project," Ann Livingston explains. ("Peers" is the health authority's term for past and present drug users.) It was actually about a month before opening day when this point of contention boiled over. VANDU threatened not only to boycott Insite, but to picket the building with drug users holding protest signs right outside its front door. Livingston issued a threat: "If there are no drug users employed on opening day, we will be picketing."

Asked today if VANDU was really willing to torpedo the continent's first sanctioned supervised-injection site, Livingston shouts back: "Fuck you! We fought for this fucking place. Are you kidding me? Of course we would have."

No one with PHS remembers a fight with VANDU on this point. "There were issues in terms of what Health Canada would allow," Liz Evans recalls. "They didn't want drug users working in the injection room. And that was the compromise we had to accept in the end, that the role of peers would be in the chill lounge."

Buchner concedes that within Vancouver Coastal Health, there was a need for a "cultural shift." He says, "There were people in the health authority who were less comfortable with it," but adds that they came around.

Today Buchner and Hay remain reluctant to point a finger at any particular source of opposition to peers working at Insite. But others say it was the nurses who were assigned to work at Insite and the union behind them.

Meetings were convened and members of VANDU, the Portland, and the health authority collected around a table. In the end, Dean Wilson was given a chair on the hiring committee for peers at Insite. Small remembers it as a prospect he was very excited about. "I had to fight and draw the line and say we were going to do it," he says. "We pushed hard on it in the background. I said, 'Heather, it's a deal breaker.'"

PHS was already employing peers at the Washington Needle Depot and had worked with them on a few other short-term projects such as at Coco Culbertson's "Thunder Box" supervised-injection trailer, for example. But Insite was different in that the risks were far, far greater.

Buchner remembers thinking that if the Canadian government allowed Vancouver to open a special facility for intravenous drug users and then shortly afterwards somebody died of an overdose there, it would likely mean no similar facility would ever open on the continent again for decades to come, if ever.

Small was cautiously optimistic. He and Wilson placed their faith in Bryan Alleyne, who was still a heavy injection cocaine user at the time. "Is it possible for someone to maintain themselves? In a hurricane of addiction, can they maintain stability?" Small recalls thinking. "Bryan was the test."

Alleyne was given the responsibility of managing Insite's chill room. He never once let them down. Today Alleyne, who stopped injecting drugs in 2005, is still there in the chill room at Insite, keeping it running as smoothly as ever.

Chapter 23

Opening Day

Heather Hay was a reluctant supporter of supervised injection. "I never actually got why we needed to have supervised-injection sites," she says. "And then, late one night in 1999, I was driving home from work. There was a young girl in a back alleyway, probably about fifteen or sixteen years old. It was raining and dark, and she was shooting up. And there was just a ton of guys around her. I thought, 'I get it. I really get it.' For health-care providers, harm-reduction can be a very hard thing to wrap your head around," she continues. "It's counterintuitive. But eventually, I realized that harm reduction gives us an opportunity to keep people alive, to give them time."

Insite was set to quietly open on September 21, 2003. PHS had done a media tour of the building one week earlier, on September 15 (which is why that date is sometimes listed as the facility's opening). Now it was time to officially open Insite's doors to the public.

One detail still remained outstanding: the health ministry in Ottawa hadn't issued the Section 56 exemption from the Controlled Drugs and Substances Act that Insite required to operate without breaking the law. PHS was promised it was coming, again and again. But it hadn't. And so on September 21, the day that they had advertised they would open, Hay stood in a back room at Insite by herself (too nervous to sit), staring at a fax machine with the number they had given Health Canada. Finally, it squawked to life and spit out the piece of paper they'd been waiting for.

On the other side of Canada, it was Jenny Kwan and Hedy Fry, the two BC politicians from different parties who had drafted the Vancouver Agreement, who finally convinced the health minister to support Insite.

Kwan remembers that they were both early supporters, but Fry said to her, "I have to sell my health minister on this." Kwan asked if she could speak to him directly and Fry, who belonged to the same party as the minister and held a position in his cabinet, said that she would set it up.

"This is really important," Kwan said to the minister, Alan Rock. "Here is what we need and what we need to do."

Rock thought about it for a moment and then said, "You know what? If you guys are all on board—the mayor, the province—we'll give you the authority and grant the exemption."

With Canada's first sanctioned supervised-injection site now truly set to open, it was time for VANDU to close the illegal injection site it was still running at 327 Carrall Street.

Christian Owen remembers not everybody thought that was the way to go. But he was paying the rent and nobody else had any money.

"We got what we wanted," he told that contingent. "They've opened Insite. That's what we wanted. We can't go on being a further thorn in their side. We have to play ball. That was the agreement I had with Larry [Campbell]."

The concern was that nobody who was injecting at 327 Carrall would use a supervised site run by Vancouver Coastal Health. Their distrust of authority was so extreme that Livingston worried they would return to the alleys before they would give their name to a nurse on their way into a building associated with the government.

"There was no trust in this new thing called Insite," she says. There was trust in the Portland. Over the previous decade, they had earned credibility with the community by housing the drug addicts whom no one else would. But the involvement of Vancouver Coastal Health made people suspicious, Livingston remembers. Most of 327 Carrall's injection-drug users were homeless, she says, struggling to explain the extent to which this group had experienced an extreme degree of marginalization at every interaction with the state.

"We had the lowest of the low down at 327 Carrall," Livingston says. "And there was nothing indicating we would have any control over Insite or whether it was any good or not."

But she knew they had made a deal with the new mayor. Just after Insite opened, 327 Carrall closed down.

North America's first sanctioned supervised-injection facility, Insite, opened in September 2003. *Photo: CommunityInsite.ca*

While the September 15 "opening" was a media circus, Insite was relatively quiet on the evening of September 21.

Liz Evans and Kerstin Stuerzbecher worked as nurses in the injection room that night. Evans explains that even with the Section 56 exemption having finally arrived, everybody remained anxious. The feeling was that nobody knew what was going to happen. There was also a sense that it was all just too good to be true. "Had they actually won?" Evans remembers thinking. It didn't seem possible. Surely at any moment, SWAT teams would kick through the door. And when they did, better that it was she and Stuerzbecher who went to jail, Evans says, than some hapless nurse who wasn't so invested in what they were doing.

Their biggest fear, however, was still that no one would show. The prospect terrified everyone involved. "Oh my God, after all this, what if no one comes?" Evans thought.

Despite her anxiety, she remembers the opening as a very special experience. "It felt beautiful and warm and cozy," she says. "I remember feeling just amazing."

The facility was absolutely spotless. The lighting Sean McEwan had paid for out of his own pocket gave it a warm glow. In the injection room, classical music played over the building's loudspeakers. Then people began to wander in.

"That these people were coming out of the alleys ..." Evans says, trailing off. "It felt like a church, it felt like a sanctuary, it felt like a very spiritual moment."

The media tour that they'd held earlier in the month had thinned the crowd of reporters that had set up camp outside hoping to catch the first injection. There was, however, one journalist present on the evening of September 21. Townsend had invited Frances Bula, a reporter for the *Vancouver Sun* who had given other harm-reduction programs fair coverage in the years leading up to Insite's founding.

"Vancouver's—and the continent's—first injection site for drug users opened quietly and without fanfare Sunday night," begins her story that ran in the paper the next morning.

"It drew an unexpectedly large number of users, given that there was no publicized opening and that official statements had said it would open sometime after today."[56]

In fact, Townsend had seen the Portland spend a small fortune advertising the site's opening. But the ads—posters and leaflets—never appeared anywhere where a middle-class reporter would see them. They were inside the Portland's hotels and the Downtown Eastside's other low-income buildings.

Bula wrote about how Dean Wilson was in the injection room and might have been the very first to use drugs there, had he not been preoccupied flirting with a Portland staffer who was doing intake at the front desk that night.

While Wilson was chatting, a man named Michel Chartrand took a seat in the booth next to him. Bula described him as "quiet."

"Chartrand unfolded the tiny envelope of paper he'd bought on the street and carefully poured the cocaine powder into his syringe.

"He turned to get water and found, to his surprise, that there was

---

[56] Frances Bula, "Drug Users File in as Injection Site Opens," *Vancouver Sun*, September 22, 2003.

already a small vial of it in the plastic kidney tray he'd been handed.

"His left leg shaking with impatience, he mixed the powder and water, tied off his right arm with the blue rubber tourniquet he'd been given, and pushed the needle into his right arm with little fumbling."

Evans remembers how important it was to Chartrand that he be there for the opening. "He had HIV and was very sick," she says. "It was too late for him, he said, to get the help that he needed. But he wanted to use there because he felt like it was such a victory for so many other people who needed Insite."

"He was a really beautiful guy," Evans adds.

After Chartrand and Wilson, people began to trickle in. A thirty-six-year-old homeless man named Bradley Clark was one of the next people to use Insite. Bula wrote that after he'd injected, he hung out in the adjoining chill room for a time and talked about his hopes for the facility and what it could mean for drug-users' access to health care. "For some people, this might be their only healthy, non-drug-related interaction," Clark told her.

Asked about that night, Kerstin Stuerzbecher laughs with joy while simultaneously beginning to cry. "All I remember are the faces of the people who died," she says. "I was standing in the IR [injection room], watching the first person come in. And all I thought about were the people who had to die, who couldn't be there, who couldn't see that day."

That evening they had a few visitors to Insite who were not drug users. Liz Evan's midwife, who had delivered their son Kes three years earlier and their daughter, Aza, the year before, came by with a bouquet of flowers. One of her own children was using intravenous drugs at the time.

"She was so grateful because now she knew where she could come to look for her son," Evans explains, "instead of sitting around at three a.m. or wandering the streets."

Evans recalls that she and Stuerzbecher spent hours on their feet, until they both were eventually overcome by emotion.

"I sat in the corner and I wept and cried and watched people coming in and how beautiful it was," Evans says. "It was our people, our community, opening this space. And it felt so obvious that we would be there doing that. It didn't feel unusual or weird. It wasn't jarring in any way. It felt completely normal."

That's the official story of North America's first sanctioned injection at a government facility designed for drug users. But Michel Chartrand wasn't actually the first person to inject at Insite.

Late one evening after the media opening on September 15 but still quite a few days before the actual "quiet opening," as it came to be called, on September 21, Dean Wilson walked through the building with Mark Townsend and Dan Small.

The three of them were standing in the chill room, taking in what they had built and what they were about to accomplish. Small looked to Townsend and said, "When do you think we should open?"

"What about right now?" Townsend replied.

Wilson gave an enthusiastic "Yeah!"

Knowing where this was going, Small turned to Wilson and said, "Do you want to be the first one?"

"Fucking right I do," Wilson said.

Wilson didn't have any cash on him so Townsend and Small reached into their pockets and together came up with enough for a flap of heroin. Wilson rushed out to the street, proceeded just one door east to where a group of dealers always stands at the edge of the alley near the Washington Needle Depot, scored a flap, and then jogged the thirty feet (nine metres) back to Insite where Townsend and Small were waiting for him.

From the chill room, they migrated over to the injection room, which was already fully stocked with supplies. Wilson grabbed a clean needle, a cooker, and a tourniquet. Townsend and Small hovered a few feet back. Wilson mixed the heroin he'd just purchased with a little bit of water, tied his arm off, sparked a lighter beneath the drugs, gave it a stir, and proceeded with North America's first sanctioned drug injection.

"That was a soft opening," he says. "Then the battle started."

Asked about that story nearly fifteen years later, Evans says she never had any idea. "Yeah, that's probably true," she concedes with a laugh, and then a long sigh. "Fuck, that's such a Dean story."

Why the big secret?

"It doesn't say that in the paper," Wilson says, laughing, "because I was playing like I was straight back then. That's because of Ann—I was trying to act like I was straight. But I wanted to be the first!"

Liz Evans and Kerstin Stuerzbecher worked at Insite for its first few weeks. They were both registered nurses and the facility felt so precious that they couldn't bear to give the responsibility to anybody else. "We just ran around pretending to actually know what we were doing," Evans jokes.

Stuerzbecher says the opening might not have been so successful if it weren't for VANDU. "It was a communal effort that made that place happen," she explains. "The VANDU peers working in the chill lounge, who are still there to this day, made it a partnership. It was the first time that community and NGO and institution and bureaucracy all came together in an attempt to be as equitable as possible."

Stuerzbecher recalls that, at first, not all of the nurses that Vancouver Coastal Health assigned to Insite loved the idea of working alongside drug users. But PHS insisted and very quickly, just about everybody came around. "Then, in less than a week, it had outperformed every expectation VCH ever could have imagined," she says.

Many of the health authority's worst fears never materialized. Bureaucrats initially worried that a safe-haven for drug users would attract people who might use violence to steal drugs from Insite clients. This led to arguments over whether the facility should employ private security guards. Again, PHS put its foot down. There are no private security guards at Insite nor at any of the Portland's hotels, for that matter. Incidents requiring police have proven rare. "It can be hard for people to understand that safety isn't about security guards or bars on windows," Evans says. "Safety is really about knowing people, having relationships, and an understanding about what somebody is going through."

On Insite's first anniversary, PHS employee Darwin Fisher took over much of the facility's day-to-day responsibilities. "It took me a little while to sort of get into the groove there," he concedes. "So Kerstin comes by and says, 'Darwin, let's go for a smoke.'"

Stuerzbecher asked Fisher what he thought the person running Insite should be doing for the people who used drugs there. Fisher told her that staff should let people feel safe, comfortable, and accepted—and she thanked him and walked away.

"I'm getting ready to go back to work, and I realize I had just described to her the job that I should have been doing since I got here," Fisher says. "So I thought, 'Okay, I've been schooled in worse ways. Thank you Kerstin.' From that point, I knew what my role was."

Insite served as a gateway to the health-care system for people who were previously marginalized. That was an anticipated outcome that activists had used to sell the concept of an injection site since the planning stages. Immediately there were improved outcomes for users' physical health: fewer abscesses and no risk of hepatitis C transmission, for example. But now operational, Insite very quickly revealed a host of other, unintended benefits.

Insite became an unlikely source of pride for the Downtown Eastside.
Photo: Travis Lupick

One of the staff's primary responsibilities was to ensure that Insite clients injected drugs in as safe a manner as possible. For some women, that had the unexpected power of freeing them from abusive relationships.

"We saw women who had been IV users for years and never self-injected," Fisher says. He explains that a pimp or boyfriend injected them and used that monopoly over their supply of opioids to exercise control. The men in these relationships could choose to alleviate the women's symptoms of withdrawal or ignore them and let a woman suffer. They could remove the emotional pain of childhood trauma or leave a woman to relive her worst memories.

By teaching women who were addicted to heroin how to safely inject themselves, Insite empowered them and freed them from those abusive dynamics, Fisher says.

"That's a difficult thing to convey because it sounds weird: 'Oh, you're teaching people how to inject,'" he concedes. "But what we're really teaching them is to take control of their own health care."

Chapter 24

Consequences

One Friday evening in late 2003, Philip Owen was driving home with his wife, Brita, travelling from downtown Vancouver to their family home in Shaughnessy. It was shortly after the opening of Insite, the greatest victory of Owen's twenty-five-year career in politics.

For most of the drive, it's a straight shot south on Granville Street, an arterial road in Vancouver that takes the Owens past the home of one of their oldest family friends. For decades, the two households had shared birthdays, anniversaries, children's graduations, and other milestones. They were as close as family.

As Owen and Brita drove past their friends' home, they saw the driveway filled with vehicles parked bumper to bumper. More cars were out on the street, on both sides and in either direction, as far as they could see.

Was there a death in the family? How could they not have heard of something like that? By this point, Owen had slowed the car to a near stop. He pulled it over to the side of the road and the couple looked to one another for an explanation.

To this day, they're both reluctant to recount the experience. Dean Wilson remembers Brita sharing the story with him.

"There were cars everywhere, all over the street and up and down the driveway," Brita told him. "And they didn't know what was going on. They found out later that it was their friends' fortieth wedding anniversary," he says. "They hadn't been invited. They knew right then and there that this had cost them a lot," Wilson continues. "Brita told me that Philip was literally stunned. He could not believe it."

Brita says they lost more than one pair of family friends over Insite. "A few of those things did happen," she adds. Philip remembers there were a lot fewer social functions to attend after Insite opened. "It was pretty rough," he says. "Some of our friends were very upset."

"So we were cut off," Owen continues. "But I was convinced that we were right."

———————

Owen's embrace of harm reduction was primarily embodied in two policy achievements: his successful push to see the City of Vancouver adopt Donald MacPherson's "Four Pillars" drug strategy, and then the establishment of the continent's first supervised-injection facility, Insite. In the early 2000s, it was groundbreaking stuff. While law enforcement led the response to drugs in every other jurisdiction in North America, Vancouver began to treat addiction as a health-care issue.

It had cost Owen more than just dinner invitations. His political career was finished.

The City of Vancouver holds elections for mayor and councillors every three years. In November 2002, Owen intended to run for a fourth term. He remained popular among the general public and stood a very good chance of winning the vote, but his party, the NPA, was done with him.

Since its founding in 1937, the NPA was a business-focused faction for conservatives. It was funded by old money, by people who embodied the status quo and wished to maintain it. Before the 2002 election, the NPA's powerbrokers told Owen that if he wanted to run for re-election, he would have to campaign for the party's nomination. It was a requirement that under normal circumstances would have been unthinkable for a popular, three-term incumbent mayor.

"It became clear to me that it was time to step aside," Owen says politely.

Brita recalls one evening around this time when George Puil, an NPA councillor and old family friend, called Owen at home to ask for a favour. She was sitting nearby and heard Owen begin to say something about how he would be happy to help. Brita got up, walked across the room, and snatched the phone from her husband's hand.

"George, my husband's got a knife in his back," Brita said to Puil. "And the blood is all over your hands." Then she slammed the phone down.

The filmmaker Nettie Wild was spending a lot of time with the Owens that year, often on the road with him, Livingston, and Wilson, promoting *Fix*. She describes how his party's withdrawal of support was much more than a political defeat.

"Philip was crushed," Wild says. "He'd lost his friends. And he loved being mayor. He *loved* it. That was a part of his identity, and it was gone."

For as long as Owen can remember, the NPA spent election night in the ballroom of the Hotel Georgia, one of the city's most prestigious venues located in the heart of the downtown core. In 1993, 1996, and 1999, the Owens had a room there, where they would watch the results come in before proceeding to the ballroom for Owen's three consecutive victories.

On election night in November 2002, he was in a hotel room again, but one so inconsequential that today no one even remembers what city it was in.

"I was with Philip the night of the election because he asked me to be there," Wild remembers. "There was me, Philip, Brita, and Donald MacPherson. Because there was nobody else he had to watch the election with."

———

Owen knew that enough of the public was onside with harm reduction to ensure that his successor would bring a supervised-injection site to the Downtown Eastside. The election was a landslide. Larry Campbell won with just less than 81,000 votes; the NPA's Jennifer Clarke got 42,000.

Thanks to Owen's groundwork, the city's next government was going to bring a supervised-injection facility to Vancouver.

Mark Townsend remembers the high he felt when Insite opened shortly after, in September 2003, and then the sense of dread that followed with the federal election that came just nine months later.

"We miscalculated," he says. "In that moment of excitement, we forgot that governments change. This one certainly did. And then we were in a very difficult position."

Chapter 25
Seattle, Washington

In 1996, Shilo Murphy was sleeping in an abandoned building in Seattle's University District. He'd passed out the night before after shooting up with a friend. When he woke up the next morning, his friend didn't.

"I went to sleep and when I woke up, he had passed away," Murphy says. "And it broke my heart."

Murphy was just twenty years old at the time. He frantically tried to wake his friend, but it's likely he had already been dead for hours. "I was hysterical," Murphy recalls. "And then I was very heartbroken." He carried his friend's body outside and set him down on a patch of grass. "I didn't want him to die in shit," Murphy explains. "I laid him outside, where he didn't have to be around garbage."

Murphy was angry. He remembers thinking that the reason they were in that abandoned building—the reason they were sleeping somewhere out of sight—was because there was a war on drugs and because police hunted people who used drugs. "There was constant harassment and we were a constant target," Murphy says. "I wasn't going to take that anymore. I wanted to start organizing."

In the late 1980s, a man named Bob Quinn started an illegal needle-exchange program in Seattle, one of the very first anywhere in the United States. In 1996, he took Murphy under his wing and let him volunteer at the nonprofit organization that the unsanctioned exchange had grown into: Street Outreach Service.

Murphy had grown up with an activist streak in him and Quinn channelled it toward harm reduction. "He taught me to always get to a meeting early, because if you come late, they'll think of you as just another drug user who they can discount," Murphy recalls. "Always give unconditional love to our participants and patients. And be a good listener, then be a good talker."

Quinn also taught Murphy about the Industrial Workers of the World, an international labour organization that was founded in Chicago in 1905. The Wobblies, as they're often called, focused on strength in numbers and the power of unions. Murphy wondered if he could take what he'd learned about the labour movement and apply it to drug users. He'd heard of a group just north of Seattle, the Vancouver Area Network of Drug Users, who had done something like that, and thought he could do the same in Seattle. (Quinn committed suicide in December 2016 at the age of fifty-four. Several obituaries ran with a photograph of him with his arm around Murphy. "He's one of the closest things I've ever had to a father," Murphy says today.)

There were a couple of failed attempts to organize drug users. "I remember talking to people and just getting them there was a struggle," Murphy says. "For a little while, people thought that we were a front for the police. We had to do a lot of convincing."

By 2007, enough of the University District's drug users were convinced that Murphy was for real. They banded with him to form the People's Harm Reduction Alliance, an advocacy group dedicated to ending the war on drugs. Then, in 2009, Murphy cofounded the Urban Survivors Union, a needle-exchange program run entirely by active drug users.

"We did a lot of protests, we did a lot of lobby efforts, and we did things like bringing drug users to meet their congressmen," Murphy says. Each week, the group met in the basement of a church on Northeast 43rd Street, just across from the University of Washington School of Law.

"One of our first campaigns was lobbying drug dealers for better quality drugs," he recalls. "We said, 'Hey, we have all these drug users who buy drugs. If you gave us better quality and better quantity and if you give us better pricing, we can guarantee you more customers.'" The idea, which Murphy borrowed from a drug-users union in London, England, experienced some success but quickly fizzled.

In 2012, the Urban Survivors Union began to discuss how to bring a supervised-injection site to Seattle. For three years, they went back and forth on different roads they could take to make it happen. Some drug users, Murphy among them, wanted to open an illegal site to test how authorities would respond. But the majority thought it would be smarter to work with local government. In November 2015, they settled on a combination of cooperation and confrontation.

"We were invited to a meeting at city hall and we said publicly, for the first time, 'We are going to open up a safe-injection room in Seattle.'"

A local newspaper's account of that meeting is slightly more colourful. "The time is now," Murphy said, quoted there. "Get on the bandwagon, or get the fuck out of our way."[57]

"Safer is better," reads an advertisement that ran on the sides of buses driving around Seattle through the summer of 2017. "Supervised consumption spaces / Reduce discarded syringes in parks and alleys."

The campaign was funded by Voices of Community Activists and Leaders Washington (VOCAL-WA), a project organized by the nonprofit Public Defender Association to educate Washington State residents about harm-reduction services.

VOCAL also used light projectors to display messages on buildings in downtown Seattle. "Overdose deaths in King County in 2015: 320," one read. "Overdose deaths in an SCS [supervised-consumption space]: 0."

"Safe Consumption Spaces Save Lives," read another message that was so large when projected, it covered an entire side of a ten-storey hotel not far from Seattle's Space Needle.

Patricia Sully is a staff attorney with the Public Defender Association and coordinator for VOCAL-WA. She says the idea behind the advertisements is to take an education campaign about harm reduction beyond activists, to the general public. "We tried to come up with messaging that would resonate with anyone standing on the street," Sully says. "Our bus ads are framed around the idea that safer is better ... Basic information that is so reasonable that in order to disagree with it, you have to accept that you are just ideologically opposed."

---

[57] Casey Jaywork, "Seattle Could Be the First City in the U.S. to Host Safe-Injection Sites for Heroin Users," *Seattle Weekly*, November 17, 2015.

Through 2015 and 2016, Sully sat alongside Shilo Murphy on the Heroin and Prescription Opiate Addiction Task Force, which was convened to assess the viability and potential benefits and drawbacks of supervised-injection services in Seattle and King County. While Murphy and the People's Harm Reduction Alliance focused on service provision, VOCAL did advocacy to educate the public about the logic and evidence that supports harm-reduction services.

Other jurisdictions in the United States that are considering supervised-injection services—California and New York, for example—are largely legislative efforts playing out in political arenas. In Washington State, local health authorities operate with significant autonomy. And a majority of key politicians already support the idea of an injection site, including Seattle Mayor Ed Murray and King County executive Dow Constantine. But there's a push to bring the issue to a public vote. Joshua Freed, a former mayor and council member from Bothell City, King County, and Mark Miloscia, a Republican senator representing the thirtieth district, are working to put supervised injection on a ballot. And so in Washington, groups like VOCAL are using buses and buildings to educate the public about harm reduction.

"We do a lot of events where we have a panel and a film screening, but those events draw people who are largely already supportive," Sully says. "We're not converting people at those events. So we've really tried to reach out and do events in places where we're encountering the general public."

In July 2016, VOCAL brought a group called Safe Shape to Washington and over one week hosted supervised-injection demonstrations at six locations around Seattle and Olympia. At different parks and outside a record store, for example, Safe Shape's Greg Scott pitched a "pop-up drug-consumption room."

It's the shape of an imperfect cube, about ten feet (three metres) long on each side. Upon entering the tent, a drug user stops at a supply station where they pick up a clean needle, cooker, and tourniquet. Then they sit at a small desk and inject. Finally, there's a sharps box for syringe disposal. Some Safe Shape demos also include an adjacent "chill room" where users who have just injected drugs can hang out for a bit to ensure they're okay and also connect with social services, such as addictions counsellors or help with housing. The chill room is just another couple of chairs or large bean bags in which people can sit.

Sully recalls one of her favourite memories since launching the education campaign. It was with Safe Shape at Victor Steinbrueck Park, along the water near Seattle's popular Pike Place Market.

"It's a beautiful, sunny day, and these little kids come running into the Safe Shape," Sully begins. "From a little kid's perspective, I guess this looks like a really cool fort. And then in the chill-out room, there are those big, brightly coloured poof pillows to sit on. So the kids run in and are sitting in this thing."

She remembers looking to Scott a bit nervously. They didn't want to just kick the kids out. The entire point was to normalize harm reduction and break down stigma. "But we're also aware that we don't know what kind of interaction we're going to have with mom or dad when they show up," Sully says. "So dad comes up and asks us, 'What is this space?'"

Dad turned out to be a state prosecutor. While his children played in the mock-injection site, Scott explained what it was and why Safe Shape thinks that bringing a functioning site to Seattle is a good idea.

"Then his two kids come up and one of them says, 'Daddy, what is this?' And the way he explained it to them was, he asked them, 'Do you ever feel like you just need to be in a place where it's calm and you're safe and you're loved and accepted, where you can just be yourself?' And the kid says, 'Yes.' And dad says, 'Well, this is a space for people who need that sometimes.'

"It was this beautiful moment of deeper recognition of what supervised-consumption spaces are," Sully continues. "People can pretty easily grasp the practical element of this—that right now, we give people clean needles and then we send them out to a dirty alley to use that needle. But it takes a deeper understanding to really get the idea of safety beyond public health—to get safety on an emotional level, safety from arrest and harassment, and safety from judgment and from stigma.

"We never would have encountered this prosecutor and his two kids at a panel," she says. "We were only going to encounter him at the park when his kids thought this thing was a fort."

Chapter 26

Drug Users with a Lawyer

I always say, there is a drug-user group, and then there is a drug-user group with a lawyer."

It's an idiom that Ann Livingston came up with in late 1999, shortly after she met a young man by the name of John Richardson.

Richardson was experiencing an existential crisis. He had just completed his final year of law school and was articling for a prominent environmental nonprofit based in downtown Vancouver. While it appeared everything was going according to his life's plan, Richardson says he actually felt totally lost. Having just spent four years and a small fortune on law school, he was considering leaving the profession and starting over—doing what, he didn't know.

"I had lots of questions about everything," Richardson recounts. "So I had this routine. Every couple of weeks, I would take a Saturday and meditate all day. And then in the evening, I would take 'shrooms and go down to the beach and just pace up and down, trying to figure my life out.

"I did that for about six months," he continues. "It was a lot of [hallucinogenic] mushrooms. And Pivot was kind of the child of that process ... The idea that I should start this organization called Pivot that would do strategic litigation on behalf of marginalized people."

Today, Pivot Legal Society has a nondescript office in the Downtown Eastside, tucked next to a trucking overpass that connects to the city's port. Over the years, its small but dedicated team of lawyers has won major victories for sex workers, homeless people, and victims of police abuse.

Pivot was founded at the old VANDU office on the corner of West Hastings and Cambie Street. "He came in and said, 'Hello, my name's John Richardson,'" Livingston recounts. Richardson told her a story about a walk he had recently taken through the Downtown Eastside, hoping to recover a stolen CD player. Faced with the neighbourhood's poverty, Richardson felt he couldn't turn away without trying to help.

"This is a social-justice issue," Livingston remembers Richardson saying. "This is just fucking nuts!"

Dean Wilson was also there at VANDU that day. "It was a Friday afternoon," he says. "It was, like, ten minutes to five and we were trying to wrap up for the day when he walked in. I looked at him, and I thought he was just another junkie."

Richardson explained that he was actually a lawyer, which made Livingston's ears perk up. "He said he wanted to use strategic litigation to advance this movement, this civil rights movement," she says. "And I said, 'Good.'"

Over the years, plenty of well-meaning people had offered to help VANDU in one way or another. After an initial pledge of support, it was rare Livingston ever saw them again. "But he never flaked out," she says.

Richardson had identified a need for legal services in the Downtown Eastside. Then he'd asked around for who might be interested in working with him on that. Livingston's name was the one that kept coming up.

She was "eternally radical," is how Richardson describes his first impression of her.

At the VANDU office, Richardson held monthly meetings with drug users. He brought food and they called them "pizza parties." He also brought a number of other lawyers as rotating guest speakers. A process of reciprocal education took shape. Drug users and VANDU members living on the street or in the Downtown Eastside's crummy hotels shared stories of persecution and police brutality—stories of such flagrant abuse of authority that at first Richardson and his lawyer friends had trouble believing them. In exchange, the lawyers answered VANDU's questions and taught members about their basic civil rights.

After a few months of pizza parties, Livingston recounts how the meetings grew more focused. She pulled out her big white chart paper and returned to the basic organizing tactics that had worked so well for her since her Back Alley days. "We asked, 'What are the issues in this neighbourhood?'" Livingston remembers. "'What's going to make the biggest difference with very limited resources? What should we do?' And what came out of it was this raw, unignorable problem: the cops."

Notes from these early Pivot meetings at VANDU actually show that four key issues were adopted as official areas of focus: drug addiction, sex work, homelessness, and police accountability. But it was problems with the cops that emerged as the most pressing.

Richardson and the lawyers he brought to VANDU were utterly shocked by the stories they heard there. Someone would tell a story about an incident where they had sworn at a police officer and then were physically assaulted. Then other VANDU members would laugh, saying things like, "You cussed him, of course you're going to get hit." Richardson explains that literally not one of the drug users there was aware that a police officer was not allowed to respond to verbal abuse with a physical assault.

The way Dean Wilson describes it, it was inevitable that police brutality was the issue to emerge from those VANDU meetings with Pivot. "It's always the issue," he explains. "It doesn't matter where. We [addicts] don't have drug problems, we have cop problems."

As flagrant as the abuse was, Richardson knew that doing anything about it would require a long and steep uphill battle. "In a credibility test, police always win," he explains. "That was their strength and they used it, mercilessly ... to see complaints against them dismissed. So we knew that if we were going to have success pushing back on that, we were going to have to come up with a pretty significant evidentiary basis."

In Vancouver, any claim of police abuse went to the Office of the Police Complaint Commissioner, a position within the same police department as the officers for which it heard grievances. How could Pivot ever get a commissioner to believe the word of a homeless drug addict over one of their own?

Richardson found the answer in Champaran, India.

In 1917, a then forty-eight-year-old Mohandas Gandhi organized a team of lawyers to collect testimonies from hundreds of farmers. The farmers were systematically abused by their British rulers and disadvantaged by colonial laws that forced them to grow indigo. The crop, used to make dyes, had become less profitable as cheaper artificial dyes were invented and overtook the market. But the British continued to force the Indian farmers to grow indigo, causing widespread hardship. Gandhi's team of lawyers documented incontrovertible evidence of this economic injustice as well as accounts of general abuse and violence perpetrated by the British Raj. For years, the local colonial authority ignored the pleas of individual impoverished farmers. But the reports of hundreds presented together, formally documented by men with law degrees, became more difficult to dismiss.

"Gandhi collected mountains of evidence," Richardson says. "And so we did the same."

His plan was to take sworn affidavits. But that was easier said than done. Champaran farmers had fixed addresses where lawyers knew they could find them. Many Downtown Eastside residents who suffered the worst of police abuses were homeless. Others who did have rooms in one of the hotels lived highly erratic lives, constantly on the hustle for drug money, in and out of jail, hospitals, and rehab.

Richardson's first attempt to collect affidavits was a failure. "At the beginning, we would say, 'We're going to do a draft and then we'll meet again in a few days and we'll have the draft ready for you,'" he remembers. Nobody ever showed up for their second meeting. So Richardson decided he would go to them.

On the corner of Main and East Hastings, just outside the Carnegie Community Centre, Richard set up a table one day in 2002. Right there in the middle of the sidewalk, out in the open and at the centre of an open drug market, he pulled up a chair, took out a laptop, and attached a portable printer that ran on batteries.

"People would sit down and I'd ask what they were here for," Richardson continues. "I would ask if they had ever been abused by police. Lots of people would tell me their stories. And then I would ask if I could take their affidavit."

It was slow going. People had to get used to a lawyer wearing a suit at the corner of Main and Hastings. At first, nobody wanted to be seen sitting down with him. But once the community figured out that he was on their side, they came around.

"The corner of Main and Hastings was a pretty reliable place where you knew people would come back, but you still had to get them in one sitting," Richardson says. "So we had the portable printer, we would type it up as they were talking, print it out, read it out to them, do any corrections, print it again, and then they would sign it right there."

One by one, Richardson filled a binder with fifty sworn affidavits written by drug users and homeless people who detailed how they had been abused by the Vancouver Police Department. Thirty-six of those accounts describe what Richardson categorized as unreasonable use of force. "She had the needle in her arm and was just pushing the heroin in when two young police officers came up from behind a garbage bin," one reads. "Without pausing, they pepper-sprayed X in the face. As they pepper-sprayed her, they said 'No fixing in the alleys.' They took the rig and broke it on ground. Then they turned and left."

A further twelve affidavits describe what Richardson argued amounts to torture. "They handcuffed my hands and my ankles. They forced me onto my knees and made me face the wall," reads one of those cases. "The woman held my neck, and pushed my face into the wall. She held me very tight. The man held my hands, and lifted them up behind me. I couldn't move. I tried to turn around to see them, but the woman pushed my face further into the wall so I couldn't. They started punching me in the kidneys. I don't remember clearly everything they did. They left me in the cell with my handcuffs and ankle cuffs on. I was very weak, and I passed out."

Richardson then compiled excerpts from the affidavits in a report and matched each incident with specific provisions of the Criminal Code of Canada that he argued officers had violated. "We filed them with the office of the police complaint commissioner," he says. "And then this becomes a very long story that stretches over a period of the next five years."

After the initial complaint, the Vancouver police chief of the day, Jamie Graham, got involved. In response, Richardson argued that the chief was interfering with the investigation and filed a complaint about that with Canada's federal police, the RCMP.

In August 2007, the embattled police chief resigned. One year after that—and six years after Richardson collected his stack of affidavits at the corner of Main and East Hastings—the series of investigations he'd sparked with Pivot finally concluded. A report that went to the city's mayor states that Graham was found guilty of discreditable conduct.

Pivot became VANDU's secret weapon.

When police confiscated the table that VANDU was using to run a needle exchange at the corner of Main and Hastings, Richardson sent the VPD a letter threatening to file charges for theft. When police officers barged into VANDU's injection site at 327 Carrall Street and refused to leave, he filed a complaint claiming trespassing.

"There is a drug-user group, and then there is a drug-user group with a lawyer," Livingston repeats.

Livingston remembers how she constantly asked Richardson, "Can we please sue somebody?"

In the summer of 2006, she finally convinced him to do so—and to aim higher than the chief of police. "We wanted to say that these massive numbers of overdose deaths and this huge outbreak of HIV is illegal," Livingston says, "and that they could not allow this to go on. We were challenging the attorney general of Canada and the minister of health." Their target was to eliminate the prohibition of illicit drugs.

It was an ambitious idea, Richardson concedes today. He explains how it grew out of conversations with one of the guest speakers that Pivot brought to VANDU, John Conroy.

For years, Richardson had taken an obsessive interest in a provision of the Canadian Charter of Rights and Freedoms called Section 7, which states: "Everyone has the right to life, liberty and security of the person and the right not to be deprived thereof except in accordance with the principles of fundamental justice."

Lawyers had used Section 7 arguments in drug cases before, notably in 1997 to successfully see laws in Canada changed to allow for the use of marijuana for medicinal purposes. Richardson thought it could be taken further. In 2002, he said so in a letter he wrote to Vancouver city council, arguing that by denying proper health services for drug addicts, the city was violating their Section 7 right to security of the person. "In this manner, Section 7 could stand as an independent cause of action against the failure of government actors to establish safe injection facilities," it read. Nothing ever came of it.

Conroy had earned a reputation in drug-policy circles by winning a number of marijuana cases and had a similar interest in Section 7 and ideas about how it could be applied to larger issues. In 2006, he and Richardson got to work drafting a legal challenge that made such a case for intravenous drug users in the Downtown Eastside. On August 30, 2006, they filed a legal challenge in the Supreme Court of BC.

"Because the sanction for possession and other conduct includes imprisonment, the constant threat of the imposition of the law and imprisonment produces in the IDU [intravenous drug user] a high level of psychologically induced stress, thereby resulting in threats to the liberty and the security of the person of the IDU that are constitutionally cognizable," it reads.

"The state action in imposing this prohibition has the grossly disproportionate effect of impairing the IDUs' health, thereby affecting the life, liberty, and the security of their persons, otherwise than in accordance with the principles of fundamental justice, contrary to s. 7 of the Charter."

Conroy concedes it was a long shot. "Obviously we were asking the court to do a pretty major thing by striking down the possession laws," he says. "But I did think the evidence was there."

Chapter 27

Protests across Canada

Stephen Harper was elected prime minister of Canada on January 23, 2006.

Dean Wilson remembers that the Conservative party taking power was like a shadow falling over the entire movement they had built to legitimize harm reduction. "We knew," Wilson says, "little by little, he would try to dismantle everything. It became this heavy weight on all of us."

For the preceding three years, Insite had operated on an exemption from federal drug laws that the Liberal government had granted. Now the Liberals were out of power.

On the campaign trail in December 2005, Harper made clear that, for him, drug policy and the government's response to addiction would be based on ideology. "Our values are under attack," he said in Vancouver's neighbouring city of Burnaby, explicitly stating that a supervised-injection facility was not something his government would support.

"We as a government will not use taxpayers' money to fund drug use," Harper said. "That is not the strategy we will pursue."[58]

When Insite's initial three-year exemption was scheduled to expire in September 2006, it looked like that would be it for the Downtown Eastside's injection site. So PHS launched a pre-emptive attack.

In August 2006, Toronto was set to host the annual International AIDS Conference, a big event that brings together health-care professionals, politicians, and stakeholders from around the world. Mark Townsend devised a plan to use the convention as a stage. The night before the conference, Townsend, Wilson, Tanya Fader, and a couple other PHS staffers flew to Toronto. The entire event had become a magnet for protests. The prime minister had declined to attend. In

---

[58] Allan Woods, "Harper's Drug Crackdown Could Cut Funds for Safe-Injection Site," *Vancouver Sun*, December 5, 2005.

his place, he sent Canada's health minister, Tony Clement. It was a major rebuff of the HIV/AIDS community as well as LGBTQ people, so many of whom were affected by the disease. The conference's co-chair even called attention to the controversy during his speech opening the event.

"We are dismayed that the prime minister of Canada, Mr Stephen Harper, is not here this evening," said Dr Mark Wainberg, director of the prestigious McGill University AIDS Centre. "Your absence sends the message that you do not consider HIV/AIDS as a critical priority, and clearly all of us here disagree with you."

There was a long list of groups planning street protests for every day of the conference. Townsend realized that if they wanted to attract attention to Insite, they were going to have do something big. But they didn't have the people for that. Toronto is a four-and-a-half hour flight from Vancouver and so he only managed to get a half-dozen PHS staffers across the country to the conference. They were going to have to get creative. Townsend's plan? Bring downtown Toronto to a standstill. All of it.

"We were trying to reach out to the minister of health, Tony Clement, and to the prime minister, and project that we had more power and more influence than we really did," he says.

The night before the conference, Portland staffer Andy Bond was out to dinner with Liz Evans, Kerstin Stuerzbecher, Dan Small, and the maintenance team. Evans's phone rang and Townsend was on the other end from Toronto. "Do Andy and Phong [Lam] want to come out here? Because we're in trouble," Townsend said. Evans relayed the message to the rest of the table and immediately, Bond and Lam rushed out to pack for the trip.

"We left the restaurant, went home, booked flights, and then went to the airport and flew overnight," Bond recounts. "We got there and we checked into a hotel at about six in the morning. We slept for two hours, and then we went to the convention centre." There they found Townsend sitting on a park bench where he brought them up to speed.

Meanwhile, Fader, Wilson, and the others were inside the conference centre handing out fliers and recruiting volunteers. Their leaflets were political but somewhat mysterious. They wanted to attract people to the demonstration they were planning but couldn't explain what it was because then the authorities would very likely mobilize police to prevent it from happening.

The fliers said things like: "Stephen Harper wants to go back to the days when Ronald Reagan was denying AIDS," and "Do you want to be part of a creative display to save Insite?"

"They were sort of vague but they said, 'Show up at this time,'" Bond says. "It was kind of alluring. But if no one showed up, it wasn't going to work."

The goal was to raise 336 large banners across intersections around Toronto's downtown core. That was the number of overdoses that Insite staff had reversed since it opened three years earlier. Townsend and Bond had calculated the math for how much ground they could cover and how many people they would need to do it.

They would deploy four banners in each of the intersections they targeted. It took two people to hold each banner, so they needed at least eight volunteers per intersection, plus another eight people to walk up and down traffic in four directions from each intersection, handing out information about Insite and the Conservative government's intention to shut it down.

It worked out to a minimum of 672 people deployed to forty-two intersections. Then, to move everybody, Townsend rented fourteen school buses. "The logistics became gigantic," he remarks.

It had already been more than twenty-four hours since any of them had slept. Townsend, Fader, and Wilson had stayed up all night preparing little activist goody bags that their volunteers would hand out to people who were stuck in their cars in the massive traffic jam PHS intended to create. Each of these bags contained a flower, a lollipop, and a pamphlet that explained Insite and how the injection facility was at risk of being shut down.

"We're sorry that we're blocking traffic today," the front page read. "But it's a matter of life and death."

Would anybody show up to help the gang hand them out?

At noon on August 17, hundreds of people did. As those mysterious fliers had instructed, they gathered in a parking lot adjacent to the convention centre. There, Townsend and Fader explained what it was that everybody was going to be doing, and then told everybody to climb on board a bus. From the convention centre, each bus was assigned to travel to three drop-off points. (The drivers were told they would be helping with an act of civil disobedience and Townsend remembers that not one of them balked, even when Toronto police began to take an interest. "I find that people quite enjoy the chance to feel like they can make a positive change," he says.)

In downtown Toronto, Bloor Street and Queen Street run parallel, east to west, about fifteen blocks apart from one another. It was along these two major arterials that Townsend had mapped two primary groups of intersections they would block off.

Secondary lines of intersections were plotted on streets running immediately to the north and to the south of Bloor and Queen, making for six parallel lines total. Those secondary protests wouldn't attract as much attention, but they would prevent anyone stuck in the main traffic jams on Bloor and Queen streets from having any hope of exiting onto side streets. When everyone was deployed at the exact same time, it would be impossible for traffic to move anywhere; there would be gridlock in every direction.

Just before two p.m., nearly 700 volunteers were in position at forty-two intersections throughout downtown Toronto. To coordinate the traffic shutdown, Fader had purchased dozens of cheap wristwatches and performed the tedious task of setting them all to the exact same time.

"It was totally like an old-school spy drama," she says. "But we had to be really on it. I remember telling the driver on my bus, 'Can you get through there and speed up!? Oh no, now you've got to slow down!'"

When all those hour-hands struck two p.m., everyone moved from the holding positions they had taken on the sidewalks into their assigned intersections. Then banners were unwrapped and draped across all four crosswalks at each of them.

"Hundreds will die if safe injection site closes," some of them read. Others carried a simpler message: "Insite saves lives."

With the banners held high, pairs of volunteers walked out from each intersection in all four directions, politely handing out the goody bags that contained an explanation of what all the fuss was about.

PHS was in every direction. Two days earlier, Townsend had hired five people to cover the city with posters that similarly called for a defence of Insite. Thousands of posters—tens of thousands, Townsend swears—covered every telephone pole and spare inch of wall space in downtown Toronto.

Now traffic ground to a halt and hundreds of drivers around the city pressed on their horns at once. Meanwhile, helicopters circled overhead to capture the chaos for that evening's news. Then an airplane flew between them, towing a sign behind it. "Support injection sites," it read.

Wilson remembers laughing when he saw that. "I was really fucked up on dope," he says. To fend off withdrawal, Wilson had found an Ontario doctor who prescribed him Dilaudid, a synthetic opioid also known as hydromorphone. It's a powerful drug, and Wilson says that day he might have underestimated it. "I remember being in the middle of fucking Bloor Street and seeing nothing but people and stopped cars," Wilson says. "We had literally brought Toronto to a standstill. And then Mark had this plane flying around."

Amidst all the chaos, Bond fondly recalls the smirk that crept across Townsend's face. Sitting at the front of one bus across the aisle from each other, Townsend looked to him. "It sounds like it's working," he shouted over the horns.

Less than five minutes later, the Portland's hundreds of volunteers left the intersections they occupied and traffic resumed. It was a very short protest by design. Townsend emphasizes that the idea was to build support, and holding people in traffic quickly works against that goal. They created a very strong visual—an entire city swept up in one cause—and that is what politicians saw on television that night and in the papers the following morning.

"All that was really just for the prime minister and Tony Clement," Townsend says. "It was to make them think, 'My god, these guys have got a lot of reach and a lot of support.'"

There was a round of drinks on a downtown patio and then they returned to the hotel, managing to stay up just long enough to watch themselves on the evening news. Almost immediately after, everybody fell asleep.

"We had pulled it off," Bond says.

Ottawa got the message. Public opinion was behind Insite, or at least it looked like it was in Toronto that weekend. Canada's new Conservative health minister caved, begrudgingly.

Insite's initial exemption from federal drug laws was scheduled to expire on September 12, 2006. On September 11, the Portland received a fax. Health Canada had granted Insite a second exemption that would run until December 31, 2007.

PHS had won that battle but was shaken.

Liz Evans remembers the September 2006 exemption as a very mixed blessing. It allowed Insite to remain open for another year, but also made it clear that Insite's fate was beyond the control of PHS. As long as an injection facility required federal permission to operate, Ottawa could shut it down. And the government of the day had signalled that that is what it intended to do.

"At that point, we knew that the writing was on the wall," she says.

Evans, Townsend, Dan Small, Kerstin Stuerzbecher, and Tom Laviolette debated what to do. A possible solution did emerge, but one with huge risks.

If the legal framework in which Insite existed left it at the mercy of Ottawa, PHS could try to change that arrangement. If the law said that the federal government could close an injection facility in Vancouver, PHS could take aim at that law. They could challenge the system in court.

PHS had opened Insite through a back door. It began as an experiment that academics were evaluating. The original exemption from federal drug laws that Insite received in 2003 actually refers to drug users as "research subjects." If PHS asked the courts whether or not an injection site was legal on its own, the courts could find that it was not, that Insite was, in fact, in violation of the law and must close forever.

The Portland's management team weighed this decision for months. Small and Stuerzbecher were in favour of going to court, but Evans and Townsend were reluctant.

Stuerzbecher says she always felt a legal battle was inevitable. "For me, it was more of a question of when we were going to trigger it," she explains. "I always thought that in order to truly enshrine it, we had to do that. Because you can't rely on governments."

Small felt the same way. "There was danger, because you can lose, and then you lose big," he remembers thinking. "But there was no other way."

Small convinced Townsend, then Townsend convinced Evans and finally pulled the trigger. "We don't have a choice," Evans remembers Townsend telling her.

Shelly Tomic knew she was addicted to drugs. She was injecting speed several times a day and recognized that the habit was beyond her control. At the same time, she had limits and there were things she promised herself she would never do. "I always looked down on people who would dig," she says.

Injecting opioids causes many people to experience a mild need to scratch themselves. It's not necessarily an unpleasant sensation. Some addicts describe it as a comforting feeling that lets them know that they are high. But over time, an addict's compulsion to gently scratch themselves can turn into picking. It's one reason why injection-drug users sometimes have open wounds or scabs. Tomic had sworn that she would never pick at herself.

"I always thought, 'If I ever get that bad, shoot me first,'" she says. "And then I had this moment. I was sitting on my bed, and it was like, suddenly I was across the room looking at myself and there I was. I was that person there with blood all over them. And I just dropped the needle down, and I cried until I fell asleep.

"I was about eleven. Eleven or twelve," she adds. "I grew up really fast ... It was at that moment that I made a conscious decision to keep using."

A sworn affidavit written and signed by Tomic states that she was born in July 1968, already addicted to methamphetamine. "My mother was addicted to speed when she was pregnant with me, so I was born addicted, too," it reads. "I have a nearly life-long history of drug use," the document continues. "My first experience with illegal drugs occurred when I was seven years old. A close relative injected me with speed. I continued to use speed throughout my childhood."

Tomic arrived in the Downtown Eastside when she was thirteen or fourteen. Six or seven years later, in 1988 or 1989, she began to inject cocaine. "I got hooked quickly and became a regular user," the affidavit says. "While I was injecting cocaine, it was not uncommon for me to fix several dozen times a day. To get the money I needed to buy cocaine, I turned tricks in the Downtown Eastside."

One day in 1994 or 1995, she bought what she thought was a flap of cocaine, but which was actually heroin. "Heroin became my drug of choice from then on," she says.

Tomic's affidavit paints two pictures: one before Insite opened and one after. "You feel unsafe in the alleys," it reads. "They are dirty. You can't get clean equipment or rigs to prepare the drugs or inject them. Also, you feel under the pressure to inject as fast as possible, in case the police bust you and take your stuff. There is no time to find a good place to inject or to test your drugs to find out how strong they [are]. So, you just jam your fix into yourself wherever you can find a vein, as fast as possible, and try to get out of the alley. The problem is that if the drugs are really potent or if there is something wrong with them, you overdose and no one is there to help you. Over the years, I have seen an uncountable number [of] people go unconscious from overdoses in the alleys."

After Insite opened, Tomic stopped using drugs on the street. "While I was using heroin, I found that I stopped getting abscesses as soon as I started to fix at Insite," the affidavit continues. "I never had a single needle from Insite break off while I was injecting, and I never had an overdose there. It is a lot less stressful to inject at Insite than it is in the alleys because there is no pressure on you to be fast. You can take your time, make sure your skin is clean, find a good vein, test your drugs, and go slowly. I found that, because I knew that I could inject at Insite any time they were open, I usually used less when I fixed. When you know that Insite is there and you can go in and inject pretty much whenever you need to, you don't feel that you need to binge to get your high."

Tomic was one of three plaintiffs named in a lawsuit against the

Attorney General of Canada. Townsend recalls that it was a complicated task to select individual plaintiffs who would best represent
the population that would be harmed by a federal decision to close
Insite. "The sad reality of it was, we had to try to pick people who
we didn't think were going to die," he says. Townsend explains that
they expected the court case to drag on for years, and the people
whom Insite helped the most were drug addicts who faced extreme
marginalization and therefore were often in very poor health. "And
we had to pick people who were passionate and who believed in this,"
he adds. "Those were the two criteria."

When Insite opened, Tomic was intensely sceptical. She was one
of the regulars at VANDU's illegal injection site at 327 Carrall Street.
She liked that it was run by users and didn't trust a facility operated
by the establishment. "Everybody thought that there was going to be
cameras," Tomic recalls. "I thought, 'This is bullshit.'"

Then she participated in a couple of consultation groups that
PHS organized with users in the neighbourhood. The idea of Insite
began to sound alright to her. Then it opened and Tomic began to
rely on the place for support, not just physically but mentally and
emotionally as well.

"I would go on in there, and I'd be on a rant or a rave," she remembers. "And they would never shake their heads at me or look different
at me. They would say, 'Okay, let's go talk. What do you need from
me?' And more than half the time—two-thirds of the time—I would
go, 'I don't know. Just what you're doing.' And then I'd walk out crying
because I was flustered. And they would stay with me."

Townsend remembers that Tomic was immediately willing to be a
plaintiff. "We asked her one day and she said, 'Sure, I'll do it.'"

The second plaintiff in the Insite case was the facility's operator,
PHS Community Services Society (the legal name for the Portland
Hotel Society). The third was Dean Wilson.

Wilson recounts that Small called one day and asked if he'd
meet him for a coffee. Wilson asked him if he could find a twenty-
dollar bill in it for him. Small said sure, he could, and the two met
at a café.

"Look, I've got a question I've got to ask you," Small said to him.

"We're going to have to do a preventive lawsuit here because they are trying to shut us down."

Wilson's response: "I'm in."

Then he got up, left the café, and used the twenty to buy cocaine. "I went and scored and that was it," Wilson remembers.

While flippant about his decision to join the lawsuit, Wilson immediately became its most vocal advocate. As the case slowly wound its way to the Supreme Court of Canada over the next four years, he was the voice for the thousands of people addicted to drugs who in literal ways depended on Insite for their survival.

"It was a constant struggle on all different fronts," he says.

On August 17, 2007, Tomic, Wilson, and PHS entered their legal challenge into the Supreme Court of British Columbia.

At issue was the application of the Controlled Drugs and Substances Act (CDSA) and, more specifically, Section 4 and Section 56. Section 4 prohibits possession and trafficking. Section 56 states that Canada's health minister can "exempt any person, class of persons, controlled substance or precursor of a controlled substance from the application of the CDSA."

According to the plaintiff's statement of claim—the document that's filed in court to initiate a legal challenge—"It is unknown whether the Minister will renew the existing exemption or provide another exemption for Insite to operate."

If Insite was forced to close because the health minister refused to grant Insite an exemption from the CDSA, it continues, "Wilson, Tomic, and other users will face a risk of death or serious harm to their physical and mental health. In particular, Wilson and Tomic will face increased risks of overdose, infection, decline in their mental and psychological well-being, and other health-related complications from drug use."

The court could not allow that to happen, the document argues, because doing so would be in violation of Section 7 of the Canadian Charter of Rights and Freedoms, which gives every citizen (and non-citizen) a "right to life, liberty and security of the person and the right not to be deprived thereof except in accordance with the principles of fundamental justice."

The health minister's refusal to grant Insite an exemption from federal drug laws would violate Wilson, Tomic, and every Insite client's rights to life, liberty, and security of the person, according to the lawsuit.

PHS also included an argument on the basis of jurisdiction. It maintained that in Canada, health care is a provincial responsibility. If the federal government interfered in how BC delivered a health-care service (in this case, supervising injection drug use), Ottawa would be exceeding its jurisdictional authority over the provinces.

On the Section 7 arguments, the judge saw obvious commonalities with the case that VANDU and Pivot had brought to the same court a year earlier, seeking to end prohibition. And so the two were granted an application to be heard together.

VANDU's lawyer, John Conroy, says this likely had advantages for PHS. "Our argument was that the problem was outside of Insite, not inside Insite," Conroy says. "That [prohibition] is not only disrupting the health of the individual addict but causing a health problem in the community."

That more radical argument made Insite's case look more reasonable by comparison, he explains. "They liked the fact that we were taking a more extreme position than them, which is always tactically interesting," Conroy says.

Notably absent from the case was the regional authority that funded Insite on behalf of the province: Vancouver Coastal Health (VCH). It was a huge setback. If the health authority had signed on alongside PHS, they would have had the provincial government's power and resources behind them.

Heather Hay, the health-authority director who had worked with PHS to establish Insite, says that within Vancouver Coastal Health, the injection facility was simply not a priority. "We didn't jump in initially, and it was very challenging to get our legal counsel on board," she says.

For the time being, PHS was on its own. Small, who was involved in strategizing the case and who helped with research, recognized that Hay was in their corner, but today is still angry when asked about Vancouver Coastal Health's refusal to help PHS. "The health board said, 'No way, we're not going to do it. And we don't want you to do it. And we're not paying for anything. We're not giving you any help,'" Small says. "They made it really hard."

Dr Patricia Daly, in 2017 the authority's chief medical-health officer and vice president of public health, recalls that it was a matter of resources and priorities. "I think that [joining the Insite legal challenge] would have been a little bit outside our comfort zone," she says. "They [VCH executives] were supportive of Portland bringing it, but it wasn't the most pressing issue at the time for VCH."

Hay maintains that she fought for Insite but was overruled. "It was something that people did not actually want to move forward," she says.

So PHS went ahead with a small team of lawyers working pro bono.

Monique Pongracic-Speier had been the Portland Hotel Society's go-to lawyer for some time and became the first legal mind that Townsend and Small contacted for the Insite case. She was joined by Andrew Schroeder and Joseph Arvay, as well as Scott Bernstein, who was just a student when the case began.

Bernstein recalls that Ottawa's lawyers wanted the sort of court proceeding that you see on television, where witnesses take the stand to field combative questions from their opponent's lawyers. PHS, however, argued for a summary trial, where a judge bases their decision on lawyers' arguments and information submitted to the court via sworn affidavits and exhibit evidence such as research papers.

"The federal government wanted to drag Dean and Shelly up on the witness stand," Bernstein says.

He notes that Tomic was in poor health at the time, in part because of decades of drug abuse, but also as a result of her long battle with endocarditis. She was confined to a wheelchair for most of this period and often in severe pain. Despite her disabilities, she seldom missed a court date.

"And Dean Wilson probably would have gotten frustrated and told the judge to go fuck himself," Bernstein continues, only half-joking. "With some work, I think we would have been able to get our witnesses there. But what we would have been doing is also opening up our witnesses to cross-examination. The idea of having Shelly drilled by the federal lawyer was not appealing."

There would have been advantages for PHS if the case had gone to a full trial. For example, the judge would have heard Wilson's and Tomic's stories from them first-hand, and experienced the emotion and passion that both of their lives carried. But Bernstein says their team felt good about the job they had done compiling their case in writing.

"With a three-foot stack of affidavits, we thought there was enough evidence in the record for the judge to get a good picture of what was going on," Bernstein says.

Arvay recounts how their work began. "We had to establish Insite as a health-care facility," he says. "But it was facilitating people taking an illicit substance. How were we going to characterize that as a health-care facility?"

They would have to go back a step. "In order to make this whole health argument, we had to first establish that addiction was an illness," Arvay says. "You might think that shouldn't have been too hard. But it was."

The judge they had drawn for the case was BC Supreme Court Justice Ian Pitfield.

Small remembers a sinking feeling upon hearing that name. "I thought he was going to show up with a shotgun and a mule ... I thought it was the good Lord working against us."

Arvay knew Pitfield was known as a conservative judge but a fair one, if tough. But from the onset of the trial, Pitfield was openly skeptical about the characterization of addiction as a disease, Arvay remembers. "Every time I would say, 'Addiction is an illness,' the judge would do air quotes around the words," Arvay says.

About halfway through proceedings in the BC Supreme Court, Arvay grew exasperated with the judge's air quotes. "I think if you ask counsel for the Government of Canada whether Canada concedes that addiction is an illness, they will concede it," he said in the courtroom.

"At which point," Arvay recounts, "the judge looked over to

Mr Hunter, who was counsel for Canada, and he said, 'What do you say, Mr Hunter?'"

Hunter stood up to respond on behalf of Ottawa. "We concede that," he said.

"That just changed the course of the trial," Arvay says. "The judge took away the air quotes."

"Now, if it is an illness, it has to be cured," he continues. "So we still had a problem of explaining how Insite was helping not cure but treat the illness. And then we had to explain the whole thing about harm reduction and what that meant. Those were the first hurdles in the case. We had to establish that addiction was an illness, and we had to establish that Insite was providing health care."

Pongracic-Speier explains how they began to build the case on two foundations. The first was the human element that Wilson and Tomic represented: the actual lives that were at stake and the stories that Wilson and Tomic brought to the case as examples of the people whose health benefited from Insite. The second was the scientific evidence that had already accumulated, which indicated that Insite does, in fact, perform its stated role of reducing harms.

To that end, the work of Evan Wood and Thomas Kerr proved crucial. When the BC Centre for Excellence in HIV/AIDS received the contract to study and evaluate Insite, the original proposal said that they would collect data and then write a report for the federal government. "They wanted us to write a big report at the end of three years," Kerr says. "But Evan had the brilliant idea to renegotiate the contract. Evan said, 'No, we want to write papers and get them published.'" Kerr and Wood feared that if they produced one single assessment attributed solely to the BC Centre for Excellence in HIV/AIDS, critics might dismiss it as the work of two starry-eyed researchers from Canada's liberal west coast.

"Anyone can diss a report," Kerr says. "But if we got a report in the *Lancet*, good luck. So we did that. It was genius. And then the papers started coming fast and furious." By the time Insite entered the courts in 2007, the pair of researchers had published more than twenty papers in a variety of reputable academic journals which, crucially, received peer review.

A paper published in the *American Journal of Infectious Diseases*, for example, found that among Insite users, "rates of syringe sharing among this population are substantially lower than the rate observed previously in the community."[59] Another, published in the journal of the *Society for the Study of Addiction*, showed "a thirty-percent increase in detoxification service use, and this behaviour was associated with increased rates of long-term addiction treatment initiation and reduced injecting at the SIF [supervised-injection facility]."[60] A third article, published in the *Canadian Medical Association Journal*, states there were "significant reductions in the number of IDUs [injection-drug users] injecting in public, publicly discarded syringes and injection-related litter after the opening of the medically supervised safer injecting facility."[61]

Pongracic-Speier says it all made for a strong case. "That there was so much uncontested science and that Insite had been so rigorously studied for a number of years was extremely powerful," she says. "There wasn't a lot of doubt about what the science was saying."

Beyond Insite, Arvay next began to build an argument against the laws for which they sought permanent relief.

"Many cases turn on some kind of epiphany that happens in the course of preparation or during the trial, and the epiphany in our case was that this law was actually contributing to the very harm and evil it was designed to prevent," he says. "This law was forcing people into the back alleys, where the evidence was that they were using puddle water to inject. So the law was instrumental in actually causing death, in causing the spread of HIV and Hep C and all that."

It was lunchtime on a weekday afternoon, and Pongracic-Speier

---

[59] Evan Wood, Mark Tyndall, Jo-Anne Stoltz, Will Small, Elisa Lloyd-Smith, Ruth Zhang, Julio Montaner, Thomas Kerr, "Factors Associated with Syringe Sharing Among Users of a Medically Supervised Safer Injecting Facility," *American Journal of Infectious Diseases* 1 (2005): 50-54.

[60] Evan Wood, Mark Tyndall, Ruth Zhang, Julio Montaner, Thomas Kerr, "Rate of Detoxification Service Use and Its Impact among a Cohort of Supervised Injecting Facility Users," *Addiction* 102 (6) (2007): 916-919.

[61] Evan Wood, Thomas Kerr, Will Small, Kathy Li, David Marsh, Julio Montaner, Mark Tyndall, "Changes in Public Order after the Opening of a Medically Supervised Safer Injecting Facility for Illicit Injection Drug Users," *Canadian Medical Association* Journal 171 (7) (2004): 731-734.

was walking down the street in downtown Vancouver looking for something to eat when, completely by chance, she bumped into Arvay.

"We won," he said to her.

Pongracic-Speier was confused. Normally, representatives for the court contact lawyers involved in a case and provide them with a date and time when the judge will release a decision. In an effort to provide clarity on whether or not Insite could stay open in the immediate term, the judge had released his decision without warning. "What are you talking about?" Pongracic-Speier asked.

"The Insite case," Arvay replied. "We won."

Pongracic-Speier remembers literally jumping up and down.

BC Supreme Court Justice Ian Pitfield's reasons for judgment stand as an extraordinary defence of the arguments that an addiction is a disease and that the response to addictive compulsions should be treated as a health-care issue. In acknowledging those assertions as facts, the court noted they were not disputed by the Government of Canada.

> In the assessment of the efficacy of safe-injection sites generally, or Insite in particular, all of the evidence adduced by PHS, VANDU, and Canada supports some incontrovertible conclusions:
>
> 1. Addiction is an illness. One aspect of the illness is the continuing need or craving to consume the substance to which the addiction relates.
>
> 2. Controlled substances such as heroin and cocaine that are introduced into the bloodstream by injection do not cause Hepatitis C or HIV/AIDS. Rather, the use of unsanitary equipment, techniques, and procedures for injection permits the transmission of those infections, illnesses or diseases from one individual to another; and
>
> 3. The risk of morbidity and mortality associated with addiction and injection is ameliorated by injection in the presence of qualified health professionals.

The judgment also addresses the extent to which drug use is a "choice," as so many people still argue it is. "The original personal decision to inject narcotics arose from a variety of circumstances, some of which commend themselves to choice, while others do not. However unfortunate, damaging, inexplicable and personal the original choice may have been, the result is an illness called addiction," it reads. "The subject with which these actions are concerned has moved beyond the question of choice to consume in the first instance."

In this situation, the judge wrote, the Controlled Drugs and Substances Act does threaten "security of the person," which is enshrined in Section 7 of the Canadian Charter of Rights and Freedoms. "It denies the addict access to a health care facility where the risk of morbidity associated with infectious disease is diminished, if not eliminated," Pitfield wrote. "While it is popular to say that addiction is the result of choice and the pursuit of a liberty interest that should not be afforded Charter protection, an understanding of the nature and circumstances which result in addiction, as I have discussed elsewhere in these reasons, must lead to the opposite conclusion. Society cannot condone addiction, but in the face of its presence it cannot fail to manage it."[62]

Pitfield's judgment even addresses criticisms of Insite and, after reviewing the evidence, vindicates the facility of the most common of those criticisms; for example, that an injection site enables or even promotes drug use and that it attracts drug users to the area where it is located.

"Observations in the period before and shortly after the opening of Insite indicated a reduction in the number of people injecting in public," it reads. "There was no evidence of increases in drug-related loitering, drug dealing or petty crime in areas around Insite; the Chinese Business Association reported reductions in crime in the Chinese business district outside the DTES and police data showed no changes in rates of crime recorded by police for the DTES; there was no evidence that Insite increased the relapse rate among injection drug users; and the cost/benefit analysis was favourable."

---

[62] *PHS Community Services Society v. Attorney General of Canada* (2008), BCSC 661.

Finally, it notes that Section 56 of the Controlled Drugs and Substances Act did exist as a tool that could have been deployed to exempt Insite from the laws with which he had found problems. But because the health minister had declined to use Section 56, "it cannot be relied upon as an antidote to the violation of s. 7 rights that had been established in relation to the users of Insite."

The blanket application of drug laws at Insite was therefore arbitrary, Pitfield found.

The Controlled Drugs and Substances Act, applied without differentiation for circumstances, was therefore not in accordance with the principles of justice. That meant it violated Section 7 of the Canadian Charter of Rights and Freedoms, the judge ruled. It violated an intravenous drug user's right to safety and security of the person.

Users and staff would be exempt from the Controlled Drugs and Substances Act, with or without Ottawa's approval.

That decision is dated May 27, 2008. On June 3, the Government of Canada filed an appeal.

Wilson laughs when he remembers how fast it came. "It was a fifty-nine-page document and they responded in two hours," he says, exaggerating only slightly. "You couldn't read that thing in two hours. It was bizarre."

Liz Evans, Mark Townsend, and children Kes and Aza, standing for a family portrait in 2002. *Photo: Lincoln Clarkes*

Chapter 28

Court Battle

The battle continued, in the courts and in the streets.

In May 2008, Leah Martin was working at Insite when Nathan Allen, another veteran PHS staffer, approached her with an idea. "Hey, do you want to drive across the country with a thousand crosses?" Allen asked her.

"And I said, 'Sure, sounds like fun. Can I bring Joey Only?'" Martin recounts. "And he said, 'Hell, yeah.' A week later, we had a U-Haul with a bunch of wooden crosses that they had used down in Oppenheimer Park."

Joey Only was something of an anti-hero in Vancouver's underground country-folk scene who had played a number of PHS-organized protests over the years. He and Martin loaded up the truck they had rented and began the drive across Canada.

Over the next week and a half, they showed up outside the offices of five Conservative members of parliament across the country and single-handedly held protests that each lasted for four or five hours. They planted the crosses, unfurled an Insite banner, and then, using a massive speaker stack they had with them, played the old Christian hymn "Amazing Grace."

Only recounts the stop at the prime minister's constituency office in Calgary. "We went into [Stephen] Harper's office and spoke to his secretary, and she was actually super nice," he says. "I expected the doors to get locked and the cops to show up, but nothing like that happened. We stood there for four hours blasting 'Amazing Grace' over and over and over again, blocking out the windows with these huge banners, and generally being a bit of a nuisance. But she never locked the doors."

Afterward, they brought her a cake. But they weren't so kind to their political targets. "Our next destination was that motherfucker

Tony Clement's office," Only continues, referring to the Conservative health minister. "We were responding to a crisis," he explains. "The Harper government had made it clear that it was going to shut Insite down. And so we were in full battle mode. We had to do anything we could to get the story out."

On June 5, Martin and Only arrived at their final destination, Ottawa, where they met up with Mark Townsend and Andy Bond.

Bond was staying with his parents at their old family home in McLarens Landing, about an hour's drive outside the nation's capital. It was an interesting group that assembled there. Bond flew in with half the Portland maintenance team—Phong Lam and Patrick O'Rourke—and then there was Townsend, who by this time had abandoned his dreadlocks but forever remained the rebel. Bond's parents' house served as a staging ground for a demonstration that PHS planned to take to the prime minister's doorstep on Parliament Hill the following day.

Martin and Only had the truck with Insite banners in the back plus a PA speaker system and hundreds of the wooden crosses that PHS and VANDU had planted years ago in Oppenheimer Park. The plan was to create a cemetery of overdose victims in Ottawa, on the front lawn of Canada's lawmakers.

"Then we realized that at the Parliament building, we weren't going to be able to spike them into the ground," Bond remembers. "We had to build bases for all of them. So we rented a U-Haul truck, drove around Ottawa, bought a ton of lumber and whatever else we needed, and then went back out to my parents' place and started to build these things."

The next challenge was transportation. Crosses are easy to move. They lie flat. Crosses with a base attached to each one are awkward and take up considerably more space. They wouldn't fit in the two U-Haul trucks they had, so Bond raced back into the city to rent a third. Then they piled in themselves and once again made the drive to Parliament Hill.

Almost immediately, the police pounced. Bond recounts trying to stall them while the maintenance team and a small group of volunteers (Bond's parents among them) hurriedly unloaded the crosses from the three U-Hauls they had parked on the sidewalk.

One officer barked: "You've got to move these trucks!"

Bond pretended he'd lost the keys, failing to actually convince anyone but somehow buying enough time for the rest of the group to empty the trucks. Then he miraculously found the missing keys and removed the vehicles from the sidewalk.

Hundreds of crosses were set in lines down a wide stone path that serves as the public entrance to Parliament. One of the Portland's unofficial documentarians, Murray Bush, had printed six-foot (two-metre) tall photographs of Insite users, but used photos taken when they were all just babies. "Before they were 'junkies' they were kids," read a line of text below each picture. A massive banner stretching sixty feet (twenty metres) across read "Stephen Harper, obey the law: Protect Insite's constitutional right to save lives!" Then Townsend hit the play button on "Amazing Grace."

Next, Townsend, Bond, and the maintenance team broke from the larger group of volunteers they'd recruited and blocked the main entrance to the prime minister's building, stretching another large Insite banner across it.

"Then my mom runs over and she says, 'Mark says to get the lawyer!'" Bond continues. He counted officers from no less than four different police agencies forming a ring around Townsend.

"Somehow, nobody ended up getting arrested," Bond says. "There was a boldness about us, for sure."

Meanwhile, in the courts, the Insite case grew in size and complexity. It moved from the BC Supreme Court in 2007 to the BC Court of Appeal and then to the Supreme Court of Canada. No less than fourteen organizations were given intervener status. Appeals were filed, and then cross appeals were filed. It dragged on for years until, on September 30, 2011, Insite was scheduled to receive its verdict.

Late at night on September 29, Liz Evans was lying awake in bed with Mark Townsend next to her. "The night before the Insite decision, it was so terrifying," Evans says. Her mind drifted to the afternoon they first met, in the English countryside in 1986. "If that one moment hadn't happened," Evans thought, "if we hadn't bumped into each other ... It was just so random that both of us were there."

The court's decision was scheduled to come at 9:45 a.m. eastern time, which is 6:45 a.m. in Vancouver. After a couple of hours in bed without falling asleep, Evans and Townsend got dressed and then woke the kids. Their son Kes was eleven by this time and their girl, Aza, was nine. It was impossible to find a babysitter. Everybody they knew planned on being with them at Insite for the announcement of the court's decision. And so the kids would come with them.

Townsend says they were ready to go to jail, and had even prepared their children for that possibility. "Liz and I had talked to our kids about what was going to happen if we lost and the risks that we would have to take," Townsend says. "The health authority could say that we had to comply with the law, but that would be crossing a line," he continues. "We could not shut it down and let people die."

Vancouver Coastal Health had told the Portland Hotel Society that if the Supreme Court ruled against them, Insite would close. It had even gone so far as to threaten to change the locks on Insite. If PHS lost the case, the bureaucrats suspected that Evans and Townsend would ignore the court's decision. In fact, Townsend had already put in motion a plan to do exactly that. At the Regal Hotel, a PHS building three blocks west of Insite, he had set up a series of tables and chairs on the ground floor and stocked a supply of clean needles and other basic equipment for injection-drug use. There was a list of local celebrities, including two former mayors, who had agreed to staff the illegal facility to act as a political shield from law enforcement.

But they had no idea to what extent that strategy would work. Dan Small had spoken with the chief of the Vancouver police, Jamie Graham, and the conversation had not gone well.

"Look, Dan," Graham said to him, "life is simple for a policeman. It is illegal or it is not. If it is illegal, we will shut it down."

Small emphasizes what that actually meant: "It would be the end of the Portland if we lost. Because we would never give up."

Ann Livingston's unsanctioned injection sites had operated in a legal grey area. Everyone assumed they broke the law, but the law had never actually been tested before a judge. Now, PHS had asked the question and, in just a few hours, would receive an answer from the Supreme Court of Canada.

At just past three in the morning, Evans, Townsend, and little Kes and Aza piled into the family's Chevy minivan and made the short drive over to the East Hastings 100 block.

A couple of hours later, people with ties to Insite from all over the city did the same. Joseph Arvay was sitting in the back seat of a taxi, coming from the opposite side of town. In September in Vancouver, the sun doesn't rise until past seven a.m. He remembers that it was still dark as his cab drove into the Downtown Eastside. "I was told that a few of us would be going down to Insite to await the results, and holy shit," Arvay says, "there was a line around the corner. I wondered, 'Who are all these people out at six in the morning?' I realized it was all people waiting for the decision."

The two former mayors, Philip Owen and Larry Campbell, were there, plus provincial and federal politicians including Bud Osborn's old policy coach, Libby Davies, as well as Jenny Kwan and Hedy Fry,

6:00am Vancouver

On September 30, 2011, hundreds of people gathered outside Insite long before sunrise, waiting for a decision on supervised injection from the Supreme Court of Canada. *Photo: Tyson Fast*

the pair of politicians from opposing parties who had come together to make the Vancouver Agreement happen. The city's drug-policy czar, Donald MacPherson, was there, as was Dr Patricia Daly and other top brass from the health authority that paid for Insite (but which had initially refused to help PHS with the case). By six a.m., Insite was absolutely packed with politicians, media, and Portland staff and supporters. Outside were hundreds of PHS tenants and other members of the community who had formed a crowd that spilled off the sidewalk and into the street.

As 6:30 a.m. passed, the crowd inside Insite grew so thick it was difficult to move. But Mark Townsend was alone. Adjoining Insite's chill room is a small office. Townsend had sneaked off and holed up in there by himself.

"Next to me, I had two banners," Townsend remembers. "One for if we won and one for if we lost."

"Insite saves lives," read the first. "Thank you so much to all who have supported Insite from day one." And the second: "Stephen Harper, we beg you, please listen ... Provide us an exemption letter to allow Insite to stay open."

The pressure of that moment was greater on Townsend than anybody else—even Liz Evans. Townsend saw himself as the Portland's fixer. When a program was placed on the government's chopping block, he would find a way to keep it running. When a community group protested against PHS moving people into a social-housing project near their children's school, Townsend addressed their concerns. Now, Townsend felt that the community had trusted him to solve the Insite question. That they were depending on him. He felt that Evans, the mother of his children, was depending on him. And that people's very lives were in the balance. If Insite closed, its users would be forced to return to the alleys, injecting with puddle water and harassed by police, where if they overdosed, there was a chance there would be no one there to save them. It could not be allowed to happen, Townsend says. But if PHS lost in the Supreme Court of Canada, how could he fix that?

"That's why I was sitting alone in a room with the phone," Townsend says. "I couldn't cope with that amount of pressure."

There was no television or radio with him. He wasn't listening to music or reading a book or the newspaper. Townsend just sat there, waiting for a call from one of their legal team's agents at the Supreme Court in Ottawa who would tell him the verdict.

Then the phone rang, but it wasn't a lawyer on the other end. It was a reporter with CBC News.

"What's your comment?" the journalist asked. "You won."

Townsend's response was to ask if they were absolutely certain. "Are you really sure that what you are telling me is right?" he asked. The reporter read him a section of the court's written decision. Insite had won.

Townsend felt only one emotion: relief.

Then he poked his head out the door of the office and called to the first person he saw. That was Bryan Alleyne, the former VANDU president and Ann Livingston's old babysitter.

"Bryan, get Liz!" Townsend shouted.

While Alleyne ran to find her, Townsend telephoned their lawyer in Ottawa and confirmed the news again. Meanwhile, Evans was in the injection room, which was packed so tight that it took a moment for Alleyne to find her.

"Bryan came and got me and told me that Mark wanted to talk to me," Evans says. Alleyne's face told her what was coming. It had a huge smile across it and was already puffy from crying. Evans hurried through the chill room to the office where Townsend was waiting for her. "And as soon as I got through the door, Mark said, 'We won.'"

"Fuck!" Evans screamed in joy. And then she hugged him.

"I couldn't believe it," she says. "I just felt this huge, incredible relief ... It was liberating."

Evans ran back to the injection room and found Tomic and hugged her and they cried. By now, the news was spreading throughout the building. Arvay received an email that he read off an iPad. He threw his hands up in the air and people around him began to cry with relief. From the injection room, Evans took word of the judge's decision through the lobby and then outside. It all happened in a matter of seconds. She stepped through the door of Insite's lobby and cried, "We won!"

And a huge roar went up from the street.

"I am so incredibly ecstatic today I don't even know how to express it," Evans said into a microphone. "Thank you all so much."

On the other side of the country, in Ottawa for the decision, Dean Wilson was outside the courtroom, pacing back and forth in the Supreme Court of Canada's massive marble lobby. When he heard the news, he stopped pacing, closed his eyes, and raised two clenched fists above his head in victory. And then he laughed.

Ann Livingston was also missing from the crowd at Insite that morning. She was at home, alone with their son, listening for news of the case to come over the radio. "It was six o'clock in the morning and I have a child," she says, somewhat bitterly. "And no one ever said, 'Oh, hey, bring Joe. We've got a babysitter ...' So I didn't come to the thing. They just ignored me."

Bud Osborn wasn't there either. Nobody knows where he was for Insite's victory.

Back in the injection room at Insite, after an initial wave of euphoria had swept through the building, the victory released a flood of very mixed emotions.

Coco Culbertson remembers how angry she felt that morning. "I hadn't slept the few nights previous as I had a constant grinding fear," she says. "We all felt raw and vulnerable. Like everything we loved was to be ripped away with the stroke of a pen. It was agonizing." Setting up that morning, Culbertson says she couldn't bring herself to make eye contact with anybody, and especially not Evans. "I couldn't bear to look at Liz," Culbertson says. "I felt like the only way to make it through to the announcement was to keep my head down and avoid the pending doom and the fight to follow. We all knew that if we didn't succeed at the federal level we would have to soldier up and start all over. All the pain I felt, all the fear and anger I had been holding broke the levy and took over," she continues. "I wasn't overjoyed. I wasn't thankful. I was fucking angry at the injustice of all of it. Fucking angry that this battle was allowed to happen. That one government mandate could cause so much harm and be so egregious that it almost was allowed to kill people. I didn't feel redemption. I felt anger."

After a little more time passed, Shelly Tomic, half-paralyzed by her endocarditis, stood up out of her wheelchair. "I was speechless for about ten minutes," Tomic says. "I was crying, I was so sad. Nobody could wrap their mind around why I was so sad. I was in my wheelchair and I couldn't walk far, but I stood up and I said, 'You guys, nobody has bothered to take a moment of silence.'"

She demanded it happen, and immediately, if only for a few seconds, the crowded room fell quiet.

"We didn't just do this for the people who are still here," Tomic remembers saying. "If we had done this sooner, the ones that we didn't save ... " She trails off. "I wanted us to all remember them."

Kerstin Stuerzbecher was standing nearby and recalls she had been thinking the same thing, feeling similar to how she did the evening when Insite first opened in 2003.

"Sad for the people who we lost," she says.

Then the sun began to rise.

The Supreme Court of Canada found in favour of Insite, upholding the BC Supreme Court's decision. But it did so on a different legal basis.

The BC court said that it was Canada's Controlled Drugs and Substances Act (CDSA) that violated Insite users' rights and therefore the country's drug laws that must be addressed. The Supreme Court of Canada did not want to tackle the ultimate question of prohibition, and found that it did not have to. Instead, it focused on Section 56 of the act—the health minister's power to exempt specific groups of people from the act's penalties.

"The exemption acts as a safety valve that prevents the CDSA from applying where it would be arbitrary, overbroad or grossly disproportionate in its effects," the decision reads.

Instead of focusing on the legislation itself, the higher court looked at how Conservative health minister Tony Clement had used Section 56 of the act to deny Insite the exemption sought by PHS. It focused on the safety valve.

"If there is a Charter problem, it lies not in the statute but in the

Minister's exercise of the power the statute gives him to grant appropriate exemptions," the decision reads.

The judges called this "the alternative." That "the Minister's failure to grant a s. 56 exemption to Insite engaged the claimants' s. 7 rights and contravened the principles of fundamental justice."

"The Minister made a decision not to extend the exemption from the application of the federal drug laws to Insite," it explains. "This limit is not in accordance with the principles of fundamental justice ... The potential denial of health services and the correlative increase in the risk of death and disease to injection drug users outweigh any benefit that might be derived from maintaining an absolute prohibition on possession of illegal drugs on Insite's premises."

The court said the Controlled Drugs and Substances Act would stand, but that the health minister must see that it does not apply where drug users receive health services required for their security of the person. "The Minister is ordered to grant an exemption for Insite under s. 56 of the CDSA," the decision concludes.

And what about VANDU's goals with the case and their ambitious play for an end to prohibition?

All the way from the BC Supreme Court through the BC Court of Appeal to the Supreme Court of Canada, no judge ever paid it any mind. In each court's written decisions, the matter was dismissed with barely more than a few paragraphs' explanation.

VANDU's lawyer John Conroy maintains that it was a missed opportunity, and one that cost lives.

"We were pleased to see that the exemption for Insite would continue and that the court had ordered the government to keep it open," he says. "But we were disappointed that they didn't see that the real problem was not inside Insite, but outside Insite. And that it was going to continue to be a problem until that was addressed."

Chapter 29

Crossing a Line

In 1991, the Downtown Eastside Residents Association gave Liz Evans ten rooms to look after inside a beat-up old building on East Hastings Street called the Portland Hotel.

In 2013, PHS Community Services Society received more than $20 million annually in government funding, operated with an additional $7 million revenue, and controlled more than $59 million in assets.[63]

The PHS management team oversaw a staff of more than 300 people. In partnership with a branch of the provincial government called BC Housing, Evans and the organization ran fifteen social-housing buildings in the Downtown Eastside, providing care for more than 1,000 tenants with mental-health and addictions issues. Then there were another seventeen contracts PHS had with the health authority, Vancouver Coastal Health. The Portland ran a bank, a half-dozen commercial enterprises staffed by PHS tenants, and Insite, still North America's only sanctioned supervised-injection facility.

When it came to social housing, PHS had become the establishment it had always sought to reject. In many ways, it operated as an arm of the government. But it didn't act like it.

On the northern edge of the Downtown Eastside is a cobblestone thoroughfare called Blood Alley. It's a beautiful, if slightly spooky place. Along much of the alley is a three- and four-storey SRO with a second-floor balcony running the length of it. When PHS took it over in 2008, it consisted of two buildings that were later connected on

---

[63] Registered Charity Information Return. "PHS Community Services Society," Canada Revenue Agency, 2013.

the inside. At the Stanley Hotel, PHS provided low-barrier housing to seventy-seven people with mental-health and addiction issues. And at the adjoining New Fountain Shelter, PHS took in between fifty and sixty people each night who had nowhere else to sleep.

Even by the take-what-we-can-get standards of PHS, the Stanley and New Fountain were falling apart. The roof leaked, there were holes in the walls, and the whole building was covered in graffiti, inside and out. Andy Bond took the lead on the New Fountain and enlisted the help of Kailin See, a younger PHS staffer who had joined the organization a couple of years earlier to help with the Insite campaign.

Together they came up with a plan to use the New Fountain Shelter to expand on PHS's old reputation as housing of the last resort. The government had come to call PHS "low-barrier." It was the bureaucracy's term for the Portland's willingness to house drug users and people with a mental illness and to not evict them when they exhibited symptoms associated with those issues. What Bond and See envisioned for the New Fountain would be "no-barrier."

"We were trying to create a shelter for people who had been kicked out of every other shelter and banned from every other building," See begins. She explains that it was winter, and while Vancouver is generally a lot warmer than most of Canada, a night on the street in November can still be dangerous. But many homeless people hate shelters even more than they do no shelter at all. Some can't deal with the rules—no shopping carts inside, for example, no couples sleeping together, no smoking, and so on. See and Bond wanted to create a space where these people felt comfortable.

"So Andy and I would drive around late at night and try to entice people to come inside," See says. She recalls finding one young man who was asleep on the sidewalk that winter, literally stuck to the ground in a frozen puddle. "We actually had to chip him out of the sidewalk," she says.

At first, nobody wanted to come with them. This group was distrustful of authority to such an extreme degree that they refused to accept help. But word slowly spread that the New Fountain was different. That even after you were barred from every other shelter in Vancouver, PHS would take you in at the New Fountain.

Sarah Blyth, another PHS staffer who worked at the New Fountain in its early days, explains that this population was a little different from that of most other PHS buildings—quite a bit younger on average and, for whatever reason, this group's drug of choice was methamphetamine, or crystal meth. "There were a lot of mental-health issues, a lot of meth users, a lot of people who just couldn't live anywhere else," she says. "The New Fountain was the last stop. You could come drunk, high—anything. There was nothing else like it."

Andy Bond recounts how they applied the Portland's trademark flexibility. People spending the night were allowed to bring shopping carts inside, for example. PHS actually creating a ticketed valet system for them. Couples were allowed to share beds. You could even smoke inside (unheard of anywhere else in Vancouver).

Kailin See describes the community that developed there as "hard and beautiful ... It could get pretty nuts," she concedes. "There were fights, there was violence, there were overdoses, there was everything that comes with working with that population."

Bond similarly says it wasn't an easy place to work. He remembers there was a two-hour period in the middle of the night when there was only one PHS staffer looking after the entire building. It wasn't uncommon for there to be five or six drug overdoses in a twenty-four-hour period, and so during those two hours just before the morning shift came on, staff prayed they wouldn't be forced to respond to more than one OD at a time. "It was insane," Bond says.

At the same time, the New Fountain's staff and clients made huge progress together. Because the shelter's population mostly consisted of regulars—people returning to the same bed each night—their lives were given some routine and stability, which led many of them to reduce their drug use. Blyth organized a group of them into a soccer team that she took to France and then Brazil for two rounds of an annual tournament called the Homeless World Cup. In barely a year, PHS took street kids who couldn't obey the rules long enough to spend one night in a homeless shelter to a mental state where they were together enough to travel the world playing on a sports team.

Then the provincial government's housing agency, BC Housing, announced it would discontinue funding for the New Fountain.

"When spring was here, we knew they were going to close it," Bond says. "But it had been so successful. We'd housed people and we started the homeless-soccer thing. So we did this campaign. And that was what really made BC Housing angry."

Blyth organized a marathon twenty-four-hour soccer match in the heart of downtown Vancouver, a location notably outside the Downtown Eastside and significantly more visible to the general population, which might otherwise have no interaction with homeless people or drug addicts.

Next PHS made a direct assault on BC Housing itself.

Early one morning in April 2011, Bond, See, and dozens of the shelter tenants themselves piled into a bus that PHS had rented and drove across town to the housing agency's headquarters in Vancouver's neighbouring city of Burnaby.

"The people who slept there at night were with us at every demonstration," See says. "They were able to communicate to people in a way that we couldn't, why the service was so essential to them. And that's who stormed the BC Housing office."

While half the group staged a demonstration just outside the building, the other half forced its way inside, occupying space on several floors in the offices where bureaucrats were working at their desks. They banged drums and used an electric bullhorn to blast a siren that made it impossible for anyone there to ignore them. Some New Fountain tenants took small posters they had printed about the shelter and walked right into people's cubicles to pin them to the walls there.

"We wanted people to feel uncomfortable, we wanted people to wish we would go away and wish we would stop," See says. "It was an absolute onslaught on all your senses. It was visual, it was visceral. They couldn't ignore this population because all of a sudden, the problem was in their offices."

PHS had always walked a fine line with advocacy and its public demonstrations. The New Fountain protests crossed that line. They were different from previous actions. Instead of targeting an entire level of government, the New Fountain campaign focused in on one agency, and not just any agency, but a primary funder of PHS programming. In 2011, the year of the New Fountain protests, BC Housing provided the organization with $7.9 million CDN, up from $6.1 million just one year earlier.[64] And now PHS was demonstrating inside BC Housing offices, literally down the hall from the bureaucrats who had written those cheques.

"It began to draw too much attention to [BC Premier] Christy Clark," Bond says. "She, basically, said, 'What the hell is going on? There is so much noise behind this shelter. Can you guys just give them the god-damn funding?'"

BC Housing caved.

"We won," Bond says. But he remembers that their government partner was angry. "It was not just a disagreement," he explains with hindsight. "BC Housing would say that it was the way that we disagreed, that it was, quote, 'frightening.'"

Just after it was announced that provincial funding for the shelter was extended, Townsend received a call from BC Housing CEO Shayne Ramsay, who lives in the Downtown Eastside and who had known Townsend and Evans for fifteen years.

"Why did you do that?" Townsend recalls Ramsay asking him. "You should have told me. I would have sorted it out."

"We did tell you," Townsend replied. "We told you twenty times. You could cut our management fee, but you could not do this [close the New Fountain]."

As an organization, BC Housing had had it with him. Ramsay generously describes the actual protests as "respectful," even when PHS held them inside BC Housing offices. He notes that they never called the police. But Townsend continued to push even after the sit-ins had ended.

"There was one time where Mark was trying to get a point across and made my vice-president of operations, a woman, afraid. He followed her out to a car and was berating her about something, as Mark would do," Ramsay says. "From that point, we would only deal with Liz or Dan.

"Staff were frightened," Ramsay adds.

---

[64] KPMG Forensic Inc. "Report to BC Housing PHS Community Services Society ("PHS")" (Vancouver, BC, July 18, 2013), 19.

Less than a block from the New Fountain Shelter is the Rainier Hotel. It opened in 2009 in response to a need. Asked what the Rainier is, Tanya Fader recounts taking one of the Portland's tenants to Harbour Light, a detox program located in the Downtown Eastside that's run by the Salvation Army.

"I walked her in there to help her do intake, and immediately she was being cat-called," Fader says. "Literally, the first thing somebody said to her was, 'Hey, baby, haven't seen you in a while.' Another guy did a whistle. Just to get inside and talk to a staff member, she had to go through this crowd of men. It was just so humiliating and demoralizing for her. So, of course, she wasn't going to stay," Fader continues. "I was surprised she even did intake."

As a woman, former sex worker, black Canadian, and recovering drug addict, she was marginalized to an extreme, Fader explains. And then she had relapsed. "She was feeling completely vulnerable. And when I walked her in there, her body just tensed up."

Fader had given the woman her cell number and received a call from her two days later. "I can't stay here," she told her. "When I'm asleep, I feel like I'm not safe. I feel like I have no privacy, like I'm constantly a target … like my whole past is up in my face." The woman returned to the street, using again, and doing everything she had to do to satisfy her addiction.

"So that was the idea behind the Rainier," Fader says. "Before the Rainier, there was no women's-only treatment down here."

Liz Evans describes the Rainier as a refuge with a unique approach to addiction. "What people think treatment is, versus what people actually need, are sometimes very different things," she explains. "What the Rainier did was give people what they needed … It was designed around the very specific needs of the most at-risk women in our community."

The Rainier was a women-only supportive-housing site and treatment centre wrapped into one. It took in former sex workers, women who had been physically abused, and those who were working on getting clean but were still struggling with addiction issues and often had mental-health problems as well. Then, instead of giving them a list of rules and a workshop schedule, Rainier staff asked the women what they felt would help them get better.

"'What do you need?'" Evans remembers asking them. "'We're going to design our program around who you are right now.'

"They'd had their guts ripped out of them and their souls beaten down," Evans says. "So the way we tried to restore balance was by giving them space and love and dignity and things to do to help them re-establish and reconnect with the part of themselves that was missing or that they'd lost."

PHS had a three-year grant from Canada's federal government and an understanding with Vancouver Coastal Health that if the Rainier's programming worked on that trial basis, the regional authority would take over funding in 2012. The Rainier opened with forty-one supportive-housing units spread over two floors. Half the beds were marked for short-term detox while the other half were for long-term treatment. There were counselling services backed by clinical staff inside the building. Living at the Rainier also came with non-clinical programming designed with input from the tenants; for example, acupuncture, grief support, counselling, and writing workshops.

After three years, PHS managers were pointing to the Rainier as one of their favourite success stories. An evaluation by the BC Centre for Excellence in HIV/AIDS described it that way. But the health authority disagreed and took issue with the study.

"At Vancouver Coastal Health, we must conclude that we do not see compelling evidence that the current way of delivering care to the Rainier's residents is leading to the best possible health outcomes for these women," the organization's executive director wrote in an op-ed published in the city's daily newspaper. The article maintains no woman living at the hotel would lose their room or support services. However, it goes on to detail how programs would change. "On-site staff will be replaced by a wider range of outside clinical staff such as counsellors, case managers, nurses and doctors operating from centres in the broader community that offer more evidence-based care," it states. "This different approach will mean some non-clinical

A Portland Hotel Society staffer named Kailin See played a central role in 2012 protests against government cuts to the New Fountain Shelter and Rainier Hotel.
Photo: Andy Bond

and administrative services that the Portland Hotel Society put in place will be reduced."[65]

PHS saw the changes as nothing less than the government abandoning the women for whom they had promised to provide care.

Kailin See had helped get a lot of the Rainier's programming off the ground. As the end of the three-year term of federal funding drew near, she met with the Rainier's tenants each Wednesday evening and asked them what they thought PHS should do. "There was a lot of conflict within the Rainier community about identifying specifically with sex work and addiction when so many of them were trying so hard to get out of that," See recounts. "So this would be about their right to be women and their right to be safe and their right to have a home."

See remembers one of the women looking down at the table they sat around, almost talking to herself. "We are not faceless," she said.

---

[65] Joanne Bezzubetz, Roland Barrios, "Vancouver's Rainier Hotel Will Continue to Be Served," *Vancouver Sun*, November 2, 2012.

"It came from constantly being tossed aside and forgotten and made to compromise," See recalls. "She just wasn't willing to do that anymore."

One afternoon in December 2012, Vancouver Coastal Health staff gathered for a conference at the redeveloped Woodward's Building, less than two blocks from the Rainier. See met with tenants at the hotel and asked them if they wanted to mount a protest against the impending program cuts. They developed a plan together. The women who were living at the Rainier felt like they didn't matter to anybody, as if they were invisible. To symbolize that, they would present themselves at the health authority meeting wearing white masks that obscured their faces.

Forty women assembled outside the VCH meeting that day, representing the forty tenants who were living at the Rainier. The group was comprised entirely of women from the Downtown Eastside, and most of them were Rainier tenants. They didn't interfere with the meeting in a physical sense. The path to the boardroom that VCH used wasn't obstructed in any way, and it was a silent protest. None of the women wearing a mask said anything to anyone. They simply stood there, lining the staircase and the hallway outside the boardroom, wearing white masks that symbolized how they felt the health authority was treating them.

"We got in a line that went all the way from the elevator to the meeting door," See recounts. "And we stood there and we waited. They were supposed to break for the end of the day and then it went long," she continues. "So we just stood there. You could hear a pin drop as we stood there forever."

Finally, VCH staff began to file out of the boardroom. They walked down the long hallway, past the women in their white masks, toward the stairwell and the building's exit. "They opened the door and filed out—and they completely ignored us," See says. "But there was power in forcing them to be ashamed when they ignored us."

In the Downtown Eastside, Vancouver Coastal Health works very closely with BC Housing. They co-fund many projects together, including the Portland's buildings and health services. Now the two government organizations were both feeling like PHS had them under siege.

Evans recalls meeting BC Housing vice-president of operations Craig Crawford at a café one morning shortly after the masked demonstration at Woodward's. He was angry. "You do realize, Liz, that Vancouver Coastal Health staff felt really intimated and threatened and very upset," Evans remembers Crawford telling her.

Evans concedes that, in response, she became frustrated. The power dynamic between these two groups of people was so imbalanced in favour of the government, she explains, and yet Crawford had claimed that the bureaucrats, who held that power, felt threatened by a group of marginalized women.

"The point was to illustrate that the women living at the Rainier didn't feel like their lives mattered," Evans said to Crawford. "Honestly, Craig, you're telling me that the same women who every day are at risk of being raped, killed, or violated, whose lives are not seen, and who people don't care about at all, that they are intimidating to bureaucrats?"

But this was just the latest in a series of actions that Mark Townsend had organized to target Vancouver Coastal Health. Townsend had spent the last twenty years of his life helping PHS provide housing to people who every other agency had said could not be housed. But there was another side to him—he had a temper. In fighting for people who could not fight for themselves, he could bully opponents and exhibit cruelty. In December 2012, Townsend unleashed this other side on the people he felt threatened to hurt the women who lived at the Rainier Hotel.

In addition to the public campaign, Dan Small recalls how hard Townsend pushed on the Rainier issue behind the scenes, repeatedly calling VCH staff. "He would call them and say, 'Hey, I'm waiting for you. It's five o'clock. You better fucking call. Because you're going home to your lovely little wife and your dinner and you're going to put your slippers on and these women don't have anything. So what the fuck?'

"Those professionals had never dealt with anything like that," Small reflects. "They had never been on the other end of that kind of heat. And that heat got turned up way high on the Rainier. Higher than we'd ever turned it."

On December 13, 2012, Jack Bibby, the president of the Portland Hotel Society's nine-member board of directors, received a letter from Dr David Ostrow, then the president and CEO of Vancouver Coastal Health.

"As you are no doubt aware, PHS, led by Mark Townsend, has been staging various protests to voice opposition to Vancouver Coastal Health's (VCH) decision to change how services are delivered to clients of the Rainier Hotel," the letter begins. "The manner in which this is occurring is completely unacceptable and undermines the credibility and sustainability of PHS as a service delivery partner to VCH. The protest activities have become increasingly disruptive, invasive, and aggressive to the extent that VCH must re-evaluate being associated with such an organization."

The letter states that these disruptions included "intimidating and harassing VCH staff and clients. Many have become fearful of coming to work and at least one has had to take sick leave because of the tactics being used as part of the protest activities," it continues. "While this may be seen as a victory for some in your organization, we consider this to be an intolerable situation."

Ostrow gave PHS an "important decision": it could continue with the protests or it could "continue to be an organization that works with VCH."

In the meantime, Townsend was banished from dealing with the health authority.

"VCH will no longer deal with PHS through Mr. Townsend," the letter states. Dan Small was appointed the health authority's sole point of contact with PHS.

The letter ends with a warning: "We will be closely monitoring any further protest activities organized by PHS and will take all necessary steps to ensure that our staff and clients are made to feel safe and supported when they come to work or to receive the clinical care they need."

Ostrow declined to grant an interview. Bibby, the PHS board's president, recalls how he and his colleagues didn't know what to make of the document. The board was aware of the New Fountain and Rainier campaigns, he says, and they knew the government was not happy about them. But Bibby says Ostrow's letter was over the top. He argues that more than anything, it underscored an ideological divide. "It was like, 'How dare somebody do something different,'" he recalls.

In spite of Ostrow's warning, PHS did not stop.

"It's not like for the sake of it we wanted to deliberately cause problems, but we had made a commitment," Townsend says. "We had made a commitment to the women at the Rainer. We had sat with them in tears. And they'd said, 'We want to do something.' So we promised that we would do something. And we were not going to renege on that."

On December 18, just five days after PHS received that letter from Ostrow, some 200 people gathered outside the Rainier Hotel for a march on VCH headquarters. They carried black coffins on their shoulders. Others dressed up like the grim reaper, wearing black robes and hoods over their heads. Most of the Rainier's tenants themselves walked among the group of protesters that day, a powerful sight, given that some of them were in frail health. They called it a "funeral procession." The message was obvious: cut funding for the Rainier and you are killing women.

Upon arriving at VCH, Small, dressed in a suit, walked into the building and presented a cake and basket of cookies. "We're not going to come into the building, there's nothing to be worried about," he told them. "This is an upsetting thing, but it's about your boss."

Outside, the group set up on a patch of grass, playing loud music and voicing demands through a megaphone. It was a standard PHS protest, of the same sort that PHS had been holding in the Downtown Eastside for twenty years. But the location was different: this one took the fight to the health authority's front door.

From there, the march proceeded to the constituency office of the BC Premier, Christy Clark. "At the premier's office, it got more out of control," Townsend says. A parade float with a band playing on it joined the marchers to make even more noise. Leaders of Vancouver's Indigenous community made speeches that emphasized how vulnerable women were in the Downtown Eastside and how important a place like the Rainier was for them.

"They were completely freaked out," Townsend remembers.

On January 25, Jack Bibby and the board received a second letter from Vancouver Coastal Health president and CEO David Ostrow. "I made it clear that while PHS has the right to disagree with the decision and voice such opinions publicly should it choose to do so, the manner in which this has been occurring not only undermines the credibility and suitability of PHS as a service delivery partner to VCH, but is intimidating and threatening to our employees," it begins. Ostrow took specific issue with posters that had appeared around VCH offices that referenced the Rainier protests and which were attributed to PHS.

"The intent of my December 13 letter was to make it clear these kinds of behaviours, should they continue, could seriously jeopardize VCH's relationship with PHS and bring into question our continued partnership," the letter continues. "The ongoing protest activities and anti-VCH comments leave us with little choice but to examine our relationship and review options."

Kerstin Stuerzbecher acknowledges that PHS had initiated a shift in its relationship with authorities. "We had started to use tactics that I think the government took personal," she says. "We didn't just march down the street or block off Main and Hastings with a Killing Fields banner or whatever ... We did things that were more direct. Our strategy did change, and I think that that had consequences."

Vancouver Coastal Health did not provide funding to continue in-house and non-clinical services at the Rainier Hotel. The building remained under the control of PHS, and the women who lived their got to keep their rooms. But the programs that PHS had fought for were cut.

"I felt devastated," Townsend says. "I felt that I'd let the women down."

PHS lost the battle and, though it would take a while before they realized it, it had also cost them the war.

Chapter 30
Sacramento, California

Somewhere in the United States, a supervised-injection facility has operated since September 2014.

In liberal cities such as San Francisco and Seattle, staff at certain needle-exchange programs have long turned the other way to let people inject drugs in their bathrooms. But this facility, which we'll call Othersite, is more than that. It's not a needle exchange. It was designed and operates specifically as a supervised-injection facility.

Alex Kral is an epidemiologist with the U.S. nonprofit organization RTI International. He's evaluated injection services at Othersite and drafted a research paper about the facility that's scheduled for publication in a forthcoming issue of the *American Journal of Preventative Medicine*. Kral, who has studied intravenous drug use for twenty-five years, declined to reveal the site's location, but there are hints it is somewhere in an urban area of northern California.

A draft copy of Kral's paper describes the facility: "The unsanctioned supervised injection site has one large room dedicated solely to injection and an adjoining room which provides post-injection monitoring/supervision," it begins.

The injection room is simple. There are five steel desks. A lamp sits on each one, and white chairs are tucked beneath them. Attached to the wall in front of each desk is a small mirror. Each injection station also has its own sharps box for the safe disposal of used needles. Most users spend between ten and twenty minutes in the injection room. They can stay longer and remain under observation in an adjacent lounge, if they wish.

"Before ... a program participant injects drugs at the site, the staff person asks twelve questions, and the answers are recorded into an encrypted survey software package via a tablet computer," Kral's paper reads. "A staff person is stationed in the injection room at all times.

Ancillary sterile injection equipment is provided by the agency, which also safely disposes of all used equipment. The staff person observing the injections has been trained in overdose prevention, resuscitation using naloxone and rescue breathing, injecting technique, and harm reduction principles."[66]

Othersite is open between four and six hours each day, five days a week. A drug user must be a member to inject there and membership is by invitation only. "There are no formal exclusion criteria," the paper says. "Once a person comes to the agency a few times, and appears to need supervised injection services, they are invited to use the supervised injection room."

According to Kral's evaluation, Othersite is a resounding success. During the first two years it was open, there were 2,574 injections by more than 100 people (the study's method of anonymizing data obscures the exact number of participants). Based on the quick interviews that users grant upon entering Othersite, Kral reports that over ninety percent of those who came to the facility would otherwise have injected drugs in a public place—a restaurant bathroom or a park, for example. "As such, this site has averted over 2,300 instances of public injection in the neighborhood during a two-year period," the paper states. In addition, sixty-seven percent of participants admitted they discard used needles on the street. Because every needle at Othersite is dropped in a safe-disposal box as soon as it is used, Kral calculates the facility has saved the neighbourhood from 1,725 dirty needles.

During the first two years that Othersite was open, there were only two overdoses. Such a low number is likely the result of two factors. The first is that users there can take a minute to properly measure each dose. The second reason is that when someone who has injected drugs at a supervised site shows signs of distress, staff are trained to intervene before an actual overdose renders them unconscious. Sometimes that means providing them with an oxygen tank, but other times an overdose can be kept at bay simply by keeping a drug user upright and talking. Both of the overdoses that staff responded to at Othersite were reversed with naloxone.

---

[66] Alex Kral, Peter Davidson, "Addressing the Nation's Opioid Epidemic: Lessons from an Unsanctioned Supervised Injection Site in the United States," unpublished draft (2017).

"Being able to inject in a clean, well-lit space equipped with sterile equipment, where there is no need to rush due to fear of detection, may also reduce injection-related injury and disease," Kral concludes.

On the phone from San Francisco, Kral says that for another research paper, he calculated that if a city like San Francisco established a sanctioned injection facility, it would not only pay for itself but actually save taxpayers $3.5 million a year.

He says his forthcoming paper about Othersite will describe the facility "as a proof of concept."

"An unsanctioned injection site somewhere in the United States has been operating now for two and a half years," Kral says, "and it's basically shown that the sky has not fallen."

The first time that Kral sat down with a politician to talk about bringing a supervised-injection site to San Francisco was 2007. He recalls that the media coverage was not positive, to put it mildly. But the occasional politician continued to seek his expertise. In May 2017, Kral took a seat on a San Francisco task force convened to assess the potential impacts of opening an injection site. The year before, he provided expert testimony for a bill that could bring injection sites to San Francisco plus seven other cities across California.

Assembly Bill 186 would make it legal for local governments to open supervised-injection sites in Alameda, Fresno, Humboldt, Los Angeles, Mendocino, San Francisco, San Joaquin, and Santa Cruz. (Legal as far as state law is concerned; federal law remains another question.)

On June 1, 2017, the California state assembly voted forty-one to thirty-three in favour of the bill, sending it on to the senate. The bill's sponsor is Susan Talamantes Eggman, assemblywoman for California's thirteenth district. "Generally, the assembly is where things that are controversial go to die," she says cheerfully. "So I have very high hopes as we go into the senate that we will be successful."

Eggman says the idea came from San Francisco. Bay Area lawyers with a group called the Drug Policy Alliance made the three-hour drive to her office in Sacramento and asked if she'd be willing to take on something controversial. They'd targeted the right assemblywoman.

Eggman is a licensed clinical social worker. Through the 1980s and '90s, she worked in several positions on the frontline of the state's response to substance abuse. She remembers the crack cocaine epidemic of the 1980s, the arrival of black tar heroin in the '90s, and the methamphetamine craze of the 2000s. Now she says the challenge is the opioid crisis, driven by prescription painkillers and made worse by fentanyl and other synthetic analogues.

"I already know about working with harm reduction," Eggman says. She recounts how she first came to understand the concept years earlier, as a social worker for women who were victims of domestic abuse. "To tell people just to leave that situation, to simply get away—it is not that easy," Eggman explains. "Instead, we ask, 'How are you going to stay safe until the next day?'" With a drug addiction, she continues, part of the answer is harm reduction.

"The best predictor for a person to make positive changes in their life is when they have a positive therapeutic relationship with a caring person and they don't feel judged," Eggman adds. "That's when they are more likely to take the next step into sobriety."

And so when the Drug Policy Alliance's lawyers from San Francisco asked her if she would help with a bill to legalize supervised injection, it didn't take much before she was willing to give it a try. "Much to the chagrin of my political advisors," Eggman says with a laugh.

In March 2017, Eggman held a meeting for activists and other stakeholders in her office in the California State Capitol building. "I have a good-sized office, but there were so many people that some were sitting on the floor," she recounts. There were a number of long-time addicts and active drug users in the room, and Eggman listened to their stories. She remembers one middle-aged man in particular. "He talked about his struggle with addiction and was very compelling," she says. The man recounted years on the street addicted to heroin. He finally got clean and told Eggman he wanted an injection site to save other people from going through what he had.

Later, Eggman continues, a few months after that meeting, the man relapsed. "By the time we actually passed that bill, he had died from a drug overdose," she says. "But he told me that many people were still out there suffering who could benefit from something like this."

Chapter 31

Prescription Heroin

David Murray was driving back to Vancouver on his way home from a harm-reduction meeting out in Abbotsford, one of the city's more distant suburbs. Ann Livingston was in the passenger seat next to him. A large kitchen knife she'd brought with them to serve snacks had slipped down in between their seats and Murray reached to look for it. When his fingers finally found the knife, he pulled it up quickly and raised it in a stabbing motion toward Livingston. He was obviously joking but made a fairly convincing show of it. Livingston laughed and they continued driving toward the Downtown Eastside.

"The next thing I know, we're cruising through Burnaby and there are police cars everywhere," Murray says. Four squad cars with lights flashing and sirens blaring forced him over to the side of the highway. With guns raised, officers surrounded their vehicle and moved in. "Get out of the car!" they shouted at him.

Murray was placed in handcuffs and questioned separately while another officer checked Livingston for injuries and ensured she wasn't being kidnapped.

"We had to stop ourselves from laughing," Livingston says. "I was worried we were going to get killed."

Livingston and Murray had been friends for a while, but after that afternoon they grew thick as thieves.

———

David Murray was in his late fifties, living in the Downtown Eastside and addicted to drugs, when he received an offer that sounded too good to be true: free heroin, three times a day, every day, paid for by Canadian taxpayers.

He'd used heroin since his late teens, and it had stopped being any fun decades ago. Court documents reveal a list of petty crimes that Murray says were related to his addiction. In the 1970s, he spent three years in a US prison for his role in a bank robbery. "I'm not proud of those days," he says. "I don't like to talk about it." Murray subsequently moved to Vancouver and held a job in the film industry for a time, but heroin got the best of him. "It led to homelessness and all the rest that goes along with everything falling apart," he says.

In February 2005, Murray walked by a clinic at the corner of East Hastings and Abbott streets where a younger guy sat behind a table he'd set up on the sidewalk. Kurt Lock, an employee of the Portland Hotel Society, stopped Murray and asked him if he was interested in participating in a study, the North American Opiate Medication Initiative, or NAOMI. "I was broke and homeless at the time," Murray recalls. "So I jumped at the idea."

NAOMI sought to test the health outcomes of methadone against diacetylmorphine, a medical term for heroin. Three times a day, Murray visited the clinic and received a free dose of pharmaceutical-grade opioids. The drugs were imported from Europe and regulated, which meant they were relatively safe and free from the uncertain qualities of street drugs and the poisons with which dealers cut them.

The experiment worked like this: At a set time, a patient knocked on the clinic's outer door. Identification was confirmed, the door was unlocked, and then, for security reasons, the patient waited for that first door to close before a second opened to let them inside. They proceeded to the injection room, which is similar to Insite's: a series of simple booths, each one with a mirror and a chair. Inside the injection room, a patient spoke to a nurse who was positioned on the opposite side of a sheet of thick glass. Identification was confirmed for a second time. Then the patient received a set dose of diacetylmorphine that was earlier prescribed by a doctor employed by the clinic. The patient took a seat at one of the booths and injected. Finally, at the end of each visit, they spent a few minutes in the clinic's chill room, where staff casually monitored them for adverse side effects. Because the drugs were pure and of a fixed dose, there was very seldom an overdose. Then the patient left the clinic and continued on with their day.

NAOMI wasn't giving out free heroin to just anyone. The eligibility

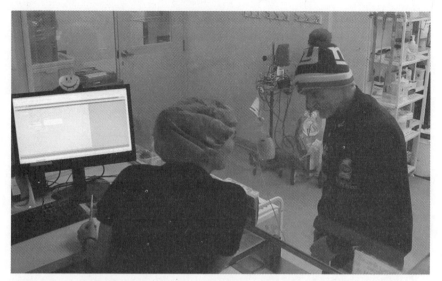

At Crosstown Clinic in the Downtown Eastside, long-time heroin addicts receive
a fixed dose of the drug from a clean supply that's regulated by the government.
Photo: Amanda Siebert / Georgia Straight

criteria was steep, designed to test the effectiveness of diacetylmorphine for the treatment of long-term addicts who had repeatedly
failed with traditional therapies such as methadone. Among the 251
participants, the average number of years they had used injection
drugs was 16.5.

Because the drugs were free, every user enrolled in the NAOMI
study could give up the daily hassles they'd been forced into to pay
for their addictions. For women, that often meant retiring from sex
work. Receiving drugs from a clinic also created a routine point of
interaction with doctors and nurses, which led to all sorts of improved
health outcomes.

When the first NAOMI research paper was eventually published
in the *New England Journal of Medicine*, in August 2009, the results
were stark. While only 54.1 percent of participants who were given
methadone remained in the study for its full term, for those given
diacetylmorphine, the retention rate was 87.8 percent. Researchers
found the group on diacetylmorphine was sixty-seven percent less
likely to use street drugs and participate in other illegal activities.

For the methadone group, that number was twenty points lower.[67]

For this group of long-time heroin addicts, the NAOMI study found that patients given prescription diacetylmorphine stayed in treatment longer, used less street drugs, committed fewer crimes, and experienced improvements in health and other social indicators such as employment. "Injectable diacetylmorphine was more effective than oral methadone," the paper concludes. "The fact that patients who received diacetylmorphine had significant improvement in these areas suggests a positive treatment effect beyond a reduction in illicit-drug use or other illegal activities."

A second paper, published in the *Canadian Medical Association Journal* in March 2012, took a look at the NAOMI data from another angle and found benefits for society as a whole. Using a mathematical research model, it calculated that fewer hospital visits incurred by participants and decreased criminal tendencies equated to enough cost savings for a prescription-heroin program to more than pay for itself.[68] "Our model indicated that diacetylmorphine would decrease societal costs, largely by reducing costs associated with crime, and would increase both the duration and quality of life of treatment recipients," it reads.

But the NAOMI trial was just that, a fixed-term research project. As soon as it ended, Murray and everyone else who had received prescription heroin at the clinic were forced to return to the alleys.

Murray remembers that it almost killed him. "I was frantic after the program," he says. "I was back on the street doing a lot of heroin again. The heroin wasn't working. I was doing a lot of pills—anything to keep the edge off. I went into detox and tried to kick it cold turkey. I went into a treatment house. And then I was back out on the street again. I tried to get serious about not using again, but nothing seemed to work."

---

67 Eugenia Oviedo-Joekes, Suzanne Brissette, David C. Marsh, Pierre Lauzon, Daphne Guh, Aslam Anis, Martin Schechter, "Diacetylmorphine versus Methadone for the Treatment of Opioid Addiction," *The New England Journal of Medicine* 361 (2009): 777-786.

68 Bohdan Nosyk, Daphne Guh, Nicholas Bansback, Eugenia Oviedo-Joekes, Suzanne Brissette, David Marsh, Evan Meikleham, Martin Schechter, Aslam Anis, "Cost-effectiveness of Diacetylmorphine versus Methadone for Chronic Opioid Dependence Refractory to Treatment," *Canadian Medical Association Journal* 184 (6) (2012): 317-328.

He acknowledges that everyone who'd participated in NAOMI was told that the trial would end and at that point they would stop receiving heroin from the clinic. "But everybody thought that they wouldn't actually do that to us," Murray adds. "They wouldn't put somebody on a drug, see that it was working, and then snatch it away from them."

Ann Livingston heard all of this from Murray as the pair of them drove around British Columbia, holding satellite VANDU meetings and teaching rural communities about harm reduction. During those hours in the car together, Livingston planted an idea in Murray's head. The Downtown Eastside was buzzing with rumours of a second prescription-heroin study on the way. Livingston said drug users should have a say in how it took shape. More than that, they wanted an exit strategy: a next step that didn't just return people to the alleys as NOAMI had. The plan Livingston and Murray came up with—really just an idea, at this point—was to eventually transform the study into a sustainable program; they wanted to establish a prescription heroin clinic.

Murray's life had improved considerably during the time he received free heroin via NAOMI. He'd found himself a room at one of the Downtown Eastside's SRO hotels and started volunteering at VANDU, keeping their office open in the evenings after most other services had closed for the day. With Livingston's encouragement, Murray also founded a group they called the NAOMI Patients Association, or the NPA, for short. (Not to be confused with the Vancouver political party of the same acronym.) His first task: find a second member.

"Some of them had really gone downhill," Murray remembers. "Some of them had died." Murray and Livingston walked the alleys, looking for people he remembered from the clinic and asking other people if they knew the whereabouts of anyone whose name he could recall. Then, once they had found a few, Murray began hosting weekly NPA meetings at VANDU.

"We did these meetings with a big sheet of paper and wrote down the names of everybody we could remember," Murray says. "Then the people who came to the meetings suggested other people. It was three or four at the beginning and then five or six and then nine or ten."

By January 2011, the NAOMI Patients Association was a group of a few dozen people and had come to agree on what it wanted from the second research project, the Study to Assess Longer-term Opioid Medication Effectiveness, or SALOME, as it was now called. The NPA wanted priority enrollment for former NAOMI participants, social services provided in conjunction with participation, and a way to keep participants on diacetylmorphine after the trial ended. But while the group had a voice, it still wasn't sure how to make that voice heard. Murray found the answer to that question in a chance encounter on the other side of the country, in Ottawa.

Susan Boyd was an old friend of Bud Osborn's who had worked in harm reduction in the Downtown Eastside since the late 1980s. Now she was working with Donald MacPherson, who had retired from his position as the City of Vancouver's drug policy coordinator and was trying to establish a new national group called the Canadian Drug Policy Coalition. To that end, MacPherson had brought both Boyd and Murray to Ottawa, and there they got talking about how the NAOMI Patients Association could influence the researchers behind SALOME.

"When we get back home [to Vancouver], maybe I'll come down to one of your meetings," Boyd told Murray. She was trained as an academic researcher. Over the next few months, Boyd tutored the NPA and helped them write a paper of their own. "I teach methodology classes and how to do research so I helped facilitate the research that they wanted to do, helped them decide on methods, and the back-and-forth process that we wanted to create."

Murray recounts the experience as liberating. He explains that during NAOMI, it felt like the power that researchers exercised over him was absolute. With SALOME, even if he was still a research subject, he wanted a piece of that power. "We wanted to do something different," he explains. "We wanted to do our own research with Susan as our mentor."

The first paper they published is titled, "NAOMI Research Survivors: Experiences and Recommendations." It describes participants' experiences with NAOMI in their own words. "The NPA hopes that this Report will guide future research studies and the setting up of permanent heroin and other drug maintenance programs in Canada," it reads. "Foremost the NPA encourages other groups to engage in creating their own research to tell their stories."[69]

Boyd also gave the NPA a copy of the Helsinki Declaration, an international agreement that governs human research ethics. It reads in part: "At the conclusion of the study, patients entered into the study are entitled to be informed about the outcome of the study and to share any benefits that result from it, for example, access to interventions identified as beneficial in the study or to other appropriate care or benefits."[70]

Murray remembers a light bulb going off: "If a drug works during a trial, they can't take it away from the people that it was benefiting," he emphasizes. With the NAOMI Patients Association involved in discussions on SALOME, they wold make sure that didn't happen again.

It's a bit of a coincidence how Eugenia Oviedo-Joekes came to work with drug addicts in the Downtown Eastside. In the early 2000s, she was an academic in her home country of Spain and was feeling like she'd hit a glass ceiling. She thought it would be a good idea to try to work in an English-speaking country for a few years. The United States was out; she didn't like the politics there. It eventually came down to the United Kingdom or Canada. "And the UK had a quarantine requirement for my dogs and Canada didn't," she recalls. "That's the reason I came to Canada."

When she was still living in Spain, Oviedo-Joekes had repeatedly attempted to contact the principle investigator of the NAOMI trial, Dr Martin Schechter, but he'd not responded. Finally, through a friend of a friend, word reached Schechter that Oviedo-Joekes had relocated to Canada. She had worked on heroin-assisted therapy in Spain, which made her one of the few academics in all of North America with that

---

[69] NAOMI Patients Association, Susan Boyd, "NAOMI Research Survivors: Experiences and Recommendations," Vancouver Area Network of Drug Users. Vancouver, BC: NAOMI Patients Association (February 20, 2012).

[70] Quoting from the declaration's sixth revision, published in 2008. (A seventh revision was subsequently released in 2013.)

experience. In 2007, Schechter finally called her up and asked if she would work with him in the Downtown Eastside.

With SALOME, Oviedo-Joekes took a lead role and sought to apply lessons they had learned from NOAMI. Her office was at St. Paul's Hospital. In a fifth-floor boardroom there, she met with Scott Harrison, director of HIV/AIDS and urban health at Providence Health Care (a partner of Vancouver Coastal Health that's not religious but was founded by Catholic nuns). She asked Harrison to work with her on SALOME. He agreed, on one condition: "The first thing we do, as soon as we start a clinical trial, is put all of our efforts toward expansion," Harrison said. It was exactly what Oviedo-Joekes wanted to hear. She recalls being devastated when she and her fellow researchers had to tell each NAOMI participant that they could no longer visit the clinic for prescription heroin and that they would have to return to dealers on the street.

"There is a saying in Spanish," she remembers telling Schechter. "The surgery has been a success, but the patient is dead."

"That's how I felt," Oviedo-Joekes says. "There was no joy in publishing in the New England Journal of Medicine. There was no joy at all."

Now, Harrison, a higher-up in the health authority, told her that with SALOME, they would find a way to save the patient. Next, they needed a physician.

Dr Scott MacDonald was brought onto the NAOMI trial not long after Schechter got it off the ground. He says that the benefits of diacetylmorphine had become clear to him and, like Oviedo-Joekes, was distraught when they had to tell patients it would no longer be available to them. "I remember one guy who did really well in NAOMI," MacDonald recalls. "He was tall, with a white beard, long white hair, [and] had been in and out of jail a few times." With NAOMI, MacDonald put him on prescription heroin and the man stopped getting into trouble with police. Then the trial ended. MacDonald continued to see him as a patient, prescribing him methadone. The man took it, but it never worked to supress his cravings for opioids. He continued to buy from dealers. "And then, on one of his relapses, he died of an overdose," MacDonald says. "If he had had access to diacetylmorphine, he would still be alive."

The doctor was on board. The next step was patient recruitment.

MacDonald explains how it is more difficult to give people free heroin than one might think. "The medical model for recruitment will not work," he says. "You cannot just open up an office with a sign that says 'Free heroin' and expect people to come in. People trust their dealers more than they trust the medical system. They have been traumatized by the medical system, almost universally. We assumed, in NAOMI and SALOME, that recruitment would be easier. But it wasn't."

Although not officially involved with the SALOME heroin clinic—which by now was named Crosstown Clinic—Mark Townsend and Dean Wilson helped behind the scenes. Wilson was connected to the streets, and Townsend had the Portland's hundreds of hotel tenants, many of whom were long-time heroin addicts who easily fit the criteria for SALOME. Townsend had actually pushed for a prescription heroin program in the Downtown Eastside for a decade by this time, but PHS prioritized supervised-injection, and his goal never got off the back-burner. He appointed Kurt Lock, a PHS employee who had worked at Insite, to assist Crosstown on behalf of PHS. Lock had played a critical role in NAOMI, swooping in to save the day when the first trial faced challenges connecting with drug users. With SALOME, he reprised that role.

"Eugenia [Oviedo-Joekes] and I visited every single agency and drug user group that we could think of to let them know that we were going to open up recruitment," Lock recounts. They obtained a telephone number that addicts could call to apply and set up tables around the Downtown Eastside where people could learn more about SALOME and register their interest on the spot. Then there were a few weeks of interviews, where applicants met one-on-one with a doctor and received a number of tests related to eligibility. Whereas with NAOMI the community was intensely skeptical, with SALOME, interest was beyond what Crosstown could accommodate.

"We had 130 people the first day and then over the course of about a year and a half while we were recruiting, we had about 560 people apply," Lock says. "So a whole bunch of them were left on the waiting list, which was pretty sad. I still get people applying."

Oviedo-Joekes remembers how angry some members of the community still were with her and her academic colleagues. At VANDU, she met with the drug-user community and addressed their concerns personally. "Listen, if we don't keep going with another clinical trial, this whole thing is going to die," she told them. "The only way to keep the torch burning, even with just this little timid fire, is another fucking clinical trial ... This is the game."

Oviedo-Joekes—who in the middle of all of this gave birth to twins—gave the room no assurance that when SALOME concluded they could continue with prescription heroin. But she said that they were going to try.

A former VANDU president named Dianne Tobin helped bring the community around. Like Murray, she had participated in NAOMI and worked as a community liaison for the clinic. Tobin remembers that it was far from a sure thing that drug users would cooperate with SALOME. Through the consultation phase, she met with Pivot Legal Society lawyers and contemplated organizing NAOMI patients into a class-action lawsuit. (Another idea that Ann Livingston played a role in shaping behind the scenes.) They were very close to suing the researchers for what they argued was denial of a proven treatment. Tobin says it was Oviedo-Joekes who convinced them that the larger picture was more important.

"As a group, we talked about it and realized that if we had a lawsuit against them that this study would never come about," Tobin says. "So we put the lawsuit on the side and decided instead that we would work with the people who were setting up SALOME."

Murray, Tobin, and the other drug users were on board.

Using the same Section 56 exemption from Canadian drug laws for which Insite had gone to court, Crosstown Clinic began administering prescription heroin for the SALOME trial. It ran for four years, from 2011 to 2015, but no one patient was enrolled for that entire period. The first group to lose access to the drug was scheduled to transition out in late 2013. It would have been NAOMI all over again. But this time, the researchers running the trial had a plan.

They turned to a federal mechanism called the special access program (SAP) that doctors and health researchers use to prescribe unconventional drugs that have not been approved for use in Canada. It's primarily used in cases where, for example, somebody is going to die of cancer and where traditional treatments have failed. In such a situation, a doctor can use the SAP to apply for a potentially life-saving treatment that's still in its research phase but which might provide some benefit to the patient.

At Crosstown, doctors attempted to use the SAP to order prescription heroin from Europe to give to long-time addicts who had repeatedly tried and failed to stabilize their lives with other drugs such as methadone.

In August 2013, Crosstown filed thirty-five SAP applications for diacetylmorphine. Staff held their breath. Then, on September 20, to everyone's surprise, twenty of them were approved. For the first time in North America outside of an academic trial, heroin addicts would receive their drugs from a doctor instead of a dealer. But just before that could happen, Ottawa got wind of what was going on over at Vancouver's little Crosstown Clinic.

The Conservative politicians who had fought Insite for so many years were still in charge of the federal government. When their new Health Minister, Rona Ambrose, heard that one of her bureaucrats had approved a SAP request for prescription heroin, she intervened.

On October 3, 2013, MacDonald received a call from a colleague at Crosstown Clinic. They told him to get online and read the news: Ambrose was shutting them down.

"This [special access] program provides emergency access to life-saving medicine," Ambrose said at a press conference. "It was never intended to provide heroin to addicts, and we are taking action to close this loophole. Our Government understands that dangerous drugs like heroin have a horrible impact on Canadian families and their communities. We will continue to support drug treatment and recovery programs that work to get Canadians off drugs in a safe way."[71]

The health ministry rewrote the special access program to eliminate the possibility that it could be applied to street drugs including

---

[71] Health Canada. "Heroin and Other Dangerous Drugs Are Banned from Health Canada's Special Access Programme," Ottawa, ON: Health Canada, October 3, 2013.

cocaine and heroin. Patients who had already exited SALOME would no longer have any route to access diacetylmorphine. "People are going to die," MacDonald remembers thinking. "For us, this is about patient care and providing good care. For those guys, it was about something else."

Oviedo-Joekes had a different reaction. "She [Ambrose] gave us the perfect platform to start the fight," Oviedo-Joekes says. "Suddenly, Rona Ambrose was taking away a right from the poorest and the most vulnerable. The nuns here at Providence Health Care said, 'No way. You're not doing that.'"

With a legal team led by Joseph Arvay, the Vancouver lawyer who had beaten the federal government once already on the Insite case, Crosstown Clinic took its prescription-heroin program to the BC Supreme Court. "Now we were having to persuade the court not only to provide [users with] a safe place to inject but to provide them with the very drug that was causing them to inject," Arvay says. "It was a much harder harm-reduction case to make. But we made it."

At the core of his argument was that it is not the drugs themselves that are most harmful to addicts; rather it is the laws that criminalize drugs that hurt people the most. "How do we characterize giving the addicts heroin as harm reduction?" Arvay recalls asking himself. "It required putting together a really interesting record to educate the court. For some people, providing them with heroin isn't necessarily going to lead to other forms of treatment or abstinence ... But at least it would start to stabilize their lives ... If the heroin is safe and administered in proper doses, a heroin addict can function and function for a long time. They can hold a job, they can keep their housing, they can keep their family."

On May 29, 2014, the court agreed, at least on an interim basis. In a thirty-four-page decision, Chief Justice Christopher Hinkson granted an interlocutory injunction. It didn't make a final determination on the issue of prescription heroin, but said that while that question is discussed before the courts, Health Canada should approve "all outstanding plaintiff requests and future SALOME requests for access to diacetylmorphine."

Crosstown Clinic's prescription-heroin program could not take on new patients or expand in any way. But for the time being, doctors could use the special access program to prescribe diacetylmorphine to those specific individuals who had previously received the drug via SALOME.

The federal government signalled its intention to continue fighting Crosstown Clinic but complied with the judge's decision and approved Vancouver doctors' SAP applications. On November 26, 2014, the first batch arrived.

MacDonald remembers his patients' general reaction: "It's about time."

Drug users at Crosstown Clinic are not required to wean themselves off of heroin, but the stability the program provides has helped many do just that.

By early 2017, twenty-five former injection-drug users had transitioned to oral therapies, according to statistics provided by Providence Health Care. Nine of those people transitioned to oral hydromorphone and sixteen to methadone, Suboxone, or slow-release oral morphine. An additional two Crosstown patients went completely free of drugs for the first extended period since they began using heroin decades ago.

Dianne Tobin was one of the first Crosstown patients to receive prescription heroin in November 2014, when it was first administered beyond the confines of an academic study. Then, in early 2017, she became one of Crosstown's first patients to give up opioids completely. Tobin went from injecting diacetylmorphine to ingesting oral hydromorphone and then to abstinence. It was the first time her body went without drugs in more than forty years.

From her family's home in Bridgewater, Nova Scotia, Tobin acknowledges it was a long road. She recounts a childhood of trauma. She came from a happy middle-class home and got along well with her parents. "But I couldn't handle society the way it was," Tobin begins.

It was the 1960s, and after repeated problems at school, the courts intervened. She was sent to the Ontario Training School for Girls, an old-fashioned institution where young women could be held for transgressions involving truancy, drugs, or promiscuity. Tobin was one of the youngest boarders there, and the older girls treated her badly.

When she was sixteen, authorities let her attend grade twelve at a public school. Terrified of being sent back to the institution, Tobin figured out a way to ensure that would never happen.

"I got married," she says. "I married the worst person in the whole world. Once we got married, I was black and blue all the time."

In 1968, the young couple moved to Vancouver, to the Downtown Eastside. At their apartment at Jackson and Pender, their neighbour was a heroin dealer. He gave Tobin the first drugs she ever tried. "It gave me courage and made me feel more like myself instead of an abused victim," she recalls. "After the first time I took heroin, from then on I was a woman of my own and I was able to stand up for myself."

Her husband drank and grew more abusive. After she tried to leave him, he tied her to a chair and confined her for six days in a room at the Downtown Eastside's Patricia Hotel. Fully addicted to heroin at the time, Tobin suffered through a cold-turkey withdrawal. "I was in total withdrawal that whole time, and it was terrible," she says. "You don't sleep, you don't sleep, you don't sleep. And then it gets worse."

By 1973, Tobin was twenty-two-years old and had two young children. She took them, ran to Edmonton, and never saw that man again. She was free of her husband but stuck with an addiction to heroin that would last the next forty years.

Vancouver's drug scene pulled her back to the Downtown Eastside. The hassles and tragedies of an addict's life followed. Tobin tried and failed to get clean. A long-time romantic partner was killed while he was in prison. She once spent three months in a coma after two guys smashed a brick over her head in a robbery that turned violent. Decades passed.

Then, on March 15, 2006, she was one of the first Vancouver residents to receive diacetylmorphine as part of the NAOMI study. SALOME came next. And then, in November 2014, Vancouver doctors began using the special access program to administer prescription heroin to patients outside of those research projects.

Prescription heroin brought stability to Tobin's life. She recounts how she became more involved in activism, for several years serving as president of VANDU. She also helped Murray organize NAOMI patients and had a hand in the clinic's successful fight against the Conservative government that eventually allowed for the program to exist as it does today. (In 2016, the Conservative government was voted out of power. Shortly after, the new Liberal government revised regulations to again allow doctors to use the SAP to prescribe diacetylmorphine. The court challenge was subsequently dropped.)

In late 2016, Tobin transitioned to oral hydromorphone and, for the first time since she was seventeen years old, spent an extended period of time without using needles. Next, with the help of her doctor at the clinic, Scott MacDonald, she lowered her hydromorphone intake in increments, from 425 milligrams per day to 125 per day and then to a seventy-five-milligram dose just twice a week. On December 5, 2016, she visited Crosstown Clinic for the last time.

Tobin remained in the Downtown Eastside for a short while after that. But the neighbourhood began to get to her. "I just finally got tired of it and I told the doc, 'I'm going home, where I don't have to hear ambulances all day.'"

Sitting beside Tobin at their home in Nova Scotia is her niece, Jenna Zinck. "It's like I finally have a chance to meet my aunt and get to know her," she says. "I'm just proud of her. With tears in my eyes right now, I am so proud of her."

There's a pause, and then Tobin responds. "To have my family trust me again, it's a gift," she says.

Still with her family in Nova Scotia today, Tobin thinks about the Downtown Eastside often and the people she knows there who used to ask her about Crosstown Clinic.

"So many of my friends wanted to get on it," Tobin says. "A lot of them died before they could."

Chapter 32

"The Assassination"

On a Friday afternoon in late February 2014, Liz Evans received an email from BC Housing vice-president of operations Craig Crawford. "BC Housing no longer has confidence in the process that we're engaged in," Evans remembers the email read.

In the preceding year, beginning shortly after the New Fountain and Rainier campaigns, BC Housing had reviewed the Portland's books. It had contracted two major accounting firms, KPMG and Deloitte, and they had been digging through PHS receipts line by line.

Evans recounts how that process became intensely frustrating. KPMG found spending issues and raised concerns about accounting practices, she concedes. But when BC Housing got involved, there didn't seem to be a genuine interest in correcting anything. "I kept going to those meetings thinking that there was going to be something specific and tangible that we were meant to address, but nothing was ever said," Evans recalls. "We were trying to get them to help us to fix stuff, but they would never come back to us and say what it was that we had to fix ... There was nothing tangible, there was nothing real about those meetings," she continues. "And then, fairly abruptly and out of the blue, I got an email [from Crawford] on a Friday afternoon."

She called BC Housing's CEO, Shayne Ramsay, with whom PHS had a long and good working relationship. The two agreed to meet face to face Monday morning. "This is what is going to happen," Evans remembers Ramsay telling her. "The Portland is going to be dismantled. We're going to burn the village. Unless you all leave."

It wasn't official notice but neither was it a chance to change anyone's mind. The decision had been made, Evans remembers. She'd known Ramsay for a long time, and he was giving her a heads-up. "That's it, it's done," Evans says Ramsay told her. "It's not working anymore."

Evans left the meeting in a state of shock. She walked to her car, got inside, and for a while just sat there. Then she called Mark Townsend and the rest of the Portland's management team—Kerstin Stuerzbecher, Dan Small, and Tom Laviolette. "We need to get together," she said. "It's urgent. We need to meet." They gathered at a hotel bar in downtown Vancouver, and Evans told them what was coming. "I was crying and didn't know how to talk about it," she remembers.

A few days later, the Portland's entire management team plus the board's president, Jack Bibby, was called to a meeting with Ramsay and Mary Ackenhusen, Vancouver Coastal Health's new president and CEO who had recently replaced David Ostrow.

Townsend remembers there was no negotiation, only a choice. "I said I would resign and then Liz said she would resign, and we asked if we could leave Dan and Kerstin," he recounts. "But they wanted everyone gone."

"They presented us with the option of stepping down," Evans says. "If we did that, they would keep the village. If we left and took the board with us and walked away, they would not dismantle the organization. They would keep it. And if we didn't ... " She trails off.

Ackenhusen declined to grant an interview. Ramsay confirms that was essentially the message, but maintains it was conveyed in very different words. "I would not have said it or presented it in that strong of an ultimatum," he explains. "I mean, they could see the writing on the wall, that there was no satisfaction in the way things were going and no belief that they could be improved. And so we suggested the way forward for the organization was that one."

Bibby's recollection of these events is closer to Evans's. "They told us, if the executive does not resign and if the board does not resign, that they would cancel every contract, one by one, until we did," Bibby recalls. "They said, 'You guys turn and walk away or we are burning the village.'" He adds, "They hated us."

Implicit in the deal was that PHS would not fight back. "The message was really clear," Evans says. "We had to be compliant, we had to do what they said, we could not fight, we could not stand up and create resistance."

News of a serious problem at PHS became public on March 4, 2014. "The unconventional partnership between government and the activist nonprofit that runs a supervised-injection site and housing for hundreds in the city's Downtown Eastside appears headed for a major rupture after a forensic audit," reads an article published in the *Globe and Mail*. "Housing Minister Rich Coleman said within ten days, his ministry will decide what action to take on the PHS Community Services Society—usually referred to as the Portland—because of significant problems discovered."[72]

Townsend is quoted in the article, expressing surprise. He acknowledged problems but claimed it was his understanding PHS was working with Deloitte auditors to correct them. "There was a sense that progress had been made," Townsend told the newspaper.

Two weeks later, Evans, Townsend, Stuerzbecher, Small, Laviolette, and all nine members of the Portland's volunteer board officially resigned from the Portland Hotel Society.

"Shock, sadness and a fervent hope for no drastic changes to services were the emotions that filtered through the Downtown Eastside with the news that the founders of a legendary nonprofit housing group had been forced out by the province," one report reads. "The organization's leaders, Mark Townsend and Liz Evans, revealed this week that they had agreed to resign under provincial pressure."[73]

The next day, on March 20, 2014, BC Housing made its financial review public. It detailed a laundry list of allegedly inappropriate spending by Evans and her team.

The newspapers crucified them. "Top managers at a Vancouver charity that's supposed to help the poor in the Downtown Eastside have racked up hundreds of thousands of dollars in limos, overseas trips, meals, parties and other perks because of lax financial oversight," reads a report in the *Vancouver Sun* newspaper. "The two audits, conducted by Vancouver Coastal Health Authority and BC Housing, paint a picture of lavish expenses for Portland Hotel Society managers and directors at a time when the society—charged with operating many services for the Downtown Eastside's at-risk population—is teetering

---

[72] Frances Bula, "Audit Findings Could Derail Downtown Eastside Non-Profit Housing Provider," *Globe and Mail*, March 4, 2014.

[73] Frances Bula, Andrea Woo, "Vancouver Non-Profit Housing Group's Programs Will Be Protected, Minister Says," *Globe and Mail*, March 19, 2014.

on the verge of financial trouble and potentially unable to pay its debts.

"Managers and directors expensed more than $69,000 over three years on restaurants, and more than $300,000 on travel to Vienna, Paris, Istanbul, New York City, Los Angeles, Banff and Ottawa, among other locations," the *Sun* article continues. "Hotel rooms of up to $880 per night were charged for trips to the United Kingdom and Austria, including flowers, alcohol and spa services. There were also more than $8,658 in limo fees in 2013, a trip to Disneyland in Anaheim, a $5,832 cruise for a PHS manager, a $917 baby shower and a $7,025 'celebration of life' for a deceased employee."[74]

Other reports attacked PHS staff on a personal level. "One of the most unpleasant interviews I have endured in four decades of journalism was a few years back with Mark Townsend," reads the first sentence of another article about PHS finances.[75]

Today Dan Small begins a conversation about the review by acknowledging that PHS's accounting was sometimes sloppy. He points out that it was the Portland's flexibility—its ability to quickly adapt to a situation and deploy a response to a problem on twenty-four-hours' notice—that made the organization such a strong on-the-ground partner for BC Housing and Vancouver Coastal Health. PHS was only able to operate that way, Small maintains, because of the very tactics that BC Housing used to justify the management team's ousting. "We were fast and loose and we did make mistakes," he says before pausing for a moment. "And some of that stuff was just complete cockups. Some of it was stupid, and I wish it had never happened."

The response from Evans and Townsend was uncharacteristically muted. Townsend offered various explanations to the press. He argued that occasional trips to somewhere warm were given to staff members who hadn't take a vacation in years. Other expenses were rationalized. What was described in the report as a limousine, for example, was actually just a larger town car that was cheaper for a group than it would have been to pay for two taxis. Townsend claimed

[74] Rob Shaw, Tiffany Crawford, "Portland Hotel Society Audit Finds Hundreds of Thousands of Dollars in Questionable Expenses," *Vancouver Sun*, March 21, 2014.
[74] Pete McMartin, "The Portland Hotel Society 'Does Not Always Play Well with Others,'" *Vancouver Sun*, March 19, 2014.

that those hotel rooms in Europe were actually paid for with private donors' money, not that of taxpayers. A lot of it could be explained, he maintained. But there were questions that the KPMG report raised that PHS didn't try tried to defend. For example, each member of the management team was paid for vacation days they never took off, unused sick time, and for statutory holidays, all on top of their salaries, something that KPMG described as "unusual."

"We were trying to deal with things that the bureaucracy found difficult to deal with," Townsend says. "So how were we going to do that? We were not going to be shaped like them or look like them."

Townsend uses his final word on the review to point to PHS administration expenses, which he says always hovered around ten percent, the benchmark for charities and nonprofit organizations around the world. Filings with Revenue Canada support his claim. In 2012, total revenue was $28.1 million and total management and administration expenditures were $2.4 million, or 8.57 percent. In 2013, that number was 10.55 percent, and in 2014, it was 9.89 percent. "Our admin fees were always fucking low," Townsend says. "Lower than anyone else, and we were doing complicated work."

Today Townsend has somewhat hardened his position on "the assassination," as he calls it. But he has expressed regret in the past. "I suppose there are many mistakes I made," Townsend told an online publication in 2014. "I am always trying to do the best I can with my heart and soul ... But one of the things that I didn't really put in my mind is that we were seen as quite scary. And I didn't feel like we had any power. So there's an illusion of that, and I was very unaware of it."[76]

There were a couple of reports on the financial review in the alternative press that mentioned the New Fountain Shelter and the Rainier Hotel, but nothing in mainstream newspapers. Townsend says no journalist ever brought either of them up and neither did he. In 2014, the team went quietly, even as the newspaper coverage continued for weeks.

Today, however, Evans is emphatic about why they were forced to resign. "I was told, pretty directly, that the government was just fed

---

[76] Doug Ward, "'We Were Seen as Quite Scary': PHS's Townsend," *Tyee*, April 2, 2014.

up with us fighting for things and embarrassing them and making them look bad," she says. "I was told, to my face by a very senior bureaucrat [Ramsay, she later reveals], that it had nothing to do with the audit, and that it had everything to do with them being sick of us fighting. And that BC Housing and VCH were done; they were sick of the power that we had gained and the voice that we had and that they needed to shut us down."

Ramsay confirms that he and Evans spoke privately about the financial review. "That was a reflection of the good working relationship we had," he says. But Ramsay denies ever telling Evans there was anything political about the financial review. He maintains that the PHS executives' ousting had nothing to do with PHS staff protests against government cuts to programming at the New Fountain Shelter and the Rainier Hotel. "There was no political interference from my side," he says. "As the audit lays out, the issues were around financial management and use of funds."

PHS had worked in partnerships with VCH and BC Housing staffers for two decades and had many friends within those organizations. Evans claims that Ramsay wasn't the only one who told her the financial review was political. "That was told to me more than once in many different ways by many different people," she says. "I was told by bureaucrats both within VCH and within BC Housing and not just once but many times."

Despite warnings from Ramsay and several other bureaucrats, Evans recalls she somehow never believed the government would actually go so far to take PHS away from them. "The truth is—maybe because I'm naïve and stupid—I never really believed in my heart that it would get followed through to the extent that it did," she says. "I'm embarrassed to admit it because there were people who told me what was going to happen. But I actually believed in my heart that people were good, that we were doing the right thing, and that people understood that."

Tom Laviolette similarly says that right until the end, he thought a compromise was going to be reached. "I knew we really pissed off some of the senior bureaucrats," he says. "I thought for sure Mark was going to have to sacrifice himself. But I was a bit surprised that they went much broader than that, that they took out Kerstin and Dan."

Laviolette says it finally became clear to him that they all were going to have to go when it was both BC Housing and VCH sitting together on the other side of the table from them. "As soon as VCH joined in, we knew we were totally screwed," he says. "We knew the game was over when the two of them got together."

Kerstin Stuerzbecher was always the least political of the group. She doesn't say much when asked about the financial review, but when asked about the Rainier protests, says this: "That was the nail in our coffin, that's for sure."

Bibby takes the view that if it wasn't the Rainier, it would have been something else shortly after. "The protests over the Rainier may have been the straw that broke the camel's back," he says. "I think they were all just absolutely tired of us."

Heather Hay, the Vancouver Coastal Health director who worked with Townsend and Small to open Insite, offers a more complicated picture. She does not suggest the Portland's activism had nothing to do with their ousting, but describes it as part of a larger transition. "Mark had a long history and was well known to have unrestrained behaviour if people disagreed with him," she says. "VCH knew for many, many years about his behaviour, and there were many, many complaints." Hay attributes less significance to the New Fountain and Rainier protests directly. She says the whole affair likely had more to do with a new executive team taking over Vancouver Coastal Health around the same time. Hay explains that those new bosses simply had less patience funding an organization (to the tune of millions of dollars) that was sending people with bullhorns and picket signs into their offices. "PHS read it wrong," Hay says. "They couldn't adapt to the new players."

Dr Patricia Daly, who in 2017 holds the positions of chief medical health officer and vice-president of public health at Vancouver Coastal Health, maintains she never once heard the Portland's political activities discussed in relation to the financial review. She was a PHS ally inside the health authority but says that, after reading the KPMG review, she felt the management team led by Evans and Townsend had to go. "If you look at the audit, they had to leave to save the organization," she says. "Remember the public: this was tax dollars."

It's clear that Evans and Townsend regard the media's coverage of the entire affair as brutally unfair. Then again, they acknowledge that in 2014, they never came out to give their side of the story. Evans adds she was pleased with one aspect of newspapers' reports. "Not in one article, not one document anywhere, ever, in the whole shit show of what went down, was there any suggestion that we were not actually doing what we said we were doing," she says. "No one ever came out and said we weren't doing a good job. No one."

Ramsay agrees with her. "The work that the Portland had done for some of the most marginalized folks in the Downtown Eastside was absolutely second to none," he says. "I quite admired them."

Daly, who was not directly involved in the removal of PHS's team of founders, remembers thinking she wasn't sure what the government would do without the organization. "Portland provided housing for some of the most challenging people in the community, hundreds that no one else would take," she says. "There are a lot of service providers down there but nobody else with their skills and expertise. So we would have been in real, real trouble if they had gone under. The deal that was worked out, whereby they left but the organization continued, that was probably the best outcome that could have happened there."

The team that Evans and Townsend had built over the years remained in place. Tanya Fader, Coco Culbertson, Andy Bond, and Darwin Fisher are all still with PHS today. But an interim board of directors appointed by BC Housing and VCH was stacked with their employees, ensuring the organization's activist days were over.

The province hadn't just taken PHS from the group that founded it; it had also labelled them corrupt, and forbade them from speaking against that narrative. Evans remembers feeling like she couldn't even discuss it with her closest friends in Vancouver.

"We knew that they were going to say things to get rid of us, with the motivation to make us look as dishonourable as possible," she says. "I tried to not care about that but was devastated."

The night after the newspapers reported on the details of BC Housing's financial review, Evans sat on her kitchen floor drinking a bottle of wine and crying. She called old friends in England, waking them in the middle of the night, trying and failing to explain what was happening.

"I did drink too much one night and was very upset," she recalls. "It was four in the morning, and I remember thinking, 'I can't talk to anyone here. I can't tell anyone what is happening.' It was really hard."

———————

Today Evans and Townsend live with their children in New York City. They work for two nonprofit organizations there, the Washington Heights Corner Project and New York Harm Reduction Educators. They're struggling within America's more conservative approach to drug addiction, running basic harm-reduction programs like the ones they started in the old Portland Hotel more than twenty years earlier.

They left Vancouver in 2016. The two were finally married in March of that year, in a small ceremony in a church just across the water from the Downtown Eastside, in North Vancouver. Evans laughs about how long it took them to get around to it. "We just never had time," she says. Two days after their wedding, Townsend flew to New York. Evans followed with the kids in July.

Their departure from the Portland Hotel Society in 2014 was the first ending of several Downtown Eastside stories that concluded that year.

In April, Bud Osborn was admitted to St. Paul's Hospital for pneumonia and a heart condition. He passed away on May 6, 2014. Osborn was sixty-six.

Ten days later, the East Hastings 100 block was closed to traffic for his memorial. It was a sunny afternoon and hundreds of people filled the street outside Insite, the sanctuary he had helped create for intravenous drug users. A small stage was erected and there above the crowd Ann Livingston recounted the power of Osborn's writing and his poetry's ability to help people feel better about themselves.

"He reassured them," Livingston said, "that their terrible anguish, humiliation, their shame, their horrid families, their drug addiction, their sexual abuse, the fact that they had traded sex for drugs—things that people don't want anyone to know—he would say, 'These are the exact things that you can say in poetry. And it creates beauty. It creates resistance, it creates pride, and it creates healing.'"[77]

Evans shared a simple memory of Osborn, of an afternoon when they sat outside a PHS coffee shop located a few doors down from Insite. She recounted how much it meant to Osborn that the Downtown Eastside simply exists, that it remains a place where anyone can feel welcome, without fear of stigma or judgment. "Bud and I sat and reflected on the fact that in spite of everything that had happened, we could still sit here on the corner of Columbia and Hastings," Evans told the crowd. "That this community still exists. That we've overcome, over and over again. That the Downtown Eastside had fought off challenges, fought off extinction, and survived and thrived, against the interests of those who fail to see the love, the magic, and the beauty in this community. Bud was so proud of this simple victory. This space that was occupied, against all odds."

Libby Davies, who had taught Osborn politics and become one of his closest friends, also spoke that afternoon. "Bud was a critical part of the struggle for the rights and dignity of drug users," she said. "He worked tirelessly for the opening of Insite. When times were dark and people felt hopeless, he gave us hope. When people felt that they had no voice, his poetry raised many voices and gave people courage. When people yearned for belonging and community, he led by example and united people in a common cause for human dignity and respect."

In December 2014, Davies announced that she was retiring from politics after representing the Downtown Eastside at the federal level for seventeen years. "I've worked very hard on issues like housing and homelessness, making sure that the rights of drug users are upheld and we don't criminalize people," she told the *Georgia Straight* newspaper that month. "It's been an extraordinary honour to serve in this community. East Vancouver is a very special place."

Davies said that her very first meeting with the Vancouver Area Network of Drug Users was one of the fondest memories of her

---

[77] Travis Lupick, "Bud Osborn Memorial Sees Insite Founder Remembered for Fighting the Good Fight," *Georgia Straight*, May 16, 2014.

career. "There were about 100 VANDU members sitting on the floor," she recounted. "We talked about a safe-injection site, and they said it would never happen. I said, 'It will. It will happen because you are involved. Your voice is finally being heard, and that's what makes a difference.'"

Davies reflected on how far Vancouver had come on harm reduction, calling it an example for all of North America to follow. Then she paused, and added: "I've learned this in life: When rights are won, you can never rest. This is an ongoing struggle."[78]

---

[78] Travis Lupick, "Outgoing Vancouver East MP Libby Davies Cautions Social Justice Victories Cannot Be Taken for Granted," *Georgia Straight*, December 12, 2014.

Chapter 33

Fentanyl Arrives

I t was the last Wednesday of August," Janet Charlie begins. She was working at a concession stand in the Downtown Eastside when her son Tyler came by. "He was walking through the market," recounts the grandmother of four. "He'd seen me working. But he knew I had an issue with his girlfriend, so he would never talk to me when she was around. He just looked at me and he walked out," she continues. "That was the last time I saw him alive."

Tyler spent the next few hours hanging out with friends on the corner of Main and East Hastings, just one block from where his mother continued her shift. "Selling cigarettes and whatever, and they drink there," she says.

Shortly after noon, a girl sprinted into the market and ran right up to Charlie. "They said, 'Your son went down,'" Charlie says calmly. "'It doesn't look good. It doesn't look like he's going to make it.' And I said, 'You know what? Don't say that, because you're not God.'"

Together, they ran up Hastings to the corner of Main, where Charlie found her son on the sidewalk outside the Carnegie Community Centre. Paramedics were bent over him, pumping oxygen into his lungs. She spent the next week with Tyler, who lay unconscious at Vancouver General Hospital.

"We thought he was going to be okay, because they had a little bit of wave in his brain," Charlie continues. "But the next day, there was nothing. So on the seventh day, we had to take him off the machines that were keeping him alive.

"He would be twenty-seven, if he was still here. He left behind an ex-wife and two kids."

———

In 1998, the peak of British Columbia's overdose crisis of the 1990s, there were 400 illicit-drug fatalities across the province. Nearly half of them were in just one city: Vancouver.

Four hundred was a number so high that it prompted activists to mobilize and, eventually, transformed how BC's government responds to the problem of addiction. Harm reduction was named a part of Vancouver's "four pillars" approach, Insite opened its doors, and researchers began looking at more radical ideas like providing clean drugs to addicts on a prescription basis. In the decade that followed, from the years 2001 to 2010, fatal overdoses in BC fell to an annual average of 212. Harm reduction worked.

But in 2011, something changed. That year, the number of fatal overdoses jumped by nearly a third, from 211 to 294. It dipped slightly the following year, to 269, but then rose again in 2013, to 333 overdose deaths. The climb continued, to 369, then 519, and then, in 2016, to 978. In 2017, BC is on track to surpass 1,500 overdose deaths, three-and-a-half times the very worst year of BC's crisis of the 1990s and nearly six times the annual average during the preceding decade.

Fentanyl had arrived.

The synthetic opioid is more than ten times stronger than heroin and at least fifty times more potent than morphine. Canada has sanctioned its use as a prescription pain killer since the 1970s. Now chemists mostly based in China and Mexico are manufacturing the drug illicitly and mixing it into North American's heroin supply. Fentanyl costs a fraction of what heroin does to produce. Just as important to dealers, its potency means it can be shipped in very small amounts, making it easy to smuggle over borders. It only has one drawback: it's so potent that it can be very difficult to accurately measure and mix into other substances for sale on the street. Police agencies often compare a shipment of heroin spiked with fentanyl to a batch of chocolate chip cookies: the baker never knows how many chips are in each treat.

In April 2016, BC's provincial government declared a public-health emergency, but no level of government took significant action to stop the tide of overdose deaths. There were half-measures. The federal health ministry dropped a prescription requirement for naloxone.

Beginning in 2011, the arrival of fentanyl and then carfentanil sent overdose deaths across British Columbia soaring. *Photo: Travis Lupick*

In BC, the provincial government then essentially made the overdose antidote widely available at no cost in at-risk neighbourhoods like the Downtown Eastside. Those initiatives undoubtedly saved many lives. But a response to fentanyl based on harm reduction, while important, is entirely reactive; it's only reaching people after they've already ingested drugs that are potentially deadly.

For the Downtown Eastside, a community that had lived through this sort of crisis once before, Tyler's death was one too many. In 2016, already five years into this new epidemic and still with little help from authorities forthcoming, the neighbourhood mobilized to take care of itself.

The alley behind the street market where Janet Charlie works is always busy with drug users. There are dealers positioned at each end and the space between them is crowded with street-entrenched addicts. There, late one evening in 2016, Ann Livingston walked the length of it, remembering how she'd seen all of this before.

Back in the 1990s, when the Downtown Eastside was breaking under the AIDS epidemic and the arrival of intravenous cocaine, Livingston cofounded the Vancouver Area Network of Drug Users and, in 1995, opened the city's first unsanctioned injection site, on Powell Street. As bad as things were back then, when the Downtown Eastside became synonymous with poverty and addiction, Livingston maintains that there is no doubt that the situation is worse today. She says that through the fall of 2016, she racked her brain for new ideas about how activists could help address the fentanyl crisis, and reveals that a state of depression began to weigh her down.

"Then, when Janet's son died, it really profoundly affected every-one in the market," Livingston continues. Since fentanyl arrived on Vancouver streets, Livingston is often found with Sarah Blyth, the former PHS staffer who helped set up the New Fountain Shelter and participated in the Rainier Hotel demonstrations. Now Blyth works at the Downtown Eastside's street market. There she's taken a lead role in the community's grassroots response to the overdose epidemic.

"The workers [at the street market] came together and said, 'We need to do something about this,'" Blyth recounts. "We cannot sit around and have this happen on our watch. We can do something about this, and we don't have to wait for red tape or the government and bureaucracy. We knew that no one could stop us, because we were doing the right thing."

On the afternoon of September 21, 2016, Blyth, Livingston, and a third Downtown Eastside activist who also works at the market, Chris Ewart, pitched a tent facing into an alley that runs just south of East Hastings Street. Inside, they set up a semi-circle of tables and chairs. On the right-hand side, they placed a jug from which people could take water to cook their drugs, clean needles and, crucially, a supply of naloxone, the overdose antidote that's used to reverse the effects of opioids like heroin and fentanyl.

"People were overdosing in the back alley and they would call to us for help," Blyth says while she's working a shift at the tent. "So here we witness them and just create an atmosphere that is safe and clean, that is not the alley and not their houses, where they would risk using alone. We're saying, "It's better to come and hang out with us here.'"

Twenty-two years had passed since Livingston set up her first unsanctioned injection site, Back Alley, at 356 Powell Street. Drugs were still illegal, users were still marginalized and pushed into the alleys, and Livingston was still stepping in where the government would not.

"No one was going to come and help," she says. "I felt really frustrated."

During the winter of 2016, overdoses occurred at the tent and throughout the Downtown Eastside with increasing frequency. There were sixty-one fatal overdoses across BC in September, the month they pitched the tent. Then seventy-four, 137, and then 161 in December. In response, Livingston, Blyth, and Ewart, now calling their group the Overdose Prevention Society, pitched a second tent in an alley one block east of the first one.

"We went from seeing one overdose a day to seeing several overdoses a day to seeing seven overdoses in one day," Blyth says. "Back to back to back. Just absolute chaos."

Still operating without any government support—but also without interference—they staffed the two tents with past and present drug users. An online fundraising campaign brought in just enough in donations to pay small stipends. At first the tents saw 100 people inject there each day, then 200, and then 300. There were dozens and then hundreds of overdoses, but every single one was reversed successfully. Nobody died at either site. Livingston describes it as a miracle.

"Two weeks ago, it was an overdose a day or every second day back here," she said in November 2016. "Then suddenly it was three every day. It's doubled. You think, 'It's so high, it's not going to get worse.' Well, it did. Next, it tripled."

On November 29, the BC Coroners Service confirmed that another synthetic opioid, called carfentanil, was detected near the body of a man who died in East Vancouver two weeks earlier. A news release warned that the drug was significantly more dangerous than fentanyl, describing it as "the most toxic opioid used commercially."

A newspaper article from December 6 quotes a representative for the coroners service confirming rumours that the city's morgues were often full. Health authorities were forced to store bodies at funeral homes. Meanwhile, the Overdose Prevention Society's tents continued to operate outside the law, without government funding or support of any kind.

Everyone who worked there in those months had a story like the one that Blyth and Livingston tell about Tyler, a moment in time when they realized they could no longer do nothing.

At the first of the two tents during those cold months, the volunteer who spent more time there than any other was Lee Tran. At the end of a ten-hour shift on November 23—a Wednesday, when welfare cheques are issued—he sheds some light on what drives the group staffing the tents.

"Previously in my life, once, I was a drug addict," Tran says. "So I feel what these guys are going through. I know what they need. And I heard about this work, so I felt like this was something I wanted to do."

As the death toll climbed through November and December, volunteers there took to calling it "the endless winter." Vancouver's weather is quite mild compared to the rest of Canada, but the winter of 2016–17 was long and brutal. The unusual cold kept residents of the Downtown Eastside inside their small hotel rooms. There, they often used drugs alone, where no one was around to help them when an overdose occurred.

Across the street from the tent, down one block, and up eight flights of stairs, Jay Slaunwhite sits in the cramped room he lives in on the top floor of the Balmoral Hotel. It's a private SRO building, one of the very worst in Vancouver, where there are no support services like what's offered at PHS hotels.

"Narcan here," reads a sign on his door. "Knock if someone is ODing. Anytime!"

Slaunwhite recounts how he came to function as the run-down hotel's de facto paramedic. "The first time, someone actually asked me to inject them," he says. "They knocked on the door, and I did. She only did half of what she had, but still she went under. She was on my bed, not breathing. So [I administered] CPR and naloxone, screaming for someone to call an ambulance. And they came, and that was that."

It was after that experience that he put the sign up on his door. Since then, Slaunwhite says, people continue to come to him for help. Several times, he adds, someone whose friend had stopped breathing knocked on his door when he was all out of naloxone.

"I don't have a lot," Slaunwhite explains. "And more people have come when I didn't have it than came when I did have it."

Asked what happened to those people, he replies quietly: "I don't know."

Slaunwhite has never been in contact with anybody representing government or even one of the Downtown Eastside's many nonprofits. He's simply a former drug user who thought it made sense to let people know he could help. He acknowledges that it might be hard for people who don't use drugs to understand why other people do, given how dangerous it's become since fentanyl arrived.

"I hear people talking, like, 'Why are these people still injecting? Are they just insane? Are they crazy? Are they stupid?'" Slaunwhite says. "That's like telling someone, 'You know the air is toxic and if you breathe in, you're going to die.' But you still need to breathe, so you're going to breathe. For a lot of people, that's what this comes down to."

Two blocks east of the Balmoral, in an alley behind VANDU's current headquarters at 380 East Hastings Street, a long-time VANDU member, Hugh Lampkin, emphasizes the extent to which past and present addicts—some of whom also struggle with mental-health issues—have come to play a lead role in the community's response to the fentanyl crisis.

He recalls an event held on November 15 in which VANDU partnered with Vancouver Coastal Health to educate drug users on overdose response. "I believe we trained about 240 people that day," Lampkin says.

VANDU also began dispatching foot patrols carrying naloxone through Downtown Eastside alleys. Lampkin estimates that those teams, working twelve hours a day, reverse more than twenty overdoses each month. He notes that it's a "train the trainers" program, where volunteers instruct the people they meet in the alleys on how to respond when somebody overdoses.

In 2017, fourteen years after Insite opened its doors on the East

Hastings 100 block, it operates at capacity, often with lineups for injection booths longer than ten minutes—a long time if you're dope sick. So people continue to use intravenous drugs in places where they lack the facility's mindful care provided by nurses.

The situation inside the Portland's hotels is better than most other places in the Downtown Eastside but has grown increasingly challenging. At the Stanley Hotel and the adjoining New Fountain Shelter, Andy Bond, now the senior director of housing for PHS, and Duncan Higgon, its shelter programs manager, speak openly about how staff are stretched to a breaking point. "Just in the last two days—in fact, in the last thirty-six hours—we have seen eight overdose interventions," Higgon says. "We are delivering multiple, multiple doses of Narcan, having to use oxygen, and for periods of time that are really difficult."

Bond says the situation is the same in most of the hotels that PHS operates throughout the Downtown Eastside. "Within our housing [sites], to give an example of just how bad the problem is, we have intervened in over 1,000 overdoses in the last twelve months, just within PHS units of housing," he says in December 2016. "That is an astronomically, alarmingly high number of overdose interventions. And that is just in housing. That does not include Insite. Everyone is overwhelmed," Bond adds. "And it doesn't seem to be getting better. It's getting worse as we go along."

Back at the Downtown Eastside street market, Janet Charlie recalls the last time her son Tyler spoke to her. "The last time I'd seen him straight was on Mother's Day [May 8, 2016]," she says. "He popped in where I was working at the street market. Him and his brother dropped off some chocolates for me on Mother's Day. That was the last time I'd seen him normal. Then he was back to drinking and selling whatever he was selling."

Charlie notes that it was only a year earlier that she lost her other son to alcohol poisoning. "Losing two sons in two years is hard," Charlie says. "I'm saving what I make. I'm saving up for headstones for both my sons. And I'm paying each month out of my welfare cheque. Trying to pay for headstones for both of them."

Ann Livingston in 2016. *Photo: Travis Lupick* / Georgia Straight

In late 2016, BC's provincial government finally sprang into action. On December 8, the health minister, Terry Lake, convened a press conference in the Downtown Eastside. The epidemic of deaths had prompted Vancouver Coastal Health to dispatch a mobile emergency room to the neighbourhood. Standing in front of the mobile ER, Lake announced that the BC government would sidestep federal drug laws, forego the application process that Insite had wrestled with, and immediately open more than fifteen new "overdose-prevention sites." These locations would function similar to Insite, he explained, but with fewer complementary health-care services in order to allow for rapid deployment.

Lake told reporters that the drastic action—possibly illegal, he later acknowledged—was inspired by Ann Livingston, Sarah Blyth, and the tent they'd set up in the alley off East Hastings Street. "I woke up yesterday at four o'clock in the morning and was thinking about the pop-up tent," he told a newspaper that month. "So we pulled the team together quickly. Vancouver Coastal had some plans in place.

And so we just expedited everything.

"We can't wait for federal changes in order to save people's lives," Lake continued. "We know people are using in alleys, they are using in their rooms, and they are not where the people who can help them are. And so in the face of this crisis, we really just wanted to do more."[79]

Within a week, there were more than a dozen so-called overdose prevention sites established across BC, five of which were in the Downtown Eastside. Government help had finally come.

Since the arrival of fentanyl and carfentanil, there are two very different groups of heroin addicts in the Downtown Eastside. Bernadette is a member of the first.

She describes her life as an endless game of Russian roulette. A half dozen times every twenty-four hours, her physical dependence on opioids, combined with an intense craving for cocaine, forces her to inject unknown substances. "I always do a little amount," she says. "Because if I use too much, I'm not going to be here to use again. But if I don't use enough, I can always use more."

At the Overdose Prevention Society's injection site in the alley behind the street market, the thin Indigenous woman describes the fear that crept into the community when fentanyl arrived. "Even if I'm buying from the same person, it doesn't matter," Bernadette says. "Just because my guy doesn't fuck with it doesn't mean the guy that gives it to him doesn't fuck with it. That's why they call it a game of Russian roulette ... And that's why I come here," she continues, looking around at the tent she sits beneath. It's just a few plastic tables and chairs, but they're always filled with people injecting or smoking drugs because of the relative safety offered there. If she overdoses, there's someone around to revive her.

As she prepares a needle, Bernadette says she worries about buying

---

[79] Travis Lupick, "Dodging Drug Laws, B.C. Unveils Plans to Immediately Offer Supervised-Injection Services in Vancouver and Other Cities," *Georgia Straight*, December 8, 2016.

heroin. She knows it probably contains fentanyl. She prays it doesn't contain carfentanil, the even more dangerous synthetic opioid that health authorities confirmed had reached Vancouver just a few months earlier. "Depending on how it's mixed, one part can be a lot stronger and the other part a lot weaker," Bernadette continues. "So every time I get it off my guy, I always test it."

Repeat overdoses have become a fact of life for members of this group of drug users. Bernadette has had two in recent months. In both instances, a friend used naloxone to bring her back to life. "That's a nasty drug," she says of naloxone. "It's like having the worst hangover that you could possibly imagine. It's like a whole bunch of bad things happening all at one time. It's just nasty. You don't want to experience that ... But it is better than dying."

Because heroin and cocaine are addictive and illegal, government policies of prohibition condemn Bernadette and people like her to find them on the streets. In addition to the chances they take with each injection, they burn through savings and sell possessions to pay for drugs. Many of the women in this group resort to sex work. Every single day is a circular hustle: wake up, get money, find drugs, use them, hopefully don't overdose, and start the process over again.

Kevin Thompson is a member of Vancouver's second group of illicit-drug users. His life is very different from Bernadette's.

Stories of past abuse or neglect are common among heroin addicts. But Thompson took a different road to the Downtown Eastside, one that is similarly shared by a lot of drug-addicted people living there. He started recreationally, using at parties and then more regularly. Eventually, when the cocaine became increasingly difficult to come down off, Thompson began using small amounts of heroin. "I'd snort a line of it, take the edge off, and go home, chill out, and go back to work the next day," he says. "Then one day I wake up thinking I'm sick and had the flu. That's the day I knew I was wired," he continues. "Haven't stopped using heroin since."

Despite his addiction, Thompson works forty hours a week at another of the city's new overdose-prevention sites. It's located inside one of the Portland's hotels but open to anyone via an entrance into an alley near the intersection of Main and East Hastings streets. He still uses heroin. But instead of buying from dealers on the street, he gets his drugs from Crosstown Clinic, the only facility in North America that dispenses diacetylmorphine, the medical term for prescription heroin.

Three times a day, Thompson visits the clinic. There, a nurse gives him a specific dose that has been prescribed by a doctor. Then he carries on with his day. Thompson wakes up to an alarm clock and is seldom late for work. He doesn't nod off on the job. The police never show up looking for him, because it's been years since he's committed a crime. "I'm living a normal life," Thompson says. "Walk next to me and you probably wouldn't even know that I use drugs. I have a full-time job. I'm a functional addict."

At Crosstown Clinic, there are virtually no overdoses. The patients enrolled there don't wake up in a panic each morning not knowing where their next fix is coming from. They don't need to steal or sell their bodies. The vast majority have found stable housing. They've left the street life behind them.

Thompson says he thinks about the first group of addicts every day and almost constantly. In his job at the overdose-prevention site, he has used naloxone to save many of their lives. "It disgusts me, really," Thompson adds, "that they don't have this [diacetylmorphine] for everybody else. It should be open to everybody."

As of May 2017, there were between ninety and 100 people in Vancouver like Thompson: long-time opioid addicts who receive prescription heroin at Crosstown Clinic. Roughly another twenty-five patients receive injection hydromorphone, an opioid better known by the brand name Dilaudid. (These numbers vary slightly as patients move from one category of the program to another and as the occasional client graduates to abstinence.)

The clinic's operator, Providence Health Care, estimates that the number of drug users in Vancouver for whom prescription heroin is appropriate likely numbers about 500. In 2017, the facility began a renovation so it could squeeze in more patients. But when that work is complete, its maximum client load will still only be between 150 and 200 people.

Vancouver's prescription-heroin program was originally designed for long-term, severely entrenched addicts who have been on opioids for decades and who have repeatedly tried and failed with more traditional treatments like methadone. The arrival of fentanyl and carfentanil has led some advocates to argue that with BC's drug supply now so contaminated with dangerous synthetics, the threshold to qualify for prescription heroin should be lowered to allow less-entrenched users to access a relatively safe supply of the drugs to which they're addicted.

Among them is Vancouver's old drug-policy czar, Donald MacPherson, who Livingston and Osborn had with them in Oppenheimer Park the day they founded VANDU so many years ago. MacPherson retired from his work with the city in 2009. He works for Simon Fraser University now, where he holds the position of executive director for the Canadian Drug Policy Coalition. Since fentanyl arrived, MacPherson has argued that access to prescription heroin should extend beyond the group of long-time addicts to whom it's offered today. "With the overdose crisis across North America, why are we withholding a clean pharmaceutical drug from people who are overdosing on toxic, poisonous substances like fentanyl and carfentanil?" he asks. "Why do we not allow people to enter some sort of program where they can acquire a clean pharmaceutical product at a dose that works for them, that doesn't kill them?"

At the time of writing, Crosstown Clinic's ninety-something patients remain the only people in North America for whom prescription heroin is available.

When Kevin Thompson entered Vancouver's first prescription-heroin study in 2006, he discovered it wasn't only the drug he was addicted to, but also the lifestyle around it.

"Some people are addicted to the needle; some people are addicted to the hustle," he explains.

Once Thompson was guaranteed three shots of heroin a day at Crosstown Clinic, he found he had so much free time on his hands that it was oddly unnerving. "I didn't have to run or chase the dope," he says. "It was overwhelming at first. Too much time. I started getting bored and going, 'Well, what does everybody do?'"

Thompson started going for walks. "I realized, 'Hey, I live on the ocean. It's a block away. And I haven't been down to the ocean and paid attention to it in twenty, twenty-five years.'"

He began visiting nearby Crab Park and then ventured farther from the Downtown Eastside to Stanley Park and the public swimming pool there. Soon enough, he felt it was time to go back to work. He was hired by the nonprofit Portland Hotel Society as a peer-support staffer. It was his first job in roughly two decades. Meanwhile, at Crosstown, Thompson slowly began to reduce his prescribed dose of diacetylmorphine.

"I'm starting to wean myself," he says. "I do want to quit one day. But it's nice to know that this is here for me if I need it."

When BC's overdose epidemic began to claim more lives over the course of the 2016–17 winter, Thompson took a new job at the overdose-prevention site attached to PHS's Washington Hotel (renamed the Maple Hotel), where he still works today. Since then, he's lost track of the number of overdoses he's reversed there. He feels good about that, adding, "I love my job." But Thompson says he also can't help but feel guilty.

"My friends that I've been with for years, they're still playing the roulette game that I'm not."

Epilogue

Before my meeting with Angel Gaeta-Hildebrandt, I spotted her across the street, standing at a crosswalk with her six-year-old son, Mikel. I was sitting outside a Starbucks, twenty minutes early for our interview. The little boy goes to school just a block away and so Gaeta-Hildebrandt, or Molly, as her friends call her, would drop him off there and then double back to meet me. Like a scene out of a movie, I watched her crouch down on one knee, lick her finger, and use it to clean a smudge of food from Mikel's cheek. Then the traffic light changed and they continued on their walk to school.

It was April 20, 2017, the first truly warm and sunny day that broke Vancouver's endless winter of fentanyl deaths. It had rained the night before, and the sun reflected off puddles and places where the pavement was still wet.

Fifteen minutes later, Molly sat down with me and told me it was Mikel's birthday. She'd just bought him a Nintendo. It's sort of a gift for both of them, she said with a smile. One of her favourite things in the world is a lazy weekend morning playing videogames with her son and his dad, who's also named Mikel. The family's favourite game is *Plants vs. Zombies: Garden Warfare*, she added. It sounded like a really nice life. Molly beamed with warmth as we talked about it.

When BC's provincial government released its 2014 financial review of the Portland Hotel Society, that was the end of Liz Evans's and Mark Townsend's work in Vancouver. But there are a thousand people who still live in their hotels in the Downtown Eastside today. Molly, for example, and her mother Mary Jack, who was one of the Portland's very first tenants. "If it weren't for Liz and Mark, we wouldn't be here," Mary told me over another coffee the following week. Tenants mourned the Portland founders' departure. But, of course, their lives continued on without them.

———————

Mary Jack was only twenty years old when she had Molly in 1980. When Molly was still a young child, their roles essentially flipped, and Molly became the voice of responsibility in their little family.

"These are the rules I'm supposed to follow," she remembers telling her mom when she was just a girl. Molly enforced those rules and would actually give herself a short time-out whenever she misbehaved.

They were homeless together, living on the streets of Vancouver for a time, though Molly didn't realize it until she was older. "We'd just walk around singing," she says. "And I had lots of babysitters."

Mary's drug dealer, an older woman named Gail, took Molly into her home for a while. Gail had two boys of her own but no daughter, and she treated Molly like the baby girl she'd always wanted. Eventually a dispute developed between Mary and Gail, and Molly was sent to live with her aunt out in Chilliwack, a rural suburb about an hour's drive from the Downtown Eastside. She hated being away from her mother.

The deal was that when Mary quit heroin, they could be together again. In 1995, when Molly was fifteen years old, Mary did quit, at least for a while. So Molly left her aunt's place and showed up at her mom's door at the Portland Hotel. "She had said, 'You can move in with me as soon as I can quit,'" Molly recounts. "So I was like, 'So now I can stay then. I'm not going back.'"

The old Portland Hotel was a sanctuary from the streets, but it was no place for a fifteen-year-old girl. So Liz Evans took Molly home to live with her and Townsend. "You can stay here for a bit," Evans told her.

Townsend remembers there was never any discussion about it. Evans brought Molly home one night, and that was that. "We couldn't leave some fifteen-year-old in the old hotel," he says.

Their house was just a short walk from the Downtown Eastside, and it wasn't uncommon for them to take in a stray. Molly remembers her first morning waking up there. It was Evans's birthday and Townsend had prepared a big breakfast and poured champagne and orange juice for everyone.

"This is kind of cool," Molly remembers thinking. "There was always tea," she continues. "I really liked that they had so many different types of music. They had a huge CD case, kind of a library ... And the first time I ever had basil was with them. I was like, 'What's this in the salad? This tastes so good!' I couldn't get enough of it. And it was just basil, but I had never heard of it before."

Evans drove Molly to school most mornings and she became a member of the family. After a few months, Townsend found Mary and Molly an apartment just outside the Downtown Eastside where they could live together. But shortly after they moved in, Mary's mother visited for a few days and passed away there. "It was hard for her to be in the same place where her mother died," Molly says. "So she kinda ran away from home for a bit."

In 1998, Molly turned eighteen and Evans let her and her mom move together into the old Portland Hotel, into two rooms on the same floor, just down the hall from one another. "It was nice," Molly says. "I had a room that was separate from everybody else that I could make my own."

Since she'd run away from her aunt's house three years earlier, Molly had always shared a bedroom with her mom or a boyfriend. This was the first time that a space was totally hers. Molly remembers there were mice, but she figured out how to live with them. Each night, she put a few scraps of food out on the side of the room opposite from her bed. The mice were going to share the room with her no matter what, she remembers thinking, so this way, she could have her space and the mice could have theirs.

Bud Osborn was hanging around the hotel a lot in those days, and Molly attended poetry workshops he held in the stairwell. "You could go there and write down your poem or whatever you were thinking or you could write about how your day was," she says. "They used to do haircuts, too," she adds. "This really awesome guy used to do my hair perfect all the time. They would always do little things like that."

Molly liked the hotel, but it was chaotic. There was always somebody high on drugs wandering the hallways or struggling with a mental-health episode. The mice didn't bother Molly much, but she didn't like the cockroaches. A couple of the older male tenants creeped her out a bit. But Molly had a room there that was her own, and it was just down the hall from her mom's.

She spent hours in the hotel's tiny lobby, chatting with Evans and

Kerstin Stuerzbecher and whoever else was around. "The old staff, you could just sit there and talk with them forever," she says. "I would talk about my boyfriends and that stuff."

Evans and Townsend had been looking out for Molly for a few years, but she'd already lived a complicated life. "When I was seventeen, that's when I started doing more drugs and stuff," Molly says. "My thing with drugs was, I wanted to try every one of them."

Molly did try them all, going through an acid phase for a while, eventually settling on cocaine, and then crack and methamphetamine. Through the 1990s, Vancouver had an underground rave scene. Teenagers and early twenty-somethings took ecstasy, acid, and crystal meth, and danced until the morning in vacant warehouses and abandoned retail stores. Molly loved it.

"I liked being awake forever," Molly continues. "I would draw and paint." She didn't realize it at the time, but she'd grown addicted to crack. She remembers how little fun it was even as she continued to smoke it. She spent night after night high on crack, in bed, hiding under the covers, convinced that any second the police were going to knock down her door. "That was my lost phase, I think, at the Old Portland." That's all she says about it.

Molly didn't like cocaine or crack anymore. They made her feel paranoid when she was high and guilty when she wasn't. On August 6, 2000, she gave them both up. It was moving day. The new Portland Hotel felt like a place where she could do without the crack that she'd smoked through her nights at the old hotel. "Getting away from all that, that was awesome," she says.

Best of all, Evans had arranged for Molly and her mother to have rooms directly across the hall from one another. "So I quit coke when we moved," Molly says. "I was like, 'This is a fresh start.' I was still doing crystal and stuff, but that was a big thing for me to do."

Molly took a job at the Interurban, a little art gallery that PHS owns on the corner just across from Pigeon Park. Then, one afternoon after a few years at the new Portland Hotel, Molly spotted a young man. She was doing her laundry when she noticed him. There weren't too many tenants in the hotel under the age of thirty. "And he was super hot," she says, laughing.

The very next day, an older guy in a wheelchair knocked on her door. "My son just got out of jail and wants to hang out with you," the man said to her. Molly was slightly nervous about the jail thing but agreed to the blind date. When she met him later that week, he turned out to be the guy from the laundry room.

Mary remembers at first being a little unsure about Mikel. "But he fell in love with my daughter," she says. "And he ended up being a good guy. He ended up being a really good guy."

A few more years passed. Mikel was hooked on heroin when he first met Molly, but together they managed to kick his habit. He started using meth and they made it into a couple's thing.

"I never really thought of it as an addiction because my cats were always fed, my responsibilities were always taken care of before I did anything else, and I would never front," Molly says. She would sometimes show up late for her job at the Interurban Gallery, but not so often that they would think of firing her. At the same time, there were signs the addiction was gaining on her. Molly would seldom sleep and started having psychotic episodes. She would hear things. Worse, it began to feel like life wasn't about much more than meth. Mikel played video games, and Molly sat beside him and filled her sketch books. "We were bored," she says.

In March 2010, it was time to move again.

The story of the new Woodward's complex is an entire book in itself. Mark Townsend, Jim Green, Bud Osborn, and a supporting cast of dozens fought for more than a decade to make it happen. Finally, the old Woodward's Department Store was torn down. In 2010, two residential towers rose in its place. They opened with 536 market-rate units, 125 units for the Portland's hard-to-house tenants, plus seventy-five subsidized apartments for families.

The Woodward's redevelopment occupies an entire square block on the western edge of the Downtown Eastside. It was one of the longest and most heated political sagas in Vancouver's history. Today, the end result remains controversial. Townsend concedes that their ultimate goal—to save the Downtown Eastside from gentrification—will likely fail, and that the Woodward's redevelopment will deserve a lot of the blame when the neighbourhood is eventually lost to higher-income condo dwellers. But for Molly and so many other PHS tenants, Woodward's remains a dream come true.

There, Molly and Mikel grew increasingly tired of drugs. For the first time in as long as either of them could remember, they felt like they could quit. It was a gradual thing. They went a few weeks without crystal, dipped back into it for a while, but then went another few weeks without using the drug. Each break lasted a little longer than the one before it.

Molly remembers that Liz Evans remained quietly supportive. Molly had used the internet to track down her father, whom she hadn't seen since she was six. He was living in Seattle, just over the border from Vancouver. So Evans bought Molly a ticket so that she could visit him. Sitting at a café waiting for the train, Evans asked Molly, "What are you doing these days?"

"Crystal," Molly replied. "Just crystal."

They continued to chat. "I think she was just making conversation, really," Molly says. She remembers it was a subtle way of Evans letting her know that she was there for her.

"She helped people help themselves," Molly explains. "She helped people feel more confident to help themselves. She never judged us. When I was messed up on drugs, she never judged me. She never made me feel like I had to hide anything I was doing. It was all about acceptance."

About a year after they moved into the Woodward's building, Molly found out she was pregnant. "And I was done," she says. Her years on crystal meth were over. When Mikel was born, his father quit drugs, too. They were married at the Interurban in a cozy ceremony attended by family, friends, and quite a few long-serving PHS staffers.

Sitting outside Starbucks, I ask Molly about their son and she begins going on about him, as mothers do.

"He's in kindergarten, right there," she says, pointing to Mikel's school just down the street. "He's into video games. I got him a little Nintendo for his birthday so now he's playing Yoshi a lot. He also likes reading. He's learning how to read. It's really cool. Each night we're going through the *Hop on Pop* book and he's getting way better at reading and that's awesome. He loves animals. He knows everything about animals, animals you don't even know about. He's obsessed."

Later, I tell Townsend about what Molly's mother said, about how she didn't think that she or her daughter would be alive today if it weren't for him and Evans.

"What you are talking about with drug use, for many people, is a sense of disconnection," he replies. Townsend says that he wishes he could have snapped his fingers and ended both Mary and Molly's addictions to drugs years earlier. "But instead we just did the best we could," he continues. "We gave them a place where they could be together and where they had someone in the world ... Where they had a connection."

Liz Evans and Mikel Gaeta Hildebrandt, a third-generation tenant of the Portland Hotel Society, in June 2017. *Photo: Angel Gaeta Hildebrandt*

They're all friends on Facebook and, from New York, Townsend remarks how much he and Evans enjoy watching Molly continue to grow up and raise her boy.

"I guess she dealt with some of her demons and she dealt with her pain," he says. "We just gave her space, and then she had her life."

Acknowledgments

There were a lot of people who helped me find my way to this project and then stick with it to completion. I think the first person I ever mentioned it to was Mark Townsend, in May 2014. He told me he didn't think anyone would read it but gave me his blessings just the same. So thank you to him. And to Liz Evans, Ann Livingston, and Dean Wilson. You all gave me so much of your time and shared with me so much of your lives. The trust you placed in me was incredible.

Thank you to Susan Safyan and Brian Lam for your edits, to Jackie Wong for your early read, always so sensitive and insightful, to Robert Lecker for your enthusiasm and advice, and to Jen Croll for tutoring me through the proposal. Thank you to Frances Bula and Lori Culbert for your wisdom, to Nettie Wild for your *Fix* transcripts, and a big thank you to Johann Hari, who so graciously shared his tapes of the last extensive interviews that Bud Osborn gave before he passed away. Thank you to Dr Gabor Maté for your expertise I sought for chapters concerning science, and to Bruce Alexander and Mallory Lupick for your help there as well. To Joseph Arvay and Sally Yee for your help sourcing documents related to the Insite case, to Sam Fenn, Gordon Katic, and Alexander Kim, for your research that went into the prescription heroin chapter, to Andrew Bell for your assistance with the six chapters that cover the United States, and to Kevin Thompson for your years of help reporting from the Downtown Eastside. For graciously giving me permission to include their photographs, I give huge thank yous to Elaine Brière, Duncan Murdoch, Lincoln Clarkes, Tyson Fast, Colin Askey, and the *Vancouver Sun*'s Carolyn Soltau. And thank you to Lost & Found Café and especially Heesue Sim for a comfortable place to work and countless free cups of coffee.

There are politicians, health-care professionals (especially nurses), and lowly bureaucrats who played significant roles in Vancouver's harm-reduction movement whom I could not give the credit they deserve. Many of these people helped me with my research and I thank them for that and apologize for the unjustified lack of attention they receive in the story I've told here. This list includes Coco Culbertson, Tanya Fader, Andy Bond, Darwin Fisher, Dan Small, Murray Bush, Sean McEwen, Nathan Allen, Russ Maynard, Sarah Blyth, Karen Ward, Dianne Tobin, Susan Boyd, Donald MacPherson, Fiona Gold, Irene Goldstone, Heather Hay, Liz Whynot, John Blatherwick, Mark Tyndall, Warren O'Briain, Maxine Davis, Gillian Maxwell, Thomas Kerr, Evan Wood, Julio Montaner, and Lani Russwurm. My apologies to the people who I've missed.

Thank you to Dan McLeod, Yolanda Stepien, Matt McLeod, and Charlie Smith for giving me a home base at the *Georgia Straight* newspaper and an education in journalism. Thank you to Sandy Stepien and Bruce Lupick for always encouraging me to learn new things and to form my own opinions, no matter how much they diverge from your own. Thank you to my love and best friend Cara Foster, for your honest feedback, early edits, and consistent reassurance that this would all eventually work out.

Finally, I am indebted to those who shared their stories to make this book possible. I express my sincere thanks to everyone whose words appear in these pages. To those who live and work in the Downtown Eastside, I also thank you for holding the place together. I love this neighbourhood. I also appreciate the burden it carries in providing space for so many people who ended up here from across Canada and the United States. Thank you for the community you've created.

References

For a complete list of references and sources for *Fighting for Space*, please visit ***tlupick.com***.

Index